ROBERTO BOLAÑO IN CONTEXT

From his first fifteen years in Chile, to his nine years in Mexico City from 1968 to 1977, to the quarter of a century he lived and worked in the Blanes-Barcelona area on the Costa Brava in Spain through his death in 2003, Roberto Bolaño developed into an astonishingly diverse, prolific writer, one of the most consequential and widely read of his generation in any language. Increasingly recognized not only in Latin America, but as a major figure in World Literature, he has come to play an integral role in the development of our contemporary imaginary on a global, planetary scale. As the wide-ranging contextual investigations of this volume's distinguished scholars attest, Bolaño's indelible influence and impact will shape literary cultures worldwide for years to come.

JONATHAN B. MONROE is Professor of Comparative Literature, and a member of the Graduate Fields of Comparative Literature, English, and Romance Studies, at Cornell University. He is the author of *Framing Roberto Bolaño: Poetry, Fiction, Literary History, Politics,* also with Cambridge University Press (2019, hardback and digital, paperback 2021); *A Poverty of Objects: The Prose Poem and the Politics of Genre*; and *Demosthenes' Legacy*, a book of prose poems and short fiction. Coauthor and editor of *Writing and Revising the Disciplines*; *Local Knowledges, Local Practices: Writing in the Disciplines at Cornell*; *Poetry Community, Movement* (*Diacritics*); and *Poetics of Avant-Garde Poetries* (*Poetics Today*), he has published widely on questions of genre, writing, and disciplinary practices; innovative poetries of the past two centuries; and avant-garde movements and their contemporary legacies.

ROBERTO BOLAÑO IN CONTEXT

EDITED BY

JONATHAN B. MONROE

Cornell University, New York

CAMBRIDGE
UNIVERSITY PRESS

University Printing House, Cambridge CB2 8BS, United Kingdom

One Liberty Plaza, 20th Floor, New York, NY 10006, USA

477 Williamstown Road, Port Melbourne, VIC 3207, Australia

314–321, 3rd Floor, Plot 3, Splendor Forum, Jasola District Centre, New Delhi – 110025, India

103 Penang Road, #05–06/07, Visioncrest Commercial, Singapore 238467

Cambridge University Press is part of the University of Cambridge.

It furthers the University's mission by disseminating knowledge in the pursuit of education, learning, and research at the highest international levels of excellence.

www.cambridge.org
Information on this title: www.cambridge.org/9781108835671
DOI: 10.1017/9781108891226

© Jonathan B. Monroe 2022

This publication is in copyright. Subject to statutory exception and to the provisions of relevant collective licensing agreements, no reproduction of any part may take place without the written permission of Cambridge University Press.

First published 2022

Printed in the United Kingdom by TJ Books Ltd, Padstow Cornwall

A catalogue record for this publication is available from the British Library.

Library of Congress Cataloging-in-Publication Data
NAMES: Monroe, Jonathan, 1954- editor.
TITLE: Roberto Bolaño in context / edited by Jonathan Beck Monroe.
DESCRIPTION: Cambridge; New York, NY: Cambridge University Press, 2022. | Includes bibliographical references and index.
IDENTIFIERS: LCCN 2022010927 (print) | LCCN 2022010928 (ebook) | ISBN 9781108835671 (hardback) | ISBN 9781108813013 (paperback) | ISBN 9781108891226 (epub)
SUBJECTS: LCSH: Bolaño, Roberto, 1953-2003–Criticism and interpretation. | Chilean literature–20th century–History and criticism. | Spanish literature–Chile–20th century–History and criticism. | Authors, Chilean–20th century–Biography. | BISAC: LITERARY CRITICISM / Caribbean & Latin American
CLASSIFICATION: LCC PQ8098.12.O38 Z835 2022 (print) | LCC PQ8098.12.O38 (ebook) | DDC 863/ .64–dc23/eng/20220421
LC record available at https://lccn.loc.gov/2022010927
LC ebook record available at https://lccn.loc.gov/2022010928

ISBN 978-1-108-83567-1 Hardback

Cambridge University Press has no responsibility for the persistence or accuracy of URLs for external or third-party internet websites referred to in this publication and does not guarantee that any content on such websites is, or will remain, accurate or appropriate.

Contents

List of Contributors	*page* viii
Chronology	xviii

PART I GEOGRAPHICAL, SOCIAL, AND HISTORICAL CONTEXTS   1

1   Mapping Bolaño's Worlds   3
       Jonathan B. Monroe

2   Chile, 1953–1973   16
       María Inés Lagos

3   The Pinochet Era, 1973–1990   33
       Michael J. Lazzara

4   Dictatorships in the Southern Cone   46
       Ksenija Bilbija

5   Mexico City, 1968   57
       Viviane Mahieux

6   Mexico City, Paris, and Life versus Art   65
       Rubén Gallo

7   Spain, Europe: 1977–2003   79
       Ana Fernández-Cebrián

8   Transnational Currents: Europe and the Americas   88
       Rory O'Bryen

PART II SHAPING EVENTS AND LITERARY HISTORY   99

9   France, Spain, 1938   101
       Juli Highfill

10	The Cold War Patrick Iber	113
11	After the Fall of the Wall: 1989–2001 Edmundo Paz Soldán	126
12	Latin American Literature Ilan Stavans	134
13	French Connections Dominique Jullien	142
14	German and Russian Precursors Thomas O. Beebee	158
15	After the Two 9/11s: Santiago, 1973, New York, 2001 Nicholas Birns	169

PART III GENRES, DISCOURSES, MEDIA — 179

16	Essays and Short Stories José Luis Venegas	181
17	Poetry I: The Ghost That Runs through the Writing Rubén Medina	191
18	Poetry II: Parody and the Question of History Sergio Villalobos-Ruminott	201
19	The Novel and the Canon Roberto González Echevarría	212
20	Detective Fiction Pablo Piccato	224
21	Journalism, Media, Mass Culture Tania Gentic	237
22	Literary Criticism and Literary History Ana Del Sarto	250

PART IV AESTHETICS, CULTURE, AND POLITICS — 263

23	The Abomination of Literature Brett Levinson	265

24	Religion and Politics *Aníbal González*	275
25	Gender and Sexuality *Ana Forcinito*	285
26	Race and Ethnicity *Juan E. De Castro*	294
27	Trauma and Collective Memory *Ryan F. Long*	303
28	Fictions of the Avant-Gardes *Michelle Clayton*	312
29	Love and Friendship *Ignacio López-Calvo*	323
30	World Literature: Twenty-First-Century Legacies *Héctor Hoyos*	333

Further Reading 347
Index 373

Contributors

THOMAS O. BEEBEE is Edwin Erle Sparks Professor of Comparative Literature and German at Penn State University. His most recent monograph is *Transmesis: Inside Translation's Black Box* (Palgrave 2012); his most recent edited collection is *German Literature as World Literature* (Bloomsbury 2014). He is editor of the Bloomsbury series Literatures as World Literature, and Editor-in-Chief of the journal *Comparative Literature Studies*. His current research project examines bibliotrauma, bibliotherapy, and belief in popular American fiction.

KSENIJA BILBIJA is Professor of Spanish American Literatures at the University of Wisconsin-Madison specializing in cultural studies, gender criticism, post-traumatic memory, and *cartonera* publishing. Her publications include *Cuerpos Textuales: Metáforas de la génesis narrativa en la literatura latinoamericana del siglo XX*, and *Yo soy trampa: Ensayos sobre la obra de Luisa Valenzuela*. She co-edited *The Art of Truth-Telling About Authoritarian Rule, Accounting for Violence: Marketing Memory in Latin America, Academia Cartonera: A Primer of Latin American Cartonera Publishers*, and most recently *Poner el cuerpo: rescatar y visibilizar las macros sexual y de genera de los archivos dictatoriales del Cono Sur*. From 2001 to 2006 she was the Editor of *Letras Femeninas: Revista de Literatura Femenina Hispánica* and from 2007 to 2012 she directed the Latin American, Caribbean and Iberian Studies Program.

NICHOLAS BIRNS is the author most recently of *The Hyperlocal in Eighteenth- and Nineteenth-Century Literary Space* (Lexington). He has co-edited *Roberto Bolaño as World Literature* (Bloomsbury), *The Contemporary Spanish American Novel* (Bloomsbury), and *Vargas Llosa and Latin American Politics* (Palgrave). He teaches at New York University.

List of Contributors

MICHELLE CLAYTON is Associate Professor of Hispanic Studies and Comparative Literature at Brown University. Her research interests range over modern and contemporary Latin American literature, the historical avant-gardes, and interdisciplinary aesthetic practices. She is the author of *Poetry in Pieces: César Vallejo and Lyric Modernity* (University of California Press, 2011), and she has published articles on modernist and avant-garde experiments, on Latin American novelists, poets, and critics, and on intersections between dance and literature in journals such as the *Revista de estudios hispánicos*, *Modernism/Modernity*, *Modernist Cultures*, and *Dance Research Journal* as well as a number of edited volumes. She is currently completing a second book project, *Moving Bodies of the Avant-Garde*, focused on the role played by dance as image and practice in the international avant-gardes. She is an editor for the Flashpoints series at Northwestern University Press.

JUAN E. DE CASTRO is Associate Professor of Literary Studies in Eugene Lang College at The New School University. Co-editor of *Roberto Bolaño as World Literature*; *The Contemporary Spanish-American Novel: Bolaño and After*; *Vargas Llosa and Latin American Politics*; and editor of *Critical Insights: Mario Vargas Llosa* and *Vargas Llosa and Latin American Politics*, he is the author of *Bread and Beauty: The Cultural Politics of José Carlos Mariátegui*; *Writing Revolution in Latin America: From Martí to García Márquez to Bolaño*; *Vargas Llosa: Public Intellectual in Neoliberal Latin America*; *The Spaces of Latin American Literature: Literature, Tradition, Globalization and Cultural Production*; and *Mestizo Nations: Culture, Race and Conformity in Latin American Literature*.

ANA DEL SARTO is Associate Professor of Latin American Literatures and Cultures in the Department of Spanish and Portuguese at The Ohio State University. Her areas of specialization include Latin American Cultural Studies, Literary, Cultural and Critical Theories, and Modern and Contemporary Latin American Literature. Among her publications are *Los estudios culturales latinoamericanos hacia el siglo XXI*, co-edited with Alicia Ríos and Abril Trigo for a special issue of *Revista Iberoamericana* and *The Latin American Cultural Studies Reader*, co-edited also with Alicia Ríos and Abril Trigo from Duke University Press. She has also published articles on Latin American discourses on criticism (literary criticism, cultural critique, cultural studies), on the interdisciplinary relations between the Humanities and the Social Sciences, on contemporary Latin American women narrative, and on Latin American cinema. Her book,

Sospecha y goce: una genealogía de la crítica cultural chilena, was published through Cuarto Propio in Santiago de Chile. Currently she is working on *Pasiones irreverentes: escritura y afectos*.

ANA FERNÁNDEZ-CEBRIÁN is Assistant Professor of Modern and Contemporary Iberian Studies at Columbia University. She has published extensively on topics related to the ideological production and the transformations of the public sphere in contemporary Spain, with a special emphasis on literature, cultural studies, film, and media. Her articles have appeared in *Bulletin of Contemporary Hispanic Studies, Journal of Contemporary Spanish Literature and Film, Revista Hispánica Moderna*, and *Cervantes: Bulletin of the Cervantes Society of America*, among others. Her book *Fables of Development: Capitalism and Social Imaginaries in Spain (1950–1967)* (Liverpool University Press, under contract) examines cultural fictions and collective social life at the time – the 1950s and 1960s – when Spain turned from autarky to industrial and tourist development. Other research interests include the impact of the accounts of progress, modernity, and scarcity on the expectations of a social majority in the current economic crisis.

ANA FORCINITO is Professor of Latin American Literatures and Cultures, and the holder of the Arsham and Charlotte Ohanessian Chair in the College of Liberal Arts, University of Minnesota. She is the author of *Memorias y nomadías: géneros y cuerpos en los márgenes del posfeminismo* (2004), *Los umbrales del testimonio: entre las narraciones de los sobrevivientes y las marcas de la posdictadura* (2012), *Oyeme con los ojos: Cine, mujeres, voces, visiones* (2018), and *Intermittences: Memory, Justice and the Poetics of the Visible* (2018). She is the editor of *Layers of Memory and the Discourse of Human Rights: Artistic and Testimonial Practices in Latin America and Iberia* (2014), and the co-editor of *Human Rights and Latin American and Iberian Cultures* (2009), *Poner el cuerpo. Rescatar y visibilizar las marcas sexuales y de género de los archivos dictatoriale*s (2017) and *Migraciones, derechos humanos y acciones locales* (2020).

RUBÉN GALLO is the Walter S. Carpenter, Jr., Professor in Language, Literature, and Civilization of Spain at Princeton University, and has written or edited more than ten books on twentieth-century Latin American Literature. His publications include: *Proust's Latin Americans* (2014), *Freud's Mexico: Into the Wilds of Psychoanalysis* (2010), *Mexican Modernity* (2005), and, most recently, *Conversation in Princeton with*

Mario Vargas Llosa (forthcoming from FSG, 2021). He is the recipient of the Gradiva award for the best publication on psychoanalysis and of the MLA's Katherine Singer Kovacs Prize. He is a member of the American Academy of Arts and Sciences.

TANIA GENTIC is Associate Professor in the Department of Spanish and Portuguese and a core faculty member of the Comparative Literature Program at Georgetown University. She specializes in the literature, history, and culture of the contemporary Ibero-Atlantic world, with a focus on literary journalism and sound media. She is the author of *The Everyday Atlantic: Time, Knowledge, and Subjectivity in the Twentieth-Century Iberian and Latin American Newspaper Chronicle* (SUNY, 2013) and articles on a variety of transatlantic topics. Professor Gentic has also co-edited two volumes: *Technology, Literature, and Digital Culture in Latin America: Mediatized Sensibilities in a Globalized Era* (Routledge, 2016), with Matthew Bush, and *Imperialism and the Wider Atlantic: Essays on the Literature, Politics, and Aesthetics of Transatlantic Cultures* (Palgrave Macmillan, 2017), with Francisco LaRubia-Prado. Her current book project is on the culture and politics of sound in post-Transition Barcelona.

ANÍBAL GONZÁLEZ is Professor of Modern Latin American Literature in the Department of Spanish and Portuguese at Yale University. He was general editor of the Cambridge Studies in Latin American and Iberian Literature Series of Cambridge University Press from 1995 to 1997, and is the founder and general editor of the Bucknell Studies in Latin American Literature and Theory Series of Bucknell University Press. A Guggenheim fellow, he is the author of seven books of criticism on topics ranging from Spanish American *Modernismo*, narrative and journalism, ethics and violence, love and politics, and religion and narrative. His latest work, *In Search of the Sacred Book: Religion and the Contemporary Latin American Novel*, was published in 2018.

ROBERTO GONZÁLEZ ECHEVARRÍA is the Sterling Professor of Hispanic and Comparative Literature at Yale University. His many books on Spanish literature of the Golden Age (Rojas, Cervantes, Calderón, Lope) and Latin American literature (Borges, Carpentier, Sarduy, Neruda) have received multiple awards. His *Myth and Archive: A Theory of Latin American Narrative*, which received prizes from the MLA and LASA, has had seven editions, and his *Oxford Book of Latin American Short Stories* has sold 35,000 copies. His work has appeared in eleven languages, including Farsi, Polish, Hebrew, Arabic, and Chinese. His online course on the *Quijote* is available through Yale Open Courses. In 2011, President Barack Obama awarded him the National Humanities Medal at the White House.

JULI HIGHFILL is Professor of Spanish Literature and Culture in the Department of Romance Languages and Literatures at the University of Michigan. In her research she focuses on the Spanish historic avant-garde, popular film in the 1920s and 30s, and cultural production during the Spanish Republic and Civil War. She is the author of *Portraits of Excess: Reading Character in the Modern Spanish Novel* (1999) and *Modernism and Its Merchandise: The Spanish Avant-garde and Material Culture, 1920–1930* (2014). Her current book project focuses on cinema and spectatorship, while tracing the turn from the avant-garde to political engagement in the 1920s and 30s: *Images in Flight: Popular and Political Affect in Spanish Film (1925–1940)*.

HÉCTOR HOYOS is Associate Professor of Iberian and Latin American Cultures and Associate Professor, by courtesy, of Comparative Literature at Stanford University. He is the author of the monographs *Beyond Bolaño: The Global Latin American Novel* (2015) and *Things with a History: Transcultural Materialism and the Literatures of Extraction in Contemporary Latin America* (2019), both by Columbia University Press. He has held visiting appointments at Freie Universität Berlin and Universidad de los Andes in Bogotá.

PATRICK IBER is Associate Professor of History at the University of Wisconsin, Madison. He is the author of *Neither Peace nor Freedom: The Cultural Cold War in Latin America*. In addition to his academic work, he is a frequent contributor to publications such as *Dissent*, *The New Republic*, and *Nueva Sociedad*.

DOMINIQUE JULLIEN is Professor of Comparative Literature and French Studies at UC Santa Barbara. Her research focuses on modern and contemporary fiction, with a particular emphasis on intertextual networks. She is the author of *Proust et ses modèles: les 1001 Nuits et les Mémoires de Saint-Simon dans la Recherche*; *Récits du Nouveau Monde: Les Voyageurs français en Amérique de Chateaubriand à nos jours*; *Les Amoureux de Schéhérazade: variations modernes sur les Mille et Une Nuits*; *Borges*,

Buddhism and World Literature: A Morphology of Renunciation Tales; as well as numerous articles on European and Latin American literature. She has held visiting positions at Saint-Gallen University, Copenhagen University, and Harvard University.

MARÍA INÉS LAGOS is Professor of Spanish, Emerita, at the University of Virginia. She is the author of *Hechura y confección: escritura y subjetividad en narraciones de mujeres latinoamericanas* (2009), *En tono mayor: relatos de formación de protagonista femenina en Hispanoamérica* (1996), and *H. A. Murena en sus ensayos y narraciones: de líder revisionista a marginado* (1989), and editor of *Creación y resistencia: la narrativa de Diamela Eltit, 1983–1998* (2000) and *Exile in Literature* (1988), and co-editor of *La palabra en vilo: narrativa de Luisa Valenzuela* (1996). She obtained her Ph.D. at Columbia University, 1980.

MICHAEL J. LAZZARA (Ph.D. Princeton University) is professor of Latin American Literature and Cultural Studies in the Department of Spanish and Portuguese at the University of California, Davis. He also serves as associate vice provost for academic programs in Global Affairs and is one of the founding faculty of the Program in Human Rights Studies. His research and writing focus on the intersections among culture, memory, history, and human rights in Latin America, especially in the Southern Cone. He is the author of various books, including *Chile in Transition: The Poetics and Politics of Memory* (2006), *Luz Arce and Pinochet's Chile: Testimony in the Aftermath of State Violence* (2011), and *Civil Obedience: Complicity and Complacency in Chile since Pinochet* (2018).

BRETT LEVINSON is a Professor of Comparative Literature at the State University of New York at Binghamton, author of *Secondary Moderns*, *The Ends of Literature*, and *Market and Thought*, as well as approximately fifty articles on Latin American literature, literary theory, and philosophy.

RYAN F. LONG is Associate Professor of Spanish and Comparative Literature at the University of Maryland. His primary areas of study are Mexican literature and visual culture, the writing of Roberto Bolaño, and the life and work of Hannes Meyer. His published books are *Queer Exposures: Sexuality and Photography in the Fiction and Poetry of Roberto Bolaño* (Pittsburgh, 2021) and *Fictions of Totality: The Mexican Novel, 1968, and the National-Popular State* (Purdue, 2008). He is currently writing a book titled *The Poetics of Place and Displacement: Hannes Meyer and Postrevolutionary Mexico*.

IGNACIO LÓPEZ-CALVO is Presidential Chair in the Humanities, Director of the Center for the Humanities, and Professor of Literature at the University of California, Merced. He is the author of more than ninety articles and book chapters, as well as eight single-authored books and seventeen essay collections. He is the co-executive director of the academic journal *Transmodernity: Journal of Peripheral Cultural Production of the Luso-Hispanic World* and the co-executive director of the Palgrave Macmillan Book Series "Historical and Cultural Interconnections between Latin America and Asia" and the Anthem Press book series "Anthem Studies in Latin American Literature and Culture Series." His latest books are *Saudades of Japan and Brazil: Contested Modernities in Lusophone Nikkei Cultural Production* (2019); *Dragons in the Land of the Condor: Tusán Literature and Knowledge in Peru* (2014); *The Affinity of the Eye: Writing Nikkei in Peru* (2013); and *Latino Los Angeles in Film and Fiction: The Cultural Production of Social Anxiety* (2011).

VIVIANE MAHIEUX is Associate Professor of Spanish at the University of California, Irvine. She teaches and writes on contemporary Latin American literature, with a focus on Mexico. She has written *Urban Chroniclers in Modern Latin America* (University of Texas Press, 2011), and published in various academic and cultural journals, including *Letras Libres* and *Nexos* in Mexico. Her past research has spanned the Latin American and European avant-gardes, the city and urban theory, the genre of the chronicle in the nineteenth and twentieth centuries, journalism, and media theory. Most recently, she has published two co-edited books, *El affair Moreno* (with Claudia Darrigrandi and Mariela Méndez, Mansalva 2020) and *Las culturas de la prensa en México* (with Yanna Hadatty Mora, UNAM 2021).

RUBÉN MEDINA is a poet, translator, and scholar. Since 1991 he has been Professor of Latin American literature at the University of Wisconsin-Madison. In poetry he has published *Báilame este viento, Mariana* (1980), *Amor de lejos ... Fools' Love* (Arte Publico 1986), four editions of *Nomadic Nation / Nación nómada, Aquel Quetzalcoalt se fue pal' norte* (2018), and *Los perdidos* (2021). He received a NEA Fellowship in poetry (1981). His scholarly books include: *Autor, autoridad y autorización: escritura y poética de Octavio Paz* (1999), *Genealogías del presente y del pasado: Literatura y cine mexicanos* (2010), a critical edition of *Consejos de 1 discípulo de Marx a 1 fanático de Heidegger* by Mario Santiago Papasquiaro (2016). In collaboration with John Burns, he translated a major anthology of beat poetry: *Una pandilla de salvajes improvisando a las puertas del infierno* (2012), and he recently translated *Memoir of a beatnik* by Diane Di Prima. In 2014 he edited *Perros habitados por las voces del desierto. Poesía infrarrealista entre dos siglos* (Mexico: Aldus), an anthology also published in Perú and Chile.

JONATHAN B. MONROE is Professor of Comparative Literature at Cornell University. Author of *Framing Roberto Bolaño: Poetry, Fiction, Literary History, Politics*; *Demosthenes' Legacy*; and *A Poverty of Objects: The Prose Poem and the Politics of Genre*, he is the editor and co-author of *Writing and Revising the Disciplines*; *Local Knowledges, Local Practices: Writing in the Disciplines at Cornell*, and two special journal issues, *Poetics of Avant-Garde Poetries II.* "Aftershock: Poetry and Cultural Politics since 1989" (*Poetics Today*) and *Poetry, Community, Movement* (*Diacritics*).

RORY O'BRYEN is a Senior Lecturer in Latin American Cultural Studies at the University of Cambridge. He is the author of *Literature, Testimony and Cinema in Contemporary Colombian Culture: Spectres of La Violencia* (2008), and co-editor of *Latin American Popular Culture: Politics, Media, Affect* (2013); *Latin American Cultural Studies: A Reader* (2017); and *Transnational Spanish Studies* (2020). He is editor of the *Journal of Latin American Cultural Studies*.

EDMUNDO PAZ SOLDÁN is Professor of Latin American Literatures at the Department of Romance Studies in Cornell University. He has published twelve novels – among them *Río Fugitivo* (1998), *Los vivos y los muertos* (2008), *Norte* (2011), and *Allá afuera hay monstruos* (2021) – six books of short-stories – among them *Billie Ruth* (2012) and *La vía del futuro* (2021) – and co-edited the book of essays *Bolaño salvaje* (2008). His novels have been translated into twelve languages.

PABLO PICCATO received his B.A. in History at the Universidad Nacional Autónoma de México, in 1989, and his Ph.D. from the University of Texas at Austin in 1997. He is Professor in the Department of History, Columbia University, where he teaches on Latin America, Mexico, and the history of crime. His research focuses on modern Mexico, particularly on crime, politics, and culture. He has taught as visiting faculty at universities in Mexico, Argentina, Brazil, Italy, and France, and has been director of Columbia's Institute of Latin American Studies. His books include *Congreso y Revolución* (1991); *City of Suspects: Crime in Mexico City, 1900–1931* (2001), *The Tyranny of Opinion: Honor in the Construction of the Mexican Public Sphere* (2010), and most recently *A History of Infamy: Crime, Truth, and Justice in Mexico* (2017), which won the María Elena Martínez Prize for the best book in Mexican History from the Conference on Latin American History.

ILAN STAVANS is the Lewis-Sebring Professor of Humanities and Latin American and Latino Culture at Amherst College and the publisher of Restless Books. His recent books include *The Seventh Heaven: Travels through Jewish Latin America* (2019), *How Yiddish Changed America and How America Changed Yiddish* (2020), *Popol Vuh: A Retelling* (2020), and *Selected Translations: Poems 2000–2020* (2021). His work, translated into twenty languages, has been adapted into film, TV, theater, and radio.

JOSÉ LUIS VENEGAS is Professor of Spanish and Interdisciplinary Humanities at Wake Forest University. He is the author of *Decolonizing Modernism: James Joyce and the Development of Spanish American Fiction* (Routledge/Legenda, 2010), *Transatlantic Correspondence: Modernity, Epistolarity, and Literature in Spain and Spanish America, 1898–1992* (Ohio State University Press, 2014), and *The Sublime South: Andalusia, Orientalism, and the Making of Modern Spain* (Northwestern University Press, 2018). He has also published articles in *MLN*, *Comparative Literature Studies*, *Discourse*, *Journal of Latin American Cultural Studies*, and *Hispanic Review*, among other venues.

SERGIO VILLALOBOS-RUMINOTT is Professor of Spanish at the University of Michigan Ann Arbor, PhD at the University of Pittsburgh (2003). Among his publications are the books *Soberanías en suspenso. Imaginación y violencia en América Latina* (La Cebra, 2013); *Heterografías de la violencia. Historia Nihilismo Destrucción* (La Cebra, 2016); *La desarticulación. Epocalidad, hegemonía e historicidad* (ediciones Macul, 2019); and *Asedios al fascismo. Neoliberalismo, revuelta y crisis* (DobleA, 2020). In 2002 he published Ernesto Laclau's conferences in Chile with the title *Hegemonía y antagonismo. El imposible fin de lo político* (Cuarto Propio, 2002). He has also translated into Spanish books by John Beverley: *Subalternismo y representación. Argumentos en teoría cultural* (Iberoamericana, 2003) and *Políticas de la teoría. Ensayos sobre subalternidad y hegemonía* (CELARG, 2011); and William Spanos: *Heidegger y la crisis del humanismo occidental. El caso de la academia metropolitana* (Escaparate, 2009). Among his latest publications are "Mito, destrucción y revuelta: Notas sobre Furio Jesi" (*Revista Diálogos Mediterrânicos*, 2018); "Chilean revolts and the crisis of neoliberal governance" (*Radical Philosophy* 2.07/Spring 2020: 9–16); and "Dirty Cosmopolitanism: Geschlecht III and the Enigma of the Black Box" (*Politica Comun* 14, Michigan, 2020). He teaches regularly on historico-political, visual, and literary aspects of contemporary Latin American culture.

Chronology
Bolaño Roberto

April 28, 1953–July 15, 2003

1953–1968

Childhood in Chile

Born Roberto Bolaño Ávalos in 1953 in Santiago, Chile, the son of a truck driver and a teacher, Bolaño and his sister spent their early years in southern and coastal Chile, the greater part of it in Los Ángeles, Bío Bío.

1968–1977

Youth and Early Career in Mexico City

In 1968, at the age of fifteen, Bolaño moves with his family to Mexico City, where he drops out of school, works as a journalist, and becomes active in left-wing political causes. Traveling to Chile in 1973 to "help build the revolution" in support of the democratically elected socialist president Salvador Allende, he is said to have been briefly arrested and detained following Augusto Pinochet's right-wing military coup, released soon thereafter by two former classmates who had become prison guards. Following his return to Mexico City in 1974, he becomes a co-founder of the "Infrarealist" poetry movement.

1977–2003

Barcelona-Blanes, Spain

Moving to Europe in 1977, eventually to Spain, Bolaño marries and settles on the Costa Brava, near Barcelona, working as a dishwasher, campground custodian, bellhop, and garbage collector. Living and writing for the next twenty-five years in the small Catalan beach town of Blanes, he wins increasing but belated acclaim as a novelist, short-story writer, poet, and essayist. Awarded the 1999 Rómulo Gallegos Prize for *Los detectives salvajes* (*The Savage Detectives*), the novel that brings him international fame, he is hospitalized with liver failure on July 1, 2003 in the Vall d'Hebron University Hospital in Barcelona, where he dies on July 15. Survived by his Spanish wife and their two children, he is posthumously awarded the National Book Critics Circle Award for Fiction in 2008 for his 2004 magnum opus, *2666*.

Major Periods and Works

In the general order of writing and by genre, rather than publication in Spanish and English translation, in the twenty-five years after his early "Infrarealist" period in Mexico City and subsequent move to Spain, Bolaño's major periods and works may be divided into the following four stages:

1. 1980–1990: The 1980s, Bolaño's First Full Decade in Blanes

Prose Poems/Prose Poem Novels/Novels

Amberes. Barcelona: Anagrama, 2002.
Antwerp. Trans. Natasha Wimmer. New York: New Directions, 2010.
El espíritu de la ciencia-ficción. Barcelona: Alfaguara, 2016; New York: Vintage Español, 2017.
The Spirit of Science Fiction. Trans. Natasha Wimmer. New York: New Directions, 2019.
Monsieur Pain. Barcelona: Anagrama, 1999; *La senda de los elefantes*, 1984, written 1981–1982.
Monsieur Pain. Trans. Chris Andrews. New York: New Directions, 2010.
Consejos de un discípulo de Morrison a un fanático de Joyce (co-written with A. G. Porta). Barcelona: Anthropos, 1984, 2006.
El Tercer Reich. Barcelona: Anagrama, 2010.
The Third Reich. Trans. Natasha Wimmer. New York: Farrar, Straus and Giroux, 2011.

2. *1990–1993: A Decisive Transitional Period from Poetry (in Verse and Prose) to Prose Fiction*

Poetry

Los perros románticos. (Prólogo de Pere Gimferer). Barcelona: Lumen, 2000.
Fragmentos de la Universidad Desonocida. Talavera de la Reina: Editorial Gráficas del Tajo, 1993.
La Universidad Desconocida. Barcelona: Anagrama, 2007.
The Unknown University. Trans. Laura Healy. New York: New Directions, 2012.

Short Stories

La Pista de hielo. Santiago de Chile: Planeta, 1993.

3. *1994–1998: An Intensely Productive Middle, Late-Middle Period*

Prose Poems/Short Stories/Novels

La literatura nazi en América. Barcelona: Seix Barral, 1996.
Nazi Literature in the Americas. Trans. Chris Andrews. New York: New Directions, 2008.
Estrella distante. Barcelona: Anagrama, 1996.
Distant Star. Trans. Chris Andrews. New York: New Directions, 2004.
Los detectives salvajes. Barcelona: Anagrama, 1998.
The Savage Detectives. Trans. Natasha Wimmer. New York: Farrar, Straus and Giroux, 2007.

Short Stories

Llamadas telefónicas. Barcelona: Anagrama, 1997.

4. *1999–2003: The Last Four Years' Explosive, Final Burst*

Prose Poems

"Un paseo por la literatura." In *Tres*. Barcelona: El Acantilado, 2000,

"A Stroll through Literature." *Tres.* Bilingual edition, trans. Laura Healy. New York: New Directions, 2011.

Novels

Amuleto. Barcelona: Anagrama, 1999.
Amulet. Trans. Chris Andrews, New York: New Directions, 2006.
Nocturno de Chile. Barcelona: Anagrama, 2000.
By Night in Chile. Trans. Chris Andrews. New York: New Directions, 2003.
Una novelita lumpen. Barcelona: Anagrama, 2002.
A Little Lumpen Novelita. Trans. Natasha Wimmer. New York: New Directions, 2014.
Los sinsabores del verdadero policía. Barcelona: Anagrama, 2011.
Woes of the True Policeman. Trans. Natasha Wimmer. New York: Farrar, Straus and Giroux, 2012.
2666. Barcelona: Anagrama, 2004.
2666. Trans. Natasha Wimmer. New York: Picador/Farrar, Straus and Giroux, 2008.

Short Stories

Putas asesinas. Barcelona: Anagrama, 2001.
El gaucho insufrible. Barcelona: Anagrama, 2003.
Cuentos completos: Llamadas telefónicas/Putas asesinas/El gaucho insufrible. Barcelona: Anagrama, 2010.
Last Evenings on Earth. Trans. Chris Andrews, New York: New Directions, 2006.
The Return. Trans. Chris Andrews. New York: New Directions, 2010.
El secreto del mal. Barcelona: Anagrama, 2007.
The Secret of Evil. Trans. Chris Andrews and Natasha Wimmer. New York: New Directions, 2012.

Essays and Interviews

"Literatura + enfermedad = enfermedad." *El gaucho insufrible.* Barcelona: Anagrama: 2003.
Cuentos: Llamadas telefónicas/Putas asesinas/El gaucho insufrible. Barcelona: Anagrama, 2013.

"Literature + Illness = Illness." *The Insufferable Gaucho.* Trans. Chris Andrews. New York: New Directions, 2010.

"Prólogo: Consejos sobre el arte de escribir cuentos" and "Discurso de Caracas." *Entre paréntesis: ensayos, artículos, y discursos (1998–2003).* Ed. Ignacio Echevarría. Barcelona: Anagrama, 2004.

"Advice on the Art of Writing Short Stories" and "Caracas Address." *Between Parentheses: Essays, Articles, and Speeches (1998–2003).* Trans. Natasha Wimmer. New York: New Directions, 2011.

"Carmen Boullosa entrevista a Roberto Bolaño." *Cadáver Exquisito.* Jan. 24, 2012.

"Reading Is Always More Important Than Writing". Interview with Carmen Boullosa, 2002. Trans. Margaret Carson, *Bomb*, Brooklyn Winter 2002.

The Last Interview and Other Conversations. Trans. Sybil Pérez. New York: Melville House, 2009.

PART I

Geographical, Social, and Historical Contexts

CHAPTER I

Mapping Bolaño's Worlds

Jonathan B. Monroe

Mapping Roberto Bolaño's worlds, "literary" and "non-literary" alike, invites the work of many hands. In that collaborative spirit, conceived and organized in four parts – "Geographical, Social, and Historical Contexts," "Shaping Events and Literary History," "Genres, Discourses, Media," and "Aesthetics, Culture, and Politics" – the twenty-nine essays that follow bring together the work of a distinguished group of scholars representing a range of disciplines. The volume itself is thus a nexus of many overlapping worlds, of locations and perspectives aligned and divergent, a site to encourage conversations about Bolaño's work for generations to come, to 2666 and beyond.

While the Chilean-born Bolaño's posthumously published *La Universidad Desconocida* (*The Unknown University*) and *Cuentos completos* (Complete Short Stories, 2010) consolidate his prodigious achievements in both poetry (in verse and prose) and short fiction, it is above all his twelve published novels (and a thirteenth, co-authored with A. G. Porta, *Consejos de un discípulo de Morrison a un fanático de Joyce* [Advice from a Morrison Disciple to a Joyce Fanatic, 1984] that have established him as the most consequential writer of his generation from Latin America and as the region's most influential novelist since Gabriel García Márquez. In his first two published novels in the early 1980s, *Amberes* (*Antwerp*, 2002/1980) and *Monsieur Pain* (1999/1981–1982; as *La senda de los elefantes* [*The Path of the Elephants*, 1984]); the five he would publish between 1996 and 2000, *La literatura Nazi en América* (*Nazi Literature in the Americas*, 1996), *Estrella distante* (*Distant Star*, 1996), *Los detectives salvajes* (*The Savage Detectives*, 1998), *Amuleto* (*Amulet*, 1999), and *Nocturno de Chile* (*By Night in Chile*, 2000); and three novels published posthumously between 2004 and 2012, *2666* (2004), *El Tercer Reich* (*The Third Reich* 2010; written 1989), and *Los sinsabores del verdadero policía* (*Woes of the True Policeman*, 2011), Bolaño demonstrates an acute sense, as I have argued elsewhere, of the transnational, cross-genre, intermedial pressures

3

facing literature in the last quarter of the twentieth century and first few years of the twenty-first. From *El espíritu de la ciencia-ficción* (*The Spirit of Science Fiction*, 2016), his first novel yet most recent to appear, dating from the same period as *Antwerp, Monsieur Pain,* and *Consejos* (1980–1984), to *Una novelita lumpen* (*A Little Lumpen Novelita*, 2002) and *2666*, the last to appear before his death in 2003 and the first to appear posthumously (2004) – these pressures would prove an enduring concern throughout his career.[1]

Hailed by Juan E. De Castro as "the most admired Latin American writer of the last decades, not only in the region but throughout the world,"[2] by Ignacio López-Calvo as "the most influential writer of his generation and the only Latin American author in the last twenty-five years to have become canonical in the United States and to have achieved world literary status," Bolaño is a writer whose "planetary consciousness" extends, as López-Calvo puts it, "beyond national projects."[3] Confirming these assessments, Héctor Hoyos observes that among writers of the "Global Latin American Novel," Bolaño is the only one to have gained "a critical mass of transnational readership.... In Spanish, and in Chile in particular, Bolaño became Bolaño only after his international canonization."[4] In the last decade, Bolaño's increasingly global influence has continued to register in such titles as Sarah Pollack's "After Bolaño: Rethinking the Politics of Latin American Literature in Translation" (2013); *The Contemporary Spanish-American Novel: Bolaño and After* (Will H. Corral, Nicholas Birns, and De Castro 2013); Hoyos' *Beyond Bolaño: The Global Latin American Novel* (2015), the edited volumes *Roberto Bolaño, a Less Distant Star* (López-Calvo 2015) and *Roberto Bolaño as World Literature* (Birns and De Castro 2017); Jeffrey Lawrence's *Anxieties of Experience: The Literatures of the Americas from Whitman to Bolaño* (2018); and De Castro's *Writing Revolution in Latin America: From Martí to García Márquez to Bolaño* (2019); as well as my

---

[1] See my *Framing Roberto Bolaño: Poetry, Fiction, Literary History, Politics* (Cambridge University Press, 2019) and "Transnational, Intermedial Pressures in Roberto Bolaño's Prose Poem Novels," in *The Oxford Handbook of the Latin American Novel*, co-edited by Juan E. De Castro and Ignacio López-Calvo (forthcoming 2022).

[2] Juan E. De Castro, *Writing Revolution in Latin America: From Martí to García Márquez to Bolaño* (Vanderbilt University Press, 2019), 134.

[3] Ignacio López-Calvo, "World Literature and the Marketing of Roberto Bolaño's Posthumous Works," in *Critical Insights: Contemporary Latin American Fiction,* ed. Ignacio López-Calvo (Salem Press, 2017), 30, 35.

[4] Héctor Hoyos, *Beyond Bolaño: The Global Latin American Novel.* (Columbia University Press, 2015), 4–5.

Framing Roberto Bolaño: Poetry, Fiction, Literary History, Politics (2019) and the present edited volume, *Roberto Bolaño in Context* (2022). As these publications attest, and as Chris Andrews rightly predicted, "all indications are that Bolaño's work is being taken up and integrated into traditions of literary and popular culture, and that coming years will see it monumentalized and officialized."[5] Referring in 2018 to both a "post-Bolaño era" and a "Bolañian Turn in Contemporary Latin/o Fiction," Lawrence characterizes Bolaño, similarly, as not only "the most important literary model for Latin American writers," but "one of the most important contemporary literary models for writers in both the English- and Spanish-speaking worlds," a writer who has "forced US and Latin American writers to confront the cultural expectations of their literary practices."[6]

Affirming the transnational character of Bolaño's literary interests and formation, in his 2002 interview with Carmen Boullosa "Reading Is Always More Important than Writing," one of the last before his death the following year, Bolaño remarked: "Needless to say, I'm not one of those nationalist monsters who only reads what his native country produces. I'm interested in French literature ... in American literature of the 1880s ... Basically, I'm interested in Western literature, and I'm fairly familiar with all of it."[7] As this self-representation and Bolaño's entire body of work make clear, including numerous essays and interviews, hybrid fictional/non-fictional prose, his literary, cultural, social, and political worlds were shaped not only by Chile (1954–1968), Mexico (1968–1977), and Spain (1977–2003), the three principal locations of his life and work, but also by the Americas, and by Europe, more inclusively.

Investigating the period of Bolaño's early formation in Chile, from his birth in Santiago in 1953 to 1968, when he moved with his family to Mexico City, through the five years leading up to the 1973 Pinochet coup,

---

[5] Chris Andrews, *Roberto Bolaño's Fiction: An Expanding Universe* (Columbia University Press, 2014), 204.

[6] Jeffrey Lawrence, *Anxieties of Experience: The Literatures of the Americas from Whitman to Bolaño* (Oxford University Press, 2018), 27.

[7] "Por supuesto, no soy de esos monstruos nacionalistas que sólo leen lo que produce el terruño. Me interesa la literatura francesa .... la literatura norteamericana del ochocientos ... Cuando era adolescente hubo una época en que sólo leía a Poe. En fin, me interesa y creo que conozco un poco de toda la literatura occidental."
    In Carmen Boullosa, "Reading Is Always More Important than Writing," Interview by Carmen Boullosa, trans. Margaret Carson, *The Last Interview and Other Conversations* (Melville House, 2009), 63; "Carmen Boullosa entrevista a Roberto Bolaño," *Cadáver Exquisito* (January 22, 2012) http://micadaverexquisito.blogspot.com/2012/01/carmen-boullosa-entrevista-roberto.html#.YJ23ky 9h3OQ.

María Inés Lagos's "Chile, 1953–1973" focuses on Chile's demographic, cultural, economic, and political conditions in the first few decades of the post–World War II, Cold War era. Encompassing issues of class and education, local, regional, and national identities, she explores legends and myths that have come to circulate about Bolaño along with his growing international reputation, especially concerning his first return trip to Chile in 1973, and the foundational identifications and complex inquiries of a specifically Chilean imaginary that later emerge in such works as *The Spirit of Science Fiction*, *Nazi Literature in the Americas*, and especially *Distant Star* and *By Night in Chile*. Extending Part I's attention in the Chilean context to the period that registers in Bolaño's work as his generation's most defining, Michael Lazzara's "The Pinochet Era, 1973–1990" focuses in particular on the ways his 1996 novel *Estrella distante* (*Distant Star*, 2004) and 2000 novel *Nocturno de Chile* (*By Night in Chile*, 2003) illuminate "the complicity of intellectuals with Pinochet's dictatorial state, ... the moral gray zones to which the dictatorship gave rise, and the myriad ways civilians and intellectuals became implicated in the regime's reign of terror."

As traumatic and shaping as Bolaño understood that context to have been, it was not until the mid-1990s, when the Pinochet era had come to an end, that he began to pursue in his writing an explicit fictional elaboration of its full impact, implications, and consequences. In *Nazi Literature in the Americas*, *Distant Star*, and *By Night in Chile*, Bolaño explores, from the perspective of a writer then in his forties who had lived in Spain for the past two decades, the complicity of writers and intellectuals inside and outside Chile, as throughout Latin America, and the ways in which the aesthetic and political choices that complicity involved were bound up with those of Europe and the Americas more generally.

Of the historical, geopolitical contexts that shaped Bolaño, none figured more centrally than the September 11, 1973 coup in Chile that resulted in the death of the democratically elected socialist president Salvador Allende and two-decade rule of General Augusto Pinochet. While Bolaño traveled only briefly to Chile during the coup before returning to Mexico City, the profound sense in his work of the Pinochet regime's enduring impact and consequences opens onto Ksenija Bilbija's larger inquiry into the legacies of European, especially German, Italian, and Spanish fascism not only in Chile but in "Dictatorships in the Southern Cone" more generally, including the relation between capitalism and communism, centers and peripheries, the role of the United States in authoritarian regimes, and left and right populisms then and now.

Turning from Bolaño's first fifteen years in Chile, the enduring impact of the Pinochet coup, and dictatorships in the Southern Cone to the principal site of Bolaño's development and career for the next decade, Viviane Mahieux's "Mexico City, 1968" elaborates the conditions of possibility for Auxilio Lacouture, the Uruguayan-Mexican narrator and central character of Bolaño's *Amulet*, the "mother of Mexican poetry" and "mother of all poets" who serves as an occasion to remember as far back as ancient Greece and as far forward as 2666. Combining both mythological and historical temporalities, *Amulet* figures a complex coming-to-terms with culture and politics, artistic movements and poetic apprenticeships, at the heart of which are the traumatic events and aftermath of the UNAM occupation and the Tlatlelolco massacre.

Transitioning briefly in 1977 from Mexico City to Paris, eventually settling in Spain, Bolaño would spend the final two decades of his life writing, in his words, "Far from the Southern Hemisphere," in Blanes, near Barcelona. Bolaño's capacious intellectual currents thus run not only between beyond Chile and Mexico City, as Rubén Gallo's "Mexico City, Paris, and Life versus Art" demonstrates in its analysis of Bolaño's short story "Labyrinth," but between Europe and the Americas. Among intellectual precursors shaping Bolaño's work, in addition to the vast number of poets and fiction writers who show up there, Marx, Nietzsche, Freud, and Wittgenstein (whom he calls "the greatest philosopher of the twentieth century") all figure prominently. In the "tax-free" language games of *Antwerp* and integral interweaving of Marxist and psychoanalytic narratives of *Monsieur Pain*; the tensions between fascism and communism, aesthetics and politics in *Distant Star* and *By Night in Chile*; the Nietzschean narrative of history, myth, and eternal return in *Amulet*; the final post-1989, post-9/11 turns of *Woes of the True Policeman* and *2666*, Bolaño develops a complex inquiry into questions of history, philosophy, and language.

Exploring the specifically Spanish, Catalonian, more broadly European contexts of Bolaño's writing in "Spain, Europe: 1977–2003," Ana Fernández-Cebrián traces their integral role in Bolaño's emergence as a major figure of world literature in the last two decades of the twentieth and the first few years of the twenty-first century. In the Costa Brava settings of *Antwerp* and *The Third Reich;* the pre–World War II Paris of *Monsieur Pain;* the co-authored, as-yet-untranslated *Consejos de un discípulo de Morrison a un fanático de Joyce* (with A.G. Porta), Bolaño established himself in the 1980s as a writer as much of Europe, of post-Franco Spain in Catalonia, as of Chile, Mexico, and Latin America, a self-understanding that remains integral through the fall of the Berlin Wall, the 1990s, and the turn of the millennium in the Rome of *A Little Lumpen Novelita*, the Barcelona, Madrid, London, Paris, Hamburg, Berlin, Milan, and other European settings of *Woes of the True Policeman* and *2666*.

As central as Chile and Mexico, France and Spain, the Americas and Europe are to Bolaño, both "in themselves" and "on their own terms," his settings, characters, plots, and concerns often move implicitly and explicitly between and among all these sites. From the Hollywood films in *Antwerp* and Vallejo's last days in Paris in *Monsieur Pain*, to the changes of scene between Santiago and Barcelona in *Distant Star* and *By Night in Chile*, between Barcelona and Mexico City, Hamburg and New York, the Eastern Front and the Sonora Desert in *Woes of the True Policeman* and *2666*, his work explores, as Rory O'Bryen's "Transnational Currents: Europe and the Americas" demonstrates, both hemispheric and trans-Atlantic connections at once historical and literary-historical, social and cultural, economic and political.

Beginning Part II's investigation of "Shaping Events and Literary History" in Bolaño's career, Juli Highfill's "France, Spain, 1938" focuses on connections between Paris, 1938, the setting of *Monsieur Pain*, Bolaño's second published novel (1981–1982), the Spanish Civil War, and the growing threat of fascism on the eve of World War II. Exploring the social, historical, economic, and political context of the exiled Peruvian poet César Vallejo's last days in Paris and Vallejo's integral, shaping role in Bolaño's literary imagination, Highfill finds that imagination encompassing "all the defeats and betrayals of twentieth-century emancipatory projects, all the dead of the European wars, all the bones of those generous youths scattered across Latin America."

Born eight years after the end of World War II, Bolaño lived almost three-quarters of his life, the first thirty-six of his fifty years, within the post–World War II, Cold War frame. Dominated increasingly until 1989 by the intractable binary choice that frame offered between the Soviet Union and the United States, the geopolitics of the half-century between the beginning of World War II and the end of the Cold War found its way repeatedly into Bolaño's work throughout his career. From the space-race-inspiredpired *The Spirt of Science Fiction* and war-gaming culture of *The Third Reich*, to the hemispheric repetitions of fascism in *Nazi Literature in the Americas*, *Distant Star*, *Amulet*, and *By Night in Chile*, to the World War II, Cold War, and post–Cold War narratives of *Woes of the True Policeman* and *2666*, Bolaño demonstrates a keen interest in that era's conjunctions of history, literary history, and politics. At its core, as Patrick Iber's essay on "The Cold War" makes clear, Bolaño's work reflects the choices and stakes, the informing role and enduring impact, of that era's aesthetic and political ideologies and regimes.

While the effects of the Cold War extended as much to the Chile and Mexico of Bolaño's youth and early adulthood as they did to the entire planet, his perspective at the time of the fall of the Berlin Wall was that of a writer who had been living in Europe, at the heart of Cold War tensions, for the past eighteen years. From that location, Bolaño registered in his work that much more acutely and personally, in *The Third Reich*, *Woes of the True Policeman*, and *2666* especially, the implications of a post–World War II, post–Cold War frame, in particular the consequences for his own poetry and fiction, in fact for all of literature as well as other media, of a gradual global transition from questions of ideology to questions of identity. Edmundo Paz Soldán's "After the Fall of the Wall, 1989–2001," explores the ways the end of the Cold War frame, and the emerging economic, cultural, and political contexts of the transitional "New World Order" of the 1990s, reshaped the conditions of Bolaño's late imaginary.

Spanish and Latin American writers too numerous to mention all figure as central influences, in some cases as characters, throughout Bolaño's work, in both his poetry and fiction as well as in his interviews and essays. In the context of Bolaño's lifelong inquiry into questions of poetic and novelistic apprenticeship, his systematic mapping of the choices aspiring writers face and continue to negotiate throughout their careers, Ilan Stavans' essay on "Latin American Literature" as, in Bolaño's metaphor, a "vast minefield," assesses the evolution and range of Bolaño's interpellations in the literature(s) of his native tongue, his stakes and strategies, his complex relations both to other individual authors and to aesthetic ideologies, movements, and schools.

At the heart of his crucial late essay "Literatura + enfermedad = enfermedad" ("Illness + Literature = Illness"), Bolaño emphasizes the enduring legacy and importance to his work of nineteenth-century French poetry, of Baudelaire, Rimbaud, Mallarmé, and Lautréamont in particular. From the early prose poem novels *Antwerp* and *Monsieur Pain* to *The Unknown University*, *Nazi Literature in the Americas*, and *Distant Star*, in his late work from *The Savage Detectives* to *Amulet*, *By Night in Chile*, and *Woes of the True Policeman*, French writers continue to inspire and inform Bolaño's literary ambitions, plots, and characters. In *Distant Star*'s Diego Soto, translator of French symbolist poets; *The Savage Detectives*' Arturo Belano, Bolaño's Baudelairean, Rimbaldian, Bretonian alter-ego; George

Perec, the framing figure of *A Stroll through Literature,* to name just a few, Bolaño demonstrates a profound lifelong indebtedness, as Dominique Jullien's "French Connections" attests, to a wide range of French literature in both poetry and prose.

Less pervasively central to Bolaño's career than Spanish-, English-, and French-language authors, "German and Russian Precursors," as Thomas O. Beebee's essay demonstrates, are nonetheless extensive and generative, including among others Goethe (*The Third Reich*), Novalis (*2666*), Kafka (*Monsieur Pain, Nazi Literature in the Americas, Distant Star, By Night in Chile*) – whom Bolaño calls the "greatest writer of the twentieth century" – and Thomas Mann (*2666*). Among Russian writers in relation to whom Bolaño situates his late work and sense of himself as a novelist in particular, the combined influences of Dostoevsky and Tolstoy (*The Savage Detectives, By Night in Chile, 2666*) are considerable.

From Chile to the United States, finally, from the Pinochet coup to the collapse of the World Trade Center and attack on the Pentagon (twenty years later the Capitol), contexts for the writing of poetry and fiction have changed radically, not only in Europe and the Americas but globally. Providing a site for reflecting on both the trajectory of Bolaño's understanding of the consequences and implications of these changes and on the contemporary status of poetic and novelistic apprenticeships, Part II's concluding essay, Nicholas Birns' "After the Two 9/11s: Santiago de Chile, 1973, New York, 2001" explores how literary cultures have evolved worldwide, in the nearly two decades since Bolaño's death in 2003.

While it is Bolaño's novels, especially the monumental *The Savage Detectives* and *2666*, that have contributed most decisively to his reputation as a representative, generational figure among writers of the last two decades of the twentieth, and the first few years of the twenty-first century, "Part III: Genres, Discourses, Media" begins with José Luis Venegas's essay on Bolaño's considerable achievements in shorter prose forms. Moving fluidly between and among prose poems, short stories, and essays, literary-critical commentary and literary history, hybrid and cross-genre writing, the condensed prose texts collected in the original in Bolaño's *Cuentos completos*, available in English in his *Last Evenings on Earth* and *The Return* (both of which offer selections from *Putas Asesinas* and *Llamadas* Telefónicas), *The Insufferable Gaucho*, and *The Secret of Evil*, demonstrate an impressive variety and mastery.

From his early Infrarealist Manifesto and first collection, *Reinventar el amor* [Reinventing Love], through the selected poems of *The Romantic Dogs*, the triptych of *Tres*, and the posthumously published collected poems of *The Unknown University*, Bolaño was a prolific poet in both verse and prose. While he devoted the final decade of his life almost exclusively to prose fiction, he remained committed to poetry, in all its forms, as Rubén Medina's "Poetry I: The Ghost That Runs through the Writing" reminds us, to the end. Situated like his novels in a transnational literary-historical frame inspired especially by poets writing in Spanish (Darío, Vallejo, Neruda, Huidobro, Borges, Parra, Cardenal, Lihn), French (Baudelaire, Rimbaud, Lautréamont, Mallarmé, Breton, Césaire), and English (Poe, Pound, W.C. Williams, and O'Hara), Bolaño's poetry encompasses in fundamental respects the full range of choices available to poets in the last three decades of the twentieth-century, and in the 1970s and 1980s in particular, from autobiographical first-person verse lyrics to experimental prose poems. Situating Bolaño's investments in poetry, in all its forms, within a broader intertextual and interdiscursive, literary-historical and historical, philosophical and political frame, Sergio Villalobos-Ruminott's "Poetry II: Parody and the Question of History" encourages readers of Bolaño to call into question claims concerning "the privileged relationship between poetry and historical truth, or, alternatively, the relationship between the saying of the poets and the historicity of the people." Challenging his "paradoxical consecration" and "undesired centrality within Latin American Studies" requires a critical response that would be free from both "the mythopoetic frame that has informed" his reception to date and "the imperatives of hegemonic thinking and calculative thought."

Arguing in favor of that very centrality, by contrast, Roberto González Echevarría's "The Novel and the Canon" affirms the literary-historical importance and value of Bolaño's late novella *By Night in Chile* (2000), and of Bolaño's work more generally, as a complex interweaving of tradition and innovation, established aesthetic regimes, and the drive for invention. From *Antwerp* and *Monsieur Pain* to *Woes of the True Policeman* and *2666*, Bolaño's work includes a remarkable variety of approaches and concerns: doppelgängers, displaced autobiography and memoir; detective, horror, and science fiction; linked prose poems and short stories; epistolary exchanges and diary entries; first-person testimonials and historical accounts; obituaries and fairy tales; stories within stories; investigative journalism, literary criticism, and literary history; poetic and novelistic taxonomies; unrestricted and disruptive temporal and historical flows; ventriloquized monological confessionals and dialogical, polyphonic, narratives; heteroglossic narratives from a variety of disciplinary, professional, and occupational perspectives (meta-linguistic and meta-textual; psychological and psychoanalytic; sociological and theological; economic, philosophical, and political); narratives of complicity, marginalization, and exile, of myth and history, progress and impasse, circularity and eternal return; narratives at once national and regional, hemispheric and transatlantic, local and global.

Of all the varieties of prose fiction in play in Bolaño's oeuvre, none figures more prominently, more integrally and centrally from the beginning to the end of his career than the detective genre, the focus of Pablo Piccato's chapter on "Detective Fiction." From *Antwerp*'s playfully metalinguistic, meta-textual, intermedial interweaving of prose poems (Baudelaire and Rimbaud), detective fiction (Arthur Conan Doyle, Agatha Christie), Hollywood and film noir, with its focus on the commodification of genres, poetic apprenticeship and the rules of art to the two Latin American detectives of *Monsieur Pain*, the Chilean detective Abel Romero in *Distant Star*, *The Savage Detectives*' amateur literary detectives Arturo Belano and Ulises Lima narrative, and the investigations of the serial murders of women at the U.S.-Mexican border in *Woes of the True Policeman* and *2666*, Bolaño's investments in detective fiction remain a signature achievement.

Registering the challenges posed to fiction in the last two decades of the twentieth century and the first few years of the twenty-first by investigative journalism in both print and electronic media, by the new journalism and the growing prestige of what's since come to be called "creative non-fiction," Bolaño engages and negotiates fiction's complex relation to non-fiction and the demands of mass culture, in such works as *Antwerp*, *Monsieur Pain*, *The Spirit of Science Fiction*, *The Third Reich*, *Distant Star*, *The Savage Detectives*, *A Little Lumpen Novelita*, *Woes of the True Policeman*, and *2666*, in a variety of ways which Tania Gentic's chapter on "Journalism, Media, Mass Culture" explores.

One of the most striking features of Bolaño's work is the extent to which he understands it as a site for an investigation of the methods and stakes of literary-critical commentary and the construction of literary history by other means. In *Antwerp*'s challenges to legibility and *Monsieur Pain*'s labyrinthine constructions; *The Third Reich*'s making visible of the novel's aesthetic regimes; the literary taxonomies of *Nazi Literature in the Americas* and *Woes of the True Policeman*; the investigative tropes of *Distant Star*, *The Savage Detectives*, and *2666*, including the latter's focus on four professional literary critics and a novelist's growing reputation; and the focus on aesthesis and poiesis in *Amulet* and *By Night in Chile*, Bolaño consistently stages questions Ana Del Sarto explores, in her chapter on "Literary Criticism and Literary History," concerning reading and interpretation.

As attuned as anyone who came of age in the post–World War II, Cold War period in Europe and the Americas to the twentieth-century's defining ideological, geopolitical conflicts, Bolaño incorporates these conflicts into his work throughout his career. Reflecting the transnational historical and literary-historical perspective of a writer who experienced these conflicts from the vantage points of three continents, including in his final decade as well as those of the post-1989 and early post-9/11 periods, his literary worlds are unthinkable – in *Antwerp, Monsieur Pain, The Spirit of Science Fiction, The Third Reich, Nazi Literature in the Americas, Distant Star, The Savage Detectives, Amulet, By Night in Chile, Woes of the True Policeman, 2666* – apart from the struggles for dominance among fascism, communism, and neoliberalism that give rise to what Brett Levinson calls, in the opening essay of the volume's concluding "Part IV: Aesthetics, Culture, and Politics," "The Abomination of Literature."

While far less pervasive a concern for Bolaño than many other issues, the relation between religion and politics, the focus of Aníbal González's essay, plays an integral role in the Chilean novels *Distant Star* and *By Night in Chile* in the complicity they explore between Catholicism and the Pinochet regime. More obliquely, but consequentially, it surfaces, post-9/11, in the Libyan friend of the narrator Bianca's younger brother in *A Little Lumpen Novelita*; the tense encounter on a train between a homosexual Spanish poet and a Maghrebi passenger near the conclusion of *Woes of the True Policeman*; the beating of a Pakistani cab driver in London by two of the four European literary critics in *2666*.

As frequent a theme as any for Bolaño, gender and sexuality figure everywhere in his work from beginning to end, from every angle (heterosexual, homosexual, asexual, pansexual) and in a wide range of registers (unrequited, romantic, pornographic, affectionate). Troublingly for many readers, as Ana Forcinito's chapter on "Gender and Sexuality" makes clear, gender- and sexuality-based violence figures prominently in Bolaño's work, from the murder of a girl at campground on the Costa Brava in *Antwerp*; to the sadism of Carlos Wieder in *Distant Star*; to the homophobic slurs, queer literary taxonomies, polyamorous critics, and serial murders of women in *Woes of the True Policeman* and *2666*. Elaborating a vast array of plots and characters, contexts and consequences, he challenges his readers to respond to the inexhaustible variations and variety of gender relations and human sexuality to their full capacity.

Less pervasively explicit in Bolaño's work than questions of gender and sexuality, questions concerning race and ethnicity nonetheless remain critical. Often playing obliquely, indirectly, implicitly on expectations associated with characters' proper names, their national origin and identity – *Distant Star*'s "Carlos Wieder," "Juan Stein," "Diego Soto"; *The Savage Detectives*' "Juan García Madero," "Arturo Belano," "Ulises Lima," "Cesárea Tinjajero"; *2666*'s "Amalfitano," "Hans Reiter," and "Archimboldi") – Bolaño rarely thematizes questions of race and ethnicity as directly as he does through such characters as El Quemado, in *The Third Reich*, the Libyan friend in *A Little Lumpen Novelita*, and perhaps most significantly, if somewhat belatedly, as Juan E. De Castro's "Race and Ethnicity" explores, through the African-American reporter Óscar Fate in *2666*.

Emerging early as one of Bolaño's central themes in *Monsieur Pain*'s focus on the last days of César Vallejo, the relation between history, psychoanalysis, trauma, and collective memory continues to play out in a variety of ways in such later works as *Nazi Literature in the Americas*, *Distant Star*, *Amulet*, *By Night in Chile*, and *2666*, as well as in the focus of Ryan Long's "Trauma and Collective Memory." Among these works' central concerns are the disorientation of life in capitalism's "Great Market"; the haunting effects of the Spanish Civil War and World War II; the violence of the UNAM occupation and the Tlatleloco massacre; the complicity of intellectuals and literary culture with the Pinochet regime; the pathologization of homosexuality; and the serial murders of women at the U.S.-Mexican border. Focusing in particular on *The Savage Detectives*, the monumental novel set in Mexico that catapulted Bolaño to international literary fame, and the forgotten legacies and enduring, unrealized promises of the historical avant-gardes that remained a pervasive preoccupation and shaping influence on his work throughout his career, Michelle Clayton explores the extent to which his "Fictions of the Avant-Gardes" open onto an international horizon encompassing avant-garde experiments throughout Europe and the Americas. Perhaps most importantly, she argues, Bolaño contributes in important ways, through such central characters as Cesárea Tinjajero and Auxilo Lacouture, to a much-needed reassessment of the contributions of avant-garde female writers and artists previously neglected, undervalued, or altogether forgotten.

Nothing is more important, and nothing more challenging and complicated to address for Bolaño, than the subject of the volume's penultimate essay, Ignacio López-Calvo's "Love and Friendship." Frequently thematizing the blurriness, fluidity, mutuality, and mutability of both terms, both in themselves and in relation to each other – in *Antwerp*, *Monsieur Pain*, *The Spirit of Science Fiction*, the co-authored *Consejos de un discípulo de Morrison a un fanático de Joyce*, and *The Third Reich*; in the poems of *The Unknown University;* in *Nazi Literature in the Americas* and *Distant Star*; in *The Savage Detectives*, *Amulet*, and *By Night in Chile*; in *Woes of the True Policeman* and *2666*, no less in his short stories, essays, and interviews – Bolaño ceaselessly demonstrates how vital a concern they remain at the complex intersection of his life and work, both personally and professionally.

In the context of Bolano's ever-expanding international reputation and increasingly secure place in contemporary world literature, Héctor Hoyos' concluding chapter, "World Literature: Twenty-First-Century Legacies," assesses his critical reception and contributions not only in Europe and the Americas, but on a global, planetary scale, situating his work in particular in relation to non-Western, especially Asian and African contexts. Given the enormous changes that have taken place worldwide in the nineteen years since Bolaño's death in 2003, the radical reframing during that time of all things aesthetic, cultural, and political invites us to continue to reimagine Bolaño's enduring legacy and futurity at the end of the first two decades of the twenty-first century, the emerging century that Bolaño saw clearly, in his final three years, had only just begun.

CHAPTER 2

Chile, 1953–1973
María Inés Lagos

"And the Chilean star rises"[1]

Roberto Bolaño (Santiago de Chile, April 28, 1953 – Barcelona, July 15, 2003) rose to international fame as the author of *Los detectives salvajes* (1998; *The Savage Detectives*, 2007), a novel that won the Herralde Prize (1998) in Spain and the Rómulo Gallegos (1999) in Venezuela. His ambiguous relationship with his native country, which he visited on three occasions after his family emigrated from Chile to Mexico in 1968, remains intriguing. While the circumstances of Bolaño's life and early death have contributed to describing him as a "myth" and "legend," it is his first trip to Chile at age twenty, which coincides with the coup d'état on September 11, 1973, that has primarily helped create his iconoclastic image. I aim here to offer a portrait of Bolaño in the context of the era and places in which he grew up. I have gathered information from diverse sources, including interviews with the author, testimonies from people who knew him, correspondence, and what he wrote in essays and texts recovered from his archive, alongside academic studies and journalistic reviews. I also refer to his three trips to Chile, particularly the first in 1973, when he would have been arrested and incarcerated for several days. This event has given rise to much speculation and even doubt, and has been considered a central experience of his biography. Bolaño includes references in a few narratives to an arrest and imprisonment similar to what, allegedly, happened to the author during his stay in Chile after the coup d'état.

I do not wish to suggest that his work is simply autobiographical or that he merely practiced autofiction. Instead, I sustain that Bolaño utilized his itinerant personal experience, "composed," to a certain extent, of his

---

[1] Rubén Darío, "A Roosevelt." The Chilean flag (1817) is known as "La estrella solitaria" (The Lone Star).

decisions that allowed him to dedicate himself to a kind of deliberately "structured" (his term) literary creation that dialogues with the Western literary tradition. I use the term "composed" that Bolaño himself uses in *Distant Star*[2] and following Mary Catherine Bateson, who proposes the notion of "composing a life," as an expression that includes agency. The critic emphasizes the subject's ability to shape her life through her decisions, a process that intertwines storytelling and remembering. Bateson writes: "The process of improvisation that goes into *composing a life* is compounded in the process of remembering a life, ... Yet this is the second process, *composing a life through memory* as well as through day-to-day choices, that seems to me most essential to creative living" (34, emphasis mine). Accordingly, it is possible to distinguish between different types of composition in relation to Bolaño, who composes his life, composes his literature, and his life within his literature. I concur with the assertion of scholars and writers such as Myrna Solotorevsky, Carlos Franz, and Jonathan B. Monroe,[3] among others, who declare the absolute necessity to distinguish between author, narrator, and character when discussing Bolaño's highly literary texts. The writer often uses autobiographical elements as resources to compose narrative voices, characters, and the ubiquitous character-narrator. Solotorevsky labels "espesor escritural" (scriptural density) that which Bolaño calls "structure" (2012, 207). She discerns in the author's narrative a set of resources that contribute to the creation of this "scriptural density." Likewise, Solotorevsky comments on Bolaño's ability to create incomplete narratives that suggest an ending, but remain in suspense through a series of strategies that simultaneously suggest ambiguity and certainty (2012, 208).

The writer's itinerant life since childhood imprints a peculiar stamp on his subjectivity which is expressed through a sense of distance. Although Bolaño was born in Santiago, as a child he lived in Valparaíso, Viña del Mar, and Quilpué (1959–1964), which at that time was a town inland of the coast in the vicinity of Valparaíso, and later in Cauquenes and Los Ángeles, where his father León had been born. At age fifteen, Bolaño's parents moved the family to Mexico City. His mother, María Victoria Ávalos, who had been to Mexico twice, convinced her husband to relocate there (Alvarez, 36). In Mexico City, the Bolaños stay firstly with friends and then settle in the Lindavista community, afterwards in Colonia Nápoles, only to later move to Samuel 27, Colonia Guadalupe Tepeyac,

---

[2] "[W]e composed the present novel" (1).
[3] Solotorevsky (2008, 1–16; 2012, *passim*), Franz (2013, 99, 110), Monroe (2019, 10).

a neighborhood in the proximity of the Basilica of Our Lady of Guadalupe. They arrive in Mexico the year of the workers' and peasants' strikes which, supported by students, culminate in the Tlatelolco Massacre of October 2, 1968.

Ávalos matriculates her son in a private Catholic school; however, at age sixteen (Herralde, 78), Bolaño decides to abandon formal education to study on his own. As he recalls in "Colonia Lindavista," this was an Opus Dei school, an elite and conservative religious order whose teachers he characterizes as fascist. His parents, he thought, surely must have been unaware of the school's ideological orientation (*The Secret of Evil*, 7).[4] This decision causes shock and malaise in his family because his parents expected that he would finish school. In his defense, Bolaño comments that his forebears on his mother's side of the family had been lazy for three hundred years, whereas his father's side had been illiterate for five hundred.[5] While his mother enjoyed reading poetry and bestsellers, his father only read pocket book cowboy novels (Alvarez, 34). Bolaño learned about Neruda's work through his mother, who read *Twenty Love Poems* to him. In contrast to the frequent moves within Chile, the relocation to Mexico implied adapting to a new country and a metropolis of 14 million people whose history and culture were unknown to him.

When the poet, essayist, and literary critic Jaime Quezada (b.1942) – also from Los Ángeles, Chile like León Bolaño – arrives in Mexico City in 1971 as a fellow at Mexican Cultural Institutions, he stays in the Bolaño house and is surprised to find that Roberto spends his days and nights reading. Quezada writes: "He read and reread all day and night (from Kafka to Eliot, Proust to Joyce, Borges to Paz, Cortázar to García Márquez) ... And was always angry with himself or someone else (which was often me) or with the world, an anger that did not match his beardless, bright white face or his attentive stare, like a precocious intellectual" (Quezada, 7–8). Aside from reading, Bolaño was already writing, and he shared the household typewriter with Quezada. Quezada collaborated on various Mexican publications, especially with articles related to the Chilean political process that was then front-page international news. For the first time, a democratic country had elected, in free elections, a socialist with Marxist leanings as President of the Republic. Later, with the awarding of

---

[4] According to Ignacio Echevarría, most stories in this posthumously published collection are autobiographical or semi-autobiographical (10).
[5] For family history, see "Dance Card" # 32.

the Nobel Prize in Literature to Pablo Neruda in October 1971, he wrote about the Chilean poet.

During that time, Quezada was not only witness to the life that his host family's son led, but he also established a good relationship with him. Recognizing his great interest in literature, he invited him to activities related to intellectual and literary life in Mexico City, and they discussed readings and literary interests. Quezada adds that "despite our always contradictory personal and literary relationships, I admired and had faith in him from the beginning" (9). Bolaño has stated that he learned about Mexico mostly through television, and since he no longer attends school and spends his days reading at home instead, the activities to which Quezada invites him – including attending a course Octavio Paz offers at the Colegio de México – allow him to familiarize himself with the Mexican cultural environment. At the same time, Quezada contributed with comments about the first months of Salvador Allende's presidency and the news that he received periodically from Chile, hence his presence surely reinforced Chilean customs, tastes, and language.

Three Trips to Chile

Bolaño made three trips to Chile after he left the country in 1968. The first was in 1973, when he stayed at Quezada's house in La Cisterna, a borough in Santiago's metropolitan area (Quezada, 10). In those years idealist, progressive, and revolutionary youths from all around the world, especially from the Americas and Europe, went to Chile attracted by the Chilean experiment. They were curious to see a country that, in free and democratic elections, elected a socialist-marxist president in 1970, even after all of the foreign and domestic efforts to impede Salvador Allende from rising to power. As such, Bolaño's trip was not at all unusual for a twenty-year-old in that historic moment. Bolaño says that his trip lasted longer than he expected.

Bolaño, after traveling by land from Mexico to Panama, embarks for Chile, arriving in Santiago on August 30, 1973 (Quezada, 2015). On board he meets Chilean families returning from Europe whom he describes as "extremely reactionary."[6] Upon arriving in Valparaíso he easily recognizes the streets, the main sites, and takes the train to the capital where Jaime Quezada is waiting for him at the Mapocho train station (Quezada, 2015). One unfortunate event related to this trip that appears in

---

[6] First letter to his parents sent from Chile.

some of his works, and even more prominently in interviews in which Bolaño repeats his account, is a traumatic detention and incarceration that likely happened when he was traveling in the south of the country. It has become well known, as it corresponds to the brutal means employed by the Military Junta to subdue young activists. Although there are some who doubt that he was incarcerated, as Bolaño affirms, and even that he visited Chile at all, exactly on those dates, others suggest that this episode shows his support for Popular Unity's revolutionary agenda and the Chilean Road to Socialism as a "young idealist" (Paz, 58). As such, I consider it necessary to explore this episode in more detail.

First, it is important to differentiate between what Bolaño says in interviews and what he writes in works of fiction. It must also be noted that the majority of his interviews were answered in writing via email (Villoro in Braithwaite, 11). In several of them, Bolaño declares that he was detained and imprisoned in rough conditions, a situation that was not uncommon in the first weeks after the coup when those suspected of supporting or contributing to the politics of the Unidad Popular (UP) were persecuted, arrested, tortured, and even murdered.[7] In his reply to Eliseo Álvarez he says: " – I was detained, but a month and a half later, in the south. *The other incident happened in Santiago.* / – And some classmates helped you escape. / – Some classmates from high school. I was detained for eight days" (Braithwaite, 37–38; my emphasis).[8] Bolaño recounts that he was not permitted to make a phone call and was given nothing to eat or drink, and that on hearing others being tortured in the room next to his he thought he would soon be the next victim. After eight days, they set him free thanks to two former classmates from his old high school in Los Ángeles, who had become police and recognized him. Once back in Santiago, he would have stayed in Chile until January 1974, that is to say, a total of five months according to his declarations (Herralde, 78; Bolaño, "I Can't Read," 85, "Dance Card" # 31, 33–35).

It is not uncommon to find erroneous information about this first trip to Chile in newspaper articles or even in scholarly writings on Bolaño. To distinguish between what could have happened to Roberto Bolaño in Chile and what actually happened, we count on reliable sources that

---

[7] After democracy was restored on March 11, 1990 two commissions investigated the crimes committed under the military dictatorship, which produced the 1991 *Rettig Report* (The National Commission for Truth and Reconciliation Report) and the 2004 *Valech report* (The National Commission on Political Imprisonment and Torture Report).

[8] Consistently, Bolaño says that his eight-day detention took place in the south in November 1973. As he does to Eliseo Álvarez, he also mentions a previous incident to Meruane (11).

corroborate what occurred – testimonies from Jaime Quezada and Lina Meruane. At the same time, it is relevant to establish what Bolaño writes in his fictional works about this topic and his responses in interviews that can also be considered texts in which he composes images of his persona for the public, whether orally or in writing. It is worth recalling here a strategy that Bolaño uses for the character Auxilio Lacouture in *Amuleto* (1999; *Amulet*, 2006), whose model is a Uruguayan woman despite the story occurring on the campus of the National University in Mexico City, an episode that evokes police presence at the University on September 18, 1968, two weeks before the Tlatelolco massacre. Solotorevsky writes that in that text, "as often happens in Bolaños' work, [we see] the exactness with which the text appropriates different elements of reality that are later poetically recreated" (28). Similarly, for Mario Vargas Llosa "fiction, [is] that other reality invented by human beings based on their lived and kneaded experiences with the leavening of their imagination and unsatisfied desires" (26). In addition, as Bolaño told Chilean writer and literary critic Lina Meruane: "My literary project is intricately related to my life. My literary project is my life. ... A literary project, a poet's poem, is the poet himself. Always. You know? Always" (Meruane, 9). Lastly, a masterful display of "scriptural density in Bolaño" and how he structures his stories can be found in the introductory note to *Distant Star*. This note may be read as a demonstration of his writing style, which uses humor to link distinct narrative levels that readers will encounter in the text, as in a self-parody.[9]

As indicated, Bolaño repeatedly mentions a traumatic encounter with the military police during his trip to southern Chile. Since he resorts to using biographical information in his fiction, when reading about this incident in a short story some readers and critics alike have deemed this information to be a representation of what happened to the author himself during his first trip back to Chile, instead of an element in a story's plot, or a strategy to portray himself in an interview. Consequently, Bolaño was considered an exile, a label that the author rejects in his essay on exile:

> I returned to Chile when I was twenty to take part in the Revolution, with such bad luck that a few days after I got to Santiago the coup came and the army seized power... I remember the days after the coup ... *five interminable months* that I lived in a state of amazement and urgency. ... *When those five months were up, I left Chile again* and I haven't been back since. /

---

[9] Gutiérrez-Mouat considers that "The autofictional and metafictional prologue is an important element for understanding the novel" (85).

That was the beginning of my exile, or what is commonly known as exile, although the truth is I didn't see it that way (*Between Parentheses*, 54).[10]

Bolaño alludes to this incident in various narratives, including his novels *The Skating Rink* (1993) and *Amulet* (1999),[11] the short stories "Detectives," "Cell Mates," "Last Evenings on Earth," and "Dance Card,"[12] and also in "I Can't Read" (*The Secret of Evil*). In the same fashion as Manuel Puig narrates his 1976 novel *Kiss of the Spider Woman* as a dialogue, in "Detectives," two police recall cases in which they participated in the past. They remember a young man who was detained and incarcerated as a foreign terrorist. It turns out they recognize the man as a former schoolmate, a very similar story to what Bolaño says happened to him in southern Chile in 1973. "Cell Mates" presents the narrator's relationship to a woman who was once his roommate. Coincidentally, they shared a similar experience on the same date, as they both spent time in jail, but while she was in Zaragoza, he was in Chile. "Dance Card" is worth examining as Bolaño tells here that the narrator, presented as his alter ego, was in Santiago at Quezada's house for the September 11 military coup. Later that day he volunteered to help with a communist cell in the neighborhood, where his duty was to keep watch in what turned out to be an empty street. He says he arrived in Chile in August 1973, and that when Neruda died on September 23 he was in Mulchén with aunts, uncles, and cousins. In November, when he travels from Los Ángeles to Concepción by bus, he is detained: "I was the only one they took from the bus" (# 31). Composed of 69 sections, very much like an itinerary in the "dance card" of life, this narrative presents under the guise of a short story reflections that the author has told in interviews, especially the sections concerning his 1973 trip to Chile and his detention by police. Lastly, in "Last Evenings on Earth" the author uses biographical information to situate the events – father and son are Chilean, live in Mexico beginning in 1968, and take a vacation to Acapulco in 1975. When at one point the father is having a good time playing cards and smiling, the son recalls that a year before, in 1974, he had returned from Chile. His father, who was in bed recovering from a broken foot and reading a sports magazine asked him about the trip: "What was it like? he asked, and B recounted his

---

[10] For another version of his experience of the coup see Mihály Dés (Braithwaite, 105–108).
[11] Grínor Rojo comments on this episode as presented in *Amulet*, and on Bolaño's evolving political views.
[12] When translated to English, these short stories were reorganized into two new collections, *Last Evenings on Earth* (which contains "Last Evenings on Earth" and "Dance Card") and *The Return* (which contains "Cell Mates" and "Detectives").

adventures. An episode from the chronicle of Latin America's doomed revolutions. I almost got killed, he said. His father looked at him and smiles. How many times? He asked. Twice, at least, B replied. Now B's father is roaring with laughter and B is trying to think clearly" (*The New Yorker*). As we can see, both characters in the story minimize the danger the son may have experienced.

After reading some of his stories and novels from the 90s – including *Distant Star* (1996) – which moved her deeply, Lina Meruane, living as a freelance in Madrid, proposed to the journal where she collaborated to interview this Chilean writer who was then mostly unknown in Chile and whose work struck her as "outstanding" (Meruane, 10). During that encounter – as she confirmed, checking her notes – Bolaño mentioned "an arrest that occurred before the coup, not during, not after, and not as it is told in 'Detectives' where two policemen from the jail turn out to be Belano's old classmates and decide to save him from a possible execution" (Meruane, 11). Meruane provides this information in her prologue to *Cuentos Completos* (2018; Complete Short Stories) titled "She Never Saw Him Again."[13] This introductory essay reads as a literary homage to the writer she admires. In her text, Meruane achieves an *imitatio* of his "espesor escritural" upon composing a celebratory parody – written in Bolaño's style – in which she narrates in third person the story of M meeting B when she traveled to Blanes to interview the writer before he became famous.

Jaime Quezada shares another testimony about Bolaño's 1973 trip to Chile in his book *Bolaño antes de Bolaño* (2007, Bolaño Before Bolaño). Although this text focuses on his relationship with Bolaño and on his own activities during the time he spent in Mexico from March 1971 to December 1972, Quezada adds a few pages about Bolaño's visit to Chile when the latter stayed at his house in La Cisterna – "September–October 1973, in Santiago de Chile" (115–117) – as well as three letters from Bolaño dated between 1995 and 1998 (119–122). In these pages Quezada refers to his friend's arrival "on the last week of August 1973" (115). He does not provide exact dates or details about Bolaño's activities during his time in Chile, except to say that the military coup finds him visiting relatives in Los Ángeles and Mulchén in southern Chile, and in Concepción. Quezada points out that at his arrival, when he sees him walking confidently and showing off "a wide and provocative leather belt,

---

[13] This expression appears frequently in Bolaño's texts. For instance, "Jim" (*El gaucho insufrible*) ends with "I never saw him again" (Bolaño, 2018, 405).

with a gold buckle made of rifle shells," he warns him: "The first thing you need to do... is take off that belt" (116), explaining that the country is already under military control and severe vigilance, especially in public places, train stations, and bus terminals. Quezada describes Bolaño's appearance as follows: "The marked Mexican rhythm of his speech and the shamelessly foreign look of his clothes, *would bring him moments of unpleasant affliction*" (116, my emphasis). Bolaño's only reply in Quezada's text is: "'I remembered your warning,' he tells me upon returning from the strong, violent, and repressive south, saved only by the fortuitous circumstances of an unknown destiny" (116–117). I want to briefly comment on the sentence I have emphasized which, if at first may be read as a warning, turns out to be an "attenuated"[14] description of whatever happened to his friend in the south when he was stopped by the police for identification. The remaining days, Quezada adds, were spent quietly at home enjoying their friendship, although his guest was just the same young man he had met in Mexico, the host remarks, a discreet form of saying he continued to be difficult. In the meantime, Quezada and Victoria Ávalos tried to find a secure way for Bolaño to go home to Mexico City. Hence, a staff member at the Mexican embassy came in a taxi at dawn to take him to the airport for his flight back to Mexico (Quezada, 117). Relieved that his friend is safe and on his way to Mexico, Quezada laments that the young man had not been able to experience the Chile he remembered and that he wanted to recover, especially the good times spent in Quilpué and Los Ángeles as a child and adolescent.

Nonetheless, in August 2015, Quezada does provide more information in his written reply to questions from Mexican writer and journalist Orlando Cruz Camarillo.[15] In his responses, Quezada confirms that Bolaño arrived to Santiago on August 30, 1973 and returned to Mexico on Tuesday October 2 of the same year, that is, after a stay of nearly five weeks. Therefore, it is true that Bolaño arrived in Santiago in August, a few days or the month before the coup, yet he did not stay for five months as Bolaño repeatedly indicates, since he left in early October on a flight arranged by Mexico's Embassy in Santiago for Chileans going into exile (Quezada, 2015). As a

---

[14] I discuss the concept of attenuation further down.
[15] I am especially thankful to Jaime Quezada for providing me his reply to Orlando Cruz Camarillo's questionnaire *(as moved from the "Further Reading"): ("Respuestas al Cuestionario de Orlando Cruz Camarillo, unpublished document, August 2015")* which contains crucial information to have a better understanding of extratextual Bolaño. In his article, the journalist of *El Universal*, Mexico, D.F. mentions most of the information provided to him by Quezada, and he also adds material from Bolaño's letters to his parents. These are now housed in the Bolaño Collection at Universidad Diego Portales, Santiago.

Mexican resident, twenty-year-old Bolaño left La Cisterna in a taxi that took him to the Mexican Embassy in Las Condes where he joined a group of Chileans to be taken by Mexican diplomatic personnel to Santiago's airport to board a Mexican flight to Mexico City (Quezada, 2015). However, since in addition to references in his fiction, the author mentions in essays and interviews having been arrested and incarcerated for eight days during his 1973 trip and avoided further punishment, even death, due to the help of two former schoolmates, it is not surprising that his own versions of the events have been considered reliable. In any case, this information has given rise to some of the myths that circulate about Bolaño, whose ambiguous and fluid accounts have raised doubts. Larry Rohter, for instance, reports on doubts regarding his presence in Chile at the time of the 1973 military coup. He asserts that, contacted by phone, "now 82 and ailing" León Bolaño told him that "he believed his son was in Chile," but he didn't remember the exact dates. Yet, the father recalls that through his employer he received assurances that the Mexican government "would evacuate his son through the embassy there." Ricardo Pascoe, a Mexican sociologist and diplomat, told Rohter that Bolaño was not at the embassy, "definitely [was] not there." Indeed, Bolaño was not staying at the embassy where people in danger of being apprehended had taken refuge, because he was at Quezada's house. As mentioned, he came to the embassy only to join the group that would be taken to the airport. In addition, Rohter says that Pascoe, who later met Bolaño in Mexico, had asked him about Allende's Chile several times and had found his answers evasive. Writing in 2009 to refute Rohter's information, and referencing his own 2003 article "Bolaño: El coraje del Cult-Pop," Omar Pérez Santiago adds that others have also written on and investigated Bolaño's 1973 trip, citing Quezada's 2007 book and Andrés Gómez's report in *La Tercera*.

After reviewing the information gathered above, I will attempt to compose an itinerary of Bolaño's 1973 trip to Chile. From Jaime Quezada we know that Bolaño arrived in Chile on August 30, 1973 and left on October 2, 1973 thanks to the assistance of the Mexican embassy in Santiago. During the days before the coup, his host took him around the city and they met Quezada's friends, mostly poets, who normally saw each other at a bar called "El Valle de Oro." On the morning of September 11, Quezada woke his guest with the news of the military coup and advised him to stay home that day, as the city was under military control, which is what they did, according to Quezada. On September 20 Bolaño traveled to Los Ángeles to visit relatives (Quezada qtd. Sánchez Mariño). In "Dance Card" Bolaño writes that the day Neruda died – September 23, 1973 – he was with family in Mulchén, a town close to Los Ángeles, from where he left for Concepción to visit a friend, but he was detained and interrogated by military police at a roadblock near the city or in Concepción's bus station. Apparently, the officer did not know what to do with a foreign terrorist, and consulted by phone with his superiors in Concepción's police station, where Bolaño was then taken ("Dance Card" #31). According to Quezada, he was kept there for a time until they checked his papers and let him go. Years later, Quezada's reaction to the dramatic story the writer had told in several interviews – his voluntary work for a communist cell immediately after the coup in Santiago, the eight days of imprisonment, his two former classmates helping him to regain freedom – was a good laugh, "long and happy," attributing the story to "his narrative power":

> Roberto always was a great storyteller, and this increases his image. He created his own story. Nothing of what he told really happened.... The truth is that he felt bound to Chile after the coup. On September 20 he went to visit with some relatives he had in Los Ángeles and then to Concepción to see a friend. He was arrested in Concepción's bus station. They kept him there for a time until they checked his papers. (Quezada qtd. Sánchez Mariño)

Regarding the unlikely story of being rescued by two classmates who recognized him, Quezada says that "those of us who lived those days we know that that was not possible.... He attracted people's attention. It was expected that he could be detained. But there was no jail, he was only interrogated and then he was let go" (Quezada qtd. Sánchez Mariño). Quezada adds that "at the time no one helped anyone, it was barbarism without god or law, except for the bloody *manu militari*" (Quezada, 2015). Afterwards, Bolaño went back to Quezada's house, made arrangements with the Mexican embassy, and returned to Mexico. Because of the deteriorating situation in Chile after the coup, Victoria Ávalos had been very concerned about her son, and she was also in touch with the Mexican authorities to get young Bolaño out as soon as possible.

Upon returning to Mexico after the dramatic Chilean experience and the definitive separation of his parents, whose relationship had been conflictive for years, Bolaño stays with his father, while his sister María Salomé and his mother leave for Spain in 1976 (Molina). In the following years, Bolaño and his friend Mario Santiago become active participants in a movement to oppose the literary establishment and to promote a break with the literary fathers, especially Octavio Paz, positioning themselves among the leaders of the group. In January 1977, Bolaño departs for

Europe intending to go to Sweden, where he presumably had a job, but he stays in Barcelona caring for his ill mother and does not make the anticipated trip.[16] He works doing anything he can, underscoring in interviews that he did all sorts of jobs, from washing dishes in Spain to loading cargo in France.[17] In Barcelona he meets young Latin American exiles, especially Chileans and Argentinians who had left their respective countries fleeing the military dictatorships of the 70s. Given his background, a Chilean coming from Mexico who was in Chile during the military coup, it is perfectly reasonable that he would have been taken for one of them. Besides, it is quite likely that Bolaño might have dramatized a story that allowed him to better integrate into the group, all of which may have ended up being part of his personal story, not just a fictitious episode.[18] Although Bolaño had followed from Mexico the effects of Allende's government in Chile, he was excited to travel to Chile and see with his own eyes what other young people who went to Chile in those years had experienced. When asked about Bolaño's story of being imprisoned for eight days in Chile, Mexican novelist Carmen Boullosa opines that perhaps "he lied" (Rohter) because he felt remorse for not having been there through the excruciating suffering others experienced (Grau, Rohter).

In several stories of *Putas asesinas* (2001),[19] the characters are often young exiles the narrator-protagonist joins.[20] Nonetheless, Bolaño does not consider himself an exile, as he extensively manifests in his essays. This is even less true of his time in Spain, where he felt welcomed (*Between Parentheses*, 32). Yet, for him "a wandering life has been crucial" (House). In 1980 he accepts an offer from his sister, who returns to Mexico with her Catalan husband, to stay in their place in Gerona. There, in 1981, he meets Carolina López, whom he marries in 1985, the same year in which they settle down in Blanes where Victoria Ávalos had started a costume jewelry business (Gutiérrez-Mouat, 3). At first, her son works part-time there; however, Bolaño is most interested in continuing to read and write. To that end, he tries to find jobs that allow him to dedicate a good portion

---

[16] According to his father and sister, Bolaño left Mexico for Europe due to a love affair gone sour. Bolaño himself also mentions that breaking up with his girlfriend, Lisa Johnson, an American poet he had met at a poetry workshop in Mexico City, was the reason he left for Europe (Meruane in Braithwaite, 111; Sanchís, in Braithwaite, 81; Gutiérrez-Mouat, 29).

[17] For Bolaño's financial situation see letters to his father. From 1993 on he lived only from his writing (Mihály Dés, 1998).

[18] Gutiérrez-Mouat writes: "[his] brief experience of imprisonment in Pinochet's Chile extended him a passport, as it were, to frequent many other exiles from Latin American dictatorships" (31).

[19] See n12.   [20] See López-Vicuña.

of his time to writing. One job that he has for several seasons is that of campground manager in Castelldefels. He points out that he feels proud of his role because while he was on watch, there were no incidents, robberies, or fights.

Through his correspondence with Soledad Bianchi, a Chilean academic and literary critic exiled in France who directed the cultural section of the journal *Araucaria*,[21] we know that from 1979 onwards, Bolaño sought ways of publishing his writing. From nearly 20 years of correspondence (1979–1997), Bianchi succeeds in gathering about 60 letters and documents that reveal his activity as a writer, a collection she hands over to Universidad Diego Portales in 2015. Bianchi, who had only known him through letters, meets him in person for the first time in Santiago in 1998 during Bolaño's second trip back to Chile.

Another aspect concerning the writer and his native country that is worth reviewing is his way of expressing opinions about Chilean literature, especially its narrative, and what happens in the country after the coup. Quezada qualifies the opinions of his compatriot as "irreverent":

> the distance from Chile ... allowed him to be the irreverent and iconoclastic man that he was in relation to the people and literature of his native country, and of other literatures and latitudes. Few escaped Bolaño's verbal or written guillotine, his irascible and ironic expressions. ... Although Bolaño did not live Chilean society *in situ*, he heard from sometimes uninformed hearsay and informants about many stories and facts that would later become topics of his novels or creative inventions. (2007, 9)

It is worth underscoring, however, that although Bolaño did not obtain the information he uses *in situ*, that same circumstance may have allowed him greater independence and freedom to create his literature, giving it a broad perspective to represent situations which were not exclusive to one country but rather the grand theme of his work: evil. As Solotorevsky affirms, "the theme of evil is reiterated in Bolaño's texts, appearing as much as a fascination with evil as a repudiation of it" (2012, 208). Furthermore, Bolaño is not interested in creating a nineteenth-century style narrative that rests on the plot, since he prefers rather structural complexity, playfulness, and the crossing over of voices, as he emphasizes in his 1999 interview with Warnken. With regard to politics, although Bolaño considered

---

[21] Although *Araucaria de Chile* (1978–1989) was financed by the communist party, Bianchi states that there was no censorship in the cultural section (Bianchi, 2017).

himself a Trotskyist in his youth, Javier Cercas remarks that Bolaño was not in any way a political activist but a writer above all else (*Babelia*).²²

The poetic and mordant expression "verbal guillotine" that Quezada uses to characterize Bolaño's language when judging Chilean narrative is better understood if we recall events that occurred during his second trip to Santiago in November 1998. After Bolaño is awarded the 1998 Premio Herralde for *The Savage Detectives* and his name acquires sudden fame in Latin America, *Revista Paula* invites him to participate in their annual short story contest as a juror. His wife Carolina López and his son Lautaro (b.1990) accompany him. In an account of this trip, the writer tells how his hosts at *Paula* treated him admirably well, he met writers and critics, received due attention, felt appreciated by the warm welcome, and was seemingly content with his 20-day stay in Chile (*Between Parentheses*, 61–71). Nonetheless, in an article for *Ajoblanco*, Bolaño denigrates Chilean narrative and its authors, and he offers intemperate opinions – which rubbed some circles the wrong way – about a dinner to which he had been invited by writer Diamela Eltit and her husband, Jorge Arrate, in their home. Once back in Spain, Bolaño writes a longer article about the same topics ("The Corridor with No Apparent Exit," *Between Parentheses*, 75–82).²³ Consequently, some of the possible personal relationships with established authors do not prosper, although the opposite happens with the younger generations that venerate Bolaño.

It seems necessary to explain the cultural context in which the apparently intolerant reaction of those who considered Bolaño's language and judgments inexcusable occurred. As Quezada's memories show, Bolaño could be difficult, and he was used to saying what he thought from an early age. Chileans, instead, tend not to use harsh remarks in professional conversations, and much less in public. This is likely due to social norms in Chile which linguist Juana Puga calls "atenuación" (attenuation). Since Bolaño leaves Chile at age fifteen, he probably had not assimilated the relevance of a practice that facilitates social harmony. While frequent in Spain, speaking frankly and directly is normally avoided in Chile, where

---

²² For Bolaño on politics and literature, see Swinburn (Braithwaite, 75–76).
²³ Echevarría comments on the repercussions of Bolaño's behavior regarding Chilean writers (*Between Parentheses*, 3). For Bolaño's own words about Chilean literature, see Braithwaite 94–96. Roberto Brodsky states that "his anger towards Chile during his second visit was a disgrace. We were friends and I had to tell him what I thought" (Ramírez Figueroa). Nonetheless, when Meruane had visited him in Blanes (January 1998), Bolaño was eager to know what Chilean authors were publishing (Meruane, 10). For Meruane's thoughts on this episode see Virginia Bautista. For Nicanor Parra's opinion, see Elisa Montesinos. Even Pedro Lemebel, who had become close to Bolaño, rebuffed his offensive comments.

instead speakers express themselves in a code characterized by evasiveness. This type of behavior circumvents confrontations and exercises criticism in an indirect way, sometimes so subtly that other Spanish speakers do not perceive that they have been criticized or given an order. The frankness of the way Spaniards unequivocally, bluntly, and confidently express themselves is striking to Chileans. On the other hand, "the attenuation of our Spanish draws attention from foreigners" (Puga). It is not in vain that Bolaño had lived in Spain for more than 20 years when he traveled to Chile in 1998, accustomed to sharing his opinions openly in press articles, which Chileans found surprising. However, for those who knew him as a contrarian, Bolaño's motto of "*Et in Sparta ego*" (Herralde, 87; Valdes) seemed more appropriate than "*Et in Arcadia ego*," as he himself points out.

Bolaño made his third and last trip in 1999 to participate in the Santiago International Book Fair (October 26 to November 7) as a special guest after having won the prestigious Rómulo Gallegos Prize. The homage in his honor included a public interview in Estación Mapocho Cultural Center. Cristián Warnken begins the conversation by reading some verses from "Land of Absence" (*Tala*, 1938) by Gabriela Mistral (1888–1957), a poem about the emotions of an expatriate who evokes her native country from a distant land. Warnken immediately asks the author how he relates to these verses by the 1945 Nobel in Literature who, like Bolaño, had not returned to live in Chile after she left for Mexico in 1922. There is no doubt that by asking this question to start the dialogue Warnken reveals the public's interest in this issue, thus offering Bolaño the opportunity to elaborate on his relationship with Chile, especially because his words in the press one year earlier had surely not been forgotten. Moreover, the warm welcome of the previous trip had changed (Valdes).[24]

Bolaño wrote that, due to his accent, Chileans do not identify him as Chilean; Mexicans consider him Chilean or Argentinian, and Spaniards as Latin American (Braithwaite, 110). On many occasions he declared that he feels Latin American, but he asserts that he feels comfortable in Spain, and also that he is not from any given place. However, he points out that he was born in Chile, is Chilean in nationality and carries a Chilean passport.

---

[24] In "I Can't Read," Bolaño writes: "Almost all the Chilean writers decided to attack me *en patota*, as they say in Chile: that is, in a gang. I guess it was their way of congratulating me for winning the Rómulo Gallegos Prize. I counterattacked.... The amazing thing about these accusations is that they were made by left- as well as right-wing Chileans ... What was it that they didn't like about me? Well, someone said it was my teeth. Fair enough. I can't argue with that" (91–92). For Bolaño on exiled Chilean intellectuals see "Perfiles de dos continentes."

In "Exiles" he writes: "the shadow of my native land wasn't erased and in the depths of my stupid heart the certainty persisted that it was there that my destiny lay" (*Between Parentheses*, 53).[25] Interestingly, in his last years he seems to have fantasized about settling in Quilpué, the town where he spent part of his infancy.[26] In terms of his use of the Spanish language, as can be heard in interviews and seen in his writing, he confidently handles different registers of Spanish and adapts his discourse to linguistic usage according to the narrative's topic and the locality where events occur. That is, he is plurilingual in Spanish.

As I have suggested, Bolaño followed what was happening in Chile from afar in Mexico and Spain. He was not exiled[27] and he did not return to live in Chile, such that his experience of Chileanness is different from that of those who spent Allende's years and later those of the military dictatorship in the country, or those who went into exile and later returned when democracy was restored in 1990. Nonetheless, his experience at a distance seems to have been emotionally profound, in a personal and literary dimension. He gave his son the name Lautaro, one of the heroes in Ercilla's *La Araucana*. Another feature, which is characteristically Chilean, is his sense of humor and vernacular wit. Chileans are always "hablando en broma," making up jokes and puns, pulling your leg.[28] Most importantly, his novels *Distant Star* and *By Night in Chile* are among his most notable works. Finally, although he published only one of his novels in Chile, *La pista de hielo*,[29] he attempted to publish *Distant Star* in Chile (October 1995), but since he received no response from the Chilean editor, in March 1996 he sold it to Spain's Anagrama (Quezada, 119–121).

Bolaño's declaration that "all literature carries exile within it, whether the writer has had to pick up and go at the age of twenty or has never left home" ("Exiles," *Between Parentheses*, 49), can be understood more clearly

---

[25] He also said: "The truth is that I'm Chilean and I'm also many other things" (*Between Parentheses*, 33); "I feel Chilean" (Soto); "I believe I am a Chilean writer," and "I am a Spanish-speaking writer" (House).

[26] Bolaño mentioned this wish to Quezada (Quezada, 2015); Echevarría also knew about it (House). A childhood friend from Quilpué points out that the old paradise does not exist anymore (Ortega Parada).

[27] Chilean citizens whose passports showed an "L" ("limited") were banned from entering Chile. This was not Bolaño's case (Cinzano).

[28] His sister remarks that her brother "invented stories with all that information [he had] only to pull your leg" (Molina). Bolaño says that he has always been very imaginative (Meruane in Braithwaite 91]), a personal trait his friend Rodrigo Fresán remembers well (House).

[29] Awarded the 1993 Alcalá de Henares Prize and published in a limited edition in Spain, it was reissued by Planeta-Chile in 1998. On the novel's launch in Santiago, see Meruane, 21.

if we consider the relationship between writing and a "nomadic aesthetics" as proposed by Rosi Braidotti. She asserts that "the polyglot is a linguistic nomad" (29), and that "writing is, for the polyglot, a process of undoing the illusory stability of fixed identities, bursting open the bubble of ontological security that comes from familiarity with one linguistic site" (43). For her, "writers can be polyglots within the same language" (44). Moreover, "becoming a polyglot in your own mother tongue: that's writing" (44). I suggest that Roberto Bolaño is a polyglot in his own mother tongue, as he translates a variety of cultural worlds and sensibilities in his writing. With regard to nomadism "as an intellectual style, nomadism consists not so much in being homeless as in being capable of recreating your home everywhere" (Braidotti, 45), an appropriate characterization of Bolaño's life experience.

Translated from the Spanish by Alexa Jeffress.

3

The Pinochet Era, 1973–1990
Michael J. Lazzara

The Latin American dictatorships and civil conflicts of the 1970s and 1980s, which played out in the midst of the Cold War, indelibly marked the lives of several generations in Chile, Argentina, Uruguay, Brazil, Peru, Guatemala, El Salvador, and other countries, and had profound effects on the intellectual field throughout the region. Realities such as torture, exile, forced disappearances, and other crimes against humanity left traumas that almost a half century later are still palpable and present in individuals and societies; these continue to surface in telling ways amid today's widespread protests against neoliberalism. This state of affairs – persistent trauma, partial truth, and incomplete justice – caused important thinkers of the postdictatorship period (Nelly Richard, Idelber Avelar, Alberto Moreiras, and others) to point out the pervasive melancholic tone of the postdictatorship period. Alberto Moreiras perhaps best summed this up with his often-cited dictum that the tenor of postdictatorship thought was, in fact, "more suffering than celebratory."[1]

The regime of General Augusto Pinochet Ugarte came to power in Chile on September 11, 1973, and put an end to the democratically-elected socialist government of Salvador Allende Gossens (1970–1973), as well as to the hope that many Chileans of the popular classes had of forging a more just and equitable society. While the Pinochet dictatorship shared characteristics with other regimes in the region, it stood apart because of the vast apparatus of political and technocratic support that it enjoyed from right-wing sectors of society.[2] Carlos Huneeus notes that

---

[1] See Alberto Moreiras, "Postdictadura y reforma del pensamiento," *Revista de Crítica Cultural* 7 (November 1993): 27.
[2] Carlos Huneeus, *The Pinochet Regime*, translated by Lake Sagaris (Boulder, CO: Lynne Rienner Publishers, 2007), 1.

"Chile's authoritarian experience brought about profound economic transformations, led by a group of technocrats known as the Chicago Boys, who changed the country's production structure [and] redefined the state's relationship to the economy and society" (2). The unique conjunction of political violence, fear, coercion, and the personalized consolidation of power in the figure of Pinochet created the conditions for neoliberalism to take deep root within Chilean society, backed by many civilians who lauded the dictator and turned a willing blind eye to the violence in the interest of preserving their power and privilege.

Although it is now well known that many conservative Chileans praised Pinochet's "economic miracle" and his regime's restoration of "order" to the country, it took more than two decades into the transition to democracy for the phrase "civilian-military dictatorship" (*dictadura cívico-militar*) to become common parlance in Chile. The complicity of civilians with the regime was one of the great taboo subjects of the transition and not a matter of widespread public debate until the 2010s. Throughout the early years of the transition it was difficult to address the topic of civilian complicity publicly given that so many of Pinochet's supporters remained in influential positions on the national scene.[3] Furthermore, the media was largely dominated by the political right, and economic power remained firmly in the grip of a few. Only more recently – following a momentary memory boom that came with the fortieth anniversary of the coup (2013) and a series of noteworthy economic and political scandals (2014–present) that have implicated public figures linked to the dictatorship in financial crimes perpetrated during the transition – have we seen a growing interest in the topic of civilian complicity (Lazzara, 2018, xvii).[4] The massive protests that broke out in Chile in October 2019 – referred to by Chileans with the term *estallido social* and that included rampant and egregious human-rights violations perpetrated by the police – have further cemented a

---

[3] My book *Civil Obedience: Complicity and Complacency in Chile since Pinochet* (Madison: University of Wisconsin Press, 2018) discusses the wide range of complicities that exist in Chile and analyzes the "fictions of mastery" that complicit figures create to assuage their shame.

[4] Perhaps journalist Javier Rebolledo's works, which include his book *A la sombra de los cuervos: Los cómplices civiles de la dictadura* (In the Raven's Shadow: The Dictatorship's Civilian Accomplices, Santiago de Chile: Ceibo Ediciones, 2015), have played the most pivotal role in sparking national discussion about forms of complicity with the dictatorship.

society-wide awareness of the many complicities that gave birth to today's neoliberal Chile.

In the literary sphere, civilian complicity is a topic that has surfaced primarily in the works of younger writers such as Nona Fernández and Alejandro Zambra, those who came of age in the 1980s and grew up as "children of dictatorship." Prior to these current examples, however, few, if any Chilean writers reflected on the theme of complicity at such length or with such scathing intentionality as Roberto Bolaño.

Bolaño, a writer who was from Chile but also very much a figure of "world" literature (as Héctor Hoyos and others have shown), was indeed ahead of his time in calling attention to and dissecting the moral gray zones to which the Pinochet dictatorship gave rise.[5] Bolaño concentrated his critique specifically on the complicities and implications of those who participated in the country's intellectual life, turning a critique of the intellectual field, as Daniuska González has pointed out, into the "epicenter" of his work.[6] Two of his texts concentrate specifically on the impacts of the Pinochet era in Chile: his 1996 novel *Estrella distante* (Distant Star, 2004) and his 2000 novel *Nocturno de Chile* (By Night in Chile, 2003).

Inspired by Michael Rothberg's formulation of the *implicated subject*, a term that is more capacious than "complicity" and useful for expanding our vocabulary about the workings of political violence, my purpose here is to illustrate how Bolaño's literature explores a range of subject positions that includes both complicity and implication. While, as Rothberg argues, complicity implies direct involvement of the subject in wrongdoing,

> implicated subjects occupy positions aligned with power and privilege without being themselves direct agents of harm; they contribute to, inhabit, inherit, or benefit from regimes of domination but do not originate or control such regimes. An implicated subject is [therefore] neither a victim nor a perpetrator, but rather a participant in histories and social formations that generate the position of victim and perpetrator, and yet in which most people do not occupy such clear-cut roles.[7]

---

[5] See Héctor Hoyos, *Beyond Bolaño: The Global Latin American Novel* (New York: Columbia University Press, 2015). See also Jonathan Beck Monroe, *Framing Roberto Bolaño: Poetry, Fiction, Literary History, Politics* (New York: Cambridge University Press, 2019).
[6] See Daniuska González, "La secta de los escritores bárbaros: Agitando el campo intelectual en *Estrella distante* de Robert Bolaño," unpublished paper, 2013.
[7] Michael Rothberg, *The Implicated Subject: Beyond Victims and Perpetrators* (Stanford: Stanford University Press, 2019), 1.

If the poet-killer Carlos Wieder, also known as Alberto Ruíz-Tagle, is clearly an accomplice to the Pinochet regime in *Distant Star*, figures such as the Opus Dei priest Sebastián Urrutia Lacroix or the belle of the literary salons María Canales in *By Night in Chile* should be more aptly characterized as implicated subjects (in Rothberg's sense) whose example brings into relief the ways in which a "civilized" culture inhabited by barbarism is part and parcel of the dictatorial state.

The Complicit Subject in *Distant Star*

Weaned in the literary workshops of the University of Concepción in the early 1970s, Alberto Ruiz-Tagle – the mysterious protagonist of Bolaño's *Distant Star* who after Pinochet's coup transmutes into the killer-poet Carlos Wieder – is the consummate example of a complicit subject. Schooled in a city commonly known to have been home to the grassroots activity of MIR (Movimiento de Izquierda Revolucionaria, or Leftist Revolutionary Movement) during Salvador Allende's Popular Unity government, Ruiz-Tagle becomes intimately familiar with Marxist doctrine and is well positioned to use that knowledge against the leftist "enemy" when he later joins the military's ranks as a member of the Chilean Air Force.[8] All that we know about Ruiz-Tagle/Wieder comes from an unnamed narrator who joined the literary workshops with him during their student years in Concepción. The narrator relates that Ruiz-Tagle, a figure of tremendous intellectual promise, was touted to be the writer who would one day "revolutionize Chilean poetry" (14). His aerial poetry, which many critics of *Distant Star* have argued is Bolaño's parody of famed Chilean poet Raúl Zurita's skywriting poems, puts Wieder on the cultural map as a figure to watch. But despite the grandiloquent nature of Weider's poetic gesture and the unconventional nature of his medium, the military poet's aerial poetics, as Jonathan Beck Monroe observes, "could scarcely be more conservative": "While

---

[8] The surname Ruiz-Tagle also brings to mind that of former Chilean president Eduardo Frei Ruiz-Tagle, a Christian Democratic president during the post-Pinochet transition to democracy whose government largely "administered" the neoliberal system that the Pinochet regime put into place. Frei's government (1994–2000) became known for its lack of judicial prosecutions of military perpetrators of human rights violations, as well as for its failed attempt to recover information about the disappeared by convening roundtable discussions (Mesa de Diálogo, 1998) between the military and civilian authorities.

innovative in its procedure, the inaugural poem of Wieder's aerial poetics [... reproduces] in Latin, unintelligible to the masses, the creation myth on which the birth of Christianity relies, a conservative myth of origin underscoring the collusion between Chilean Catholicism, the Pinochet regime, and German fascism."[9]

The pinnacle of Wieder's fascist art actions comes in chapter six, roughly the center-point of Bolaño's novel. The chapter focuses on the killer-poet's artistic endeavors of 1974 – a year notoriously known to be the most violent of the Pinochet years and an important one for the consolidation of the regime. One of his art actions is a photographic installation set up in a Providencia apartment. The installation consists of images of disappeared leftist militants, likely taken just prior to their deaths. To "launch" the exhibit, the aviator-poet throws a party at which Tatiana von Beck, the only woman in attendance, enters a dark bedroom where the photographs hang on display. She emerges visibly ill and vomits in the hallway. Guests at the party speculate that Tatiana is drunk, but the reader sees past this and understands that the same photographs that are capable of bringing a smile and a "growing air of satisfaction" to a military captain's face are so reprehensible that they can cause another to vomit (86–87). Among the missing persons whose photographs hang on the wall are those of the Garmendia sisters, two women who, like the narrator, took part years earlier in the Concepción literary workshops and for whose murders Wieder is the likely culprit.

Of all the details the apartment scene contains, two speak volumes to the context of the Pinochet era. First, the photographs of the missing persons hang on the apartment wall in an orderly fashion: "The order in which they were exhibited was not haphazard: there was a progression, an argument, a story (literal and allegorical), a plan" (88). This detail reminds readers of the methodical and intentional nature with which the Pinochet regime carried out its violent acts and flies in the face of the military's tired argument that human rights violations were merely "excesses" of a few rogue actors. Second, a photograph of "a young blonde woman who seemed to be dissolving into the air" evokes disappearance and the phenomenon of the "death flights," in which bodies of drugged prisoners were thrown alive into volcanos, lakes, or the Pacific Ocean, never to be seen again (89).

---

[9] Monroe (2019, 89).

Following the aviator-poet's party, an air of silence and intentional oblivion reigns. One lieutenant makes a list of all the attendees and encourages them to swear not to speak of anything they have seen. The guests, like the real-life Chilean "military family" and its civilian accomplices, enter that night into a *pact of silence*. One person at the party casually remarks that the danger of breaking the "oath," or pact of silence, "lay not with the soldiers but with the civilians," a detail that shows Bolaño's heightened awareness – long before the phrase *dictadura cívico-militar* was commonly used – that the regime's consolidation and projection in time depended not just on the military but on the civilians who supported their "civilizing" mission.

Justice took a long time to materialize after Pinochet's dictatorship. The 1990s were largely a decade of impunity, with counted exceptions. Prosecutions of military officers ramped up only after the watershed moment of Pinochet's 1998 detention in London. Like Pinochet in his nonage, Wieder tries to portray himself as a valiant soldier who sacrificed for the nation and did "his duty as a Chilean," a rhetorical move that is still commonplace among Chilean military officers seeking to save themselves from the clutches of justice. Bolaño wryly expresses frustration with the plodding, uphill battle for justice and the inertia toward forgetting, noting that: "Finally, a courageous and pessimistic judge indicted Wieder in a case that would never get very far ... The country had too many problems to concern itself for a long time with the fading figure of a serial killer who had disappeared years ago. Chile forgot him" (110–111).

Wieder, at bottom, is a complicit subject, but also an emblem of impunity. He lives on in the lore of Chile's popular imagination, still a hero in the eyes of some, out of sight and out of mind for others. In the end, he would pay no price for his crimes.

The Implicated Subject in *By Night in Chile*

Bolaño's *By Night in Chile* confronts readers with intellectuals (or pseudo-intellectuals) who were "implicated" in the state's machinery of terror, subjects whose acts may not have risen to the level of overt criminality but who nevertheless occupy a place on the broad spectrum of moral grays that authoritarian governments create. Evocative of Primo Levi's famous concept of the "gray zone" (here extrapolated beyond the circumscribed universe of the concentration camp), the novel reminds us that authoritarian regimes and the exercise of absolute power cannot be understood through a Manichean lens. Though victims and perpetrators always exist, there is also a vast array of subject positions situated in between those poles. Bolaño's main character and narrator, Father Sebastián Urrutia Lacroix, an Opus Dei priest and literary critic who goes by the pen name of H. Ibacache (a protagonist fashioned after Father Ignacio Valente, the real-life, "official" literary critic for the conservative, pro-Pinochet *El Mercurio* newspaper) is one of several characters in the novel who embody the tremendous hypocrisy and inconsistency of values of cultural elites. His stream-of-consciousness, deathbed confession speaks to a world in which ethics, politics, and the cultural field are in crisis.

If the Allende years (1970–1973) saw an effervescent explosion of culture, the massification of literacy (symbolized most profoundly by the emergence of the popular press known as Editorial Quimantú), and a scenario in which "writing literature and criticism was perceived as inseparable from building a new society," the Pinochet years brought censorship, book burnings, and a "stereotypical and paralyzing mass media culture geared toward larger sections of the population."[10] This is not to say that contestatory cultural practices disappeared completely under Pinochet. To the contrary, many writers of the Allende years went into exile and continued to produce works that drew attention to the realities of dictatorship and repression, while within Chile an underground art and literature scene evaded the censors and produced complex and challenging works from the margins of society.[11]

In *By Night in Chile*, Bolaño is less interested in reminding readers about the rich contestatory artistic practices that existed in Chile under Pinochet than in critiquing the "oscillating scale of [ethical] values," opportunism, and chameleonic morality that characterized the behaviors of so many Chileans.[12] As Bolaño told Dominique Aussenac in a 2002

---

[10] Ideber Avelar, *The Untimely Present: Postdictatorial Latin American Fiction and the Task of Mourning* (Durham: Duke University Press, 1999), 45, 44, 46.
[11] On the alternative art scene, see, in particular, Nelly Richard, *Márgenes e instituciones: arte en Chile desde 1973*, 2nd Edition (Santiago de Chile: Ediciones Metales Pesados, 2007).
[12] Here I am paraphrasing some ideas expounded by Nelly Richard in *Residuos y metáforas (Ensayos de crítica cultural sobre el Chile de la Transición)* (Santiago de Chile: Editorial Cuarto Propio, 1998), 39.

interview, he wanted to call attention to the "lack of guilt" (*la falta de culpa*) in Chilean society.[13] This lack of guilt is channeled through Urrutia Lacroix's vertiginous, deathbed internal monologue – full of dreams, delirium, stories, memories, and reflections detonated under the watchful eye of the *joven envejecido* (wizened youth), the priest's superego and conscience that torments him throughout the novel. As the priest reviews his life, the reader gains insight into how he becomes indoctrinated into a world of literary posers, all of whom jockey for position, declare themselves acolytes of Neruda and others, and crave the unbridled approval of Farewell, a character based on the real-life Hernán Díaz Urrieta, otherwise known as Alone, who worked as a literary critic for the newspapers *El Mercurio* and *La Nación* for over fifty years. Alone's impressionistic literary criticism and sought-after approval, informed by his Francophile taste, was a required "blessing" for any writer or critic in Chile hoping to gain notoriety or become someone.[14] Ironically, or not so ironically, Urrutia Lacroix, whose literary "baptism" occurs during his frequent visits to Farewell's *Là-bas* estate – a clear symbol of the connection between the landed aristocracy and "high" (or civilized) culture – turns his back on the poor farmer-peasants who work at the ranch, chiding them and effectively relegating them to the position of subaltern barbarians. Whenever Urrutia Lacroix senses the judgment of the wizened youth or feels an iota of shame for his attitudes or implications, he averts his gaze to assuage his conscience. Forgetfulness and evasion become his keys to survival: "How pleasant to hear nothing. How pleasant not to have to prop myself up on an elbow, on these poor old weary bones, to stretch out in the bed and rest and look at the grey sky and let the bed drift in the care of the saints, half closing my eyes, to remember nothing and only hear my blood pulsing."[15]

The implication of intellectuals with conservative forces perhaps most stands out in two episodes of the novel that I will touch on briefly. The

---

[13] This line from Aussenac's September 2002 interview with Bolaño, originally published in *Le Matricule des Anges*, is reproduced in Andrés Braithwaite ed., *Bolaño por sí mismo: entrevistas escogidas* (Santiago de Chile: Ediciones Universidad Diego Portales, 2006), 114.

[14] Luis Nitrihual Valdebenito and Juan Manuel Fierro Bustos, "*Nocturno de Chile* de Roberto Bolaño: Metáforas y horror," *Letras* 53.84 (2011): 60. These authors also call attention to Alone's "supposed homosexuality," a characteristic also attributed to Bolaño's Farewell, who makes advances toward Urrutia Lacroix as part of his indoctrination.

[15] Roberto Bolaño, *By Night in Chile*, translated by Chris Andrews (New York: New Directions, 2003), 57.

first of these episodes, which takes place on the eve of Allende's election, speaks of the cooptation of intellectuals by the regime's henchmen. Roughly three-quarters of the way through the novel, the reader meets two characters named Oido and Odeim (Odio and Miedo, hatred and fear spelled in reverse), who recruit Urrutia Lacroix for a civilizing mission to Europe; later these men will become members of Pinochet's secret police organization. The aim of the priest's mission is to preserve historic churches whose facades are deteriorating because of the excrement of doves. The collusion among Oido, Odeim, and Urrutia Lacroix in upholding a Eurocentric, civilizing mission, in a way, evokes the behind-the-scenes machinations of the coup plotters, who readied themselves to bomb La Moneda palace in September 1973. While Urrutia Lacroix is in Italy, a fellow priest, Father Pietro, teaches him to unleash falcons to destroy the doves. This barbaric practice evokes a number of symbolic meanings ranging from the infamous death flights to the Hawker Hunter fighter planes that bombed La Moneda, Operation Condor (a consortium of terror through which Latin American dictatorships cooperated with one another to execute their repressive tactics), and the ways in which forms of fascism traveled from Europe (Italy, Spain) to Latin America. The novel's European episode leaves readers contemplating two searing lessons: that all human institutions need rapacious birds (their henchmen) to do their dirty work and that the preservation of culture and particular ways of life are staked upon the elimination of the weak.

Upon his return to Chile, Urrutia Lacroix lives through Allende's election and the Popular Unity government isolated in his room, voraciously devouring the Greek tragedies. The distancing of the intellectual from the country's social realities is telling and summons critiques that are still frequently levied today against Chilean elites who act and legislate in ways that are out of touch with the realities of people's lives. The coup transpires for the "implicated subject" as something that happens *to* him and for which he does not take responsibility. About the coup itself, Urrutia Lacroix observes: "And we went on living day by day in accordance with the abnormal conventions of the dream-world: anything can happen and whatever happens the dreamer accepts it" (83). Here the state of exception has become the norm and the implicated subject stands by in tacit approval, lacking the courage to speak up or trade his tranquil life as a beneficiary of the dictatorship to denounce injustice. Shortly thereafter, passive implication turns to active implication when Oido and Odeim recruit Urrutia Lacroix to teach classes on Marxism to none other than General Pinochet and the junta. Doing this at first gives the priest pause, but his hesitation turns quickly to acquiescence and eventually to pride in his work. Bolaño's prose captures the sting of moral relativism as the priest's cassock – which generally functions in the novel as a shield behind which he hides his true self – now chameleonically accommodates the "colors" (ideology) of the military: "From the corner of my eye I could see myself reflected in a mirror. The [military junta's] uniforms shimmered a moment like shiny cardboard cut-outs, then like a restless forest. My black, loose-fitting cassock seemed to absorb the whole spectrum of colors in an instant" (91).

Another of the most memorable episodes of implication comes late in the priest's monologue. Urrutia Lacroix recalls his attendance at the workshops of María Canales, a character based on the real-life Mariana Callejas, a literary writer who hosted the crème de la crème of Chile's literary establishment at her Lo Curro mansion, located in the foothills of the Andes outside of Santiago. Callejas was an ideological adventurer whose youthful flirt with socialism gave way to a visceral anti-Marxism when she eventually married Michael Vernon Townley, an American, wannabe CIA-agent who was complicit with some of the most egregious international crimes carried out by Pinochet's secret police, most notably the 1976 assassination of Allende's former minister Orlando Letelier and his assistant Ronnie Karpen Moffitt. Bolaño casts Townley as Jimmy Thompson in a move that metonymically reminds readers of the complicity of the United States not only with the Pinochet regime but also with other authoritarian regimes in Latin America and around the world. One night while the writers of the Chilean vanguard imbibe and exchange ideas in Canales's living room, a theoretician of the avant-garde who happens to be attending the party wanders off and discovers a hidden torture chamber in the basement where he sees a man convalescing on a metallic bed. The theoretician quietly makes his way back to the party and never speaks of what he saw. Though the existence of the torture chamber is *vox populi* – even Canales assuredly knew about it – everyone associated with her turns a blind eye to its existence in a way that makes them all implicated subjects. Bolaño seizes the occasion to offer one of the novel's most pithy insights about complicity and implication: "all horrors are dulled by routine" (122, *la rutina matiza todo horror*). This sentence becomes a way of restating the dynamic of the state of exception: violence becomes the norm and people are willing to tacitly or actively approve of it to maintain the status quo.

The real-life Callejas hosted writers of the 1980s generation at the infamous Lo Curro mansion. Some of them have spoken about the experience, remembering Callejas as a gifted writer and charismatic personality and claiming that they were unaware of Callejas's complicity and criminality; these included Gonzalo Contreras, Carlos Iturra, Enrique Lafourcade, and Carlos Franz, among others.[16] Urrutia Lacroix, however, does feel something like shame that causes him to return to the Lo Curro mansion and confront María Canales in the novel's final pages. He confesses that he knew, secondhand, about the killings that took place in the house's basement. Bolaño's prose foregrounds Canales' evasiveness. She tells the priest that all she wants to discuss is literature and complains that people keep pressuring her to talk about politics.

As the conversation between Urrutia Lacroix and Canales progresses, a question arises that brings the priest profound discomfort.[17] "Do you want to see the basement?" Canales asks (125). Urrutia Lacroix suddenly becomes evasive, turns his head away, and closes his eyes. But Canales insists: "Do you want to see the basement?" For a woman who wishes nothing more than to forget, the question, which arises from an impulse buried deep within her, startles the reader. Her insistence on seeing the basement, despite her desire to look away, speaks to the persistence of shame. It is as if the wizened youth were interrogating her, too, taking her to task, calling out to her to act responsibly. Yet Canales is too weak. Like the real-life Callejas, she would remain haunted by her "implicated" past for years to come.[18]

Take Off the Wig

Roberto Bolaño's novels about the dictatorship era unveil pervasive, long-silenced phenomena such as the complicity and implication of civilians

---

[16] Carlos Iturra fictionalized the case of Callejas and Townley in his short story "Caída en desgracia," in *Crimen y perdón: Cuentos* (Santiago de Chile: Catalonia, 2008), 183–219. Pedro Lemebel also offered his famously scathing caricature of Callejas's literary soirées in his chronicle "Las orquídeas negras de Mariana Callejas (o 'el Centro Cultural de la DINA,'" in *De perlas y cicatrices: Crónicas radiales* (Santiago de Chile: LOM, 1998), 14–15. A more recent creative riff on the Callejas story can be found in Nona Fernández's play *El taller*, in *Bestiario: Freakshow, temporada 1973/1990*, ed. Marcelo Leonart, Ximena Carrera, and Nona Fernández (Santiago de Chile: Ceibo Ediciones, 2013), 135–203.

[17] My reading of the encounter between Urrutia Lacroix and María Canales derives from *Civil Obedience*, 51–52.

[18] The real-life Mariana Callejas eventually paid a judicial price for her complicity in the 1974 assassinations in Buenos Aires of General Carlos Prats (who was loyal to Allende) and his wife, Sofía Cuthbert. In 2009 Santiago's Ninth Appellate Court sentenced Callejas to two consecutive ten-year jail terms for her role in the car bombing. Chile's Supreme Court overturned that ruling in 2010, letting Callejas off with only five years of house arrest and no prison time.

and intellectuals with the dictatorial state. As the epigraph to *By Night in Chile*, taken from Chesterton, suggests, Bolaño's writing implores complicitous individuals and institutions to "take off the wig" and show their true stripes – something we know almost never happens. In launching this mandate, Bolaño leaves no group unscathed, reminding us that complicity and implication occur across the political spectrum and are privative neither of the political left nor the political right.

For Bolaño, not even the institution we call *literature* escapes his invective, something which both Patrick Dove and Ignacio López Vicuña have signaled eloquently. While Dove hones in on Bolaño's view that certain institutionalized modes of literary production can indeed "deaden our sensibilities" more than awaken us to critique or insight, López Vicuña admires Bolaño's capacity to "out" the bureaucratized, civilizing, and marketeering aspects of both literature and the literary establishment: "Stripped of its civilizing aura ... literature can serve to force us to examine those dark and savage dimensions at the heart of every culture, gesturing toward the vanishing point where the borders between civilization and barbarism appear to converge."[19] Bolaño, in short, removes the proverbial wig from both literature as an institution, as well as from the authors and critics who hypocritically routinize and exploit it, especially under conditions of authoritarianism and dictatorship.

While Patrick Dove acknowledges the merits and complexities of Bolaño's writing about states of exception, he does not squander the opportunity to turn Bolaño's critique back on him by asking if in some moments Bolaño's writings also risk "routinizing" the horrors of dictatorship. Recalling the moment in that novel in which the avant-garde poet who attends María Canales's literary soirées discovers a torture chamber in the basement, Dove remarks: "[I]n the figure of a torture victim lying handcuffed to a bed, it would seem that Bolaño himself could not have chosen a more traveled, well-worn cliché to exemplify the contemporary experience of terror." He continues: "Does Bolaño somehow repeat the very crime of which he accuses others of the 'post-Boom' generations, as if to demonstrate despite himself that literature *cannot avoid* 'routinizing' whatever it touches even when it protests against the deadening of our moral and aesthetic sensibilities?"[20] Whether Bolaño is falling into his own trap or signaling its existence, he brings us face-to-face with well-worn questions and debates about the disaster and its representability. He also seems to be asking us as readers to examine our own responses to the

[19] López Vicuña (2009, 164). [20] Dove (2009, 150).

metaphors, images, and language we consume and replicate, perhaps suggesting that the act of reading implicates us both through our interpretations and the actions that derive from them.

Just as Bolaño lays bare the implications and complicities of people, institutions, and ideologies, his injunction is for us all to take off our wigs and consider that the ways in which we speak, think, interpret, and act constantly plunge us into morally and ethically fraught terrain. His novels about the dictatorship era disentangle and obviate the webs of complicity that dictatorships create, while acknowledging how difficult it is for implicated subjects to locate their moral compass and find a way out.

CHAPTER 4

Dictatorships in the Southern Cone
Ksenija Bilbija

Roberto Bolaño's literary fictions come to us from the realm of failed human rights and ineffective state justice systems. Haunted by violence – political, criminal, economic, and psychological – Bolaño's novels and short stories are flagging sites of the ghostly presence that lies beneath: the NN, *nomen nescio*, name unknown, and the *desaparecido*, the disappeared. Language is by its nature perennially haunted by what cannot be conceptualized and rendered textual, by what is lost in translation from the writer's interior landscape to the reader's lettered sign. The Spanish word *historia* – denoting both fictional and historical accounting, story as well as history – is itself marked by the ghostly presence of the letter *h*, visually present yet silenced, haunting the reader's mind. The mute *h* reminds the reader that the unspeakable is embedded in stories and histories even as it resonates in the materiality of the sign. The *h* stands for voiceless stories that don't find their way into histories, the *h* stands for haunting. It also stands for horror that must be translated from an abstraction to a ghostly tale that can be animated in the reader's eye. Although brutally silenced, the ghosts of Bolaño's fiction don't seem to be speechless.

A similar slippage is sustained in the transitive use of an intransitive verb *to disappear*, a verb that should not have a direct object. Through brutal, unforeseen practice, the ghostly direct object rendered possible the idea of "disappearing" someone. As the ghostly, muted *h* recalls that which has not found its way into stories and histories, so the ghostly direct object denotes the illegal abduction and enforced disappearance of persons, a sequence of torture, murder, and concealment through which the authoritarian regimes in Southern Cone enacted the elimination of the body as evidence of a crime committed on that body. The disappearance of evidence rendered repression more powerful (in the absence of visibility) and its victims more ghostly (in the absence of visible bodies). "They are just that...*desaparecidos*. They are not alive, neither are they dead. They are just missing," declared convicted Argentine state criminal General Videla in his often-cited definition of the term.[1] Bolaño's writing exposes the social and political fabric crafted in nations marked by state-sponsored terror, nations haunted by those Videla struggles to capture in his torturous wording. But allowing the voices of the disappeared to be heard – conveying their missives – is not a matter of simple ventriloquism. Bolaño voices the stories and histories of the disappeared by triggering in the mind of the reader a recognition of the silent haunting that animates her pursuit of justice.

Much of Bolaño's writing referencing the human rights abuses in the Southern Cone unpacks the relationship between literary ethics and literary politics in relation to repressive political regimes. Although his poetics have been shaped by the legacies of military terrorism and impunity in Latin America, Bolaño distances himself from other writers of post-dictatorship literature in two ways: he does not employ reparation narrative as a means of coming to terms with trauma, nor does he attempt to speak on behalf of victims. His fictions only rarely center on traumatized victims who seek a suitable language for restitution. Instead, his literary mind charts the social web that allowed for violence and disappearances to happen and seize hold of the society that followed the reasoning of the military state.

Bolaño's books describe the writer's responsibility to account for the complicity between artists and repressive forces, invoking reader skepticism against writers' claimed protagonism in the struggle for human rights, justice, and social memory. His narrative imaginaries posit fascism as ubiquitously present in the contemporary world, and they cynically depict complacent *literati* characters in tacit and active collusion with the perpetrators of violence: the air force pilot/vanguard artist/murderer who is a protagonist of *Estrella Distante* (*1996; Distant Star,* 2004); the poet/literary critic/Opus Dei priest character from *Nocturno de Chile* (2000; *By Night in Chile,* 2003) who hypocritically collaborated with Pinochet's dictatorship; or a compendium of writers and literary entrepreneurs featured in the mock encyclopedia *La literatura Nazi en América* (1996; *Nazi Literature in America,* 2008), writers whose incursions into literary spheres indicate the currency of European Nazi ideology in the New World.

What literary authors confront and make legible regarding human rights abuses matters ethically, because fiction has the capacity to be restorative in channeling repression – state repression as well as the self-repression of

---

[1] BBC News, "Death of Argentina's Videla evokes painful memories," May 17, 2013. www.bbc.com/news/world-latin-america-22578356 (accessed March 15, 2020).

desire – into political critique and social action. And from everything we know about Bolaño – from reading his books and getting entangled in his intertextual traps – he was an avid reader of fiction. He valued literature's power to reflect, refract, realign, and resignify life, its ability to articulate that which escapes us as we keep living. Yet in Bolaño's narratives writers are not saviors who give literary shape to oppressive forms of violence; writers are at best passive, if not parasitic and self-aggrandizing, profiteers of the establishment. The fragmentary autofictional worlds – their ambiguity eluding binary categorizations – that Bolaño extends to his global audience are anything but redemptive, restorative, and action-driven. These worlds do, however, embrace those readers willing to deconstruct the narrative ethics of his fictional representations, engage in literary speleology, and bring the ghostly matter of complicity and evil to the surface. These tasks of deconstruction and excavation are ones that Bolaño's global readers – constituted under the neologism *bolañomaniacs* – have mastered as they have consecrated him as a bestselling and paradigmatic, even cult, author of the literary post-boom era. These readers seem to enjoy, and even to crave, access to the mind of the author – even though that access has never yielded a single happy, liberating, or totalizing ending.

Bolaño is the first writer from post-boom Latin America to transcend intercontinental borders and achieve international recognition on the scale of the 1960s and 1970s literary boom produced by writings of the Peruvian Mario Vargas Llosa, Mexican Carlos Fuentes, Argentine Julio Cortázar, and most of all, the Colombian Gabriel García Márquez, whose *One Hundred Years of Solitude* became a generational emblem. This prior generation's totalizing (and quite exoticizing) fictions – which undoubtedly became the global trademark of Latin American writing – did address the social and political violence in the region and did construct powerful and mythical images of strongmen and dictators. But Bolaño's post-boom opus[2] looks at authoritarian repression through the prism of complicity by the citizens of *the lettered city*, those whose states invested them with cultural power but who failed to undermine those states' practice of repression. His narratives are thus about the unsettled debt

---

[2] Although *McOndo*, an anthology by Alberto Fuguet and Sergio Gómez that is considered an attempt to break with the boom tradition and expectations of Latin American writers, was published in Spain in 1996 (the same year that Bolaño broke into the Spanish-language literary market with his two major works *La literatura nazi en América* and *Nocturno de Chile*), Bolaño's writing was not included in their roster of iconoclastic innovators, nor does it share any traits of the post-boom writing that Fuguet and Gómez featured in their collection.

that remains between responsible literary practices and institutionalized totalitarianism.

Bolaño was born in 1953 in Chile but saw himself as a more broadly Latin American author whose generation was indelibly marked by the dictatorship's repressive violence. While his family moved to Mexico City the year of the government's 1968 Tlatelolco Plaza massacre, Bolaño happened to be in Chile during Pinochet's 1971 coup and was briefly imprisoned there. In 1977, two years after the end of Franco's dictatorship, he relocated to Spain and lived in coastal Catalonia until his early death in 2003. The three countries – each marked by violence, state-sponsored silence, and illegal silencing of opponents – feature prominently in his fiction, each contributing its own history to Bolaño's articulation of ghostly matters of authoritarian legacies. These three are, in some of Bolaño's works, supplanted by the numerous other Latin American nations that have regularly subscribed to regimes of exception.

The apocryphal encyclopedia-like book on *Nazi Literature in America* features fictional biographies of infamous literary authors from nine Latin American countries – Argentina, Colombia, Brazil, Cuba, Chile, Peru, Mexico, Venezuela, Uruguay – who lived between 1894 and 2029 and were inspired by European-born ideology and the aesthetics of fascism. From this fictional accounting of writers moved by fascist ideals emerges the notion that while the line connecting them may not be straightforward, it does not mean that it is nonexistent. These are citizens of the apparitional world that Bolaño's writing brings into fictional existence without referential backing. No one has ever read their writing, and no publisher has evaluated their talent. They are the ghosts of Bolaño's mind, specters of cultures that once took away people by brutal force and annulled their existence. Bolaño's exploration of human rights violations stems from a desire to illuminate these crimes against society – including a need to demonstrate both the imprecise nature of causation and the fluidity of temporal boundaries (such crimes have persisted even as dictatorships have morphed into a neoliberal order). Violence, in Bolaño's work, seems to hold sovereign immunity and cannot be circumscribed by law. Meanwhile its victims, the disappeared, become spectral appearances that haunt Bolaño's narratives. Further contributing to the apparitional character of his writing is the trajectory of Bolaño's literary career: global literary acclaim came only after the posthumous publication of his colossal masterpiece *2666* in 2004, and new books have since continued to appear around the world, both in Spanish and in translations into numerous languages.³ Much of what Bolaño tells us has thus been told after his own death.

In Bolaño's literary register of Nazi ideas, Latin American fascism is a European import that has achieved an autonomous existence in the New World. Despite its undeniable transatlantic journey, Nazism is not limited by history and politics, nor can it be explained through the fascist ideology of number of authoritarian states that periodically thrived in Latin America. In Bolaño's writing universes, we see embodied Deleuze's and Guattari's argument that fascism operates on a "molecular" level (*A Thousand Plateaus* 214) and is not bound by a binary and schematic logic that posits Right and Left, fascist and revolutionary ideologies, as necessarily opposed. In Bolaño's narratives, fascist tendencies seem ever alive and abundantly spilling into the future: not even the 1996 publication date of *Nazi literature in America*, Bolaño's fake compendium of Nazi literature, limits narrative temporality, because the careers of featured writers, including Willy Schürholz, extend to the year 2029.⁴ The signifying plane thus extends towards contexts with which the encyclopedia compiler could not have been acquainted. Bolaño's book seems to suggest that the ghosts of Nazism are not just any ghosts, as many of those featured in the book are still quite alive in the world of the reader and will remain so for years. The longevity of national socialist ideology evidenced in this apparent lack of closure and in its overreaching power in both Americas – eleven writers are related to Argentina, nine to the United States, and the rest come from eight other Latin American countries – suggests its global hegemony. The rhizome of fascism, also seen as "cancerous" in Deleuze and Guattari's wording of its workings, obliquely proliferates through mass movements and is accommodated by hosts who may not even recognize its presence within. Foucault summarizes his view in the preface to the English translation of Deleuze and Guattari's *Anti-Oedipus* as "fascism in us all, in our heads and everyday behavior, the fascism that causes us to love power, to desire the very thing that dominates and exploits us" (xiii). Although the implication of fascist universality is daunting, Bolaño's narrative explores and depicts this unaccountable molecular violence,

---

³ The following books were published posthumously: *2666* in 2004 (in March 2009 *The Guardian* newspaper announced the discovery of the sixth part of the book), *The Third Reich* in 2010 (*El tercer Reich* English 2011); *Los sinsabores del verdadero policía* in 2001 (*Woes of the True Policeman, 2012*); *El espíritu de la ciencia-ficción* in 2016 (*The Spirit of Science Fiction*, 2019); *El secreto del Mal*, 2007 (*The Secret of Evil*, 2010); *Los perros románticos*, 2006 (*The Romantic Dogs*, 2008).

⁴ The epilogue will push the narrative history to 2060, the year when Elizabeth Moreno, the last wife of Argentino Schiaffino, dies.

anachronistic in its core, that resurfaces, escapes, and affects the human construction of society, culture, and arts, all the spheres and practices in which the politics of power operate. While doing so, through a carefully selected range of characters, he also signals the dangers of any utopia of social justice. Nazism, as Bolaño sees it, is adaptable to a variety of national contexts, although it thrives in environments that favor violence, as he illustrates via the Argentine-born Schiffiano brothers, whose passions included both literature and soccer: while invested in their clubs, they also found it natural to offer their skills to the forces of dictatorship and to participate in the illegal kidnapping and torture of their fellow citizens.

Several writers included in Bolaño's encyclopedia colluded directly with Southern Cone dictatorships: Juan Mendiluce Thompson supported both Peronist and military governments, while his sister Luz, who authored the poem "I was happy with Hitler," only considered changing her fascist ideology to please a twenty-five-years-younger Trotskyite poet, Claudia Saldaña, who is later disappeared, and not because she no longer subscribed to the ideological underpinnings of Nazism; Italo Schiaffino, an anti-Semitic literature-soccer fanatic, works for the Argentine press during the 1978 World Cup; Italo's brother Argentino shares both literary and soccer passions and, like Brazilian Amado Cuoto, participates in death squads; Willy Schürholz, who was fascinated by designs of concentration camps and grew up in an isolated Nazi colony (which the encyclopedia's narrator tells us ceased to be newsworthy after the 1973 military coup) that was integrated in Pinochet's Chile; the infamous Ramírez Hoffman was a pilot of the Chilean Airforce and found artistic inspiration in killing mostly women.

The spectral presence in *Nazi Literature in the Americas* is twofold: On the one hand, although the literary lives of many included writers were fully analyzed and put into historical perspective, others were still alive in 1996 (when the book was published) and a few are ostensibly still among us in 2020, a fact that makes us intermittently feel their eerie presence around us, in our own countries. On the other hand, and beyond the fact that (if we are to believe the encyclopedia's author) these were not very good writers, their literary opus is non-existent, ghostly, and only intermittently revived in the encyclopedia's direct quotations.

Starting even from the epigraph of *Nazi Literature in America* – Augusto Monterroso's microfictional postulation against the Heraclitean predicament that one cannot swim twice in the same river, proposing that under certain muddled circumstances "it *is* possible to bathe twice (or even three times, should your personal hygiene so require) in the same river" – Bolaño sarcastically recalls the redemptive demand of "Never Again" as raised after the Holocaust and then repeated following each new violent regime of state terror, most prominently in the Southern Cone and Central American countries of the New World. The undeniable reality that the human rights slogan of Never Again, calling for an end to violence, is repeated again and again and again, to the point that it almost sounds hollow, suggests that humanity indeed does swim repeatedly in the same muddy river of history while consciously displaying its will to silence and forget. Along the same lines of ever-repeating violence, Bolaño's novel *Distant Star* features an experimental poet and murderer Carlos Wieder, whose last name, as the narrative explains in great detail, in German means "again." And while human rights appeals indicate an endless deferring of a just social order, literature is failing in its prerogative of exposing social ills. "Take off [your] wig," demands the epigraph from Chesterton that Bolaño uses to head the novel *By Night in Chile*, insinuating to the reader that another disguise will be removed through the fiction. And yet, Chesterton's words inevitably recall the letdown experienced when priest-detective Father Brown removes the suspicious Duke's wig to reveal only his shiny bald head and nothing else. What, then, is there for literature to unearth? Faulkner's words – echoed as the epigraph of *Distant Star* ("What star falls unseen") and recalling the national flag, nicknamed *La Estrella Solitaria*, The Lone Star – remind us that the stars we see today are ones that fell long ago. Their light, if we look at the right time and in the right direction, eventually reveals the existence of these extinguished stars. Reading literature, similarly, will make us see the ghosts of the past. The body of the disappeared Garmendia sister, killed by a malicious aviator/artist (Carlos Wieder) whose art needed a mutilated female body to inscribe its sublime impulse, appears many years later in a mass grave – and we see the appearance of this ghostly form of the disappeared star in the spectral configuration of Bolaño's novel.

Spectral haunting is the essence of Bolaño's writing. Nothing ever concludes nor achieves closure in Bolaño's fiction.[5] Regimes of exception recur endlessly. Characters migrate from one book to another. Fictional authors often share his very name – as in Arturo Belano, Arturo B, or simply B, iterations that undoubtfully make one think of Bolaño. Autofiction and fiction indistinctly bear witness to past horror. The unconscious keeps intruding in spite of being repressed and kept at bay

---

[5] As many of Bolaño's books were published posthumously and continue to be extracted from the memory of his computer, not even the death of an author can imply an end to his opus.

so that the subject can attempt to function. It is as if those who populate his texts could not be contained within just one story, or they need more space to act and thus transition to a new novel. Or even, as if they exist independently from the novel and Bolaño occasionally captures their ongoing activities. The infamous protagonist Ramirez Hoffman, the last entry of *Nazi Literature in America*, then becomes the main character of the novel *Distant Star* and is also remembered by the moribund right-wing conservative priest who collaborates with the military government in *By Night in Chile*. We assume that the priest dies, and we imagine that the infamous Ramírez Hoffman is killed by the hired detective, but consequences remain always inferred, as none of these transpire within the fiction. Bolaño's is an absent end, assumed but not legible, insinuated by the year of Hoffman's death in the encyclopedia entry. This constant inconclusiveness and repetition of uncompleted scenes, this elliptical storytelling that – much as portions of the unconscious that reach the conscious mind tend to omit a segment or two of the events' sequences – obsessively displaces stories and characters, this narrative cyclicality and open-endedness, the compulsive irruptions of violence, together, these urge the reader to look historically and geographically beyond military dictatorships in Paraguay (1954–1989), Brazil (1964–1985), Chile (1973–1990), Uruguay (1973–1985), and Argentina (1976–1983), in search of an indirect connection between the manifestations of violence and those manifestations' oblique causes. One of those rhizomatic "thought ideas," proposed by Deleuze and Guattari, is mapped out in the *Nazi Literature in America*'s fictional archive, which Bolaño constructs to suggest a ubiquity of fascism in both North and South America.

The ghosts lurking in the pseudo–encyclopedia entry titled "The Infamous Ramírez Hoffman" needed and eventually acquired a more spacious narrative, installing themselves in the novel-length account of the assassin aviator published the same year as *Distant Star*. Also, among the apparitional substitutions in the novel is a narrator called "Bolaño," who now takes a secondary position and collaborates with a certain Arturo B. (a pseudonym that Bolaño often used in his narratives and that many critics consider to be his alter ego), who has a direct experience, a *testimonio* to share. He is also a Chilean poet, "veteran of Latin America's doomed revolutions," who expands the story of Carlos Wieder, the military pilot who murders for the sake of authentic artistic inspiration. The prologue of *Distant Star* explicitly invokes another "animated ghost," that of Borges's Pierre Ménard, "author of the Quixote," who rewrote *Don Quixote* several centuries after Cervantes. While textually identical, Borges frames

Menard's anachronistic work as richer in meaning and more open to interpretations, in particular in unintended contexts. Bolaño's spectral framing proposes taking a second look at the military dictatorship and recognizes its neoliberal component as a legacy that Chilean society has not properly addressed.[6] In *Distant Star* he brilliantly depicts a first-person narrator, Arturo B., who would recognize Carlos Wieder from the pre-coup Allende era literary gathering that both writers attended. An anonymous contractor residing in Chile hires Arturo B. to read obscure avant-garde sources in the hope of identifying Carlos Wieder through his writing. He successfully accomplishes the identification and, the novel implies, Wieder is executed. The alleged murderer Wieder is not, however, convicted by any court – Chilean, international, or otherwise. By participating in his extrajudicial killing, Arturo B. (Bolaño in the encyclopedia's shorter version) actually becomes accomplice to a murder;[7] moreover, he is accomplice to the murder of a character whom earlier – in a telling moment where he dreams of the soon-to-be-dead aviator assassin, he has recognized in an uncanny sensation as his own double. Arturo's unconscious has spoken to him through a dream, in the image of a shipwreck in which Arturo and Wieder find themselves collectively overturned: while the pilot "may have conspired to sink it, he [Arturo] had done little or nothing to stop it from going down" (122). And while the novel implies Wieder committed his killings for the (morbid) sake of artistic authenticity and inspiration, Arturo B., unsure of the exact price for his literary research project of identifying the workshop participant but deeming three hundred thousand pesetas "too much" (149), seems to be employed in this task by another profiteer of Pinochet's neoliberal miracle who "made a fortune in the last few years [...] and in Chile too, not abroad" (137). The ghost of Wieder (again and again) can return or has already returned, possibly through the narrator's reading of Wieder's death – inspired verses (a process that turns Arturo B., a silent witness, into an accomplice to Wieder's murder) – and potentially even speaking to us, the readers of Bolaño's novel, regarding the stories we tell ourselves.

---

[6] Banners and graffiti reading "It's not about 30 pesos, it's about 30 years," which have surfaced during ongoing social protests in Chile, explicitly link the dictatorship's legacy of wealth inequality to the truncated social reparations process.

[7] Bolaño's novel was published in 1996, some five years after the Rettig Report of the Chilean Truth and Reconciliation Commission (1991) accounted only for cases of those who died under the dictatorship while excluding the cases and testimonies of torture survivors. While clarifying from the beginning that the Commission had no legal bearing or legal competence, the report identified victims but failed to identify individual perpetrators as responsible for those victims' injury.

The ending of *Distant Star* is paradigmatic in Bolaño's focus on a Chilean writer in exile who is hired to assist with the vigilante-type murder of a Pinochet-era assassin (and elusive vanguard poet) living in Spain. While Bolaño leaves the reader to guess the true market value for assisting in murder, monetary compensation features prominently in the discussion between Arturo B and the detective who is in charge of identifying the target and hiring the narrator to help him (since allegedly, nobody less than a poet can successfully read the tracks of another poet). Monetary compensation from a mysterious entity based in Chile serves as restitution for the job that ostensibly only a man of letters can perform. The neoliberal state's global market economy thus seems even to have a place for poets – even though the place thus made for them seems immersed in "literature's bottomless cesspools" (130) or the *mar de mierda* of literature, as the Spanish original reads. The freedom inaugurated by the free market seems immoral and the free subject, as exemplified in the poet whose name the novel evolved to resemble, though no longer directly echo, Bolaño's, is left feeling ethically compromised. The reader is haunted by the irony of the circumstances that prepare a poet who once had revolutionary ideals to be complicit in a murder. Bolaño leaves unresolved whether this act may inspire his poet's future literary production, but the picture it does paint of violence as a legitimate response to the failure of the state justice system is unambiguously ominous. The novel consequently projects a cynical vision of the relationship between individual and society.

Bolaño's novel *By Night in Chile* features yet another kind of ghostly presence – in this case, the wizened youth that haunts the Opus Dei priest Urrutia Lacroix and prompts him to trace his own life's ethical trajectory. The wizened youth might represent a refraction of the priest's own identity, confronting him with the person he imagined he would become versus the person he indeed became in a self-centered rationalization of his past. Or we might read the encounter as an interrogation by a ghostly presence of the tortured and disappeared who were brutally vanished in the very spaces where tacit collaborators with the dictatorship attended poetry soirees with the powerful leaders that gave them an audience? In either scenario, the priest's confession is addressed neither to the victims/disappeared nor to any other audience that would benefit from that confession in the project of advancing reparation and reconciliation. Although this novel – structured as a single 150-page paragraph, plus one concluding sentence – adopts an apparently confessional tone, its textual content is nothing more than a prominent member of the Chilean religious and literary society justifying his choice to accept, silently and willingly, the dictatorship's offered hand and to close his eyes to the regime's obvious human rights abuses. Although he has one eye on his impending death, and the other on a hoped-for personal salvation, Father Urrutia speaks words that are more directly and actually prompted by the ghostly presence of Bolaño's own spectral generation, enormously desecrated by military forces, as this ghostly presence makes itself visible and emotionally present throughout the priest's solipsistic attempt to find peace. This force, this seething presence, lurks in the underground spaces of María Canales' home and might be identified, towards the end of the priest's self-serving introspection, as the ghostly presence of the disappeared.[8] The holy ghost that Father Urrutia has intended to invoke is replaced by this other, deeply unsettling spectral presence. Urrutia Lacroix's account of the past, while denying any contrition and in no way representing his ethical atonement, eventually brings back to life this brutally silenced apparition and tells the story of thousands of ghosts. Together these ghosts make up the history of the Southern Cone dictatorships.

Bolaño's writing subverts narrative expectations. His unsettling literary accounting for violence perpetrated by the military dictatorships in the Southern Cone Latin America is about conjuring up a ghostly world of the disappeared and showing his readers how to hear and listen to those ghosts, as well as to read between the lines. All of us who lay eyes on his writing will remain not just haunted by his ghostly configurations of justice but hopefully also animated to denounce human rights abuses and build a stronger democratic culture.

---

[8] It is not hard to recognize in the novel's character María Canales the Chilean poet Mariana Callejas, wife of Michael Townley, who worked with the CIA and participated in the 1976 assassination of Chilean politician and diplomat Orlando Letelier in Washington, DC. Both torture interrogations and poetry gatherings took place at Callejas' house in the Lo Curro neighborhood, often simultaneously.

CHAPTER 5

Mexico City, 1968

Viviane Mahieux

A brief note at the end of Roberto Bolaño's short novel *Amulet* tells us where and when the work was completed: "Blanes, septiembre de 1998."[1] The detail is significant, for it distances the novel – both geographically and chronologically – from the historical events it explores, namely, the two-week military occupation of Mexico's most important public university, UNAM (National Autonomous University of Mexico), in September 1968, and the subsequent massacre at the plaza of Tlatelolco on October 2nd, when government forces opened fire on peaceful protesters. While the exact death toll is yet unclear, hundreds of people were killed that night, and thousands of others were arrested, tortured or jailed, ten days before Mexico entered the world stage as host to the Olympic Games.

This distance – thirty years and an ocean away – situates Bolaño's novel within a late wave of works that approach '68 Mexico through a global lens. The most prominent early representations of this period – which include works published in the 1970s and early 1980s by Carlos Monsiváis, Elena Poniatowska, José Revueltas, Luis González de Alba, Octavio Paz, Luis Spota and Fernando del Paso – focused on the collective effervescence of the political movements, offering a testimony of the physical and emotional suffering felt by students, labor organizers and activists as a result of brutal state-led repression. Without renouncing the intimacy of the deeply subjective narrations that characterized these early depictions, Bolaño also takes a step back.[2] *Amulet* links Mexico to Spain, Uruguay and Chile through a cast of dislocated characters, all of whom have been marked by political violence. The novel's openness extends to its chronology – it connects 1968 to other crucial dates of conflict and loss for

---

[1] This note appears in the Spanish edition, but was removed from the 2006 English translation.
[2] In Jorge Volpi's novel *El fin de la locura* (2003), '68 is narrated between Paris and Mexico City. In the novel, this year represents a turning point, marking a closure that establishes an ordering system on a global scale. On the contrary, *Amulet* arguably works to counter the possibility of closure regarding '68. For a sharp reading of Volpi's novel, see Steinberg (2016).

the political left: the 1936 Spanish Civil War, the 1973 Pinochet coup in Chile, the Southern Cone dictatorships of the 1970s in Argentina and Uruguay – and even to its form: historical characters and events are intertwined with clearly fictional scenes so that every claim to truth is countered by surreal, dream-like episodes.

Amulet is narrated by Auxilio Lacouture, a Uruguayan woman who emigrated to Mexico City sometime in the mid 1960s. Her narration frequently confuses dates and locations, and as a character, she is equal parts out of place and anachronistic. Auxilio spends her days frequenting older male Spanish poets – the exiled Pedro Garfias and León Felipe – for whom she does odd domestic chores, and young male Mexican poets, whose longwinded diatribes she listens to in smoky, crowded bars. Younger than the Spaniards and older than the Mexicans, a reader more than a writer, the lone South American woman in primarily homosocial environments, Auxilio does not fit into any predetermined group or role. In fact, it is easier to describe her by what she is not: a student, a professor, a writer, a muse, a feminist, an artist, an activist, even an exile.[3] Although she dubs herself "the mother of Mexican poetry," her mothering skills are often put into question, and it is also unclear to what extent she lives up to her name, Auxilio, a relatively common name in Spanish-speaking countries that translates as "help" or "assistance."[4]

When the military occupies UNAM, Auxilio hides in the fourth floor bathroom of the Faculty of Philosophy and Literature, where she remains for the duration of the occupation, approximately from the 18th to 30th of September.[5] Auxilio portrays herself as a defender of university autonomy, even though it is unclear if her choice to remain in the bathroom is an act of willful resistance, the result of paralyzing fear, or a bit of both. Her undiscovered presence ensures that a small part of the university remains untouched by military power, even if the space she protects is, after all, just a bathroom. Auxilio's choice to hide is framed in relation to her female body. First, it is presented as an act of self-defense against a metaphorical

---

[3] Medina (2009) draws a convincing connection between exile and anachronism, and proposes that for Bolaño, "exile is not so much a circumstance as an ethics of life and writing" (547). While I agree with his reading, it is important to highlight the fact that Auxilio herself explicitly refrains from calling herself an exile, insisting that she chose to travel to Mexico (3). Thus, she retains the ethical aspect of exile, while undermining the heroically charged label.

[4] Ryan Long (2010) develops a convincing reading of the notion of "intemperie" – a sense of abandonment, isolation and menacing exposure – as it relates both to the novel's sense of time and to Auxilio's ambivalent role as mother.

[5] As did Alcira Soust Scaffo, the Uruguayan poet and educator who inspired the character of Auxilio. For more on Scaffo, see Long (2010).

sexual assault. When the autonomy of the university is *violated* (a word that appears repeatedly in the Spanish original), she resists this violation – this rape – by staying put in the gendered space of the bathroom. Locked in a stall, leafing through a book of Pedro Garfias' poems with her underpants around her ankles "like a pair of handcuffs" (29), she hears a soldier coming in. To hide, she lifts her legs into a birthing position so that they cannot be seen underneath the stall. When the soldier steps out without noticing her, she concludes: "the birth was over" (31). Auxilio survives the next two weeks by drinking tap water and chewing toilet paper. This unique, solitary experience of '68 marks her profoundly: the embodied symbolic violence of rape and birthing brings together trauma, poetry and storytelling into the unlikely space of a public bathroom.

Because of her confinement, Auxilio is a witness who sees very little: "I saw it all," she states, "and yet I didn't see a thing" (22). She glimpses the UNAM occupation from afar: "I was the last to realize that the riot police were on campus and that the army had occupied the university" (23). She misses the defining event of Mexico '68, namely, the brutal occupation of Tlatelolco: "Not many people were killed at the University. That was in Tlatelolco. May that name live forever in our memory!" (22). This shift away from narrating the violence of October 2nd creates an interesting tension with the genre of *testimonio*, associated with the event ever since the groundbreaking publication of Elena Poniatowska's *Massacre in Mexico* (1971). Auxilio cannot speak for a collectivity – she is either a loner or a satellite who hovers around a group she does not belong to – nor can she give an eyewitness account, both essential markers of a testimonial narrative.[6] By not explicitly addressing the massacre, *Amulet* breaks with the notion of this event as a turning point in Mexican history, thus steering away from a linear, chronological narration with a clear before and after.[7] This is not the tale of a transition to democracy, nor the story of a cyclical return to a premodern sacrificial violence, as proposed in Octavio Paz' *Posdata* (1970).[8] If anything, Tlatelolco haunts *Amulet* while only appearing in a handful of passing mentions. This hollow core – Tlatelolco is at the center of the novel yet it remains mostly absent – ensures that the event

---

[6] For an illuminating reading of *Amulet* in relation to the genre of testimonio, see Marinescu (2013).
[7] In *Photopoetics at Tlatelolco* (2016) Steinberg argues that October 2nd represents an organizing, dividing line that structures the archive of '68. As has persuasively been argued by Long (2010), in conversation with Steinberg's thought, *Amuleto* works precisely to undermine any intent of narrative order, thus reconfiguring the archive of '68.
[8] For a comparative reading of Paz and Poniatowska's narratives of '68, see Sorensen (2007).

cannot be fixed into a straightforward, transparent narration, ripe for appropriation as a symbol, be it of resistance, sacrifice or progress.

So, it is Auxilio's two-week ordeal in the university bathroom that structures *Amulet*, not Tlatelolco. The unspeakable horrors of October 2nd are displaced towards the slightly less traumatic ordeal of voluntary solitary confinement. The enclosed space of the bathroom, paradoxically, also becomes a point of departure for exploration.[9] It serves as a prism through which Auxilio imagines and remembers both past and future. Both actions – imagining and remembering – are purposefully interchangeable, as we can see, for example, in the surreal scene in which Auxilio visits the Spanish exiled painter Remedios Varo at home, even though the artist had died two years before the Uruguayan arrived in Mexico. Or how, as she hides in the bathroom, Auxilio remembers events that would happen years later, such as her meetings with Arturo Belano, Bolaño's autobiographical alter ego, that wouldn't take place until well into the 1970s. The echoes of Borges' story "The Aleph," in which the mediocre poet Carlos Argentino Daneri can see across space and time through the aleph hidden in his basement, are unmistakable. Both Borges and Bolaño refer to ominous enclosed spaces that provoke a sense of dread, and at the same time, remain full of infinite possibilities, in a fusion of horror and wonder. That the character of Auxilio Lacouture first appeared in a brief episode within Bolaño's novel *The Savage Detectives*, and was then developed in this separate novel, adds yet another level to the parallel with "The Aleph." The bottomless *mise en abîme* of the aleph, where infinity can be perceived from one single point, here doubles as literature, where the fragment of a novel births another novel.

As we return yet again to the act of giving birth, some crucial questions remain. To whom, or to what, did Auxilio give birth in the toilet of the Faculty of Philosophy and Literature? Was this the moment she effectively became "the mother of Mexican poetry"? Did she give birth to a generation of poets? To Literature? To History? Or simply to a story, which once told would no longer be hers? While there is no straightforward answer, we do know that Auxilio, in the subservient, gendered attitude which is belied by her name, exists for and through others. *Amulet* is not about her, nor does the intensely personal subjectivity of her narration set the scene for

---

[9] Draper (2012) proposes that one of the singularities of Auxilio lies in her focus on what could have happened, or on impossible happenings such as a meeting between the poets Darío and Huidobro, rather than on events themselves. Thus, Auxilio's narrative, according to Draper, leaves open the possibilities of political imagination.

her evolution as a character. The focus of Auxilio's story is not her own transformation, but rather, the transformation of others. She channels the emotional trauma and the yearning for a different future of an entire generation to which she did not belong. Arguably, this is possible precisely because she does not see anything: since she is not present during the era's most traumatic event, Auxilio does not have the historical responsibility to narrate what happened. Consequently, she can draw out the emotional experience that lingers long after the blood on the Tlatelolco plaza has been cleaned up. Her narration evokes the ongoing ripple effects of '68, rather than the happenings themselves, even though they are constantly alluded to through the emotions that remain: trauma, loss and even residual hope.

Auxilio's experience of having missed a defining moment, yet still having to grapple with its aftermath, also applies to Arturo Belano, who appears in *Amulet* as a young aspiring poet. When he returns to Mexico from Chile in 1974, after traveling to his home country in support of Allende's government and surviving Pinochet's 1973 coup, Belano begins frequenting a crowd of adolescent poets. Auxilio describes them as a lost, abject, but beautiful group: "the mere sight made me shudder, as if they weren't creatures of flesh and blood but a generation sprung from the open wound of Tlatelolco, like ants or cicadas or pus, although they couldn't have been there or taken part in the demonstrations of '68" (77). In a horrific doubling of Auxilio's birthing scene, these new poets emerge from the festering wound of Tlatelolco. They are pus, crawling insects – the visual evidence of the impossibility of healing – and yet, they never experienced the violence that birthed them. Much like Auxilio herself, these young poets are marked in perpetuity by an event they did not experience firsthand.

Autobiographical coincidences surface throughout many of Bolaño's works, so it comes as no surprise that he also evoked this feeling of being out of place, of having missed a historically defining moment while inheriting the trauma that it created. In an essay on Bolaño's relationship to Mexico, his contemporary, the writer Carmen Boullosa, describes in similar terms her own entry into Mexico's literary scene as a young poet: "I had arrived too late. Everything that mattered seemed to have ended in 1968." To the sense of anachronism evoked by Boullosa, Bolaño adds the dismay of a generation that did not live the defining moment of a political movement, and yet gave everything for a cause that did not recognize its commitment. In his "Caracas Speech," read when he received the 1999 Rómulo Gallegos prize for his novel *The Savage Detectives*, Bolaño describes his cohort of activists and writers as a lost, sacrificed generation. The idea of sacrificing in vain, which recurs throughout Bolaño's work, is often evoked by critics debating the author's disenchantment with the left.[10] Did his feeling of individual disconnect from this period, defined precisely by the collectivity of cultural and political movements, distance Bolaño from the ideals that fueled the '68 movement? Did he give up on the left? Or did this very sense of disjunction strengthen his commitment to literature as a form of political engagement? Literature, after all, is anachronistic by nature, and throughout his works, Bolaño repeatedly plays with the obsolescence or actuality of literary practice. It is hardly coincidental that during the time Auxilio spends in the bathroom, she only has with her a book by Pedro Garfias, the exiled poet of the Spanish generation of '27 who died before witnessing the upheaval of '68 and whose writing could never have grasped the particularities of the moment.

What are the effects of the recurring anachronisms and displacements so prevalent in *Amulet*? Such temporal and geographic disorientations render it impossible to define, not just Tlatelolco itself, but also the greater epoch of '68, in its multiple manifestations of effervescence and tragedy. In his analysis of *Amulet*, Rory O'Bryen convincingly argues for a melancholic reading of Auxilio's narrative: if mourning implies the possibility of closure, and hence of a collective moving on, melancholia, on the contrary, renders this impossible. Melancholia thus can explain the overflowing temporality of the bathroom episode, which stands in both for the trauma of Tlatelolco and for the broader effects of violent dictatorships throughout the 1970s Latin America. It also helps us grasp the absence of a character arc for Auxilio, as one can find in other first-person narratives such as a memoir or a bildungsroman. If melancholia means permanently living with loss, it also means refusing, not only to forget, but also to change: it is a commitment to living anachronistically.

In the aftermath of '68, living with loss, for the political left, was akin to living with failure. As Ana María Amar Sánchez has argued in her sweeping analysis of what she terms "narratives of defeat," failure implies a refusal to

---

[10] Critics such as Franco (2009) and Medina (2009) see in Bolaño a renunciation of the left and a turn towards the global literary market. Others, such as Marinescu (2013), O'Bryen (2011) and Draper (212), argue for Bolaño's continued political commitment. Engaging with such debates is beyond the confines of this chapter.

negotiate with the winners, and as such, it is the only possible ethical stance that does not capitulate to a dominant narrative.[11] Being a loser, like being melancholic, thus means not moving away from defeat but, on the contrary, embracing it. Reading Auxilio as a defeated figure is not farfetched. She steers clear of a heroic subjectivity, preferring to pass unnoticed and downplaying her abilities. Auxilio's physique reinforces this antiheroic presence. Tall, skinny, with graying page-boy hair and a set of missing front teeth that she discreetly hides with her hand when she smiles, she bears an uncanny resemblance to a female Don Quijote (25). In true Quijote form, her solitary and tragi-comic defense of university autonomy from the confines of a bathroom is tinged with madness and absurdity. The notion of sacrificing in vain surfaces once more, since the battle Auxilio waged was soon eclipsed by the much more significant episode of Tlatelolco, but in her case, political disenchantment does not arise. On the contrary, the bathroom episode becomes the defining element of her identity.

Some of the sharpest readings of *Amulet* highlight the link between Auxilio's last name, Lacouture, and culture, "la cultura" in Spanish" – Auxilio, by implication, comes to the rescue of culture. While the connection is accurate, the direct translation of the French "la couture" is either "sewing" (in Spanish, "la costura"), or a "seam" that joins together two distinct pieces of fabric. The name "Lacouture" clearly harks back to the chores Auxilio does for the Spanish poets, the invisible and unvalued domestic work that enables others to create, as does her self-described role as mother – facilitator of others.[12] The idea of sewing also highlights Auxilio's role as a bridge between people, locations, historical events, and political contexts. Rather than being a savior, she is an auxiliary figure, a discreet mediator, who stands in direct contrast with Arturo Belano, the "machito latinoamericano," or young *macho* whose political militancy is inextricable from his masculine sense of self and the attachment to a narrative of heroism and transformation.[13]

---

[11] For Ana María Amar Sánchez (2010), the loser functions as a metaphorical figure through whom alternate versions of history can be told. See *Instrucciones para la derrota. Narrativas éticas y políticas de perdedores.*.

[12] Monroe (2019) highlights this traditional, subservient aspect of Auxilio's character in the chapter "Making Visible the Non-Power of Poetry."

[13] Chris Andrews translates "su terrible conciencia de machito latinoamericano" (55) as "he'd been a brave Latin American boy" (73). While functional, the translation obscures the tensions around masculinity that are clear in the original Spanish version. For a convincing contrast between Auxilio's narration and Ernesto "Che" Guevara's memoir of political transformation, see Marinescu (2013).

Auxilio creates connections – she sews – by listening, another gendered activity that implies the care for others, and that is generally labeled as passive and feminine. Sound is of primary importance in *Amulet*, especially in the final, dreamlike chapter. The novel ends, tellingly, with Auxilio reaffirming her commitment to listening. A multitude of ghost children sing while marching towards an abyss. Unable to intervene, Auxilio fails to save them: "The only thing I could do was to stand up, trembling, and listen to their song, go on listening to their song right up to the last breath, because, though they were swallowed by the abyss, the song remained in the air of the valley" (184). This song becomes the amulet that gives title to the novel. This final chapter is a striking rearticulation of Elena Poniatowska's *Massacre in Mexico*, where orality is essential, from the original subtitle "Testimonios de historia oral" (testimonies of oral history) to the chant of marching youth that begins the book. In *Amulet*, sound ensures an open ending: the song is never transcribed nor fixed, it remains in the air as a metaphor of '68, ensuring the continued need to listen, to remain aware. Even though the novel ends with an image of tragedy and loss, the commitment to an ongoing ethics of listening leaves an opening for a future.

Amulet's powerful ending recalls how Bolaño closed his 1999 "Caracas Speech." Here, he describes how his insomnia enables him to listen, in the dead of night, to the song of countless crickets: "Don Rómulo can't appear to me in dreams for the simple reason that I can't sleep. Outside, the crickets are chirping. I calculate, very roughly, that there are some ten or twenty thousand of them. Perhaps don Rómulo's voice is in one of their songs, confused, joyfully confused, in the Venezuelan night, in the American night, in the night that belongs to all of us, to those who sleep and to those of us who can't." Insomnia, and the subsequent possibility of continued listening, here links to the relevance of literature, and the importance of continuing to write about this, and other, lost generations. The doubling between the fictional Auxilio's commitment to listening, and Bolaño's evocation of the night song "that belongs to all of us," return us to Blanes, exactly thirty years from Mexico '68. The inclusion of the postscript creates an ambiguity: where does the frame of fiction end? Does it extend to this date and location, or does it stop just before it? Fiction and non-fiction here touch, contaminate each other, interpellating listeners and readers years into the future and across oceans. Yet what also remains in the air, along with *Amulet*'s song and the chirping of crickets, is the unspoken question of whether listening is ever enough.

CHAPTER 6

Mexico City, Paris, and Life versus Art
Rubén Gallo

In Roberto Bolaño's œuvre, the short story "Labyrinth" stands out as somewhat of an anomaly, as it is his only incursion into the world of French literary theory, a subject far removed from the usual themes explored in the rest of his published work: Latin American politics and violence, minor literatures written by marginal and forgotten authors, and the alcohol-fueled sexuality of young bohemians who are not bound by full-time or even part-time jobs. After reading this piece, readers might wonder what led the Chilean writer to compose a short story – never published during his life – devoted to a group of intellectuals who rose to prominence in the 1970s, during the heyday of structuralism.[1]

Like other Latin American experiments of the 1970s and 1980s – Guillermo Cabrera Infante's *View of Dawn in the Tropics* and Julio Cortázar's "Blow-Up," to name two works – "Labyrinth" is an exercise in photographic ekphrasis: it takes as a point of departure a photograph taken in Paris, in the 1970s, of several members of the Tel Quel group seated at a café. In the center of the group we find Philippe Sollers, the avant-garde novelist and editor of the group's journal, and his wife, the Bulgarian-born linguist Julia Kristeva. Around them, other minor figures, less familiar to English-speaking readers, gather around the table: Jacques Henric, Jean-Joseph Goux, Marie-Thérèse Réveillé, Catherine Devade (in the story she is called "Carla Devade"), Marc Devade, as well as Pierre Guyotat, known for his sadomasochistic novels.

Bolaño's narrator scans the photograph, commenting on each of the figures, analyzing their clothes, their expressions, and their gazes. He then embarks on what reads like a creative writing experiment: imagining the daily life of each of these intellectuals over the course of several days and nights. The static figures come alive as we see them working at the Tel

---

[1] Bolaño, "Labyrinth," *The Secret of Evil*, trans. Chris Andrews and Natasha Wimmer, New York: New Directions, 2012, 55.

Quel office, walking through the streets of Paris, having dinner with their respective partners, making love, going to bed, starting a new day.

A good part of the story revolves around a figure who is not included in the photograph but whom the narrator imagines as being just outside the frame: "Z," a Central American author who once visited the Tel Quel office, most probably in the hope of getting his work published in the journal, only to see his dreams dashed by an indifferent though polite Philippe Sollers. The narrator imagines that, while the group is seated at the café, Cathérine Devade and Marie-Thérèse Réveillé recognize the Central American and their gazes converge in a spot outside the frame.

It would be tempting to read this story as Bolaño's commentary on avant-garde fiction– novels like Sollers' *Nombres* – and the theoretical texts published by the Collection Tel Quel, a prestigious series that included many books by Kristeva, Jacques Lacan, Roland Barthes, and Michel Foucault among others. Is this piece an homage or a parody, a serious engagement with the ideas promoted by the group or simply a lighthearted jab at their stance?

Chris Andrews, Bolaño's biographer, reads "Labyrinth" as a tale about the relation between margin and center, and the resentment expressed by the Central American when confronted with the Parisians' indifference: "The visitor," Andrews writes, "comes from a part of the periphery that has no cachet for these central intellectuals, and he resents their indifference, his nullity in their eyes." In this analysis, the resentment is unjustified, since the Latin American writer belongs to the type of the "Arriviste (*el trepa* in Spanish), the writer intent on using literature as a social ladder, who is irresistibly attracted to the holders and wielders of symbolic power."[2] "Labyrinth" would thus be a moral tale about literary hubris, the story of a Central American who elbowed his way first to Paris and then to the Tel Quel office only to find his inflated sense of self punctured by the Parisians' rejection. Andrews' reading gives center stage to the Central American and his unbounded ambitions, while the members of Tel Quel recede into the background as representatives of French intellectual life.

Bolaño's story, however, reveals both a fascination with Tel Quel and an in-depth knowledge of both the group and the dynamics among the members. The story offers extensive commentary, albeit in code, on the literary theories advanced by Julia Kristeva and other authors associated

---

[2] Chris Andrews, *Bolaño's Fiction: An Expanding Universe*, New York: Columbia University Press, 2014, 66–67.

with the group. To see what Bolaño does with these figures, we should recall a few important aspects of the group's history.

Tel Quel, a journal named after one of Nietzsche's declarations: "I want the world and I want it as is, *tel quel*" – the expression could be translated as "as is" – was founded in 1960 by the publishing house Éditions du Seuil. It was the brainchild of Philippe Sollers and François Wahl, a legendary editor who published Lacan, Barthes, Foucault, and Kristeva, among many others, during the 1960s and 1970s. Wahl was actually much more than an editor: in the case of Lacan, he literally forced the analyst to write his book: by the 1960s, Lacan had gained fame as an analyst and public speaker, but had barely published anything since his 1932 thesis on paranoia; he dismissed publishing as "poubellication" (a pun on "pou-belle," garbage); it was not until Wahl asked Lacan to rent a house in the mountains and spend the summer months transforming his lectures into a book that Lacan completed *Écrits*, which became an instant bestseller.[3]

In 1960, Sollers, then a young and rebellious avant-garde novelist, approached Wahl with a tempting request: would Seuil sponsor a new journal, devoted to publishing the youngest and most experimental writers, along with figures who had been long forgotten – like the Marquis de Sade, Stéphane Mallarmé, and Georges Bataille – as well as theoretical discussions informed by structural linguistics, sociology and psychoanalysis? The journal – on "literature, philosophy, science, politics," as the frontispiece announced – published its first issue in spring 1960, featuring a wide array of authors and texts: Francis Ponge and Claude Simon, Virginia Woolf and Albert Camus. The editorial announced that a heterogeneous group of writers had come together in the pursuit of "literary beauty" and against the grain of "moral and political imperatives."[4]

The journal continued publishing until 1982, and in those two decades its pages featured articles by Artaud, Barthes, Bataille, Michel Butor, John Cage, Jacques Derrida, T. S. Eliot, Paul Éluard, Foucault, Jean Genet, Friedrich Hölderlin, Luce Irigaray, James Joyce, Mao Tse Tung, Ezra Pound, Alain Robbe-Grillet, Nathalie Sarraute, Tzvetan Todorov, and Paul Valéry, among many others, as it came to occupy a privileged place

---

[3] Elisabeth Roudinesco, *Jacques Lacan & Co.*, trans. Jeffrey Mehlman, Chicago: The University of Chicago Press, 1990, 413–414.
[4] "Déclaration," *Tel Quel* 1 (Spring 1960): 3–4.

in the cultural scene during one of the most creative and daring periods in French intellectual life.[5]

As one can see from the above list, Latin American literature was absent from the pages of Tel Quel: not a single article is devoted to the writers of the Boom generation – Carlos Fuentes, Gabriel García Márquez, Mario Vargas Llosa – who made waves with novels like *One Hundred Years of Solitude* (1967), or even to Latin Americans who lived and worked in Paris like Julio Cortázar. The two exceptions are Jorge Luis Borges – a French translation of "Narrative Art and Magic" was published in issue 7–[6] and the Cuban novelist Severo Sarduy, who contributed nine texts to the journal, including excerpts from his novels *Cobra* (1972) and *Maitreya* (1978), as well as critical articles on Góngora and baroque literature, and became the single Latin American author to have a sustained presence in Tel Quel.

The journal's lack of interest in Latin America is not surprising, as it mirrors Sollers' preferences. Though he grew up speaking fluent Spanish – he was raised in Bordeaux by a Spanish nanny – he was notoriously dismissive of Latin American writers. One of his novels depicted Octavio Paz, "the surrealist Mexican poet," as an interloper into the Parisian scene, and, in general, Sollers showed no interest in any of the dozens of Latin American writers who made Paris their home during the 1960s and 1970s. Tel Quel's – and Seuil's – attitude contrasted sharply with those of other French publishers. Gallimard, for instance, launched "La Croix du Sud," a collection devoted to Latin American literature, founded by Roger Caillois in 1952, and published works by Borges, Guillermo Cabrera Infante, Ernesto Sábato, Mario Vargas Llosa, among many others, in a list that continues to grow today.[7]

The notable exception to Soller's and Tel Quel's indifference to Latin American letters was Sarduy, a Cuban novelist who left the island in the wake of the Revolution and settled in Paris in 1960: Sarduy had a privileged position in the group: not only did he publish regularly in the journal; his novel *Cobra* was translated into French by Sollers– a translation that was awarded the prestigious Médicis prize.

But why was Tel Quel so partial to Sarduy? There are at least two reasons, one literary, the other, personal. Since its inaugural issue, Tel

---

[5] Tel Quel, *Index des auteurs, Index thématique des articles, numéro 1 au numéro 49*.
[6] Another story by Borges, "Degrees," was published in issue 11.
[7] Philippe Sollers, *Femmes*, Paris: Gallimard, 1983, 467. See also Sollers, *Casanova, the Irresistible*, Urbana: The University of Illinois Press, 2016, 131.

Quel promoted writers influenced by the *nouveau roman*, who were willing to perform radical experiments with the novelistic form. Most Latin American novelists – from Vargas Llosa to Cortázar – wrote novels that followed the expectations readers associated with the genre: there were recognizable characters, a clear plot, and a mimetic effect that sought to recreate external reality. In contrast, Sarduy published novels that were much closer in spirit to Tel Quel's avant-garde sensibility: characters change names, genders, and shapes; pages become, like painting, canvases for experimenting with the colors and shapes of words; and all mimetic intent is forsaken in favor of linguistic play. As Kristeva might have put it, Sarduy's fiction brought the materiality of the signifier to the foreground.

The second reason for Sarduy's privileged position in the group had to do with his private life. He arrived in Paris in early 1960 with a grant from the Cuban government to study art at the Académie des Beaux Arts in Paris, moved into a room at the Cité Universitaire and, a few months after his arrival, met a Frenchman who would become his lover, introduce him to the bustling artistic and literary scene, and change his life forever: François Wahl. When they met, Sarduy was a 22-year-old and Wahl, at 35, was already an influential figure in French letters, known primarily for his role as editor of the Tel Quel collection at Seuil. Soon after they moved in together and lived together for thirty-three years, until Sarduy died of AIDS in 1993 (Wahl lived another twenty years and died in 2014, at age 89).

When Sarduy arrived in Paris he was, like Z in Bolaño's story, a total outsider: though he had published a few poems and articles in newspapers and journals in Havana and in his native Camagüey, he was completely unknown to European readers. He spoke broken French with a thick Spanish accent – he continued rolling his Rs until the end – and his Caribbean manners – he moved his hands and his body as he talked – would have put him out of place in most Parisian social settings, ruled by an elaborate intellectual etiquette.

Without Wahl, Sarduy's experience in the Parisian literary scene would have been exactly like that of Bolaño's Z: he could have arrived one day at the Tel Quel offices, writing portfolio in hand, only to be received and soon after dispatched by an extremely polite and almost effusive editor, who would have not even cast a glance at his poems and stories.

As it turns out, Sarduy's experience was the exact opposite of Z's. After he moved in with Wahl, he saw Sollers, Kristeva, and many of the other members of Tel Quel – along with Barthes, Lacan, Foucault, and other figures whose books were edited by Wahl – on a regular basis. He would meet Sollers and Kristeva at least once a week: in a late interview, Wahl remembers that Sarduy and Kristeva would often stroll in the garden while he and Sollers discussed the upcoming issues of Tel Quel.[8]

Sarduy was funny, brilliant, and charismatic, and in the end his tropical demeanor conquered Sollers. The French novelist read the Cuban's work and offered to translate him. The two collaborated on the translation of *Cobra*, an experimental work that appears, at first glance, untranslatable, given its use of Cubanisms and its experiments with language. Together, they extended the novel's literary games as they invented neologism after neologism to render obscure Cubanisms into French (one example: *grande finasserie*, an expression meant to denote a grand mess, was coined as a jab against Lucette Finas, a novelist whose work was not appreciated by Sollers).[9]

In the end, Sarduy led the kind of life in Paris that Bolaño's Z could only dream of. The history of Latin American literature is full of writers – Rubén Darío, Amado Nervo, César Vallejo, to name only a few – who arrived in Paris full of dreams and ambitions only to find themselves ignored by the French literary scene. José Donoso, the Chilean writer, devoted a brilliant story – "El tiempo perdido" – to the trope of the aspiring Latin American intellectual whose dreams are shattered by Parisian indifference and returns home bitter and disappointed at the unwelcoming reality of a city that has long been imagined as a literary Mecca for Latin Americans.[10]

Could Bolaño have been thinking of Sarduy when he wrote "Labyrinth"? If so, the story imagines what historians call a counterfactual narrative: how would the Cuban writer have fared in Paris without Wahl as a partner and literary godfather? But "Labyrinth" is not only a story about Z, an anonymous Central American writer who arrives in Paris only to see his literary dreams smashed. It is also a story about literary scenes, and, specifically, about Tel Quel and its role in the Parisian intellectual scene of the 1960s and 1970s, a golden age for French letters and criticism.

Since his teenage years, Bolaño was fascinated with literary scenes. In *The Savage Detectives*, he portrays Mexico City's intellectual world, which made a deep impression on him when he lived there in the 1970s, as a vast and complex universe, featuring, at one extreme, Octavio Paz, a giant who

---

[8] Rubén Gallo, "Severo Sarduy, Jacques Lacan y el psicoanálisis: entrevista con François Wahl," *Revista Hispánica Moderna* 59.1–2 (2006): 51–60.
[9] Severo Sarduy, *Cobra*, trans. Philippe Sollers, Paris: Éditions du Seuil, 1972.
[10] José Donoso, "El tiempo perdido," *Cuatro para Delfina*, Barcelona: Seix Barral, Biblioteca Breve, 1982, 150–209.

won the Nobel Prize in 1990 and who ruled over a literary empire built around his journals *Plural* and *Vuelta*. As Jonathan Monroe puts it, echoing one of the characters in *The Savage Detectives*, "the situation of Mexican poets is 'unsustainable, trapped ... between the reign of Octavio Paz, and the reign of Pablo Neruda.'"[11] On the margins of this world the reader discovers the young, irreverent, and experimental poets of "real visceralismo" who emerge as central characters of the novel. The literary universe is so vast that there are even figures who get lost in it, like Cesárea Tinajero, who becomes the object of desire for the bohemian writers.

In one of the most intriguing scenes in the novel, the two extremes of the Mexico City literary world meet: Octavio Paz asks his secretary to drive him to a park where he runs into Ulises Lima, who introduces himself to Paz's secretary as "the penultimate real visceralist poet in Mexico," and was perhaps part of a group that had once hatched a plan to kidnap the venerable Mexican poet. Bolaño describes the encounter with the precision of an entomologist detailing the mating rituals of two specimens of the insect world: Paz and Lima walk in circles as they approach each other and finally stare at each other in silence, before exchanging some words that are not reported by the narrator.[12]

Bolaño was fascinated with Paz and with the literary empire he built over the years through his journals *Plural* and *Vuelta*. The Chilean poet wrote his first texts during the years he spent in Mexico City, and during this time he witnessed how Paz towered over Mexican letters. Bolaño's friends and fellow poets were minor figures who published in obscure magazines and who inhabited a very different world from Paz, who had traveled the world, lived in Europe, Asia, and the United States, and had become friends with Nobel laureates, politicians and diplomats – figures who became contributors to *Plural* and *Vuelta* – and, by the end of his life, was courted by Mexican presidents who hailed him as a glory to national culture.

If a young Bolaño had ever dared approach Paz's journal, his experience would have been similar to Z's, minus the French courtesy. *Plural* and then *Vuelta* became literary citadels, protected by intellectual gatekeepers who spent considerable energy keeping interlopers and gawkers at bay. If Bolaño had visited the journal's offices to submit a poem, he would not have made it past the receptionist. But he could have crossed paths with

---

[11] Jonathan Beck Monroe, *Framing Roberto Bolaño's Fiction*, Cambridge: Cambridge University Press, 2010, 126.
[12] Roberto Bolaño, *Los detectives salvajes*, Barcelona: Editorial Anagrama, 1998, 501–511.

many of the writers in Paz's circle – Homero Aridjis, José de la Colina, Juan García Ponce, Salvador Elizondo – in the cafés and restaurants frequented by the intellectual establishment. One could imagine a scene like the one described in "Labyrinth," but with a young Bolaño gazing from afar at a terrace where a different cast of characters –Paz, Marie-José Tramini, Juan García Ponce, Ramón Xirau, and Julieta Campos – were busy debating the latest literary trend or political scandal.

Though Bolaño would have never been invited to join Paz's friends at their table, the scene at Parque Hundido in *The Savage Detectives* stages an imaginary – if fleeting – meeting of the two worlds, the *Plural-Vuelta* circle and the real visceralistas, represented by Lima and Paz. It imagines an Octavio Paz who has left his gatekeepers and lieutenants behind and, for once, can meet a fellow poet on equal – and neutral – ground. "Their conversation was relaxed, serene, tolerant," recounts Paz's secretary in the novel (510). This scene continues to fascinate readers because it presents a human and vulnerable Paz who shows that he remains, in essence, a poet. "Labyrinth" presents a much darker vision of literary scenes: in this story there is no equivalent to the Parque Hundido encounter: Z never gets to see Sollers on neutral ground, away from his army of acolytes, and they never connect as fellow writers. Bolaño spent most of his life as a literary outsider, and his fiction demonstrates great empathy towards characters like Z, who inhabit the margins and are snubbed by mainstream figures. He belongs to the same class as Arturo Belano, Ulises Lima, and Cesárea Tinajero – bohemian poets who would be turned away by *Plural*, *Vuelta*, *Tel Quel*, or *The New Yorker* but who, in Bolaño's view, inhabit the space where true literature is created.

"Labyrinth" can also be read as a manifesto of sorts in which Bolaño engages with Tel Quel's literary theories. The French group was best known for promoting structural analysis, a form of criticism that focused exclusively on textual matters and excluded the consideration of biographical material or any material related to the author's life. Barthes summed up this stance in his 1967 article "Death of the Author," which declared: "the text is a tissue of citations, resulting from the thousand sources of culture" and thus "it is language which speaks, not the author."[13] Two years later, Foucault expressed a similar idea in "What is an author?": "We can easily imagine a culture where discourse could circulate without any

---

[13] Roland Barthes, "The Death of the Author," *Image, Music, Text*, New York: Hill and Wang, 1977, 142–148.

need for an author."¹⁴ For over two decades, Tel Quel promoted a form of literary analysis that privileged texts, discourse, and linguistics while avoiding authorial or biographical questions.

"Labyrinth," in contrast, depicts the protagonists of Tel Quel as authors, going against the grain of the theories these figures promoted in real life. Bolaño's narrator tells us nothing about their work, and a naïve reader could very well finish reading "Labyrinth" without getting a sense of Soller's novels, Kristeva's articles, or Guyotat's journals. Kristeva, for instance, rose to fame as a linguist with the publication of *Sèméiotikè* in 1969, followed by her doctoral thesis *The Revolution of Poetic Language* in 1974. "Labyrinth" skips over these works – they are not mentioned in the story – to depict Kristeva as a coquettish woman, certainly the most appealing character in the group, perhaps because Bolaño believed her Bulgarian origin placed her in the margins of an otherwise entirely Parisian circle. Rather than exploring their work, "Labyrinth" examines how the group's members lived their lives, fell in love, got entangled in complicated relations. "The author is well and alive," Bolaño seems to retort to Tel Quel.

From the first paragraphs, "Labyrinth" engages in an imaginary debate on the role and function of literature. Immediately after introducing the characters in the photograph, the narrator explains that "they're sitting at a table" and then adds: "It's an ordinary table, made of wood, perhaps, or plastic, it could even be a marble table on metal legs, but nothing could be less germane to my purpose than to give an exhaustive description of it" (55). Most readers would take this as a random comment, but in it the narrator engages with one of the central ideas of the *nouveau roman*, the "new novel" promoted by Tel Quel. In his manifesto *Pour un nouveau roman*, Alain Robbe-Grillet lambasted the traditional novel's centuries-long insistence on adopting a human perspective. Against this "anthropocentrism," Robbe-Grillet called for experimenting with alternate points of view, including those by inanimate objects. He imagined a novel told from the perspective of an ashtray and, in his novel *The Erasers,* the protagonists are erasers who constantly undo the narrative, erasing it even as they advance it.¹⁵

---

¹⁴ Michel Foucault, "What Is an Author?" *Language, Counter-Memory, Practice: Selected Essays and Interviews,* Ithaca: Cornell University Press, 1977, 113.
¹⁵ Alain Robbe-Grillet, *For a New Novel: Essays on Fiction,* Evanston: Northwestern University Press, 1989, 29; 51–57.

The novelists associated with Tel Quel – including Sollers and Guyotat – took Robbe-Grillet's criticism to heart and wrote novels that aspired to break with all the conventions of traditional narrative, including the centrality given to human perspective. In contrast, Bolaño's narrative playfully announces at the very beginning that he will not seek to evade the anthropomorphocentric pull by turning the table into the center of the story. "Nothing could be less germane to my purpose," he declares, as if reminding the reader that a table is a table is a table is a table.

"Labyrinth" includes many other jabs at other literary ideas promoted by Tel Quel. Much of the criticism published in the journal's pages was structural analysis: a quasi-mathematical analysis of the relation between different elements of the text that almost never delved into content. Playing on these ideas, Bolaño's narrator playfully engages in a parodic form of structuralism: his discussion of the various members of Tel Quel seated at the café table focuses on the differences and similarities among the garments they are wearing, with special attention to the morphology of turtlenecks: Of Sollers, for instance, he tells us that "Like J.-J., he is wearing a turtleneck sweater, though the sweater that Sollers is wearing is white, dazzlingly white, while J.-J.'s is probably yellow or light green;" and Carla (as Bolaño calls Catherine Devade in the story) "is wearing a turtleneck sweater, like J.-J. Goux, Sollers, and Kristeva," while Marie-Thérèse Réveillé "is the first person so far not to be wearing a turtleneck sweater." Pushing his comparative analysis further, the narrator asks "Who are the most warmly dressed?" before answering: "J.-J. Goux, Sollers, and Marc Devade, without question: they're wearing jackets over their turtleneck sweaters, and thick jackets too, from the look of them" and adding that Guyotat "[is] the only one wearing three layers," while "Kristeva is a case apart: her turtleneck sweater is light, more elegant than practical, and she's not wearing anything over it" (55).

At this point Bolaño's readers might wonder why they have been told so much about the characters' turtlenecks, even before knowing who these people are or what they are doing in the café, but the reason for this excess in sartorial analysis (and not only sartorial: we also learn that Sollers is the only one smoking and Kristeva is the only one showing her teeth) becomes clear when we consider the narrator is simply poking fun at the structuralist theses defended by Kristeva and other members of Tel Quel.

"Labyrinth" offers an elaborate refutation of Tel Quel's ideas about the relationship between literature and life. Whereas members of the group proclaimed the death of the author and argued that literary texts should be read as a series of structural relations – theses debated passionately in works

Mexico City, Paris, and Life versus Art 75

like Kristeva's *Sèméiotikè* and *The Revolution in Poetic Language* – Bolaño's narrator cheerfully ignores the content of their theoretical and critical works: he tells the reader, in passing, that Sollers is the author of *Nombres* and *Paradis* and that Kristeva has published *Powers of Horror*, but omits any information about the ideas expressed in these works, their reception, or the debates they generated, opting instead to embark on a comparative analysis of their dress, posture, and complexion.

The narrator devotes the rest of the story to imagining the Tel Quel members' daily routines in a sort of extra-diegetic excursion meant to reveal "a more complex and subtle web of relations among these men and women." The reader is offered glimpses of J. Henric riding through the streets of Paris on his Honda motorcycle while J.-J. Goux stays at home reading a book; of Sollers writing in his study while Kristeva teaches her courses at the university; of Carla and Marc Devade bickering and giving each other the silent treatment, while Guyotat sodomizes Marie-Thérèse Réveillé. We are even allowed a peek into the characters' dreams, learning, for instance, that at night Philippe Sollers fantasizes about a beach in Brittany while Kristeva revisits a German village where she once participated in a conference.

Bolaño used a similar strategy in other works: *The Savage Detectives* focuses on the private lives of Arturo Belano, Ulises Lima, and their fellow real visceralists, without telling the reader much about the contents of their work. We see these young men and women drinking mezcal, staying up late, having trysts, gossiping, recounting anecdotes, and wandering the streets and parks of Mexico City. The novel aligns with the Romantic view of the writer as a *poète maudit*, whose life is as much of a work of art as his literary production.

But there is an important difference between the characters appearing in *The Savage Detectives* and the protagonists of "Labyrinth": Lima and Belano live wild, hyperbolic adventures in a Latin American megalopolis where everything seems possible: meeting Trotsky's granddaughter, having a tryst with a waitress in a cafeteria's bathroom, driving through the Sonora desert in search of a lost avant-garde poet. The members of Tel Quel, in contrast, live entirely uneventful lives and their daily routines differ very little from that of the average accountant or engineer: they cook dinner at home, have sex with their partners, meet friends in a café. Even their conversations are devoid of the outrageous topics debated by real visceralists. In a turn of events that departs from the Romantic ideal of the *poète maudit*, the published works of these Parisian intellectuals are much more interesting than their private lives... though their contents remain opaque to the reader.

This surprising inversion of Romantic values can be read as a jab against Tel Quel: the group insisted on the primacy of published work over lived experience – Bolaño seems to intimate – because their lives outside writing and publishing were utterly boring. Once we peek into their inner realms, we get the sense that for these characters, writing is like a job like any other – once they leave the Tel Quel office they do not seem particularly invested in intellectual work; their interests lie elsewhere: in cooking, seeing friends, and carousing with their partners and lovers. The moral of the story seems to be that life will always be more important that theory, even when theories are revolutionary and lives are conformist.

If "Labyrinth" is structured like a counterpoint between art and life, between theory and lived experience, the appearance of Z, the Central American, marks the *punctum* of the story. The narrator tells the reader very little about this character: we see him arrive at the Tel Quel office, being greeted and soon after dismissed by Sollers, and we get a sense of his bitterness and disappointment. Unlike what happens with Sollers, Kristeva, and the other members of the group, the narrator never gives the reader a glimpse of this Latin American's private life. Does he live alone? Is he seeing anyone? Can he cook? Does he ride a motorcycle? Does he have a sadistic streak in bed? Who are his friends? In his presentation, the narrator seems to adopt the point of view of the Parisian intellectuals, who see Z as a curious and slightly amusing specimen of an exotic foreigner but would never consider getting to know him in a more intimate setting.

One could imagine that in his home country, the Central American might lead the kind of life portrayed in *The Savage Detectives*, spending his days with friends and lovers, reading and discussing literature, even embarking in an adventure to a remote place in search of an author he has read an admired. As happens with Lima and Belano, life – especially the lives of his favorite authors – is central to his interest in literature. What pains him most about his disastrous visit to Tel Quel is his inability to connect with Sollers on a human level: after praising his literature, he attempts to move to a more intimate register by mentioning Julia Kristeva and celebrating "the matchless beauty and grace of French women," only to discover that the French novelist has completely lost interest in the conversation.

This encounter is but one of many Z had in France that ended in a similar disappointment: the narrator explains that "if he's a Central

American in Paris, in addition to being ambitious he may also be bitter." His inability to connect with writers on a human level – to have the kind of conversations that make the bulk of *The Savage Detectives* – have filled him with "horror and fear" and awakened in him murderous impulses, though the narrator concedes that "[t]his Pol Pot won't kill anyone in Paris. And actually back in Tegucigalpa or San Salvador, he'll probably end up teaching at the University." What is it about Tel Quel that can turn a mousy academic into a potential mass-murderer? The abyss between literature and art, the narrator seems to intimate.

It would not be too difficult to read Z as a stand-in for Bolaño, who experienced Paris as a South American author, and who privileged lived experience over bookish learning ("My life," he once said, "has been infinitely more savage than Borges's.")[16] "Labyrinth" is packed with small details that reveal Bolaño had spent much time reading and thinking about Tel Quel: aside from the titles of the books published by members of the group, the story mentions the street in which the journal had its office – rue Jacob – the disposition of Soller's study – upstairs from their apartment – and even Kristeva's life at the university, where we see her "surrounded by a retinue of students, quite a few of whom are foreign (two Spaniards, a Mexican, an Italian, two Germans)." All of these details reveal an intimate knowledge of the lives of these figures.

Did Bolaño – like Z – try "at some point ... to write an article about the group?" Did he translate Denis Roche? Did he visit the Tel Quel office on rue Jacob only to be given the cold shoulder by Philippe Sollers? Interestingly, neither the story nor Bolaño's published work has anything to say about the one member of Tel Quel, Severo Sarduy, who managed to live a colorful, bohemian life that would not be out of place in the pages of *The Savage Detectives*.

Did Bolaño actually meet with Sollers to discuss collaborating with the journal? Or did he simply imagine the missed encounter with the editors? If the encounter had truly happened, his experience would have been the same as Z's, but he used the power of fiction to imagine a different outcome: though Z is ushered away, "Labyrinth"'s narrator finds a way to peek into the apartments of Sollers and Kristeva, Guyotat and Marie-Thérèse, Marc and Carla Devade, and is able to give the reader a chronicle of their private lives, just like he did with the Mexican writers, old and young, that appear in *The Savage Detectives*.

---

[16] Qtd in Francisco Goldman, "The Great Bolaño," *The New York Review of Books*, July 19, 2007, 10.

"Labyrinth" is a manifesto for reading all literature as an extension of life. It is also a portrait of a group of French intellectuals who insist on erecting a wall between the two: "Literature brushes past these literary creatures and kisses them on the lips, but they don't even notice," as the narrator says, at one point in the story, of a different cast of characters — those not visible in the frame of the photograph.

CHAPTER 7

Spain, Europe: 1977–2003
Ana Fernández-Cebrián

In the summer of 1979, Roberto Bolaño and Catalan writer A. G. Porta (Antoni García Porta) started writing *Consejos de un discípulo de Morrison a un fanático de Joyce*. The novel, one of many projects they created together, was published in 1984 and re-released in 2006 together with another one of their stories, *Diario de bar*.[1] *Consejos* narrates, through the voice of its protagonist, the life journey of a young delinquent couple in the city of Barcelona, together with their shared experience of sex and drug use. The initial motive of the violence, an assault on an elderly woman for money, culminates with her brutal murder. This detonates an escalation of ever more extreme violence, which connects with the climate of citizen insecurity described in the media:

> The following day the press only spoke of one thing, the violence in Barcelona and insecurity in the city ... It was as if the city had become immersed in a gangster film that terrified it, and yet, at the same time, made it happy. In general, the public opinion was of one mind: the reign of terror was back – at the end of the day, these crimes wanted to de-stabilize-democracy. (*Consejos*, XI Las Perspectivas)

The violence unleashed by the lead characters will also appear in the locations in Barcelona and the Costa Brava described in *Antwerp* (written in 1980, and published in 2002).[2] It is inserted within the social crisis which characterized the end of the Spanish Democratic Transition, and whose protagonists were the younger generations. At the beginning of the 80s, major youth sectors found themselves destined to social marginalization as a result of a complex geometric figure of factors, the edges of which were unemployment, petty crime, and drug use and addiction. In this context, the criminal court cases attributed most of the legal causes and

---

[1] Roberto Bolaño, *Consejos de un discípulo de Morrison a un fanático de Joyce. Diario de bar*, co-written with A.G. Porta (Madrid: Penguin Random House, 2016), Kindle e-book.
[2] Roberto Bolaño, *Antwerp*, trans. Natasha Wimmer (New York: New Directions, 2010).

prison sentences to property crimes, which, in those years, grew "from 2,400 in 1977 to over 12,000 in 1986."[3] As is the case with the crimes committed by the protagonists of *Consejos*, it was mainly petty theft that was part of the typical dynamics of the cycle of crime associated with drugs. It is estimated that in 1980 Spain had nearly 80,000 heroin addicts, a figure which, by 1984, had grown to 125,000. Thus, one in every twenty youths born between 1960 and 1970 got to know this drug intimately, and the figure of the junky turned into "the incarnation of the nihilism of an era of self-effacement of whole sectors of youth" (*Por qué fracasó* 290). This massive drug use, and the huge amount of youth casualties, was a social tragedy that left its mark on collective memory, a phenomenon to which Roberto Bolaño dedicated, in the year 2000, the short story "Playa" ("Beach"), told from the vantage point of a drug addict in rehab.[4] The experience of a whole generation, destroyed by drugs and AIDS, was also included among the memories of the writer of the young communities he came in contact with when he arrived in Spain:

> My first friends in Blanes were almost all drug addicts. That sounds like an exaggeration, but it's true. Today most of them are dead. Some died of overdoses, others of AIDS. When I met them they were young, good-looking kids. They weren't good students, none of them went to college, but they lived their lives – short lives, as it turned out – as if they were part of a vast Greek tragedy.[5]

The situation of the protagonists of *Consejos*, a Latin American female migrant and a Spanish boy, was the same as those of thousands of youths that lived through the dramatic effects of an economic crisis that had, since the end of the 70s, torn up the working class and the industrial fabric that had formed during the years of Francoist "desarrollismo." Around 1982, the year of the Spanish Worker's Socialist Party (PSOE) victory at the ballots, youth unemployment "among those under 20 was over 70%, and among those under 25 was close to 50%" (*Por qué fracasó* 291). Unemployment and a case of low pay and temporary job opportunities were synonymous with the lack of future, with an idle time suspended in a void present tense, as manifested by the narrator of *Consejos* in their

---

[3] Emmanuel Rodríguez López, *Por qué fracasó la democracia en España. La Transición y el régimen del'78* (Madrid: Traficantes de Sueños, 2015), 297.
[4] Roberto Bolaño, "Beach" in *Between Parenthesis: Essays, Articles and Speeches (1998–2003)*, trans. Natasha Wimmer (New York: New Directions, 2011), 260–269.
[5] Roberto Bolaño, "*Town Crier of Blanes*," in *Between Parenthesis: Essays, Articles and Speeches (1998–2003)*, trans. Natasha Wimmer (New York: New Directions, 2011), 249–250.

reflection on the precariousness to which the youth from Southern Europe were condemned:

> The last dreams of youth had turned into nightmares ... And the future? It was marvelous! To work and work in order to build up some country, the kind of stupid ideas that only Germans and Belgians, or Belgians and Danes, believe in. Forty more years of that, and then retirement with a modest state pension ... an increasingly remote possibility. (*Consejos,* IV Mitos de bolsillo trasero)

Bolaño and Porta's stories deployed their narrative within the same imaginary that informed the phenomenon of the so-called "quinqui" petty crime towards the end of the Spanish Transition. In mass culture, "quinqui," as a reference to the small-time delinquency and other social practices of a marginalized youth, became a dominant lifestyle and a form of resistance, a mass-cultural sign of the times. Since the end of the 70s, the media, the film industry and literature started to tell the stories of the new heroes of youth, with an epic tone determined by a life full of action, prison sentences, unbreakable friendships, as well as shared practices of drug use and dealing. The life stories of these "quinquis" consisted in exemplary teachings on the sacred nature of private property, and on the regime of monopoly on violence exerted by the State, and were targeted at an audience that watched this phenomenon with a mix of terror and fascination. All of this resulted in a spectacularization of a series of limit-case, extreme lifestyles which coincided in time and procedure with a wider process of social disciplinarization of those youth sectors. In parallel, as was the case with Bolaño's works from the beginning of the 80s, such as *Consejos, Antwerp* and *A Little Lumpen Novelita* – a story set in Rome – what was being elaborated in these narratives was the exaltation of a criminal imaginary.[6] This criminal imaginary was, in turn, nothing else but the expression of the resistance to social misery which went in parallel to the expansion of the neoliberal model during the end years of the Spanish Democratic Transition and the so-called Lead Years in Italy.

In 1977 Roberto Bolaño had moved from Mexico City to Paris, and later, to Spain. Much like the characters in his novels, as a young man, the writer had held down a series of precarious jobs in Barcelona and Castelldefels, a small coastal town close to the Catalan capital. There, he worked during the summers and some winters between 1978 and 1981 at the "Estrella de Mar" camping site, a location relevant to the plot of

---

[6] Roberto Bolaño, *A Little Lumpen Novelita*, trans. Natasha Wimmer (New York: New Directions, 2014).

Antwerp and other novels. The Costa Brava landscape and the town of Blanes, where he resided permanently from 1985 onwards, would become the settings of *The Skating Rink*, published in 1993, and *The Third Reich*, written in 1989 but not released until 2010.[7] In *The Third Reich*, a coastal town very similar to Blanes will be the destination chosen by the young German-born Udo Berger to spend the holidays with his girlfriend Ingeborg at the "Del Mar" hotel, where the protagonist used to spend summers with his family when he was a child. During his free time, Berger, a writer and a wargame champion in his country, befriends another German couple, and also characters like the local workers nicknamed el Lobo, el Cordero, and el Quemado, the latter being a Chilean who lives and works at the beach, renting out pedal boats. This character, called "el Quemado" due to the scars left on his skin after being tortured by a group of Germans in the past, will be a wargaming rival with whom Berger starts an increasingly intense game of The Third Reich in his hotel room. What will be played out in this game between a Western European citizen and a Latin American exile will be the power relationship between metropolitan and peripheral subjects, between a descendent of the twentieth-century European Fascisms and a victim like el Quemado, who embodies the historical trauma of the Latin American dictatorships, and who, in the mind of the German character, acquires "the ominous character of the return of the past in the form of an Other that demands reparations."[8]

The gaze of the protagonist couple on the workers in the coastal town unites the gaze of the Northern-European tourist with the gaze of the colonizer who dehumanizes those communities that they consider should be under their dominion. Thus, in a moment of anger, Berger expresses his opinion of his new friends el Lobo and el Cordero in the following terms: "They live off of other people's holidays, they attach themselves to other people's holidays and leisure and make tourists' lives miserable. They're parasites." In the same manner, through the voice of the narrator, we have access to his girlfriend Ingeborg's opinion of the Spaniards as a tourist who "hardly gave them a second thought" and "spoke of them as if they were invisible." She also considers that men like el Lobo and el Cordero "are nothing but a couple of pathetic Latin lovers." According to the analysis of Antonio Córdoba, Berger believes that "he lives in an amnesiac Europe

---

[7] Roberto Bolaño, *The Skating Rink*, trans. Chris Andrews (New York: New Directions, 2009), and *The Third Reich*, Trans. Natasha Wimmer (New York: Picador, 2011).

[8] Antonio Córboba, "(De)Mythologizing the Disabled. Chilean Freaks in Roberto Bolaño's 'El Tercer Reich' and 'Estrella distante'," *Hispanic Issues on Line* 20 (2018): 77–96, 77.

that has no sense of the heroic," so that, by turning, in his imagination, el Quemado into a killing monster, he would be able to embrace a kind of recovered identity: "dying the way that Germans died as war criminals will allow him to re-enter the transhistorical realm of the German nation" (128, 114, 115, 86).

The xenophobia towards the Latin Americans residing in Spain will also be present in *The Skating Rink*, but, in this case, through the figure of Enric Rosquelles, the novel criticizes the attitude of the Catalan bourgeoisie towards migrants. Rosquelles is a civil servant who works in the town council of a Catalan coastal town governed by the PSOE, who decrees the building of an ice-skating rink with public funds, in honour of a professional ice-skater he falls in love with. Through a gaze charged with xenophobia, Rosquelles compares the migrant population residing in the town with the young marginalized "quinquis" and junkies, and considers both subaltern groups as a kind of "surplus" population that should be disciplined through its exploitation as work force in the agriculture sector:

> I don't like Africans. Especially, if they're Muslims. Once, in passing, I suggested to my team in Social Services that we could gather up all the street kids in Z and give them jobs on the farms: sowing, harvesting, driving tractors, even working on the market stalls each morning. It would have been marvelous to see that generation of future delinquents and junkies working the land. (80–81)

When, at the end, the dead body of an elderly woman appears in the building where Rosquelles had ordered the skating rink to be built, and he is arrested as a murder suspect, the civil servant defends his innocence by reclaiming the superiority of his Catalan identity. An identity which will allow him to present himself as a citizen endowed with an implied innate capacity to obey the law in the face of other places in the world associated, according to his Eurocentric imaginary, with crime: "I am a Catalan and this is Catalonia, not Chicago or Colombia." The crime of embezzlement committed by Rosquelles, who sees himself as "the driving force behind the Z city council, its muscles and its brain" (*The Skating Rink* 149, 6), would become part of the repertoire of cases of institutional corruption that took place within the PSOE and the Spanish government during the 90s, which had a dire impact on the credibility of the country's political class. The corruption during the second and third mandate of the PSOE (1986–1992) was connected with those social sectors in which Spanish capitalism found its way in a historical period in which Spain became a privileged site of the European financial and real estate bubbles. In this context, some of the so-called "structural defects" of the Spanish economy, such as the excessive capacity of its tourist sector or its real-estate market, became financial advantages, capable of capturing and temporarily holding on to a large amount of global floating capital in the coastal and metropolitan real-estate markets. The economic party went on until 1992, a year of the celebration of events that reinforced the entry of Spain in the Global Modernity as one of the European democracies with the largest potential for global investment. A series of celebrations that included the World Expo in Seville, the celebration of the Fifth Centenary of the Discovery of America, and the Olympic Games in Barcelona. This was the final touch of a context of an imagined economic riches during which the abundance of money was considered a measure of success, and which the Socialist Minister of the Economy, Carlos Solchaga, had summarized in 1988 by referring to Spain as "the country where the most money can be made in the short term in the whole of Europe, and maybe one of the countries where the most money can be made in the world." This phenomenon, which came to be known at the time as the "cultura del pelotazo" (the get-rich-quick culture), and which the character of Rosquelles is part of, can be framed within a political and economic reality in which those declarations by the minister had been nothing if not a good old call to speculative capital.

The context of the 1992 celebrations would be the very scenario in which Bolaño situates one of the protagonists of *Distant Star* (1996), in an episode in which the clash between the national identities of Latin American and European subjects is left behind. One of the chapters tells the story of Lorenzo, a gay artist who has lost both arms in an accident and who, after attempting suicide, leaves Chile and moves to Europe. Once in Spain, Lorenzo has two prosthetic arms implanted, and ends up in the role of Petra, the mascot of the Paralympic Games of Barcelona.[9] The narrator of *Distant Star* manifests their critical and ironic vantage point towards the Olympic event represented by the mascot designed by Catalan illustrator Javier Mariscal, who becomes the greatest admirer of Lorenzo's acting: "when Mariscal saw Lorenzo leaping about in his skin-tight Petra costume like a schizophrenic principal from the Bolshoi Ballet, he said: the Petra of my dreams" (75). As Edgar Illas explains, these Games had the purpose, among others, of reinforcing the Eurocentric identity of Catalonia and Barcelona as a global showcase: "[t]ogether with the Mediterranean label, the embrace of Europe was another key component of the official

---

[9] Roberto Bolaño, *Distant Star*. Trans. Chris Andrews (New York: New Directions, 2004).

marketing of Barcelona during the Olympics."[10] In this manner, with his role as Petra, Lorenzo becomes integrated as a subject within the new model of citizenship, ruled by the cultural logics of the spectacle and of transnational capital. A model that was part of what writer Rafael Sánchez Ferlosio called "a 'State marketing operation,' in order to boost the sales of the 'Spain Brand,'"[11] and which culminated in a deep economic crisis in 1993. At the end of this chapter of *Distant Star*, the narrator tells us how the life of this character unfolds after the end of his successful interpretation as an Olympic mascot: "Three years later, I found out he had died of *AIDS*" (76). Lorenzo thus becomes part of the precarious lives left out of public representation by the media over-exposure of the 1992 celebrations in Spain. A series of events that projected the spectacular image of a socially progressive, technologically sophisticated, and morally virtuous nation, while at the same time erasing the impact of the social costs of neoliberalism in the lives of a series of generations destroyed by unemployment, drugs, and AIDS.

At the beginning of the twenty-first century, Bolaño would explore the global dimensions of transnational capital in *2666*, a novel in which the contradictory unity of the diverse geographies in different parts of the book is that of a neoliberal modernity which connects bourgeois literary critics from Europe, experts in the work of German writer Benno von Archimboldi, with the textile workers in the North American periphery.[12] In an inversion of the movement of the exiled poets from *The Savage Detectives*, the artists and intellectuals in *2666* move from Europe to America, from the centres to the periphery. The story of Archimboldi, whose identity as a German soldier on the Eastern Front is revealed in Book Five, connects Nazi Germany with the contemporary textile industry in Ciudad Juárez. In this way, Bolaño refers to the Fascism of the 1930s in order to suggest that Santa Teresa is the new geographic and historical site of the systematized forms of genocide and femicide of neoliberal globalization. In "The Part About the Crimes," the connections between the interleaved stories that refer back to the Holocaust and to the assassination of women in Santa Teresa thus engage the causes of a structural violence which unfolds the continuity of its logics in different historical contexts, as part of a post-global dystopian narrative. In *2666*, the protagonist of "The

---

[10] Edgar Illas, *Thinking Barcelona: Ideologies of a Global City* (Liverpool: Liverpool University Press, 2012), 106.
[11] Peru Egurbide, "Sánchez Ferlosio ve en los fastos del V Centenario un 'marketing' de Estado," *El País*, April 9, 1992.
[12] Roberto Bolaño, *2666* (Barcelona: Anagrama, 2004).

Part About Amalfitano" is Óscar Amalfitano, a Chilean-born Philosophy professor who has lived, with his daughter Rosa, in Argentina, France, and Spain, and who is also the protagonist of *Woes of the True Policeman*, a novel published in 2011.[13] In the beginning of the novel, Amalfitano finds himself in a new stage of his life, after being sacked from the University of Barcelona, and discovering his homosexuality at a late age, in a moment in which his heterosexuality, like the Berlin Wall that also names the first chapter, becomes a hard-to-maintain fiction. In constant transition through different territories, the narrator presents this character's diaspora, which represents the conflict of those who cross the established borders in the logic of the map traced by the West, transgressing national identitary configuration itself. At the same time, as has been pointed out by some critics, the "madness" of the character of Amalfitano is a narrative thread that operates as an allegory in the cracks of symbolic plotlines of global geography, and which accompanies him in his process of deterritorialization: "madness is the sole visible 'thing' that Amalfitano carries from Chile to Spain to Mexico, from Pinochet to Franco to the Juárez murders, from time to time."[14]

In Roberto Bolaño's fiction, those lives in exile sometimes imply a temporal dislocation when characters migrate, transplanting the account of their political struggles from one country to the other. This is the case of the characters of *Monsieur Pain*, which narrates the last days of poet César Vallejo, militant communist and active defender of the Spanish Republic, over "the nine days leading up to Vallejo's death on April 15, primarily the five days from April 6 to April 11, concluding in its final pages with the day after his April 19 funeral at Montrouge Cemetery organized by the Communist party."[15] Both the character of César Vallejo and that of Amalfitano embody, as is the case with so many other characters in the Chilean writer's work, different vantage points on the idea of exile. An idea that, as Alberto Medina reminds us, "is not so much a circumstance as an ethics of life and writing."[16] It is not only a case of a geographical, but also a chronological exile, so his narratives are also conceived as "exercises of

---

[13] Roberto Bolaño, *Woes of the True Policeman*, trans. Natasha Wimmer (New York: Farrar, Straus and Giroux, 2011).
[14] Brett Levinson, "Case Closed: Madness and Dissociation in 2666," *Journal of Latin American Cultural Studies*, 18.2–3 (2009): 177–191.
[15] Jonathan Beck Monroe, *Framing Roberto Bolaño. Poetry, Fiction, Literary History, Politics* (Cambridge; New York: Cambridge University Press, 2019).
[16] Alberto Medina, "Arts of Homelessness: Roberto Bolaño, or The Commodification of Exile," *Novel* 3 (2009): 546–554, 547.

remembrance, tributes to a generation, his own, often portrayed as anachronistic, unable to realize the loss that had already happened." As has been pointed out by some critics, the expansion of Bolaño's work as a commodity in a globalized world makes the author's own position regarding exile as a site of enunciation more complex, since "the anglophone literary field has commodified Bolaño's translated fictions, marketing an exilic sensibility that appeals to exoticist stereotypes of Latin America and that distorts the political content of his work."[17] As has been made manifest in these pages, Bolaño was capable of showing himself as an icon of the global writer, while at the same time offering his readers a complex reflection on Spanish and European reality at the end of the twentieth and beginnings of the twenty-first centuries, as well as on the potential, the limitations, and the cracks within these transatlantic connections.[18]

Translated from the Spanish by Kamen Nedev.

---

[17] Sharae Deckard, "Peripheral Realism, Millennial Capitalism, and Roberto Bolaño's 2666". *Modern Language Quarterly* 73.3 (2012): 351–372, 371.

CHAPTER 8

Transnational Currents: Europe and the Americas

Rory O'Bryen

Many of Bolaño's novels can be, and often are, read with reference to their ingenious engagement with the histories of those two nations, Chile and Mexico, where he spent much of his life. Written long after his move from Mexico to Spain in 1977 (nine years after leaving his native Chile), *Distant Star* (1996), *The Savage Detectives* (1998), *Amulet* (1999), and *By Night in Chile* (2000) return, both directly and obliquely, to key events in both nations' historical unfolding in the second half of the twentieth century: to the CIA-backed coup that toppled Salvador Allende's government in September 1973 and initiated the violent restructuring of the Chilean nation and state;[1] and to the repression of student and labour movements in 1968 that helped consolidate the PRI's hegemony in post-Revolutionary Mexico.[2] However, while they make important contributions to the sense-making of these events, and to national literary histories in which these events serve key historicizing functions – contributions not to be overlooked in enthusiastic identifications of Bolaño as the representative of a

---

[1] On Chile 1973 see Ignacio López-Vicuña, "The Violence of Writing: Literature and Discontent in Roberto Bolaño's 'Chilean' Novels," *Journal of Latin American Cultural Studies* 18.2 (2009): 155–166; Gareth Williams, "Sovereignty and Melancholic Paralysis in Roberto Bolaño," *Journal of Latin American Cultural Studies* 18.2 (2009): 125–140; Patrick Dove, "The Night of the Senses: Literary (Dis)orders in *Nocturno de Chile*," *Journal of Latin American Cultural Studies* 18.2 (2009): 141–154; and Ignacio López-Calvo, "Roberto Bolaño's Flower War: Memory, Melancholy, and Pierre Menard," in Ignacio López-Calvo ed. *Roberto Bolaño: A Less Distant Star* (NY: Palgrave Macmillan, 2015), 35–64.

[2] On Mexico 1968 see Ryan Long, "Traumatic Time in Roberto Bolaño's *Amuleto* and the Archive of 1968," *Bulletin of Latin American Research* 29.1 (2010): 128–143. For broader engagements with Mexico 1968 in literature, see Dolly J. Young, "Mexican Literary Reactions to Tlatelolco 1968," *Latin American Research Review* 20.2 (1985): 71–85; Ryan Long, "Tlatelolco's Persistent Legacy: A Comparative Analysis of Three Mexican Novels," *Bulletin of Latin American Research* 24.4 (2005): 513–26; and Samuel Steinberg's deconstruction of Tlatelolco's status as "event" in *Photopoetics at Tlatelolco: Afterimages of Mexico, 1968* (Austin: University of Texas Press, 2016).

new "world" or "global" literature –[3] they should not be read as "national novels."

It is not in itself surprising that Bolaño's more overt engagements with Chile or Mexico should come *after* his relocation to Spain. For, it reminds us, first, of the transnational circumstances in which many canonical Latin American works were written: from Argentina's founding text, *Facundo, Civilization and Barbarism* (1845), written in exile in Chile by future president Domingo Sarmiento, and in a recycling of various European travel writings; through José Eustasio Rivera's *The Vortex* (1924), whose patriotic denunciation of the savage capitalism of the Amazonian rubber boom grew from his involvement in a Swiss-led commission to resolve a border dispute with Venezuela; to the transatlantic collaborations that spawned the Latin American "Boom."[4] The fact that Bolaño's European-based works, *Antwerp*, *Monsieur Pain*, and *The Third Reich*, were written prior to but only published *after* these ostensibly "Latin American novels" may indeed reflect the consolidation of expectations, by the "Boom" phenomenon itself, that Latin Americans write *about* Latin America. It is also important to remember that literature in Latin America was *formally* (if not always avowedly) transnational long before the "Boom," in its drawing on the cultures of European, autochthonous, and diasporic subjects thrown together by the long imperial history that forged the entities "Latin America," "Europe," and "Africa" as we now know them.[5]

Although some of Bolaño's best-loved works exemplify this dialectic whereby Latin Americanness enters "narration" at a temporal and geographical remove, their transnational emplotments also explicitly foreground the overdetermination of the national by the transnational. *Distant Star*, for example, may well be preoccupied with Chile's post-dictatorial "grey zones" where "civilization" becomes "barbarism," and where left and right politics become indistinct.[6] But its culmination in a scene of recognition outside Barcelona – long-time rival of Buenos Aires and Mexico City for the title of "capital city" of Latin American

---

[3] On Bolaño as "global Latin American novelist" see Héctor Hoyos, *Beyond Bolaño* (NY: Columbia University Press, 2015), 1–32, and Will H. Corral, *Bolaño traducido: Nueva Literatura Mundial* (Madrid: Escalera, 2011).

[4] On the "Boom" novel as a transnational literary phenomenon see Mario Santana, *Foreigners in the Homeland: The Spanish American New Novel in Spain, 1962–1974* (Lewisburg: Bucknell University Press, 2000).

[5] See Mark Thurner, "The Names of Spain and Peru. Notes on the Global Scope of the Hispanic," in Catherine Davies and Rory O'Bryen eds. *Transnational Spanish Studies* (Liverpool: Liverpool University Press, 2020),

[6] See in particular Williams, "Sovereignty and Melancholic Paralysis."

publishing – also ties its descent into so much ethico-political "murk" to the international publishing business's dissolution of the "conflicting universals" of Cold War ideology.[7] *The Savage Detectives*, similarly, may encode a national drama of loss and political defeat in its "farewell" to *Infrarrealismo*'s dream of "revolutionizing Mexican poetry."[8] Yet the global dispersion of its poet protagonists – notably in the second part's loose assembly of globally-scattered witness reports of last sightings of Arturo Belano and Ulises Lima – also charts the "Mexican" writer's disappearance *into* the dispersed global multitude *against* which he was once tasked with shoring up a unifying imaginary of the nation as an enclosed signifying entelechy.[9]

As Jonathan Monroe has shown, Bolaño's *oeuvre* circulates freely between the geopolitical *and* literary histories of Europe and the Americas, thereby calling for a "prismatic" combination of alternately "Latin Americanist," "hemispheric," and "global" heuristic approaches (2–3). Yet, from his Rimbaldian beginnings, with their poetic leave-taking of Nerudian- and Casa de las Americas-inspired third-world nationalism, through the tri-continental *Savage Detectives*, with its polyphonic scattering of characters across Europe, Africa, and the Americas, to the global *2666*, which hints at the "secret" of a new world order emerging in the collision of post-war European and American histories on the deadly border between "First" and "Third" worlds, Bolaño maintained an "exilic" distance from literary and political nationalism.[10] This he makes explicit in his 2002 prologue to *Antwerp*, where he situates his writing practice in a "wild" space "a la intemperie" (of which more below) "equally distant from

---

[7] I owe this point to Jonathan Monroe's reading of *Estrella distante* in *Framing Bolaño: Poetry, Fiction, Literary History, Politics* (Cambridge: CUP, 2019), 86–101, which traces the novel's reversals not only of communism and fascism, but also literary autonomy and investment in the rules of the literary market. This final reversal, he argues, is encoded in the final chapter's turn to the detective fiction format, always a synecdoche, as Monroe shows, for investments, returns, and the rules of the literary game in Bolaño. On the "conflicting universals" of the Cold War and their reshaping of the Latin American *ciudades letradas*, see Jean Franco, *Decline and Fall of the Lettered City: Latin America and the Cold War* (Cambridge: Harvard University Press, 2002).

[8] See Philip Derbyshire, "*Los detectives salvajes*: Line, loss and the political," *Journal of Latin American Cultural Studies* 18.2 (2009): 167–176 and Monroe's sustained discussion of Bolaño's prose poetics and poetics of prose.

[9] See Benedict Anderson, *Imagined Communities: Reflections on the Rise and Spread of Nationalism* (London: Verso, 1991) and Doris Sommer, *Foundational Fictions: The National Romances of Latin America* (Berkeley and Los Angeles: California University Press, 1991).

[10] In "Literature and Exile," Bolaño maintained that literature and exile were two sides of the same coin, that to talk of literature *and* exile amounted to a tautology. *Between Parentheses*, trans Natasha Wimmer (NY: New Directions, 2011), 38–45.

all the countries in the world."¹¹ And it is palpable across his *oeuvre* as it maps, under the aegis of the most heteroclite assembly of writers, a dispersion of "ghosts" whose wanderings trace the contours of a cosmos in turmoil. These "ghosts," he writes, "are the only ones who have any time because they live outside time," and are identified as his companions and addressees (ix).¹²

Beyond his own transnational trajectory and explicitly transnational plots, then, a defining feature of the transnational in Bolaño can be found in his poetic cosmopolitics of the ghostly "underdogs" who drift across Latin America in the pursuit of dreams of emancipation, before being scattered beyond Latin America, around Europe and the rest of the globe. These make a memorable appearance in the title poem of *The Romantic Dogs* (1993) in its evocation of the *Infrarrealistas*' withdrawal into a space of exilic loss. From the start, however, this loss is gathered under the sign of a gain. In "losing a nation," the poet announces, "I had gained a dream," thanks to which "nothing else mattered. / Neither work nor prayer/ nor study in the early hours."¹³ What Monroe identifies, via Agamben, as Bolaño's pursuit of a poetry beyond "the end of its lines" (65–85)¹⁴ here finds its complement in what, also via Agamben, we might call the underdog's "destituent" potential. Envisaging a "belonging together of life and form, being and action, *beyond all relation*,"¹⁵ the dream of the romantic dogs encodes a will to "become ungovernable": a withdrawal that "deactivates and renders works (of economy, of religion, of language etc.) inoperative," and that suspends and redirects in so doing, understandings both of art's "proper function," and of community as a closed distribution of "factical vocations" (69, 74).

Across his *oeuvre*, of course, poetry bears the weight of a double "destitution." In a literal sense, most of his poets are dirt-poor and live in precarity. Poetry is tied to suicide – by the mutilated transgender Lorenzo/Petra in *Distant Star*, who surmises that suicide is "redundant" when one could "become an undercover poet";¹⁶ and to disappearance – the case of Juan Stein, also in *Distant Star*, who is buried in a grave that

---

[11] Roberto Bolaño, *Antwerp*, trans Natasha Wimmer (NY: New Directions, 2011), ix–xi.
[12] In the same prologue he writes of his debt to Alice Sheldon, Sade, Manrique, to unknown science fiction writers, and to the occasional pornographer.
[13] Roberto Bolaño, *Los perros románticos* (Barcelona: Acantilado, 2006), 3
[14] See also Monroe's chapter on *The Savage Detectives*, which traces Bolaño's development of a post-Baudelairean prose-poetics into the novel's dismantling of narrative "drives," 105–129.
[15] Giorgio Agamben, "What is a destituent power?" trans. Stephanie Wakefield, *Environment and Planning D: Society and Space* 32 (2014): 65.
[16] Roberto Bolaño, *Distant Star*, trans. Chris Andrews (London: Harvill Press, 2004), 73.

can't be found, and deprived after death of his single ennobling claim: to be descended from a war hero from a "family of dirt-poor Ukranian Jews" now scattered all over the globe (64). In *The Savage Detectives*, which also ends in disappearance, poetry is the circulating currency in an antieconomy of diminishing returns, and binds the illicit and the counterfeit to the shadow-worlds of crime, prostitution, and death. And in *Amulet*, poetry is connected to destitution – via the associations that the displaced, childless Auxilio Lacouture forms with the exiled Spaniards, León Felipe and Pedro Garfias, and with Belano's drifting poet-groupies: "kids, who seemed to have graduated from the great orphanage of Mexico City's subway rather than from the Faculty of Philosophy and Literature."[17] Yet in this last text, poetry also reveals a second sense of destitution, which lies in its "destituent" potential to suspend narratives of history and identity, to render them inoperable, and to free them in so doing from the economy of "ends" to which they are commonly put.

Ryan Long perceptively points out the semantic density of the term *intemperie* used by Auxilio to describe her "exposure," during the UNAM's military occupation in 1968, as exposure *to* the traumatic "untimeliness" of the event. *Intemperie*, he notes, encompasses meanings at once meteorological ("inconstancy of weather"), ethico-moral ("intemperance, lack of moderation"), spatial ("an absence of shelter from the elements"), and temporal (from the Latin root, "*tempus*," of the Spanish "tiempo" meaning weather and time). On this basis, he persuasively reads *Amulet* as one instance, in an archive of writings about Mexico's '68, of a narrative that captures the "untimeliness" of the event (as a "cut" in the teleological unfolding of historical time) while also guarding (in its refusal to reassemble a fractured set of memories) against the "suturing" of the event-as-cut into national narratives of progress.[18] While Long's reading outlines where Auxilio's poetic vision may "deactivate" and render "inoperative" a progressive historical narrative, I should like to develop further, and with reference to the transnational wanderings of Bolaño's underdogs, his observation that *intemperie* (in *Amulet*) makes exposure "an at once historical and *geographical* condition of being unsettled" (133).[19]

Life as it is lived by Bolaño's underdogs entails exposure not only to the "untimeliness" of *intemperie* – defined by Long, with Derrida, as an

---

[17] Roberto Bolaño, *Amulet*, trans. Chris Andrews (NY: New Directions, 2006), 77.
[18] Long, "Traumatic Time in Roberto Bolaño's *Amuleto*," *Bulletin of Latin American Research* 29.1 (2010): 128–143.
[19] Emphasis added.

experience of being "out of joint," on the wrong side of history – but also to what Homi Bhabha defines as the anomic "unhomeliness" of the nation today, whose imagined closure is internally riven by geographically-scattered populations as they gather "on the edge of 'foreign' cultures [...] in the half-life, half-light of foreign tongues, or in the uncanny fluency of another's language."[20] This scattering of migrants is a unifying feature of the short stories in *Llamadas telefónicas* (1997) and *Putas asesinas* (2001). In these, characters like "Lalo Cura" (born to a Colombian porn star and a priest, and who later appears in northern Mexico as a cop in *2666*), Mauricio "the eye" Silva (a doubly-exiled gay Chilean photojournalist who rescues two boys from an underground brothel in an unnamed city in India), and "Buba" (a footballer from an unnamed African country hired to play in the Spanish championship league, who performs a strange blood ritual with his team mates, the Chilean Acevedo and the Spanish Herrera, before dying in an accident), join the ranks of the wandering "orphans" that Auxilio gathers under her wing. The lines drawn by their wanderings fade into the unknown just as suddenly as they come into view, like the lights on the desert highway that the narrator of "Gómez Palacio" watches in the half-light of dusk.

While in *Amulet* this "gathering," which is also a "scattering," offers (following Long) "a profoundly unsettled [...] unstable vantage point" on Mexican memory and history (134–135), in the short stories, Bolaño's wandering characters radically displace the nation as a heuristic frame. Making up what Ignacio López-Vicuña calls a new cast of "cosmopolitans" – "maquiladora workers, prostitutes, football players, political exiles, reporters, detectives, traveling artists, wandering poets and revolutionaries" –[21] they open up instead the perspective of an "in-between space of overlapping nation claims and cultural norms" (90). For Bhabha, such "in-between spaces" typically void the national "Heim" as the "daemonic double of [melancholic] introjection and identification" (236). For López-Vicuña, Bolaño's transnational wanderers place nations and imagined "national communities" more radically in abeyance. For, as social, sexual, and racial outsiders vis-à-vis those displaced Latin Americans held together by "the melancholic folklore of exile," they inhabit something closer to the wild underside of global, transnational space, where the "regulative fictions

---

[20] Homi K. Bhabha, "DisseminNation," in *The Location of Culture* (NY: Routledge, 1994), 199–200.
[21] Ignacio López-Vicuña, "The Part of the Exile: Displacement and Belonging in Bolaño's *Putas asesinas*," *Hispanófila* 164 (2012): 82.

for relating to others and organizing the national community – such as *mestizaje* or multiculturalism'" – are "suspended" (90).

Amulet enriches this view of the suspension both of the nation and of the "regulative fictions" of transnationalism's multicultural dimensions. Auxilio's story, for example, is narrated in such a way as to forewarn against critical efforts to sever Mexico from Latin America and from Europe. The storm (*intemperie*) that blows over Mexico in the novel, for example, is also the storm blowing north from the rest of Latin America, and connects the traumatic events of Tlatelolco in 1968, via the dust from the *pampas* that it deposits on Auxilio's books (4–5), with the horrors of the dictatorial Southern Cone occurring in the 1970s. This storm also converges, in the novel's kaleidoscopic temporal unfolding, with the winds of post-war Fascism that drove many European artists to Mexico in the first half of the century. This last convergence is of course a "known" in the story of the transnational genesis of the European *and* Latin American avant-gardes.[22] Yet by decentring the protagonism of figures like Breton, Rivera, Picasso, Chagall (albeit not Carrington or Varos), Bolaño locates our perspective on this transnational history in the "unknown universe" of those underdogs who lived in its wings, and in the dimly lit worlds of "the subway, the underworld, the sewers." Life in these *inframundos* is assumed not as a tragedy but as a boon, for that submerged "beloved university," his protagonist Auxilio muses, is "waiting for its day to come" (78, 122).

How should we read this announcement of the becoming-universal of the cloaca, and of the becoming-historical of the "known" university? As a provocation, like Baudelaire's spleen-filled suggestion that those insensitive to poetry should be given not "delicate perfumes [...] but carefully chosen manure"?[23] Or as confirmation of the "sovereignty *d'en bas*" that Baudelaire maintained in his indifference to all social forms?[24] Bolaño often invokes this "cloacal" undercurrent as a rising tide and destructuring force, notably at moments when the "known university" is in crisis: in the "barbaric writers" defilement of books in pursuit of an intimacy "that broke all the barriers imposed by culture, the academy and knowledge" (*Distant Star*, 131–132); in the "sea of shit of literature" into which *Distant Star*'s narrator vows never to submerge himself again;[25] and in the "storm

---

[22] See Tatiana Flores, *Mexico's Revolutionary Avant-Gardes: from Estridentismo to ¡30–30!* (New Haven: Yale University Press, 2013), which includes a reading of *The Savage Detectives'* engagement with the legacies of these transnational collaborations, *Estridentismo* in particular 4–7.
[23] Charles Baudelaire, *Le Spleen de Paris* (Paris: Gallimard, 2010), 25.
[24] Roberto Calasso, *La folie Baudelaire* (London: Penguin, 2008), 37.
[25] In Andrews' translation, "cesspools."

of shit" unleashed when the prattling Urrutia Lacroix is finally silenced by the "wizened youth's" inaudible "no."[26] Aren't these scatological figures, in effect, figures for the unknown university's potential to "unworld the world"?[27] Ciphers for how what Monroe calls a poetry "at the end of its lines" might expose "world" and "work" to the elements (*intemperie*), and render both inoperative in a radical "opening" towards something beyond (65–85).

These figures, of course, demand a reflection on form, and on the narrative configuration of the "unknown universe" in relation to the world as we know it. For while thinking *with* our emissions may, as Timothy Morton argues, introduce *différance* and dispersal into those foreground-background, hither-yonder distinctions which guarantee the phenomenological unity of "worlds,"[28] the "worlding" of *différance* into neat demarcations of identity/difference is also determined along political and economic lines: by capitalism's deterritorializations and reterritorializations of capital and labour, and by the extension of external national borders through the biopolitical management of internal social borders.[29] Yet, if for Bolaño the nation is *essentially* indeterminate as a form (as underscored by his satire of "Nazis" like Irma Carrasco and Silvio Silvático in *Nazi Literature in the Americas*, who believe that literature can secure the nation's borders), then the "world" is even more so. Indeed, following Monroe, who emphasizes Bolaño's deconstruction of the novelistic "impulses towards linearity and closure" – in favour of formal openness, modularity, and inconclusion – his novels appear as the formal counterparts of a world which is itself "set adrift [...] on a vast ocean" of fragmented forms (81, 108).

---

[26] Roberto Bolaño, *By Night in Chile*, trans. Chris Andrews (London: Harvill Press, 2003), 128–130.
[27] On "worlding" see Gayatri Spivak, "The Rani of Sirmur: An Essay in Reading the Archives," *History and Theory* 24.3 (1985): 247–272, which analyses the internalization, by colonial subjects, of the colonizer's view of colonized lands as alien and in need of domestication. For a brilliant account of "a cosmopolitanism that reckons with the experience of the *unworlding* of the world," see Mariano Siskind's reading of "El Ojo Silva" and its "displacement of the very stable notion of world as globe produced by hegemonic discourses of cosmopolitanism and financial and consumerist globalization," in Gesine Müller and Mariano Siskind, eds, *World Literature, Cosmopolitanism, Globality* (Berlin/Munich/Boston: de Gruyter, 2019), 206–207. And for a further discussion of the folding of "scatology" into "eschatology," see Dove's "The Night of the Senses."
[28] Timothy Morton, "Deconstruction and/as Ecology," in Greg Garrard, ed. *The Oxford Handbook of Ecocrticism* (Oxford: OUP, 2014), 291–304.
[29] On these points, see Zygmunt Bauman, *Globalization: The Human Consequences* (New York: Columbia University Press, 1998) and Étienne Balibar, "What Is a Border?," in Étienne Balibar, *Politics and the Other Scene* (London: Verso, 2002), 75–85.

Monroe's reference to the "oceanic" here is propitious, and not only for its evocation, in negative form, of those "oceanic feelings" which Freud, in his critique of religion, had dismantled as sublimations of the destructive instincts that flourished in war.[30] For as well as underscoring Bolaño's pursuit of unity in *fragmentation* – rather than in eirenic oneness: for Siskind, the guiding figures of "a Christian, gendered notion of cosmopolitan piety that is now in crisis" (224) – it also invites parallels between Bolaño and two transatlantic interlocutors, particularly with respect to his balancing of part and whole, fragment and totality, the "known" and the "unknown," and of what remains in between. The first is Baudelaire, who in "The Painter of Modern Life" stated his interest "in the whole world," yet ceaselessly underscored that the "correspondences" between part and whole had sunk into obscurity, leaving man on a "hunt for images, without beginning or end" (Calasso 9, 12). The second is Melville, whose exploration of man's orphanhood in *Moby Dick* gives form to the *emptiness* of his world as he is cast adrift on the world's seas. It does so by "looming" (or weaving) its digressive "fugues" (on whales in art, literature, religion, and philosophy) in such a way that when the sublime whale finally "looms" over the horizon, reducing Ishmael's ship to nothing and leaving him circling the vortex, it has already wholly "consumed" both reader and protagonist.[31]

Amalfitano's citation of *Moby Dick* as the emblem "of the great, imperfect, torrential works, books that blaze paths into the unknown,"[32] may constitute an invitation to read *2666* as a return to the "total novel" ("Boom" or otherwise):[33] as a novel which, like *Moby Dick*, swings open "the great flood-gates of the wonder-world" to "chart" the winds that "blow Moby Dick into the devious zig-zag world-circle of the Pequod's circumnavigating wake" (5, 180). But, like *Moby Dick*, its opening out from the known "university" of literary criticism onto an unknown "universe," leads not to the revelation of a hidden "chart" or "transcript," but to a vortex. Thus, its cast of unmoored "cosmopolitans"– the four European critics, an exiled Chilean philosopher and his daughter, an African American journalist, and a former Nazi-turned Nobel-nominated

---

[30] Sigmund Freud, *Civilization and Its Discontents* (London: Vintage, 200), 61–73.
[31] On the polysemy of "loomings" in Melville, see Tony Tanner's introduction to *Moby Dick* (Oxford: Oxford University Press, 1988), vi–xxxii.
[32] Roberto Bolaño, *2666*, trans Natasha Wimmer (London: Picador, 2009), 227.
[33] For a compelling reading of Bolaño's reworking of the "Ulyssean" Boom novel format, see Patricia Novillo-Corvalán, "Transnational Modernist Encounters: Joyce, Borges, Bolaño, and the Dialectics of Expansion and Compression," *The Modern Language Review* 108.2 (2013): 341–367.

author – are drawn, much like the cast of the Pequod in its zig-zagging, world-circling voyages, into the baleful "wake" of yet another vortex: the cloacal body-dump in the desert. The "secret of the world" said to await decipherment at the centre of this scene, is of course never revealed. Or perhaps the secret is instead the very dehiscence or implosion of the "world" that the novel formally performs – the gathering together, as Brett Levinson astutely observes, of an accumulation of severed stories, which in their serialization and repetition, "bind" the world in the form of a self-differing, self-deferring "unbinding."[34]

Bolaño had, of course, been exploring this "binding-unbinding" of world and work long before he sat down to work on his *magnum opus*. Gathering together a loosely-arranged series of fragments, and from the titular place of a place which (like its many other European locations) may in fact be an empty reference or a misnomer, *Antwerp* had already enacted the event of a kaleidoscopic concatenation of erasures and scatterings. From its titular report of a man run over by a truckload of pigs who then flee along a highway, through "People walking away," which announces that "Nothing lasts, the purely loving gestures of children tumble into the void," to the self-reflexive exposure of its "synopsis" – "... hunchback in the woods near the campground... In Barcelona a South American is dying ... Cops who fuck nameless girls ..." – to the "wind" that "whips up sand and buries them" all, *Antwerp*, like *2666*, performed not a reconstitution but a *deconstitution* of the novel. Collapsing the work into a dispersion of photographs, intervals of silence, indecipherable signs, and lines that lead nowhere – and into a space of "total anarchy" that thwarts its very "operativity" as a novel – it registered, as Baudelaire had done years before, the nervous shocks that make it so hard "to get a fix on the frequencies of reality." And with that, perhaps, the gutting of a whole aesthetic "edifice" of which, for some time now, all that remains is the façade (*Antwerp*, 68, 51, 29, 30, 3).

---

[34] Brett Levinson, "Case Closed: Madness and Dissociation in *2666*," *Journal of Latin American Cultural Studies* 18.2 (2009): 177–191.

PART II

Shaping Events and Literary History

CHAPTER 9

France, Spain, 1938
Juli Highfill

Bolaño's early novel, *Monsieur Pain* (1999), opens by situating readers in a precise place and time – Paris, April 6, 1938 – and much of the action takes place during a scant five days of perpetual rain. Through its atmospherics of gloom we find ourselves submerged in those tense times of dread and uncertainty. The Spanish Civil War is raging, fascism is on the rise; Europe is looking back at the devastation of the Great War and forward to another world war that will bring mass death on an unfathomable scale. The hapless protagonist, Pierre Pain – a World War I veteran, now a dabbler in the occult arts – narrates in the first person a series of misadventures, recounting how he was drawn into a noirish labyrinthine intrigue, which he never manages to comprehend.

 A sense of menace erupts on the first page, as Pain encounters on the stairway two shadowy men wearing dark trenchcoats and speaking Spanish. He goes on to meet with Madame Reynaud, a widow whose husband he tried and failed to heal with acupuncture and hypnosis, and who now asks him to treat her friend's husband, a South American who is dying of a mysterious illness, stricken by incessant hiccups. The patient is César Vallejo – the impoverished Peruvian poet, still relatively unknown, persecuted by the regime in his native country, exiled in Paris since 1923, a Communist deeply committed to the anti-fascist struggle and consumed with the fate of the Spanish Republic. Monsieur Pain's narration, as it unfolds, will pivot around the presence/absence of the hiccupping poet, Vallejo – an abyssal figure who occupies the incomprehensible and catastrophic "now" of that moment in time.

 Given the poet's posthumous fame, Bolaño's readers will likely experience a jolt of recognition, once Madame Reynaud utters Vallejo's name. Bolaño, in his "Preliminary Note" to the novel, calls attention to the biographical underpinnings of the novel: "Almost all the events related actually occurred: Vallejo's hiccups, . . . the doctors who were so negligent in treating Vallejo. Even Pain is real. Georgette mentions him on a page of her passionate, bitter, defenseless memoirs" (11–12).[1] And indeed, Vallejo's widow, Georgette Philippart, names the callous doctors who maltreated him, as well as Pierre Pain, the mesmerist and acupuncturist, whom she summoned to his bedside. She describes how Pain suspended his hand above Vallejo's forehead, transmitting magnetic energy to the feverish, hiccupping patient, and how his efforts seemed to yield results; Vallejo's hiccups ceased and he fell into a deep restful sleep. As Pain left, she reports, he said, "There is hope," and agreed to return in two days (Georgette de Vallejo 1978, 131). The mesmerist failed to return, however, and Georgette later learned that he was turned away at the door. Vallejo, after showing improvement, worsened in the following days; the hiccups, fever, and delirium returned and he died on April 15.

Based on Georgette's account, Bolaño weaves an expansive, hallucinatory tale of intrigue. Mysterious, malevolent forces are at work to ensure that Vallejo does not recover. The Spanish agents (fascists, we presume) return and bribe Pain not to treat Vallejo and to forget the whole affair. Immediately after taking the bribe, however, Pain regrets his "abominable act" (37); he proceeds to visit Vallejo, to treat him and to calm his hiccups, exactly as Georgette described. Through the rest of his increasingly fantastical narration, Pain – at once a melancholic *flâneur* and a sad-sack detective – wanders the streets of Paris under a "sinister" sky, "like a mirror hanging over a hole," as he attempts to unravel the impenetrable plot against Vallejo (83). In the end, Pain's failure is complete: already a failed poet, he fails professionally in not saving Vallejo; he fails ethically in accepting the bribe; he fails romantically with Madame Reynaud; and he fails cognitively to untangle the intrigue. Arguably, every character in the novel fails; an "Epilogue of Voices" offers brief testimonials that recount the fates of various characters, including Pain. Some will die in the Second World War, others will lead banal, futile lives in the postwar years. Pain will fall further into abjection, joining a trio of performers and eking out a living in cheap cabarets and circuses, reading "blood-stained" palms and tarot cards (132). Altogether, these multiple failures reflect a historical and existential conundrum: the impossibility of truly apprehending a given historical moment, not only for those living on the threshold of a cataclysm in 1938, but also the impossibility for all of us, in our own given

---

[1] Translations from *Monsieur Pain* (1999) and other texts are my own. For Georgette de Vallejo's account of her husband's last days, see *¡Allá ellos, allá ellos, allá ellos!* (1978, 115–140). Refer also to Stephen Hart's literary biography of Vallejo (2013).

contexts, to comprehend the obscure, myriad forces at play in what Walter Benjamin called "the darkness of the lived moment."[2]

Contextual markers of catastrophe abound in Pain's narration, the most pervasive among them being fascism itself. A sense of dread haunts the novel, infusing the shadowy, damp, and oppressive atmosphere with deadly certainty. Fascism, Cory Stockwell observes, "is often thought of as a nocturnal politics that appeals to emotions and to those darker elements within us"; the novel's "nocturnal sensibility" emerges not only from the noirish atmospherics, but also from key motifs, namely: Pain's own practice of the occult arts and the innumerable darkened, mysterious, and labyrinthine sites (2019, 344). And fascism, of course, remains a perennial preoccupation for Bolaño, omnipresent in his novels – *La literatura nazi en América*, *Estrella distante*, *El Tercer Reich*, *2666*, among others – and appearing as a transhistorical, transcontinental ideology of evil.[3]

In Pain's immediate historical context, Spain – that first battleground against fascism – is an ongoing topic of conversation in the cafes. The denizens speak of the unprecedented aerial bombing of civilians, carried out by the new German *Stukas*, each mounted with three machine guns and loaded with over one thousand kilos of bombs. "The damned Germans are testing their arsenal" (65). Pain, his lungs seared by poison gas at Verdun, recalls his own war: "the bombs, the gas, the diseases [that] devastated us, a terrified, brutalized troop of deluded peasants, workers, and petits bourgeois" (66). Later, in another café, Pain encounters an eerie representation of mass death that gestures towards wars past and wars to come. Gazing into an aquarium, a "marine cemetery" created by twin avant-garde artists, he discerns wrecked ships, trains, and planes, with miniature, dismembered bodies scattered about, half-buried in the sand, while above them red fish swim about like "flags of death" (57–58). Pain,

---

[2] Benjamin cites Ernst Bloch's, "darkness of the lived moment" on at least two occasions in the *Arcades Project*. Like Bloch, Benjamin was seeking a utopian opening within that darkness, and in so doing, relates that darkness with the "dream consciousness of the collective" as opposed to a "waking consciousness" that could read allegorically the traces of the past in the present and advance (consciously) into the future (1999, 858, 883).

[3] For the historian Federico Finchelstein, "Bolaño's work frames fascism at the center of politics and literature. His work presents fascism as a historical event but also as an object with meaningful ramifications into the structural violence and inequalities of the present" (2017, 23). Therefore, "Reading Bolaño should be a must for historians of fascism" (24). However, Finchelstein also finds Bolaño's notion of fascism to be "problematic because it is sometimes too much rooted in an 'ahistorical' notion of evil that basically turns fascism into a transcendental object," reduced to "the essence of evil" (39).

ever the spectator, peruses this submerged scene of horror, uncomprehending and stunned.

Indeed, "spectator" is a term which he repeatedly uses to describe himself. After breaking with his mentor, Monsieur Rivette, Pain reflects: "the old man and I were alike not only in our stance before the labyrinth but also in our shared condition as spectators" (87). In another moment, as he stands in a dark room in the labyrinthine hospital, he searches in vain for a light switch so that he might be seen through the window, and thereby confirm his presence as a "humble but punctual spectator" (115). In a key scene in the novel, Pain finds himself among the spectators of a film, *Actualidad* (the present) – the title a wink at the French newsreels of the period, *Actualités*. Paula Aguilar regards this film screening as "a mise en abyme for the novel's central axis," consolidating Pain's status as a mere spectator, paralyzed, trapped in a labyrinth, unable to comprehend, unable to act (2014, 495). At this point in the narrative, Pain has spent hours walking in circles, drenched by rain, as he pursues one of the Spanish agents, who finally enters a cinema and joins a companion. Pain takes a seat beside them, and by chance, the companion happens to be an old acquaintance, Pleumeur-Bodou, once a fellow student of mesmerism, and now an avowed fascist on leave from service in Spain, where he puts his skills to use as an interrogator. Amid the protests of other spectators, Pleumeur-Bodou and Pain carry on an extended conversation – their words interspersed with the actors' lines on screen – a mish-mash of dialog that creates a markedly disorienting effect.

Adding to the confusion, *Actualidad* is a temporal mélange, its representation of the present infused with images of the past and intimations of the future. The action begins as the protagonist Michel, a former scientist, walks with his fiancée along the beaches of Normandy – an obvious allusion to D-Day, reinforced by the intermittent explosions heard in the background. As it happens, these explosions are taking place in Michel's own tormented mind. Guilt-ridden, he is haunted by memories of a deadly blast that killed twenty young scientists in his laboratory, where he conducted radioactive experiments – again a signal of the war to come and the first atomic bomb. Inserted into this "sinister melodrama" is grainy documentary footage of scientists at work in a laboratory years before – a past that Pleumeur-Bodou and Pain share as well (97). For one of the scientists is Terzeff, another of the "sorcerer's apprentices" who had studied under Rivette, the master of mesmerism, and who later committed suicide (85). Peumeur-Bodou, in his running commentary, calls the film a hybrid, noting that the director embedded the documentary footage to portray Michel's memories and dreams.

We might read this confusing hodgepodge of a film, with its repeated explosions that bespeak historic disasters (past, present, and yet to come), as a metafigure for the novel itself. It bears noting that Bolaño, on more than one occasion, likened literary works to time bombs, having the potential of exploding not only in their own time, but also in the future, in other contexts.[4] *Monsieur Pain*, like the film, is a hybrid, a "documento fantástico," its factual, contextual substrata – the documented existence of Vallejo, Pain, the doctors – all intermixed with fictional, oneiric elements. In turn, the impenetrable intrigue unfolding within the diegesis stands as a figure for the obscure geopolitical forces at play in that *actualidad*, that historical present, forces that neither Pain nor those who lived these events could unravel. By extension, we as readers share Pain's condition as spectator, our interpretative endeavors stymied by the increasingly hallucinatory and indecipherable narration.

The film, with its transtemporal references, also reflects the more expansive multiplication of contexts at play in *Monsieur Pain*. For while April, 1938 – and more broadly the interwar period – constitutes the explicit timeframe of the novel, other implicit contexts become quite obvious to readers. Layered upon that moment of extreme geopolitical tension are moments that form part of Bolaño's own (directly or indirectly) lived experience: the Cuban Revolution, the Latin American liberation movements of the 1960s, the Tlatelolco massacre, Pinochet's coup, the Dirty War in Argentina. Bolaño, in an acceptance speech for the Premio Rómulo Gallegos in 1999, made an anguished statement that revealed the driving force behind all his work. "Everything I have written," he asserts, is to a large extent either "a love letter or a farewell to my own generation, those of us born in the 1950s and those of us who, in a given moment, chose [...] militancy" (*Entre paréntesis* 2004, 37). With mixed emotions of pride, indignation, regret, and mourning, Bolaño recounts how he and his comrades gave their youth to a cause which they believed to be "the most generous of causes in the world, and which, in a certain way was, but in reality was not," and he goes on to evoke the enormity of the betrayal (37):

---

[4] In a commentary on Jonathan Swift, Bolaño describes certain classics "cuya principal virtud, cuya elegancia y vigencia, está simbolizada por la bomba de relojería, una bomba que no sólo recorre peligrosamente a su tiempo sino que es capaz de proyectarse hace el futuro" (*Entre paréntesis* 2004, 166). Other references to time bombs appear in *Entre paréntesis* (95, 167, and 172). Bolaño expressed a similar idea in his infrarrealist manifiesto of 1976: "La verdadera imaginación es aquella que dinamita, elucida, inyecta microbios esmeraldas en otras imaginaciones" (2010, 149).

we fought tooth and nail, but we had corrupt leaders, cowardly leaders ... we fought for parties that if they had won, would have sent us straight to forced-labor camps ... we put all our generosity into an ideal that had been dead for fifty years, and some of us knew it ... but we did it anyway ... and now nothing remains of those youths ... All of Latin America is sown with the bones of those forgotten youths. (*Entre parénthesis* 2004, 37–38)

Bolaño's ongoing preoccupation with the failure of these liberation movements, with the incalculable loss of all those "stupid and generous" youths, with the enduring, deadly forms of fascism and totalitarianism – all this anguish, as so many scholars have noted, permeates his novels and haunts his melancholic, defeated protagonists.[5] For Paula Aguilar, "They are the nuclei of a constant obsession with unpacking the forms of evil that have so marked the Western world, which culminate in his great posthumous novel, *2666*" (2014, 504). *Monsieur Pain*, an "allegory of defeat," in Aguilar's words, represents an early attempt at addressing the questions that would reverberate through his work thereafter (501).[6] Vallejo and Pierre Pain are twinned figures of failure and paralysis, bound by "un campo magnético" (magnetic field) and replicated by the twin artists who create those tableaus of disaster, with corpses strewn across the aquarium floor, like the bones of all those Latin American youths sown across Latin America.[7]

Vallejo, in his death throes, clearly stands for the destruction of Spanish democracy, the failure of an international Popular Front to make Spain "the tomb of fascism" and forestall world war. The betrayal of the global anti-fascist movement would come just four months hence, when the Nazi–Soviet Non-Aggression Pact revoked the Popular Front, paving the way for the invasion of Poland and the onset of World War II. The Spanish people would live under a brutal dictatorship for thirty-five more years. It bears noting that Bolaño, like Vallejo a writer in exile, penned *Monsieur Pain* (1981–1982) while living in Spain during a tense period of transition from dictatorship to democracy, largely pacific but punctuated

---

[5] An earlier expression of these same sentiments appears in Bolaño's "Primer manifesto infrarrealista": "Soñábamos con utopía y nos despertamos gritando" (We dreamed of utopia and awakened shouting) (2010, 150).

[6] Aguilar draws here from Idelber Avelar's *Alegorías de la derrota: La ficción postdictatorial y el trabajo del duelo*, the Spanish edition of *The Untimely Present*. Sergio Franco also remarks on this layering of multiple defeats – in Spain and in Latin America (2014, 483–485).

[7] Emerson analyzes multiple instances of doubling in *Monsieur Pain* and relates it to the uncanny. Doubling appears in the form of doppelgängers, twins, doubled sounds, paired characters, and double names (2017). Gutiérrez Mouat, in "Vallejo en Bolaño," remarks on the "campo magnético" established between Bolaño's text and Vallejo's poetry (2020, 2).

by the attempted coup of 1981. Spain's fascist past was thus very much in the air, adding still another contextual layer to the novel's labyrinthine field of reference. If the defeat of multiple emancipatory political projects – in Spain, Latin America, and in the Soviet Block at large – constitutes the ultimate context of *Monsieur Pain*, any apprehension, or coming-to-terms with the enormity of that failure remains unrealized. It lies in an abyss enswathed by the dense, hyper-referential *contexture* of the novel.

Up to this point, I have failed to examine the term, "context," having deployed it simplistically to denote the historical circumstances (*circum* around + *stare* to stand) referenced in the novel. But context – deriving from the Latin *contextus*, to weave together or connect – is a slippery and imprecise term, its semantic field traversing the historical, empirical, and verbal domains. In literature, strictly speaking, context comes down to intertext. Mikhail Bakhtin famously remarked:

> For the novelist working in prose, the object is always entangled in someone else's discourse about it, it is already present with qualifications, an object of dispute that is conceptualized and evaluated variously, inseparable from the heteroglot social apperception of it. The novelist speaks of this "already qualified world" in a language that is heteroglot and internally dialogized. Thus both object and language are revealed to the novelist in their historical dimension, in the process of social and heteroglot becoming. (1981, 330).

Julia Kristeva coined the term *intertextuality* as a means of synthesizing for a Western audience Bakhtin's notions of dialogism and heteroglossia.[8] For readers, a sense of context emerges as we navigate the network of *intertexts* explicitly or implicitly referenced in a given work. An impression of lifelikeness, a "reality effect" (to borrow from Roland Barthes), arises as a function of recognition, as readers *recognize*, not the world, but an "already qualified world" – a myriad of citations of familiar bits of discourse – be they literary, historical, journalistic, scientific, or simply the social scripts and common knowledge of daily life (Barthes 1986). Regardless of whether a text makes claims to realism, its readability still depends on this process of recognition amid a tissue of voices absorbed from prior discursive and worldly encounters – "the already read, seen, done, experienced" (Barthes 1988, 20). However, avant-garde texts like *Monsieur Pain*, which owes much to surrealism, interfere with this process of recognition by flaunting their own dense intertextual webs and thwarting readers'

---

[8] See Todorov's chapter on intertextuality in *Mikhail Bakhtin: The Dialogical Principle* (1988).

interpretive efforts.[9] In the case of this novel, the maze-like expanse of its fictional space performs this function – with Pain repeatedly lost in labyrinthine sites (the hospital, the warehouse, the streets) and admitting "the pleasure he takes in the labyrinth" (112). The Borgesian motif of the labyrinth thus serves as its most obvious intertext and central metaphor, representing the overcrowded and opaque intertextual web in its entirety.

Critics have called attention to the profusion of intertexts that echo throughout the novel, like an enactment of the "demented radio-theater" with its "inferno of voices" that Pain hears in a nightmare (43). In terms of genre, Sergio Franco remarks on its hybridity, its kinship with the gothic novel, *noir*, and detective fiction (albeit with the case never solved).[10] Poe's "Mesmeric Revelation" emerges as the most explicit intertext, cited in the epigraph and referenced in a cafe conversation. Planted throughout the hallucinatory tale are sly references to mesmerism, among them, the Meersburgh Express, the locomotive submerged in the aquarium, which names the city where Franz Mesmer died (Aguilar 2014, 501). As Jonathan Monroe points out, Pain's status as melancholic *flâneur* hearkens back to Baudelaire, while his ceaseless wanderings through the city and his bizarre, chance encounters also gesture towards Breton's *Nadja* and Aragon's *Paris Peasant* (2019). An explicit reference to surrealism appears in the novel when Pain describes Vallejo's hiccup as "a surrealist found object" (50). But more pervasively, Monroe observes, the novel displays its affinity to surrealism through its fragmented and labyrinthine form and structure, creating a "dream-like collage," that "simultaneously constructs and unhinges, articulates and disarticulates the dissociative state – at once real, imaginary, and symbolic; referential and self-referential" (2019, 40–41). Also in synchrony with surrealism – specifically, with "objective chance" – is the "intricate punning," which adds additional layers of intertextuality to the narrative (43). Monroe offers a concise list: *Pain* as suffering in English and bread in French; the *Clinique Arago*, evoking both *argot* and Aragon; *Place Blanche* suggesting *page blanche*; the term *engaged* in the context of the character Jules Sartreau, alluding to Sartre; and Pleumeur-Bodot, which plays on *plumes*, *flâneur*, and Baudelaire (43). All this wordplay, whether homophonic or homographic,

---

[9] See Suleiman's discussion of how avant-garde texts defy readability (1981).
[10] Franco goes on to describe the novel as a critique of instrumental reason. Antoine Dechêne includes *Monsieur Pain* in a study of "metacognitive" detective narratives, "unreadable mysteries, that enact interpretive failure (2014, 3–4).

works to foreground the materiality of language, by densifying and further expanding the intertextual web.

The punning with the protagonist's name also serves to point readers directly to Vallejo's poetry. For readers familiar with Vallejo's work, multiple fragments of verse will inevitably come to mind, drawn from those poems composed during his years of penury in Paris – poems that so tenderly evoke everyday life and the material life of the body, stripped down, destitute, and seeking sustenance.[11] The surname, Pain, coincides with the persistent expressions of suffering in Vallejo's work: "El dolor nos agarra, hermanos hombres,/ ... / y nos aloca con boleto en los cinemas"[12] (The pain that grabs us, brother men/ ... / and drives us mad with a ticket in the cinemas) (1988, 412); "Tú sufres, tú padeces y tú vuelves a sufrir horriblemente,/ desgraciado mono,/ jovencito de Darwin"[13] (You suffer, you endure, and again you suffer horribly,/ wretched monkey,/ Darwin's little man) (422). The French meaning of *pain* also brings to mind the perennial theme of hunger and sustenance in Vallejo's poetry, so often expressed with the image of *pan* (bread)[14]: "dadme,/ por favor, un pedazo de pan en que sentarme"[15] (give me,/ please, a piece of bread to sit upon) (364–365)"; and "llegar/ a ser lo que es uno entre millones/ de panes, entre miles de vinos, entre cientos de bocas"[16] (to become/ what one is among millions/ of loaves, among thousands of wines, among hundreds of mouths) (433). Even the name *Pierre* (*piedra*, stone) resonates in Vallejo's poetry, famously in "Parado en una piedra" (Sitting Idle on a Stone), a devastating portrait of a jobless, hungry man in the midst of capitalist crisis (354–355).[17] Indeed, the sonnet, "Piedra negra sobre una piedra blanca" (Black stone on a white stone), might well have inspired Bolaño's *Monsieur Pain*. Beginning with the verse – "Me moriré en París con aguacero, / un día del cual tengo ya el recuerdo" (I will die in Paris in a sudden shower, / a day of which I already have the memory) – the poem

---

[11] Gutiérrez Mouat, in "Vallejo in Bolaño," offers a detailed overview of these intertexts (2020).
[12] "Los nueve monstruos" (1988, 411–413). Translations of these lines are my own, although I also consulted Clayton Eshleman's translation.
[13] "El alma que sufrió de ser cuerpo" (1988, 422–423).
[14] Giovanni Meo Zilio quantifies the many images of hunger and bread in Vallejo's poetry (1988, 644–645).
[15] "La rueda del hambriento," (1988, 364–365).
[16] "Ello es el lugar donde me pongo," (1988, 432–433).
[17] Regarding the punning with both given name and surname, Antoine Dechêne writes: "This is Pain's sublime source of suffering, the alienation that he carries in his own name, like a stone (Pierre), eternal and unfathomable" (2019, (269).

ends with three words that encapsulate Pain's experience: "la soledad, la lluvia, los caminos..." (the loneliness, the rain, the streets) (339).

But it is the hiccup, above all – that seemingly non-signifying "sonic ectoplasm" – that remains the most significant referent in the novel, calling attention to the cruel joke played by life on a poet so preoccupied with the physical, physiological struggle for expression (Bolaño 1999, 50).[18] Ubiquitous in Vallejo's poems is the mute animal within the human body, coughing and spitting, unable to dislodge that lump of anguish lodged in the throat: "Considerando en frío, imparcialmente/ que el hombre es triste, tose y ... / que es lóbrego mamífero y se peina"[19] (Considering coldly, impartially/ that man is sad, he coughs ... / that he is a gloomy mammal that combs himself) (1988, 350); "Quiero escribir, pero me sale espuma,/ ... / quiero escribir, pero me siento puma"[20] (I want to write, but I spit out foam,/ ... / I want to write, but I feel like a puma) (400). Another animal reference on Vallejo's part may shed light on the curious, original title of *Monsieur Pain*, first published as *La senda de los elefantes* ("The Elephant's Path") and retained in the subtitle to the epilogue.[21] The poem "Telúrica y magnética" includes the lines: "Paquidermos en prosa cuando pasan/ y en verso cuando páranse" (Pachyderms in prose when they pass/ and in verse when standing still) (360).[22] According to the Vallejo critic, Michelle Clayton, these verses suggest that "if prose walks alongside history, poetry attempts to interrupt it – resisting the march of history, yet still consciously inscribed within it" (2011, 15).

Clayton's remarks on this distinction between poetry and prose offer a clue to the unsettling experience of reading *Monsieur Pain*, at least for readers familiar with Vallejo's work. For in summoning these lines of verse to our minds, a striking discordance emerges; Bolaño's prosaic language and absurdist tone collide with Vallejo's spare poetic eloquence – among the most powerful expressions of human anguish and solidarity ever penned. Perhaps, however, this asynchrony is the point; perhaps the plodding

---

[18] Monroe also remarks on Vallejo's affliction with the hiccups as a "bad joke," a "sick joke" (2019, 39, 44).
[19] "Considerando en frío, imparcialmente" (1988, 350–351).
[20] "Intensidad y altura" (1988, 400).
[21] Bolaño recounts the editorial history of his novel in the "Nota preliminar" to *Monsieur Pain* (1999, ix).
[22] Manzoni posits a curious intertext relating to the original title, "La senda de los elefantes." She suggests a parallel between the embedded film, *Actualidad*, with its theme of destruction, and a Hollywood film, *Elephant Walk* (1954), which ends with the total destruction of a colonial plantation by a herd of elephants (2011, 117). César Vallejo makes other references to elephants in his posthumous poems: "mi noche de elefante en descanso" (1988, 333); and "infame paquidermo" (425); la hormiga/ traerá pedacitos de pan al elefante encadedo/ a su delicadeza" (452).

"elephantine" prose of the novel serves to lead readers directly to Vallejo's poetry, to a literary language with the power to "interrupt" history, as Clayton suggests. Bolaño would surely have posited a reader familiar with Vallejo's work, one who would be struck by the disparity in the evocative power of Bolaño's prose and Vallejo's poetry. For such a readership, Bolaño's language "fails" perhaps by design, adding still another level of failure to this "allegory of defeat" (Aguilar, 2014, 501). We have seen how within the diegesis, Pain utterly fails – professionally, ethically, and cognitively – how he never manages to unravel the intrigue that enmeshes him. And we have seen how the novel sets up readers for failure by thwarting our efforts to navigate the dense intertextual web and by foreclosing resolution. On the level of its literary language (its poetics, broadly conceived), the novel admits and indeed announces its own failure as written expression, I would suggest. And in so doing, it points us directly to an abyss, to "el pozo que era Vallejo" (the pit that was Vallejo), to the tragic absurdity of this consummate poet afflicted with the hiccups, as he lies dying (Bolaño 1999, 51).

That abyss where the hiccupping poet lies is the site of catastrophe, of catastrophic failure; and as such, it designates the ultimate context of this novel – all the defeats and betrayals of twentieth-century emancipatory projects, all the dead of the European wars, all the bones of those generous youths scattered across Latin America, all this historical *circum-stance* that cannot be fully apprehended or expressed, and yet is uttered, absurdly, in Vallejo's hiccups. Given the density of the intertextual web that enswathes that context of failure, signaling its locus while foreclosing access, the novel might lend itself to a post-structuralist reading, one that foregrounds our "linguistic predicament," defined by Paul de Man in these terms: "what we are deprived of is not life but the shape and sense of a world accessible only in the privative way of understanding" (1979, 930). However, Vallejo's hiccups, resounding through *Monsieur Pain*, complicate the notion of our entrapment in a linguistic order that allows only privative access to a reality beyond. For the hiccups, at once involuntary and imperative, erupt from that reality beyond; they are, in the final analysis, utterances, albeit in an "undecipherable tongue" (Bolaño, 1999, 83).[23] By emitting a guttural, uninterpretable sound, a "toz hablada," (a "spoken cough" in Vallejo's

---

[23] Both Monroe and Stockwell offer compelling readings of Vallejo's hiccups. Monroe describes them as "eruptive, disruptive (non-)utterance[s]," observing that the trope of the hiccup, along with the many puns, signals the text's "investment in the serious play of signification" (2019, 39–40). For Stockwell, Vallejo's hiccup comes "close to what Blanchot theorizes as the 'murmur' inherent to literary space" (2019, 350); it "is not separate from the breathing it interrupts," but rather, "is the breathing of this novel" (352).

words), the mute animal engages in the primal struggle of meaning-making.[24] Not yet poetry, that "spoken cough" is nevertheless the commencement of poetic *articulation*, which simultaneously entails *disarticulation* – an ongoing breaking and remaking of the complex, vascularized web of relations among people and things, ideas and texts, words and world.[25]

This novel, so consumed with failure and seemingly devoid of any glint of redemption, nevertheless leaves us with Vallejo's hiccups. "There is hope," Pierre Pain had said to Georgette, after calming her husband's hiccups. César Vallejo in his prose poem, "Voy a hablar de la esperanza" (I'm going to speak of hope) repeats: "Hoy sufro desde más abajo... Hoy sufro desde más arriba. Hoy sufro solamente." (Today I suffer from the deepest depths ... Today I suffer from the highest heights. Today I simply suffer) (1988, 316). It is the hiccup that erupts and interrupts history, demanding to be heard, acknowledged, and deeply felt. That "spoken cough" bespeaks the pain of mass death, of mass mourning, of emancipation forestalled, and the torment of that unanswered question bequeathed by all those catastrophic failures; yet in that very convulsive act, there resides the faint possibility of hope.

---

[24] From "Intensidad y altura" (Vallejo 1988, 400).

[25] In addressing articulation, I am drawing from Bruno Latour's *Pandora's Hope* (1999) and Lawrence Grossberg's *Cultural Studies in the Future Tense* (2010), in which he discusses his notion of "radical contextualism." Also see Rita Felski, who draws from both Latour and Grossberg in "Context Stinks" (2011).

CHAPTER 10

The Cold War

Patrick Iber

In the address he gave in 1999 on receiving the Rómulo Gallegos Prize, Roberto Bolaño declared that "to a great extent everything that I've written is a love letter or a farewell letter to my own generation."[1] But what was that generation, and what experiences shaped it? Bolaño was born on April 28, 1953 in Santiago, Chile, a year he later described as that of the deaths of Stalin and the Welsh poet Dylan Thomas (15). And it was that combination of politics and literature that defined his experience of the Cold War, as he and his cohort grew into adulthood in some of its darkest years in Latin America.

The Cold War, at its most rudimentary, was a contest for global leadership between the United States and the Soviet Union. It began under a nuclear cloud, the U.S. having used atomic weapons over Japan in August 1945. The Second World War over, in February 1946 Stalin gave a speech in which he blamed the outbreak of the Second World War on inevitable frictions in monopoly capitalism, which was widely interpreted as a prediction of future conflict with the capitalist "West." The next month, Winston Churchill declared that an "iron curtain" had descended across Europe. By March 1947, President Truman announced that it would be the policy of the United States to "support free peoples who are resisting attempted subjugation by armed minorities or outside pressures." In 1949, the Soviet Union successfully tested its own atomic bomb. Though there is no agreed-upon start date for the Cold War, any hope of postwar cooperation had clearly vanished by the end of the 1940s.[2]

Fear of nuclear devastation proscribed open warfare, and so the Cold War took on different forms. There were proxy battles around the world

---

[1] Roberto Bolaño, *Between Parentheses: Essays, Articles, and Speeches, 1998–2003*, ed. Ignacio Echevarría, trans. Natasha Wimmer (New York: New Directions, 2011), 35.
[2] There have been many schools of interpretation of the Cold War that have assigned responsibility for it in various ways. A superb guide to the literature is Steven Hurst, *Cold War US Foreign Policy: Key Perspectives* (Edinburgh: Edinburgh University Press, 2005).

that make the "Cold" War seem like a misnomer. "Cold War interventions," historian Odd Arne Westad has written, "were most often extensions of ideological civil wars, fought with the ferocity that only civil wars can bring forth."[3] But the conflict went beyond armed combat. It also took place at the level of symbols: in the race into the vastness of space, in the exertions of athletes at the Olympics, in performances at chess boards or piano recitals. Both the U.S. and U.S.S.R. wanted to claim that their system of government and economy offered the world a future of prosperity. Both propagated messianic visions of the future driven by different ideas of social and economic justice.[4]

Both also insisted on maintaining a security perimeter consisting of friendly states. For the Soviet Union, the most important were the Eastern European "people's democracies." But if the Soviet Union stretched the meaning of "democracy" past its breaking point in describing Communist autocracies as democratic, so did the United States in its own areas, where it muddled democracy and anti-Communism. The United States claimed both Western Europe and Latin America as essential to re-establish a functioning capitalist economy and maintain its position of security and power. The traditional Monroe doctrine in U.S. foreign policy, dating back to the early nineteenth century, called for European non-interference in the Americas. Updated for the Cold War, it defined Communism as an inherently foreign doctrine: something to be driven out of the hemisphere.[5]

For Latin America, the Cold War meant that U.S. aid and diplomatic relations would now be directed to fundamentally anti-Communist priorities. The boundaries of what was politically possible, and what was impossible, had changed. In Bolaño's Chile, for example, the Communist Party had operated legally and participated in Popular Front governments alongside partners in the Socialist and Radical parties. In 1946, Gabriel González Videla was elected president with the support of the Communist Party. But by 1948 the logic had changed: needing economic aid from the United States, González Videla moved against

---

[3] Odd Arne Westad, *The Global Cold War: Third World Interventions and the Making of Our Times* (Cambridge; New York: Cambridge University Press, 2005), 5.
[4] See especially Westad, *Global Cold War*; Odd Arne Westad, *The Cold War: A World History* (New York: Basic Books, 2017).
[5] A general synthesis is Hal Brands, *Latin America's Cold War* (Cambridge, Mass.: Harvard University Press, 2010). An excellent discussion of the historiography of Latin America's Cold War, including varying interpretations, is Vanni Pettinà, *Historia mínima de la Guerra Fría en América Latina* (México: El Colegio de México, 2018).

striking miners with violence and against the Communist Party with a law that banned its participation in politics or unions. With the official, Orwellian name of "Law for the Permanent Defense of Democracy," Chile's Communist Party simply called it the *ley maldita*, "the accursed law." In the year Bolaño was born, it had been in place for five years.[6]

Neither Communism nor anti-Communism, of course, were new to the region. Communist Parties in Latin America were founded in the years after the Russian Revolution, typically as splinters of existing socialist parties and with relatively tenuous connections to the Soviet Union.[7] In the 1930s, there were uprisings in El Salvador and Brazil led by Communist organizers. They were overlaid on existing lines of authority, conflict, and inequality. The Salvadoran movement of 1932 led the government to order widespread massacres of indigenous men. "There are no Indians who aren't Communists," imagined one threatened landholder.[8] With this in mind, some looking at the region have seen the Cold War as fundamentally a struggle over social rights, with anti-Communism providing a consistent justification for repression.[9] Mexico's left-wing former president Lázaro Cárdenas, writing in his diary in 1961, declared that "anticommunism has been an instrument in the fight against freedom and democracy in the countries of Latin America."[10] From that perspective, the Cold War in Latin America is defined more by antagonism between Communism and anti-Communism than U.S.–Soviet conflict as such. If so, then it is easy to see the Cold War as spilling over the traditional dates that define it.

This point of view illuminates important continuities of the prewar period, the social and political conditions out of which it was possible to build Cold War conflict. But it is important to register changes as well. In the 1930s and 1940s, U.S. policy in Latin America was not singlemindedly anti-Communist. In the 1940s, Communists joined governments in Cuba, Ecuador, and Chile, and were legal in other places. The

---

[6] Andrew Barnard, "Chile," in *Latin America between the Second World War and the Cold War, 1944–1948*, ed. Leslie Bethell and Ian Roxborough (Cambridge: Cambridge University Press, 1992), 66–91.

[7] Manuel Caballero, *Latin America and the Comintern, 1919–1943* (Cambridge; New York: Cambridge University Press, 1986); Robert J. Alexander, *Communism in Latin America* (New Brunswick, N.J.: Rutgers University Press, 1957).

[8] Jeffrey L. Gould and Aldo Lauria-Santiago, *To Rise in Darkness: Revolution, Repression, and Memory in El Salvador, 1920–1932* (Durham: Duke University Press, 2008), 231.

[9] This argument is most associated with Greg Grandin, *The Last Colonial Massacre: Latin America in the Cold War* (Chicago: University of Chicago Press, 2004).

[10] Lázaro Cárdenas, *Apuntes, 1957–1966* (México, D.F.: Universidad Nacional Autónoma de México, 1973), 241.

U.S.–Soviet alliance against Nazi Germany during the Second World War made possible odd arrangements. At a time when the U.S. government was working to ensure that pro-Allied sentiments were shared as widely as possible, Communists could be partners: U.S. government money even supported the Mexican painter David Álfaro Siqueiros' 1943 mural in Havana, Cuba, which portrayed José Martí and Abraham Lincoln together.[11]

The Cold War's arrival would make such an arrangement unimaginable. Though Communism and anti-Communism were not new, during the Cold War the international system was structured by U.S.–Soviet conflict in a way that it had not been prior to the Second World War. The political opening experienced in the mid-1940s in many countries of the region – of democratization, labor mobilization, and a shift to the political left – made possible by the global conjuncture of having aligned with a war for democracy and against fascism, snapped shut.[12] The speed of the change varied by location: it lasted the longest in Guatemala, which had two consecutive democratic elections in 1944 and 1950, elevating reformist presidents. Yet the political reaction was also stronger there than almost anywhere. When the second of the two presidents, Jacobo Arbenz, began an ambitious land reform affecting the interests of the United Fruit Company, the Central Intelligence Agency decided to work to undermine him. Guatemala's Communist party was small, but had an important advisory role, and the CIA calculated that the land reform would redound to its benefit. In 1954 he was removed.[13] Roberto Bolaño, thousands of miles away, was one year old: his generation was born into the dynamic of reform and counter-reform, revolution and counter-revolution.

Those political dynamics necessarily affected the world of the arts and literature that Bolaño would eventually join. When he did so, as a poet in Mexico City in the 1970s, he would do so by rejection: mocking the established pieties and conventions of the literati of the Cold War, regardless of what political inclination they professed. To understand what produced that reaction, it is important to understand not just the Cold War but the *cultural Cold War*. All wars produce propaganda, and enlist

---

[11] Claire Fox, *Making Art Panamerican: Cultural Policy and the Cold War* (Minneapolis: University of Minnesota Press, 2013), 70–71.
[12] Leslie Bethell and Ian Roxborough, *Latin America between the Second World War and the Cold War, 1944–1948* (Cambridge; New York: Cambridge University Press, 1992).
[13] In the voluminous literature on this subject, the best book is probably Piero Gleijeses, *Shattered Hope: The Guatemalan Revolution and the United States, 1944–1954* (Princeton, N.J.: Princeton University Press, 1991).

the talents of artists to their causes. But the Cold War presented states with an opportunity to organize artists and intellectuals on behalf of views that they already held, heightening the authenticity of the messaging: all the better if the propaganda is sincere. The CIA would later describe the cultural Cold War as the "battle for Picasso's mind."[14] Picasso, probably the most famous artist in the world at the time, had joined the French Communist Party in 1944.

Many artists with mature careers in the early years of the Cold War had come of age during the Great Depression and had been drawn to leftist political activism of one variety or another. Aesthetic vanguards often embraced political radicalism, and artists often challenge conventional, "bourgeois" standards of behavior. Additionally, in the 1930s the Soviet Union had organized artists into anti-fascist movements, cementing the loyalties of some while causing others to see them as manipulative and opportunistic, leading some to adopt anti-Stalinist forms of left politics. Chilean poet Pablo Neruda helped to organize anti-fascist congresses in Spain in 1937, for example, and became and remained a Communist for the rest of his life; Mexican poet Octavio Paz attended too, as a young leftist, but was disturbed by official silences around Communist repression and the treatment of artists, he would take the anti-Stalinist path.[15]

In the Cold War era, the Soviet Union resurrected similar work with an initiative that placed the defense of "Peace" at the center of its appeal to artists and intellectuals. (Picasso's painting of a pigeon was upgraded to a dove for a 1949 Paris conference, becoming the symbol of the movement.) The Soviet Union's own internal cultural policy of socialist realism – of broadly realistic works that showed the heroic efforts of building future socialism – spilled over into the works of its followers elsewhere. Neruda, who organized a conference for Peace in Santiago in 1953 and participated in many others, wrote paeans to Stalin during this time and completed his *Canto General*, a broadly socialist realist epic of Latin American history.[16]

---

[14] Greg Barnhisel, *Cold War Modernists: Art, Literature, and American Cultural Diplomacy* (New York: Columbia University Press, 2015), 27. For a general guide to the historiography of the Cultural Cold War, see Patrick Iber, "The Cultural Cold War," in *Oxford Research Encyclopedia of American History* (Oxford University Press, 2019), https://doi.org/10.1093/acrefore/9780199329175.013.760

[15] David Schidlowsky, *Las Furias y Las Penas: Pablo Neruda y Su Tiempo* (Berlin: Wissenschaftlicher Verlag, 1999), 130–135; Octavio Paz, *Itinerario* (México, D.F.: Fondo de Cultura Económica, 1993), 59–67.

[16] Pablo Neruda, *Canto General*, trans. Jack Schmitt (Berkeley: University of California Press, 1991). On the cultural Cold War in Latin America, see especially Jean Franco, *The Decline and Fall of the Lettered City: Latin America in the Cold War* (Cambridge, Mass.: Harvard University Press, 2002);

Artists whose views diverged from the interpretation of world affairs of the Communist party often diverged both politically and aesthetically. Peace politics attacked the "cosmopolitanism" of capitalist culture and trends like abstract art. In the absence of a culture ministry in the United States, the Central Intelligence Agency played the role of promoting arts (including abstract expressionism in painting, for example), as art that could not have been produced under totalitarianism. It was presented as the art of "freedom," in contrast to the artistic policy of the Soviet Union.[17] The CIA helped create and sustain the "Congress for Cultural Freedom," a body with a headquarters in Paris and a global publishing network. Though it included some right-wing figures, its dominant politics was intended primarily to appeal to provide an alternative to Communism that could appeal to the left. Many of those who joined with repentant former Communists or came from other branches of the left, though some had moved to the political center. In Latin America, it published a magazine in the 1950s called *Cuadernos*, published anti-Communist literature, and sponsored meetings preaching both anti-Communist and anti-dictatorial goals. The Cold War thus created two paths towards institutionalized artistic political activism: one organized around sympathy for Communism and another of anti-Communism. They each carried the possibilities of integration into larger networks of exhibitions, conferences, translations, and publications. Octavio Paz never joined the Mexican branch of the Congress for Cultural Freedom, for example, of which he was rightly suspicious. But he shared the anti-Communist politics and anti-Communist aesthetics, championing the work of abstract art in Mexico and rejecting the artistic prerogatives of socialist realism.

The next major turning point in Latin America's experience of the Cold War came in 1959, when Bolaño was five years old. Then, revolutionaries in Cuba succeeded in dislodging the dictator, Fulgencio Batista, and established a new government. The Cuban Revolution was not the beginning of the Cold War in Latin America, but it intensified it. Cuba's early reforms were transformative, providing an existence proof of the possibility of major social change. Cuba inspired and trained guerrillas to try to repeat their experience elsewhere. Fearful of his growing closeness with the Soviet

---

Patrick Iber, *Neither Peace nor Freedom: The Cultural Cold War in Latin America* (Cambridge, Mass.: Harvard University Press, 2015).

[17] Frances Stonor Saunders, *The Cultural Cold War: The CIA and the World of Arts and Letters* (New York: New Press, 2000); Hugh Wilford, *The Mighty Wurlitzer: How the CIA Played America* (Cambridge, Mass.: Harvard University Press, 2008).

Union, the U.S. tried to overthrow Fidel Castro with a CIA-supported exile army at the Bay of Pigs in 1961. When this attack failed, it showed that a small country could turn back the nearby empire. The Cuban Missile Crisis the next year brought the world close to nuclear war, and for the United States, reinforced the fear of Communist countries in the hemisphere.

Cuban Communism redistributed property more widely and equally while concentrating political power in the party apparatus and the person of Fidel Castro. It had an ambitious artistic agenda: bringing films and literacy to the impoverished countryside and opening up spaces and institutions for Cuban artists and writers. Nervous about censorship, Cuban artists got a message from Fidel in 1961 that he would not interfere with artistic freedom or lay down a "line" in the Stalinist manner. "Within the Revolution, everything," he said, before adding: "against the revolution, no rights."[18] For international projection, the artistic space of Casa de las Américas, and the magazine of the same name, put forward a vision of committed revolutionary nationalism. The Casa de las Américas prizes brought writers from around Latin America to serve on prize juries, and they, in turn, defended the revolution abroad.

Cuba's vision did not pass without challenge. The CIA-sponsored Congress for Cultural Freedom retooled its Latin American operations. It shut down *Cuadernos* in 1965 and started a new magazine, *Mundo Nuevo*, in 1966. *Mundo Nuevo* published many of the emerging writers of the "boom," like Gabriel García Márquez and José Donoso, and even left-wing legends like Neruda. In its first issue, an interview with Carlos Fuentes established the magazine's intended tone, when Fuentes argued that the purpose of the writer's freedom was in "maintaining some room for heresy," and against the McCarthyists of both left and right. It did not take an explicitly anti-Cuba stand, but it did provide an alternative vision of what a writer should be: someone for whom taking up a pen was more important than taking up a machine gun. But it was precisely in 1966 and 1967 that the Congress for Cultural Freedom was publicly confirmed to have been CIA-sponsored, reinforcing for those inclined to revolution that "maintaining some room for heresy" was really little more than "maintaining some room for imperialism" (Iber 2015, 201).

Cuba also suffered loss of prestige in some corners as the decade wore on, as the more authoritarian aspects of its revolution became more widely

---

[18] Julio García Luis, *Cuban Revolution Reader: A Documentary History of 40 Key Moments of the Cuban Revolution* (Melbourne; New York: Ocean Press, 2001), 76–82.

known. In 1971, the detention and self-criticism of the poet Heberto Padilla led many prominent writers to sign an open letter declaring that the affair recalled "the most sordid moments of ... Stalinism," solidifying a rupture.[19] The next years, from 1971 to 1976, were of deep cultural and intellectual repression.[20] In Bolaño's works, set in those years and those beyond, Cubans make their appearances largely as cultural bureaucrats rather than heroic revolutionaries. In a fictional 1976, in *The Savage Detectives*, a young Mexican poet wins a Casa de las Américas poetry prize that he hasn't applied for, and writers are excluded or included from compilation on the basis of their statements about Cuba. "Literature isn't innocent," he muses.[21] In the profile of one of the imaginary right-wing writers from *Nazi Literature in the Americas*, Bolaño makes a sly joke in positing that one of the founders of "Artists and Writers of the Counterrevolution," is "included in the *Dictionary of Cuban Authors* (Havana, 1978), which omits Guillermo Cabrera Infante."[22] Cabrera Infante was a significant writer, but a critic of the revolution, its censorship practices, and a close collaborator with the Congress for Cultural Freedom and *Mundo Nuevo*.

When Bolaño was fifteen years old, in 1968, his family left Chile and moved to Mexico City. Mexico occupied a unique place in the regional Cold War architecture. As a nominally post-revolutionary state, its single-party government had to watch its left flank. It was a haven for left-wing exiles: tens of thousands arrived from Spain after the defeat of the Spanish Republic in 1939 and in the 1970s new refugees from the Southern Cone dictatorships made their homes there. But these refugees also served to do a kind of "redwashing" for the Mexican government, obscuring the ways in which its revolution had been institutionalized. Mexico City was also a haven for spies and would-be spies: a kind of "Casablanca" of the Western hemisphere. In *The Savage Detectives*, the "visceral realist" poets Arturo Belano and Ulises Lima publish a literary magazine called *Lee Harvey Oswald*. The significance of the name goes beyond Oswald having been

---

[19] "Text of the Statement," *New York Times*, May 22, 1971, 8.
[20] John M. Kirk and Leonardo Padura Fuentes, *Culture and the Cuban Revolution: Conversations in Havana* (Gainsville: University Press of Florida, 2001).
[21] Roberto Bolaño, *The Savage Detectives*, trans. Natasha Wimmer (New York: Picador/Farrar, Straus and Giroux, 2010), 154.
[22] Roberto Bolaño, *Nazi Literature in the Americas*, trans. Chris Andrews (New York: New Directions, 2008), 58.

the assassin of President Kennedy: Oswald had been through the Mexico City scene, hoping and failing to secure Soviet or Cuban support.[23]

In 1968, the year of Bolaño's arrival, the government violently suppressed a student movement, massacring them in the plaza at Tlatelolco in the weeks before hosting the Olympics. The president who assumed office in 1970, Luis Echeverría, tried to tack to the left to mollify critical students and intellectuals. He hosted soirées with the country's leading writers and thinkers, and increased spending on education. Carlos Fuentes argued that the choice was "Echeverría or fascism."[24] Octavio Paz, who had resigned from his ambassadorship to India in 1968 over the massacre at Tlatelolco but defended Echeverría, would later describe the ruling Partido Revolucionaro Institucional as a "philanthropic ogre."

If an older generation mostly made peace with Echeverría, radicals rejected him. Guerrillas in the countryside still hoped to overthrow the government. And the possibility of violent revolution was still attractive to many. Bolaño himself felt it. Leftist hopes swelled with the election of the Marxist Salvador Allende in his home country of Chile in 1970; opening what seemed to be an electoral path to socialism. The Nixon administration responded with hostility: "I don't see why we need to stand by and let a country go Communist due to the responsibility of its people," said National Security Advisor Henry Kissinger. Shortages and social polarization intensified. On September 11, 1973, the military set a coup in motion; Allende made a final radio address and committed suicide with the machine gun gifted to him by Fidel Castro.[25]

According to Bolaño's later recollections, when he heard that Allende had been overthrown, he immediately went in search of arms. He described the situation as confused, chaotic: an absurdity out of a Marx brothers movie. There was a plot to blow up a pedestrian bridge with Molotov cocktails, which would never have worked. Two months later, traveling in southern Chile, he was picked up and arrested and accused of being a foreign terrorist. He feared that he would be killed; thrown into the sea. But two of his guards turned out to be classmates of his before his

---

[23] Jefferson Morley, *Our Man in Mexico: Winston Scott and the Hidden History of the CIA* (Lawrence: University Press of Kansas, 2008). In general, see Renata Keller, *Mexico's Cold War: Cuba, the United States, and the Legacy of the Mexican Revolution* (New York: Cambridge University Press, 2015).

[24] Enrique Krauze, *Redeemers: Ideas and Power in Latin America*, trans. Hank Heifetz and Natasha Wimmer (New York: Harper, 2011), 219.

[25] See especially Tanya Harmer, *Allende's Chile and the Inter-American Cold War* (Chapel Hill: University of North Carolina Press, 2011).

family had left for Mexico, and after eight days he was let go and left the country.[26]

It was after his return to Mexico that Bolaño helped found the Infrarrealist poetry movement (represented in *The Savage Detectives* as "visceral realism"). His friend Mario Santiago Papasquiaro (the basis for the character of Ulises Lima from Bolaño's works), wrote in a 1975 manifesto: "WHAT DO WE PROPOSE? NOT TO MAKE A CAREER OUT OF ART." Bolaño's own manifesto, written the following year, was playfully militant: "As Saint-Just told me in a dream I had some time ago: even the heads of the aristocrats can be our weapons."[27] It was titled "Leave it all behind, again." In the *Savage Detectives*, a young poet who has just joined the "visceral realists" writes "Our situation (as far as I could understand) is unsustainable, trapped as we are between the reign of Octavio Paz and the reign of Pablo Neruda" (21). It was a rejection of the literary camps created and sustained by the Cold War politics of literature, in its international and national dimensions. The infrarealists, member Rubén Medina has written, were part of a neo-vanguard that declared itself against "the whole system of literary and cultural power" (26). Ulises Lima's determination to finance the magazine *Lee Harvey Oswald*, for example, by selling weed, represents a determination to steer clear of official sources of patronage.

The years of Bolaño's adulthood were the nightmare years of the Cold War in Latin America. Military coups displaced governments across the region. At their height, a transnational surveillance and murder network, Operation Condor, linked the dictatorships together. Bolaño's novellas *By Night in Chile* and *Distant Star* deal directly with the writer as accessory to fascism. The narrator of *By Night in Chile*, the priest Father Urrutia started out in Chile's literary circles. (He gets his start at the home of the literary critic "Farewell," based on the real Hernán Díaz Arrieta, whose pseudonym was the English word "Alone.") Urrutia ends up as the tutor to the dictator Augusto Pinochet, who flatters himself as an intellectual (though he falls asleep during his lessons) and wants Urrutia to tutor him in the fundamentals of Marxism, in order, he explains, to "understand Chile's enemies, to find out how they think, to get an idea of how far they are

---

[26] Roberto Bolaño, Andrés Braithwaite, and Juan Villoro, eds., *Bolaño por sí mismo: Entrevistas escogidas*, 2nd ed., revisada, Colección Huellas (Santiago, Chile: Ediciones Univ. Diego Portales, 2011), 37–38, 105–107.

[27] Rubén Medina, ed., *Perros habitados por las voces del desierto: poesía infrarrealista entre dos siglos*, Segunda edición (Ciudad de México: Matadero, 2016), 81–89.

prepared to go."²⁸ Similarly, *Distant Star*, featuring a fascist sky-writing poet, contains characters who host events in a house holding political prisoners for torture in the basement based on the American-born agent Michael Townley, who orchestrated assassinations for the dictatorship.²⁹

In the 1980s, as some of the Southern Cone dictatorships returned to electoral democracy, the killing fields of Latin America's Cold War moved to Central America. Guerrilla insurgencies faced off against death squads and pitiless armies, often backed by the United States. In El Salvador, the decade was marked by stalemate; in Guatemala, by government murder of the indigenous population. According to his own accounts, Bolaño had passed through El Salvador in 1974, and met Roque Dalton, the country's prominent left-wing poet as well as the guerrillas who killed him in 1976 in internecine conflict.

In Nicaragua, the guerrillas had triumphed in 1979 and there was a revolutionary government, inspired in significant ways by the experience of Cuba. The poet and priest Ernesto Cardenal, a practitioner of the left-wing interpretation of Christianity known as liberation theology, became Minister of Culture. The government struggled to promote the arts without seeming to be prescribing an official artistic line. One of Bolaño's most significant poems, "Ernesto Cardenal and I," imagines him encountering Cardenal and asking the priest if there will be a place in "The Kingdom of Heaven" for homosexuals, impenitent masturbators, "for those who can't take it anymore, those who really truly can't take it anymore?" Cardenal assures him there will be, while the branches of the trees shake menacingly (Bolaño, Braithwaite, and Villoro 2011, 92).

In the late 1980s, the tension between the United States and the Soviet Union that defined the global condition of Cold War began to ease. The Berlin Wall fell in 1989; the Soviet Union collapsed in 1991. Pinochet left office in 1990, having lost a plebiscite in 1988. The Sandinistas in Nicaragua lost an election the same year. Peace accords brought El Salvador's civil war to a close in 1992. Cuba's economic collapse in the 1990s laid bare how much its socialist economy had depended on Soviet subsidies. But debt crises across the capitalist countries brought their own kinds of misery too, and the dismantling of state-led development and the

---

²⁸ Roberto Bolaño, *By Night in Chile*, trans. Chris Andrews (New York: New Directions Books, 2003), 92, 100.
²⁹ Chris Andrews, *Roberto Bolaño's Fiction: An Expanding Universe* (New York: Columbia University Press, 2014), 150; John Dinges, *The Condor Years: How Pinochet and His Allies Brought Terrorism to Three Continents* (New York: New Press, 2004), 30.

widespread adoption of "neoliberalism" bridged the pre- and post–Cold War periods.

In the 1990s, many interpreted the end of the Cold War as a triumph of liberal, democratic capitalism, now devoid of competing ideologies on the world stage. It was in this time, widely (if incorrectly) seen as post-ideological, that Bolaño composed the prose output that brought him global fame, before his early death in 2003. Often looking back onto the years of Cold War trauma – or, in the femicides of the northern Mexican border region of *2666* in the 1990s, the years just after, parts of his work highlight continuities and legacies of violence that serve as a reminder of the uneven distribution of the "end of history."

But there are ways in which Bolaño appears as a post–Cold War writer. The cavalier and independent radicalism of his youth had been sanded smooth. Bolaño did not believe that literature could deliver social transformation. "Writers have no purpose. Literature has no purpose," Bolaño said towards the end of his life. "With respect to injustice and such things, well, a writer, in addition to being a writer, is a person, a citizen, and as such should speak out against situations that put dignity, freedom, and tolerance at risk" (Bolaño, Braithwaite, and Villoro 2011, 108; Krauze 2011, *Redeemers*). Bolaño always denied that he was "disenchanted," but in his fiction he is decidedly uninterested in presenting writers as heroic "redeemers," a role into which Latin America's artists have often been cast. "What things bore you?," Playboy magazine asked him, and he replied: "The empty discourse of the Left. I take for granted the empty discourse of the Right" (*Between Parentheses*, 365).

When Bolaño became a novelist in the 1990s, one of his major preoccupations was the invention of imaginary literary lives. But he makes them neither heroic nor politically "engaged" in any traditional sense. They are frequently detectives seeking out other writers: a layered joke, perhaps, on the work of the writer inventing imaginary writers. He invents a whole bestiary of fascist writers; and even the sought-after Archimboldi of *2666* is hiding a Nazi past. But if Bolaño seems to be commenting on the ultra-right, he has stated his inventions were also a way of commenting on the perversions he saw on the left. He offered scathing assessments of the writers of the "boom" generation and their descendants. "I always wanted to be a political writer – of the left, of course – but the political writers of the left seem dreadful to me," he told another interviewer (*Between Parentheses*, 365). Emilio Sauri has argued, in an interpretation of *The Savage Detectives*, that "Whereas the modernisms of ... generations of Latin American writers and critics have previously conceived the literary as an opening onto [a future capable of redeeming the past], Bolaño's novel signals the end of this particular aesthetic ideology, if only to suggest that history must now be found beyond it."[30]

Perhaps the most heroic character in all of his works is Auxilio Lacouture, a Uruguayan exile (based on the real-life person of Alcira Soust Scaffo) who survives the occupation of Mexico's National University in a bathroom, flushing away pieces of toilet paper on which she had written poetry. At the end of the novella, she is having a hallucinatory vision of a mass of ghostly children walking towards an abyss into which they fall. "And although the song that I heard was about war, about the heroic deeds of a whole generation of young Latin Americans led to sacrifice, I knew that above and beyond all, it was about courage and mirrors, desire and pleasure."[31] Like the writers he invents, like the characters who seek them out, Bolaño was struggling to make meaning of heroism and solidarity that had produced so much less justice than had been hoped for in the years of the Cold War. A "love letter or a farewell letter," and sometimes both.

---

[30] Emilio Sauri, "'A La Pinche Modernidad': Literary Form and the End of History in Roberto Bolaño's Los Detectives Salvajes," *MLN* 125, no. 2 (2010): 431.
[31] Roberto Bolaño, *Amulet*, trans. Chris Andrews (New York: New Directions, 2006), 184.

CHAPTER 11

After the Fall of the Wall: 1989–2001

Edmundo Paz Soldán

The first section of *Woes of the True Policeman*, the posthumous novel of Roberto Bolaño published in 2011, is titled "The Fall of the Berlin Wall." In it, we meet Amalfitano, a fifty-year-old literature professor who finds himself in Santa Teresa, México after the Barcelona university where he worked fires him for having a homosexual relationship with a student. In the fifth chapter of that section, he looks back on his life: "I who was expelled from the Party and who kept believing in the class struggle and the fight for the revolution of the Americas ... I who kept up my ties with leftist groups ... I who discovered my homosexuality at the same time that the Russians discovered their passion for capitalism ... (27–30). The chapter can be read as a synopsis of the life of a central character in Bolaño's works – who reappears in a more complex form in *2666* – at the pivotal historical moment of the end of the Cold War, which brings with it the installation of a new world order marked by the triumphant deployment of capitalism and globalization. As in other texts by Bolaño, there is a melancholic settling of the score with a past committed to the fight for social change, at the same time that the defeat of those forces is made clear.[1]

Among the specific vectors of the historical transition of 1989, marked by the fall of the Berlin Wall, Bolaño highlights the Chilean situation, where a plebiscite on the continuation of the dictatorship of Augusto Pinochet is held, and the global defeat of progressive forces. If Bolaño celebrates Pinochet's loss, he isn't very enthusiastic, as he is quite conscious of the harm that has been done to an entire generation and to the psyche of the country, and senses that the neoliberal economic forces installed by the dictatorship will only expand across the continent during the nineties. In the late eighties and nineties, his preoccupation with the Chilean situation

---

[1] Jonathan Monroe remarks on the "sadness and disappointment, if not utter disillusionment ... on the entire synecdochic history of [Amalfitano's] failed political commitments and engagements, consistently aligned, like the dominant in Latin American poetry, with the radical left" (2020, 160).

connects with his interest in writing fiction that recounts that loss, along with the establishment of the central pieces of the new economic world order, which, due to the free trade agreement of 1994, places Mexico and the grind of the border as a central axis.[2]

For Bolaño, the fall of the Berlin Wall unleashes energies associated with a new world map in which the American continent is key to the necropolitics of the end of the century. Bolaño will become the main Latin American author of this period marked by multilateralism, though he is certainly not alone. In fact, one of the central characteristics of Latin American literature of the end of the century is a "search for globality" (Hoyos, 20), which can be found in writers like César Aira, Diamela Eltit, and Mario Bellatin, and in movements like the Crack and McOndo.[3]

In the beginning of the nineties, Roberto Bolaño was known as a neo-vanguard poet in a small literary circle, lived in Spain, and remained relatively estranged from the literary currents of his country even if he did show interest in them. In the literary panorama of Chile, what stood out were neo-vanguard movements like the *Escena de Avanzada*, which brought together artists like Eugenio Dittborn and Carlos Altamirano and viewed critic Nelly Richard as a central referent, and the *CADA (Colectivo de Acciones de Arte)*, which included writer Diamela Eltit, poet Raúl Zurita, and photographer Lotty Rosenfield (Gutiérrez Mouat, 85). Through their interventions in the streets and work with photography, these groups articulated a potent critique of the dictatorship of Pinochet throughout the eighties.

Among these groups, *Yeguas of the Apocalypse*, which emerged at the end of the eighties, should be included. Formed by Francisco Casas and columnist Pedro Lemebel, whom Bolaño admired, they put on provocative performances, attacking the aims of the *Escena de Avanzada*, and defended queer identity from a dissident stance. The end of the eighties (1987) also saw the appearance of *Biblioteca del Sur*, a commercial effort by the publishing company, Planeta, to install a Chilean narrative on the market. This Spanish publishing company will become the spearhead – later to be joined by Alfaguara – that will bring to Chile "una voluntad, un proyecto publicitario, comercial y editorial que avanza y se [va] concentrando, y ensanchando" (a drive, a commercial, editorial publicity project

---

[2] This is a central theme in *2666*, a novel that dialogues with *Woes of the True Policeman*.
[3] In *Beyond Bolaño: The Global Latin American Novel*, Héctor Hoyos argues that the "*novela global latinoamericana*" (global Latin American novel) is the main narrative phenomenon of the nineties. These novels "are works that may contribute to consolidating, simultaneously, both the world and Latin America as their chambers of resonance" (2015, 7).

that progresses and expands as it becomes more focused) (Bianchi). Among the most notable names of what came to be known as the "new Chilean narrative" are Carlos Franz, Gonzalo Contreras, Marcela Serrano, and Alberto Fuguet. The return of democracy sparked an interest in reading local authors, and the consolidation of the country as an important literary market in a Hispanic landscape dominated by the presence of Spanish publishers. For some of these writers, the approval of the market seemed fundamental to bring about literary legitimacy.

At the end of the eighties, Bolaño begins to write his main poetic work, *The Unknown University* – he publishes the first part in 1993 and the complete edition in 2007 – and establishes a genealogy inspired by his admiration for the works and anti-establishment gestures of Nicanor Parra ("el que sea valiente que siga a Parra," "brave ones follow Parra," *Entre 92*) and Enrique Lihn ("un lujo inmerecido," "an undeserved luxury," *Entre 88*), distancing himself from the totem pole that Pablo Neruda represented for Chilean poets. Meanwhile, Bolaño developed his narrative voice in novels like *The Third Reich* – written in 1989, published in 2010 – and *The Skating Rink* (1993), in which he suggests that the historical past – in contrast to what is represented by the democratic transition – should be critically revised.[4] It's in the mid-nineties when his genius as a narrator explodes with two books he publishes in 1996: *Nazi Literature in the Americas* and *Distant Star*. In both, he processes classic Latin American influences (Borges's *A Universal History of Infamy*) and others that are not so well known (Rodolfo Wilcock's *The Synagogue of Iconoclasts*), at the same time that he reveals his fascination with the avant-garde, offers a satirical glance towards the work of *CADA*, and parodies Raúl Zurita's *Anteparadise*.

Beyond literary influences, however, are his historical and philosophical inquiry into Pinochet's Chile – in *Distant Star* – extended to the "destino terrible de nuestro continente" ("terrible fate of our continent") (*Entre* 31) in *Nazi Literature*, in which he establishes an alternative history of reactionary forces that is as sardonic as it is lethal. Evil is represented as a banal yet tenacious figure, an ivy that spreads its roots in magazines and poems by mediocre authors from the far right and flowers dramatically, in both books, beneath a politics of the state (meanwhile, those who incarnate evil

---

[4] Díaz Klaassen points out that *The Third Reich* suggests "la necesidad de rebelarse contra un pasado en apariencia clausurado, de abrirlo para enjuiciarlo (en esta novela, literalmente) y para hacerse cargo de él y tomar responsabilidad" (the need to rebel against an apparently closed past, to open it, examine it (literally in this novel), and to take care of and responsibility for it) (2020, 52–3).

transcend that politics, as if the chance events that cause history were added to the casual nature of individual free will). There is also the bitter conclusion that the neoliberal trend has consolidated in Chilean society; no one wants to relive collective utopias, preferring instead individual projects.[5]

Bolaño's fame explodes in Latin America and Spain with *The Savage Detectives*, a novel that is awarded the prestigious Herralde and Rómulo Gallegos prizes in 1998. At the end of 1996, he applies for a Guggenheim fellowship with the intent of writing the novel, stating that he would begin it in the middle of '97 and that it would take him a year to write. In the novel, which deals with the illusions and disillusionments of an entire Latin American generation – the one that dreamed of social reform in the seventies and was confronted by savage dictatorial repression – critic Héctor Hoyos finds "a literary map to navigate a new consciousness of the world as a whole" (20) appearing precisely after the fall of the Berlin Wall: the idea of literature on a global scale, with characters who move from Mexico to Managua, Luanda and Tel Aviv, framed by encounters with "puzzling forms of fascism" and an enormous "variety of sexual experience" (14–15).

In *The Savage Detectives*, Bolaño also contends with the influential tradition of the Boom, the iconic movement of writers who brought Latin American literature international status in the beginning of the sixties through expansive novels with complex linguistic, symbolic, and formal registers. Because of the totalizing ambition of his novel, Bolaño has been known as "the last Boom writer." However, the truth is that while *The Savage Detectives* is informed by some Boom texts – notably Julio Cortázar's *Rayuela* – it also initiates a new narrative paradigm that is more countercultural and approximates certain avant-garde poetic movements like surrealism and dadaism, which were already present during the infrarealist movement of which Bolaño formed a part in the seventies.

One of the questions hovering over the novel is the role of poetry – and of literature – in a cultural field that is increasingly dominated by the pressures of the market.[6] Facing the impossibility of finding a liberated space for the work of art, Ulises Lima and Arturo Belano, poets who

---

[5] Romero, the detective of *Distant Star*, wants to return to Chile to open up a business: "hay bastante gente que se está haciendo rica" (210). It's significant that the business is a funeral parlor: "Romero, literalmente, volverá para enterrar a los muertos en un país empeñado en olvidarlos" (Romero will literally come back to bury the dead in a country set on forgetting them) (Díaz Klaassen 2020, 190).

[6] Bolaño makes a significant effort to work with poetic tradition through prose. Monroe argues that his "work centrally involves the construction of literary history by other means at the intersection of poetry and fiction, of the prose poem and the novel" (2020, 9).

pertain to the visceral realist movement – clearly inspired by infrarealism – opt not to leave any work at all; their lives in themselves are poetic gestures. Bolaño is critical of all of those writers who are willing to make concessions to the market so that their books will find a space; in a section of the novel that occurs in the Madrid Book Fair of 1994, his sharp critique of editorial globalization and what he considers the accommodating character of the writer of the nineties is palpable. For Pere Ordoñez, who participated in the Fair, writing is "a way to climb up the social pyramid, settling while being very careful to not transgress anything" (485). As Cobas Carral and Garibotto say, Bolaño suggests that "any poetic practice ends up being coopted by the market, becoming functional in the system; the editorial industry leads to the erosion of the subversive character of literature; its conversion into merchandise brings with it a depolitization" (178–179). *The Savage Detectives* can thus be read as a poetic and an ethics, an instruction manual for contending with the market without making concessions. It's about adopting a radical stance, which sometimes implies assuming silence.

When he received the Rómulo Gallegos prize, Bolaño gave a speech in which he said that his entire career was a "love letter or farewell song" to his own generation, those born in the 1950s who "gave the little that we had, the much that we had, which was our youth, to the cause we believed was the most generous cause of the world, and in a way it was, but in reality it wasn't" (*Entre* 37). In that love song there was also fury, as Bolaño was very drawn to controversy. His recognition across the continent allowed him to be more explicit with his intervention in the Chilean and Latin American canon. In his columns and articles, he drew up his own map of literary affinities and rejections. On one side were the obvious: writers associated with the new Chilean narrative and authors who, as part of the globalizing editorial expansion, had turned "magical realism" into a registered brand of the continent's literature (Isabel Allende, Luis Sepúlveda). On the other were the less obvious figures, writers like Diamela Eltit or Raúl Zurita, with whom he assumed more complex and ambivalent stances. He recognized Eltit's literature as "among the most complex written today in Spanish" (*Entre* 75). At the same time, it disturbed him that she was married to a minister even though the minister was a socialist. This had to do with his extreme distrust of power: "That is what I learned from Chilean literature ... Don't fight because you'll always be defeated. Don't turn your back on power because power is everything" (*Entre* 66). That was part of his way of understanding literature as a mechanism of war: if Eltit was the main writer in Chilean literature of the nineties, he had to find ways to attack this respected figure with whom he was incompatible.[7]

In the continental panorama, Bolaño's canon included authors like Wilcock, Osvaldo Lamborghini, and Felisberto Hernández and writers of their generation like Horacio Castellanos Moya, Rodrigo Rey Rosa, César Aira, and Carmen Boullosa; in the newer generations, he was very close to Rodrigo Fresán. Although many of these writers were already known before Bolaño acknowledged them, almost all are now important figures in the Latin American constellation, which speaks to his critical eye and the weight of his words in promoting or reinforcing an author's reputation.

At the end of the nineties, already an acclaimed author in Latin America and Spain, admired by readers and rapidly turning into the most influential writer for those of newer generations, his works began to take off around the world through their translations. It is during these years that Bolaño continues his investigation into the traumas of Latin American history (*Amulet*, 1999) and the Chilean dictatorship (*By Night in Chile*, 2000) while preparing to take on *2666*, published in 2004, with the global paradigm again upset by the attack of the Twin Towers in 2001. He also published a novel written in the early eighties (*Monsier Pain*, 2000), and two powerful books of short stories: *Llamadas telefónicas* (1997) and *Putas asesinas* (2001).[8]

During these years, Bolaño struggled with continual tensions, as he had to contend with the contradictions that came with becoming a literary star in the hypermarket of the culture that he had so strongly reviled. His trips to Chile provoked constant conflicts. Critic Ignacio Echevarría points out that in the report of his first visit, at the end of 1998, "he wounded, with good reason, all types of susceptibilities" (*Entre* 9), and that the second, in 1999, "occured in a stormy climate, full of bitter interjections and boycotts on the part of the cultural establishment" (9). Through the public posture he took, increasingly "disturbing, irreverent, more unsettling," Echevarría believes he can make out the tutelary figure of Nicanor Parra, who is central to Bolaño's universe (10).

---

[7] He was also ambivalent about Zurita: "crea una obra magnífica, que descuella entre los de su generación y que marca un punto de no retorno con la poética de la generación precedente, pero su escatología, su mesianismo, son también los puntales de un mausoleo o de una pira funeraria hacia la que se encaminaron, en los años ochenta, casi todos los poetas chilenos" (he has had a magnificent career, standing out among those of his generation and marking a point of no return with the poetry of the previous. But his scatology, his messianism, are also the posts of a mausoleum or a pyre towards which almost all Chilean poets are headed in the eighties") (*Entre*, 89).

[8] In English, *Last Evenings of Earth* (2006) is a selection of stories from both books, and *The Return* (2010) collects all the stories from both books not included in *Last Evenings on Earth*.

Many of the works Bolaño wrote in the second half of the nineties can be read as a constant investigation into evil, a reflection on the traumas produced by that evil in their Chilean, Latin American, and global particularities, and an intent to put together a genealogy of evil through time and space. On one hand, Pinochet's dictatorship is connected to Nazism; on the other, the contemporary global landscape unites places as diverse as Blanes and Santa Teresa. *By Night in Chile* is narrated by a melancholic character, ethically blind and deaf, who has been marked by the trauma of a history that has gone through him and in which he is incapable of acting. He is a representative of a Latin American republic of letters whose main characteristics are hypocrisy as a form of conduct, consent to serve those in power, and the capacity to focus on his own survival while perverse events surround him.[9]

A story from 1997, "Detectives" (in *Last Evenings on Earth*), structured as a dialogue between two detectives, speaks to the primitive trauma of Chilean society, taking as a starting point the author's memories of the few weeks he spent in detention at the beginning of Pinochet's dictatorship. The dialogue begins with an exchange about their preferred type of weapons and then focuses on the nostalgic memory of the coup of '73. There is a cocky tone: "that's when we killed them all," says one (42). Little by little, however, their post-traumatic disorder reveals itself:

> the dead turn up in my dreams, and I get them mixed them up with the ones who are neither dead nor alive … And I blame Chile, and call it a country of faggots and killers [...] Then I think this country went to hell years ago, and the reason we're here, those of us who've stayed, is to have nightmares, just because someone had to stay and face up to them. (43–44)

The policeman does not assume his responsibility in the construction of the trauma, instead generalizing, looking for collective guilt. It's clear that those deaths matter and Chile is not responsible for them, but in the master–slave dialectics that Bolaño works with, neither the assassin nor the victim emerge unscathed.

A detective recalls that one of the political prisoners, Arturo Belano – Roberto Bolaño's alter ego – his ex-schoolmate, appeared through a mirror

---

[9] In the home of poet María Canales – wife of Dirección de Inteligencia Nacional (DINA) agent Michael Townley – the parties and receptions of writers continued during the dictatorship: "Los artistas se reían, bebían, bailaban, mientras afuera, en esa zona de grandes avenidas despobladas de Santiago, transcurría el toque de queda" (135) (The artists laughed, drank and danced, while outside, on the wide, empty avenues of Santiago, the curfew was in force) (116). Meanwhile, in the basement, opponents to Pinochet's regime are tortured, something that a friend of the narrator discovers by accident: one night he went downstairs to look for the bathroom, drunk, and found a cot with "un hombre desnudo, atado de las muñecas y los tobillos" (139).

in a prison hallway and he couldn't recognize him: "en efecto, me dijo, no era él, era otra persona" (130) (and sure enough, he said, it wasn't him, it was someone else) (53). To calm him down, the detective tells him that he will look in the mirror next to him. He places himself before the mirror, closes his eyes, opens them:

> I opened my eyes right up and looked at myself and saw someone ... scared shitless, and behind him I saw a guy about twenty years old, but he looked at least ten years older ... and to tell the truth, I couldn't be sure, I saw a swarm of faces, as if the mirror was broken, though I knew perfectly well it wasn't. (55–56)

The mirror reflects back broken images, and the policeman does not recognize himself. "Joder," he says, "Jesus, we really have fucked up, haven't we, Contreras?" (56). The tough man sees a ghostly, terrorized figure in the mirror. There is as much fear in the victim as in the perpetrator. That experience of the uncanny shows the rupture in the Chilean psyche produced by the appearance of evil.

In this world of Bolaño's later work, which prefigures *2666*, divinity does not exist: irrevocable, "radical evil" – the "corrupt inclination" of man – roams on the same plane as freedom, understood as "the rational core of human subjectivity" (Dews 2012, 18).[10] Through the construction of his autonomy, in the search for complete freedom, man places his maliciousness before the overwhelming good of society and the majority of the time ends up acting according to selfish motives. There is no antidote for his poison. If at the end of the nineties Bolaño's apocalyptic aesthetic changes the appearance of trauma and shows the melancholia in the broken Chilean psyche, art could attempt to transcend that melancholia by returning to it again and again, in search of something new. Nonetheless, most likely, Bolaño suggests, all pathways have been exhausted and there is nothing new to say about horror. However, shortly after, at the beginning of the new century, with the monumental *2666*, Bolaño will show that there is still much to say about that horror.

Translated from the Spanish by Julie Lind.

---

[10] Dews refers to the concept of "radical evil" as developed by Kant.

CHAPTER 12

Latin American Literature

Ilan Stavans

"Literature was a vast minefield occupied by enemies," Roberto Bolaño, who enjoyed accruing enemies in the pantheon of Latin American letters, writes in the short story "Meeting with Enrique Lihn" (*The New Yorker*, December 22, 2008).

> except for a few classic authors (just a few), and every day I had to walk through that minefield, where any false move could be fatal, with only the poems of Archilochus to guide me. It's like that for all young writers. There comes a time when you have no support, not even from friends, forget about mentors, and there's no one to give you a hand; publication, prizes, and grants are reserved for the others, the ones who said "Yes, sir," over and over, or those who praised the literary mandarins, a never-ending horde distinguished only by their aptitude for discipline and punishment – nothing escapes them and they forgive nothing.

Aptitude for disciple and punishment Bolaño himself had aplenty, too. And in spite of his precarious health, he had stamina. At a young age, he had made up his mind he would die. So who cared if he annoyed others. His mission, as is clear from *The Savage Detectives* (1998), was to upend that tradition, to take it by the neck and expose its platitudes. What is the use of sacred cows if not to be desecrated? Indeed, every tradition needs an *enfant terrible*, maybe more than one. When was the last time a rebel rouser came along in Latin American literature? As Bolaño put it in *2666* (2004), "if you're going to say what you want to say, you're going to hear what you don't want to hear."

I write these paragraphs in the middle of the COVID-19 pandemic. (Though I really don't know how to measure the length of the calamity. Might I still be at the beginning?) The whole planet is upside down, taken by the neck. Infectious are rampant. The general feeling is of despair. Death is everywhere at the door. Of course, there is no interest in sacred cows now.

I can't but imagine how Bolaño would have thrived in this environment, the bile he would have enjoyed spilling. His essay "Literature + Illness = Illness" (*The Insufferable Gaucho*, 2003) is an insightful meditation into why death should be welcomed, not shunned. He wrote it knowing his prognosis was grim. In it, he talks of Kafka realizing his bouts of tuberculosis will soon draw him flat, when there is nothing between him and eternity. Bolaño dedicated the essay to his friend Dr. Víctor Vargas, an hepatologist who tried fruitlessly to save his life. In the superb *Playboy* interview (July 2003) with Mónica Maristain, he is asked what he wishes to do before dying. "Nothing special," Bolaño responds:

> Well, clearly I'd prefer not to die. But sooner or later the distinguished lady arrives. The problem is that sometimes she's neither a lady nor very distinguished, but, as Nicanor Parra says in a poem, she's a hot wench who will make your teeth chatter no matter how fancy you think you are.

It goes without saying that in death, Bolaño has become a mandarin. That's the effect death has on *enfants terribles*: it turns them into myth. He is at the center of the very literary tradition he sought to sabotage. The vast minefield occupied by enemies has been turned into a memorial park, with mausoleums, statues, murals, and other paraphernalia. It is ironic how the subversive has metamorphosed into a Che Guevara–like model among middle-class readers and creative-writing factories, not only in Latin American but everywhere. Yet his scream-and-shout strategy, his mantra of face-Goliath-without-fear remains his alone, since rebellion is not for the faint of heart.

The parade of Bolaño's tantrums against Latin American icons is plentiful. So is his reverence toward other agitators. At one point in *The Savage Detectives*, he describes an attempt by his alter ego, Arturo Belano, along with his pal and partner in crime Mario Santiago (aka Ulises Lima), to kidnap Octavio Paz, the Nobel Prize–winning poet and essayist, near Parque Hundido, in Colonia Benito Juárez, not far from Paz's Mexico City apartment. The endeavor is designed to be another iteration, like those the Infrarrealistas orchestrate in Casa del Lago and other sites, against Mexico's literary establishment.

In every national culture Bolaño irritatingly inserted himself in – Chile, Argentina, Mexico, and Spain – he made sharp, uncompromising critiques. He ridiculed Diamela Eltit for being impenetrable (she is!) and Isabel Allende for being square and unadventurous (ditto). In *Between Parenthesis* (2011), he affirms, with venomous panache, that she's nothing if not tacky:

Asked to choose between the frying pan and the fire, I choose Isabel Allende. The glamour of her life as a South American in California, her imitations of García Marquez, her unquestionable courage, the way her writing ranges from the kitsch to the pathetic and reveals her as a kind of Latin American and politically correct version of the author of *The Valley of the Dolls*...

Blah blah blah. Bolaño scorns Paolo Coelho ("a soap opera Rio with doctor"). He poked fun at Mario Vargas Llosa for jogging his way to success (he meditates on two of the Peruvian's novels in *Between Parenthesis* [2011]) and teased Carlos Fuentes for fashioning himself as a prima donna (César Aira also licked his fingers on this idea, turned it into a novella). And this doesn't include the Latin American authors he snubbed by not even acknowledging their existence: José Donoso, Laura Esquivel, Ariel Dorfman, etc.

Schadenfreude, a useful German term, implies the joy that results from the troubles of others. Bolaño not only loved trouble; he also knew his invectives were a spectacle. The world is too complacent, with too many people getting accolades with little effort. He learned the tricks from fellow Chilean Nicanor Parra, a physicist and poet whose oeuvre is an equal rat-a-tat against all sorts of targets, not only literary: the hypocrisy of the bourgeoisie, the guilt of the Catholic Church in the decimation of indigenous peoples and its closeness to power since the colonial period; the tendency of the rest of the world to see Latin America as exotic; Neruda's myopic Stalinism; and so on.

In his contrarianism, Bolaño also emulated other Chilean poets, like Lihn himself – the country is one of the most fertile poetic grounds in the region, with two Nobel Prizes – the art of saying NO. But he also went against other NO-sayers, such as Raúl Zurita, who is an inspiration behind Alberto Ruiz-Tagle, the performative pilot who writes sky poetry during the Pinochet dictatorship in *Distant Star* (1996), a novella, by the way, told from the perspective of Arturo B. (Belano), fleshing out the last chapter of *Nazi Literature in the Americas* (1998).

However, this index of condemnations run the risk of eclipsing Bolaño's far more cuddled relationship with the Latin American literary canon. An inveterate reader, he knew the continent's tropes almost better than anyone, keeping up, through books reviews, newspapers columns, interviews, and other writing artillery, on what was new and forthcoming. He generously – and effusively – dispensed praise for the work of acquaintances and others (Manuel Puig, Juan Villoro, Rodrigo Rey Rosa, et al.), engaged in conversations with insightful readers (Ricardo Piglia, for instance, who, by the way, also adored Puig), and unreservedly celebrated the books that had influenced him (in *Playboy*, he mentioned *Don Quixote* [1605–1615], Adolfo Bioy Casares' *The Invention of Morel* [1940], Julio Cortázar's *Hopscotch* [1963]).

The novella *Monsieur Pain* (1994), originally written between 1981 and 1982 and published under the title *La senda de los elefantes* (The Path of the Elephants), is about Peruvian poet César Vallejo's death – by hiccups! – in Paris in 1938, just as the Spanish Civil War was unfolding. It is a solemnly humorous homage to the author of *Spain, Take This Chalice from Me* (1939), at a time, in the Reagan years, when his fervent Communism almost made him a second thought.

What strikes me as *sine qua non*, maybe even nearsighted, is Bolaño's silence on Gabriel García Márquez. Not that he doesn't mention him; he does, in *Between Parenthesis* and elsewhere. Accumulatively, these references are, in my view, tame, not to say dismissive. I say it because I believe *One Hundred Years of Solitude* (1963) is unquestionably the best and most important novel ever published in Latin America. In its scope and complexity, it is the region's Bible.

Bolaño's indifference (Piglia has a similar attitude) has an explanation. He came about at a time when Latin American letters were exhausted with Macondo. García Márquez has received so much adulation abroad, internally its shadow felt ominous. Sensing its exoticism as an imposition, they protested against it through movements like McOndo (Alberto Fuget, Edmundo Paz Soldán), an embrace of exactly the opposite: American culture of the cheapest kind. Although Bolaño didn't fall for this paganism, he did keep his distance from the Buendías.

At any rate, obviously it is Borges who is at the epicenter of Bolaño's universe. Starting with *Nazi Literature in the Americas*, an invented encyclopedia that is an overt tribute to the semi-historical profiles of Monk Eastman, Billy the Kid, Ching Shih, and others in *A Universal History of Infamy* (1935), he made sure his bookishness, time and again, referred back to the author of "The Aleph" (1945).

He inherited his passion for detective fiction from Borges too (*The Savage Detectives* is a bit Dashiell Hammett and Raymond Chandler and a lot Borges), as he did his interest in philosophical pursuits that are nurtured by a desire to apprehend the world in full (one might say that in *2666*, the elusive Prussian Hans Reiter, aka Benno von Archimboldi, author of *The Leather Mask*, *Lethaea*, and a dozen other titles (and others presumed to be by him as well), has nothing of Borges; still, it is possible to trace in his veneer the Argentine's propensity for authors who insist on disappearing before our eyes, as in "The Approach to Al-Mu'tasim" [1936]). And his loyalty to science-fiction is more rooted in stories like "Tlön, Uqbar, *Orbis Tertius*" (1940) and "Shakespeare's Memory" (1983) than in anything by Bioy Casares, who is actually a second-rate author.

Bolaño also received from Borges his Gaucho obsession. "The Insufferable Gaucho" owes much to Domingo Faustino Sarmiento, Hilario Ascasubi, and, especially, Argentina's 2,316-line national epic, José Hernández's *The Gaucho Martín Fierro* (1872). The frantically-multiplying rabbits are traceable to Cortázar's story "Letter to a Young Lady in Paris" (1951). Which brings me to Cortázar. Bolaño not only cherished *Hopscotch*. He also borrowed handsomely, to name a few tales, from "Bestiary" (1951), about a private zoo of fantastic beasts, and the exploration of criminal fandom in "We Loved Glenda So Much" (1980).

Cervantes, obviously, wasn't Latin American but, in his capacity to turn the banal into a metaphysical system, it's as if he was. Let's say he was, for convenience's sake and to correct a wrong made by fate. Long before Bolaño came along, Borges had already figured out how to relocate – or, if you wish, "appropriated" – him with his disquisition on plagiarism in "Pierre Menard, Author of the *Quixote*" (1939). Bolaño, who would doubt it, is exhibit #1 in Menardism,[1] the capacity to rewrite someone else's original, often surpassing it in quality, or at least forcing a vertiginous rereading of it.

Arturo Belano and Ulises Lima are surrogates of Don Quixote and Sancho Panza. They are in constant (if unwritten) dialogue, each proposing a worldview that depends, in dialectical terms, on the other. In fact, what happens, at the end, in *Don Quixote* is replicated in *The Savage Detectives*: just as Sancho becomes Quixotized and Don Quixote Sanchotized – e.g., their personalities are reverted – so does Belano become Lima-like and vice versa. That's the nature of any true friendship.

There are countless other celebrations of *Don Quixote* in *The Savage Detectives*: the narrative designed as a journey of *iter autem intellectualis inventa*; the parallel surveying of inner and outer geography; the use of novelistic devices to engage in philosophical disquisitions; the indulgence in linguistic playfulness; and so on. I will leave the fertility of this contrast for another occasion.

Yet, as it is for all of us, the most important feature in Bolaño's love-and-hate bond with his Latin American wound was what I call his

---

[1] I explore two contrasting terms, "Menardism" and "Macondism," in my book *Quixote: The Novel and the World* (New York: W. W. Norton, 2015).

ventriloquism. Unfortunately, it doesn't come across sufficiently in the translations of his oeuvre into languages I know (English, Italian, French, Portuguese, German, and Hebrew), not because of a lack of talent from the translators. (I especially like Chris Andrews and Natasha Wimmer.) On the contrary, the majority are first-rate. Rather, it is because accents are rather difficult to convey in translation. And Bolaño is one of the few writers in world literature I know to have had various registers within his own language.

In this paragraph I'm engaging in an aside, one sufficiently valued not to ghettoize it in a footnote (although, mind you, I life footnotes). There is a specific section of *The Savage Detectives* – concretely, of part II: 1976–1996 – that strikes me as genial. It is chapter 10, delivered by Norman Bolzman, sitting on a bench in Edith Wolfson Park, in Tel Aviv, on the edge of Yad Eliyahu, October 1979. Looking for Claudia, a Mexican student in Israel who shares an apartment with Daniel and Norman, two other Mexican students, Ulises Lima knocks at their door. What transpires in the next few weeks is a complicated relationship in which Lima, in an alien land, depends economically, culturally, and linguistically on Claudia and her friends.

The episode showcases Bolaño's extraordinary talent to delve into alienation in all its forms. I don't know when exactly he visited Israel, but he must have. I have lived there on numerous occasions. The feel is authentic. So is the depiction of Mexican Jews finding themselves in it without fully breaking the umbilical cord. I don't know of any other contemporary Latin American novel offering a similar glimpse of life in the Middle East. This is one paragraph deep in the chapter, pages 267–268:

> Then there was the question of money. Claudia, Daniel, and I were in school and we each received a monthly allowance from our parents. In Daniel's case this allowance was barely enough to live on. In Claudia's case it was more generous. Mine fell somewhere in between. If we pooled our money, we could pay for the apartment, our classes, and our food, have enough for the movies or the theater or to buy books in Spanish at the Cervantes Bookstore, on Zamenhof. But having Ulises there upset everything, because after a week he had hardly any money left and all of a sudden we had another mouth to feed, as the sociologists say. Still, as far as I was concerned, it was no big deal. I was prepared to give up certain luxuries. Daniel didn't care either, although he continued to live his life exactly as he had before. It was Claudia – who would've thought? – who chafed at the new situation. At first she tackled the problem coolly and practically. One night she told Ulises that he needed to look for work or ask to have money

sent from Mexico. I remember that Ulises sat there looking at her with a lopsided smile and then said that he would look for work. The next night, during dinner, Claudia asked if he'd found work. Not yet, said Ulises. But did you go out and look? asked Claudia. Ulises was washing the dishes and he didn't turn around when he said yes. He'd gone out and looked but had no luck. I was sitting at the head of the table and could see his face in profile, and it looked to me like he was smiling. Fuck, I thought, he's smiling, smiling out of sheer happiness. As if Claudia was his wife, a nagging wife, a wife who worried about her husband finding work, and he liked that. That night I told Claudia to leave him alone, that he was already having a hard enough time without her getting on his case about work. Anyway, I said, what kind of job to you expect him to find in Tel Aviv? as a construction worker? a porter at a market? a dishwasher? What do you know, Claudia said to me.

I say the feel is authentic because I know: I was Ulises Lima in Tel Aviv.

Back on track, in Bolaño's Chilean books, say *By Night in Chile* [2000] and *Distant Star*, and in countless stories, he sounds Chilean through the cadence of the words. The same goes for his Argentine work, like "The Insufferable Gaucho." In his Mexican titles, especially *The Savage Detective* – to me is the best Mexican novel of the end of the twentieth century – he outdoes, and even supersedes, Elena Poniatowska and Carlos Monsiváis, not to mention Paz and Fuentes. And for readers who access him in Spanish, in *2666* Bolaño sounds a little Iberian and a lot pan–Latin American.

In that sense, he was, and here's the rub, an entire literary tradition on his own. As a voyager across the tradition, and through his irritability, he cannibalized his victims, spitting out their bones in the form of mimicry. That parody, that impersonation ruffled feathers and deflated egos to acknowledge its pomposity, forcing the Latin American literary tradition like a corpse that thought of itself as vigorous.

In "Caracas Address" (included in *Between Parenthesis*), upon receiving the Rómulo Gallegos Prize, Bolaño attested to the act of writing as an experience *de profundis*. "It's possible to have many homelands," he stated,

> it occurs to me now, but only one passport, and that passport is obviously the quality of one's writing. Which doesn't mean writing well, because anyone can do that, but writing incredibly well, and not even that, because anyone can write incredibly well. So what is top-notch writing? The same thing it's always been: the ability to peer into the darkness, to leap into the void, to know that literature is basically a dangerous undertaking. The ability to sprint along the edge of the precipice: to one side the bottomless abyss and to the other the faces you love, the smiling faces you love, and

books and friends and food. And the ability to accept what you find, even though it may be heavier than the stones over the graves of all dead writers. Literature, as an Andalusian folk singer would put it, is danger.

It's good to be crabby and offend when offense is what is needed. It's good to speak with utter conviction – in fact, with the conviction of a criminal. In *Playboy*, he confessed that he would much rather have been a homicide detective than a writer. "That's the one thing I'm absolutely sure of. A homicide cop, someone who returns alone at night to the scene of the crime and isn't afraid of ghosts. Maybe then I really would have gone crazy, but when you're a policeman, you solve that by shooting yourself in the mouth."

And again, there is wisdom in being ill. In *2666*, Bolaño states:

> The diseased, anyway, are more interesting than the healthy. The words of the diseased, even those who can manage only a murmur, carry more weight than those of the healthy. Then, too, all healthy people will in the future know disease. That sense of time, ah, the diseased man's sense of time, what treasure hidden in a desert cave. Then, too the diseased truly bite, whereas the healthy pretend to bite but really only snap at the air. Then, too, then, too, then, too.

Fitting words from the grave in the age of COVID-19.

CHAPTER 13

French Connections
Dominique Jullien

Introduction: Plots of Globalization

Roberto Bolaño is often described as a global writer, and much of his success can be explained by the appeal of his cosmopolitan narratives. Bolaño was an uprooted writer (born in Chile, he spent his formative years in Mexico and most of his adult life in Spain); his stories and his characters are wanderers too, whether the four European academics whose paths intersect in Northern Mexico in their quest of the missing writer Archimboldi, or the American woman, Anne Moore, who drifts from city to city, or the Chilean photographer Mauricio "The Eye" Silva, whose wanderings take him to Mexico, India and Germany. Alexander Beecroft mentioned *2666* as one example of the new global novel, alongside Amitav Ghosh's *Ibis* trilogy or González Iñárritu's film *Babel*. These narratives all share a pattern of intersecting plots ("Plot of globalization") which exhibit an acute awareness of the interconnectedness of the world.[1] This is also Héctor Hoyos's view: the success of *The Savage Detectives* (which made Bolaño famous almost overnight) was due, he argues, to its synchronicity with the image of Latin American literature in conjunction with a sense of globality after 1989.[2] Jonathan Lethem praised *2666* as "a landmark in what's possible for the novel as a form in our increasingly, and terrifyingly, post-national world."[3] Rebecca Walkowitz also points to a linguistic particularity of Bolaño's writing: because of his multinational life (from Chile to Mexico and Spain), his novels combine several regional idioms and seem translated, a multilingualism that is also communicated narratively in the transnational plot which typically moves across several continents.[4]

---

[1] Beecroft, *An Ecology of World Literature*, 283.   [2] Hoyos, *Beyond Bolaño*, 164.
[3] *The New York Times Book Review*, November 9, 2008.   [4] Walkowitz, *Born Translated*, 17–20.

Given this strong transnational claim, the question of "French" connections – indeed, of national connections of any kind – may seem contradictory, and perhaps even a misleading way of thinking about Bolaño. It will quickly become apparent, though, that Bolaño's affinity for "French" models of writing has little in common with a cultural identification, a fondness for the language, culture or history of France. Instead, his many French "connections" (Baudelaire, Rimbaud, the Surrealists, Marcel Schwob, Georges Perec, François Bon, or Pierre Michon are all important references, as will be seen) tend to focus on themes that transcend national parameters, such as life writing in connection with chance and destiny, or the pull towards what Perec called the "infra-ordinary," or, for several of the writers, the theme of illness.

Flâneurs on a Global Scale

While the French intertext is only one among several in Bolaño's transnational universe (Poe, Kafka, Vallejo and Borges come to mind as key points of reference; references to both German literature and German history play a capital role),[5] French models clearly occupy a place of choice. For Bolaño, who thought of himself as a poet rather than a novelist, the first of these intertextual models is undoubtedly Charles Baudelaire, the iconic poet of nineteenth-century Paris. As the inventor of the term "modernité," as the poet who articulated the organic link between the new hybrid form of the prose poem and the new experience of urban anonymity and serendipity, as the unlucky, unappreciated poet ravaged by illness and carried off by an early death, Baudelaire is in many ways a foundational figure for Bolaño.[6] If Baudelaire could be crowned first poet of the "capital of the nineteenth century," in Walter Benjamin's famous phrase, it is because he captured a condition of modern capitalistic societies, in which the poet occupies an untenable position both as an unproductive outsider given to leisurely rambles through the frantic city (a *flâneur*, "on the threshold of the city as of the bourgeois class"),[7] and an essentially

---

[5] See Thomas Beebee's essay on Bolaño's German precursors, Chapter 14 of this volume.

[6] A rich intertextual triangulation links Baudelaire to Vallejo; this exceeds the limits of the present essay. See Efraín Kristal, "*Les Hérauts noirs* de César Vallejo: entre Rubén Darío et *Les Fleurs du mal* d'Eduardo Marquina," *La Parole impossible. Regards croisés autour de la traduction de César Vallejo, Marina Tsvetaeva et Paul Celan*, L. Brysse-Chanet, I. Salazar & R. Béhar (eds.) (Paris: Hermann, 2019), 83–98.

[7] W. Benjamin, "Paris capital of the 19th century," *Reflections*, 156; see also Benjamin's well-known discussion of the connections between Baudelaire's *flâneur* and Poe's Man of the Crowd, *Illuminations*, 172.

privileged insider able to convey the lyrical truth of the city dweller's experience.

The four academic protagonists of Bolaño's *2666* can be read as contemporary versions of the Baudelairian *flâneur*: marginally integrated into the productive circuit of the modern economy, they roam the world in search of a fellow writer (the elusive German author Benno von Archimboldi) just as their predecessor Baudelaire roamed the streets of Paris in the throes of Haussmannization, in search of words and poetic inspiration, "trébuchant sur les mots comme sur les pavés."[8] No longer bounded by national borders, they form a European quartet (one is French, one English, one Italian, and one Spanish) whose peripatetic quest for the missing German writer takes them all the way to the fictional town of Santa Teresa on the US–Mexican border, where their stories become entangled with the stories of a Chilean philosopher and an American journalist. Bolaño conveys the late twentieth-century experience of wandering and transnational *flânerie*: the experience captured by early nineteenth-century writers such as Baudelaire (or indeed, even before him, Balzac) of circulating and getting lost in an anonymous, fluid, urban landscape, is expanded, in Bolaño's narratives, to the confines of the planet.

Another important facet of the Baudelairean legacy is its turning away from the novel. In this respect, the prose poem, promoted by Baudelaire, Rimbaud, Mallarmé and other late nineteenth-century French writers, provides serious competition to the novel as the genre most suited to modern urban reality, since it is the offspring, as Baudelaire famously claimed in the preface to his *Petits poèmes en prose,* of the "fréquentation des villes énormes."[9] As Jonathan Monroe shows in his recent book *Framing Roberto Bolaño*, Bolaño, who thought of himself as a poet first and foremost, had a troubled relationship to the novel, avowedly tying his choice of the genre to the need to support his family rather than to an intrinsic aesthetic imperative. The boundary between prose poem and short story, always blurry, took on a new meaning for Bolaño: generic ambiguity became essential in his own aesthetic quest. The core of Bolaño's writing, Monroe argues, is the prose poem, in particular the prose poem in the tradition of Baudelaire and Rimbaud, with its characteristically generative hybridization of poetry and narrative.[10] In Bolaño's

---

[8] Baudelaire, "Le Soleil," *Les Fleurs du mal,* 13.
[9] Baudelaire, *Petits poèmes en prose,* Dédicace à Arsène Houssaye, 22.
[10] Monroe, *Framing Roberto Bolaño,* especially 1–3.

longer novels, prose poems live on; Monroe points out their fragmentary construction, the collection of disjointed texts that resemble Baudelaire's *Petits poèmes en prose*. (More on the episodic structure of Bolaño's novels below.) The Baudelairean DNA and the influence of the Parisian prose poem speaks to something foundational in Bolaño's writing process – the connection to the modern urban experience, of course, and also a choice of the brief and the fragmentary over the ampler flow and dramatic architecture of the nineteenth-century realist novel.

Surrealists Lost and Found

Bolaño's allegiance to the serendipitous poetry of big cities also overlaps with his love of Surrealism. Rimbaud, the Surrealists' patron saint, triangulates both the practice of worshiping chance encounters as poetic events, and an extreme view of poetry as a tension towards its own demise. Living poetry rather than writing it eventually became Rimbaud's destiny: some of the same gamble defined the Surrealists (who sought to overcome the divide between art and life and make their poetry a form of praxis) and Bolaño, whose complicated love–hate relationship to literature (both his own writing and that of his fellow writers) was always shot through with the contrarian wish to "give up" literature at last.[11]

Actual Surrealists also appear in Bolaño's texts. In the short story "Last Evenings on Earth," Bolaño recounts a melancholy road trip to Acapulco with his father. The adolescent narrator, "B," spends most of his time reading and thinking about the minor surrealist poet Gui Rosey (1896–1981). Remarkably, it is not Gui Rosey's work that fascinates the young narrator (nor is the reader treated to any Gui Rosey quotes; in fact, the narrator admits he's not very interested in his poems), but rather the mystery of his disappearance. The young man imagines that Gui Rosey, fleeing Nazi-occupied France and finding himself stuck in Marseilles without a visa, committed suicide or vanished into a forged identity, when in fact the poet survived the war, moved to Switzerland, and continued publishing into the seventies. His collected poems were published by José Corti in 1963, and he produced a handful of works in collaboration with Man Ray and René Magritte. The choice of a minor poet whose life shows some loose ends and a degree of mystery points to the most constant structuring plot device in Bolaño's work: the protagonist's quest for a

[11] Bolaño, *2666*, 785; quoted in Monroe, *Framing Roberto Bolaño*, 191. This provides the title for his tenth chapter: "What a relief to give up literature" (173–197).

minor, dead, or disappeared writer, as many critics have noted. In *The Savage Detectives*, the protagonists embark on a search for the elusive poet Cesárea Tinajero; in *2666*, four European academics follow the trail of German writer Benno von Archimboldi; other narratives display the same fixation under various guises, the story pursuing a vanishing photographer ("Mauricio ('The Eye') Silva"), an elusive Belgian writer ("Vagabond in France and Belgium"), or a dying Spanish poet (*Monsieur Pain*).

In "Last Evenings on Earth," Gui Rosey's life itself, and the open-ended questions it raises, also takes the place of the "found object" of which the Surrealists were so fond. In addition, the obsessive device of the quest for a missing poet also defeats the rules of the well-constructed plot in favor of a looser episodic arrangement or stringing together of scenes. The search for a missing poet, then, is not only a structuring device used over and over throughout Bolaño's fiction: it also provides a serviceable image of a quest for the validation of narrative. The question of what happened to the poet echoes the more general question of the purpose of that individual life, and of life more generally.

Writing Lives

Marcel Schwob occupies an important intertextual place in Bolaño's work. Schwob is mentioned in Bolaño's late text, "Un paseo por la literatura," which takes the form of 57 ultra-brief, numbered prose poetic fragments narrating dream encounters with writers. In fragment 49, the fleeting vision of Marcel Schwob passing in a coach offers a fitting metatextual image of his presence in Bolaño's fictional universe. Many of Bolaño's narratives suggest the model of Schwob's *Imaginary Lives*, which were to become so influential for a generation of Latin American writers, most prominently Jorge Luis Borges. The book is a collection of brief lives of characters both historical and fictional. Famous artists (Uccello), writers (Petronius), princesses (Pocahontas), pirates (Captain Kidd) and criminals (Burke & Hare) are next to invented, obscure characters, such as the poor murdered prostitute "Katherine la Dentellière" (on whom more below).

As S. Jill Levine pointed out, many Latin American writers found in Marcel Schwob's short book a model that allowed them to pursue intertwined ideals of brevity and narratives focused on destiny. Two aesthetic principles stood out in Schwob's imaginary lives: the biographer's art is an "art of selection" (as Roger Caillois, friend and early translator of Borges, put it), and contrary to the historian's task, it requires imagination in the selection of historical episodes. Borges perfected this technique by condensing the life of his "infamous" heroes into a characteristically small number of pivotal episodes.[12] More recently, Cristian Crusat describes a Latin American lineage leading from Schwob to Alfonso Reyes, Borges, Bolaño and beyond.[13] Crusat's example of choice is the fictional anthology *Nazi Literature in America*, perhaps the most explicitly Borgesian of Bolaño's books, a collection of biographies of imaginary fascist writers across the American continent. Written exactly 100 years after Schwob's *Imaginary Lives*, it is arguably also the most clearly "Schwobian" of Bolaño's books (Crusat 2019, 249). These narratives reinvent both Schwob's artistically inclined criminals and Borges' lives of infamy, in which crime and depravity are ironically described in the grand register. Crime is treated in aesthetic terms: in Schwob's last story, "Mssrs. Burke and Hare, Assassins," which Borges hailed as the most accomplished), the body-snatchers' grisly murders are described as the refinements of an artistic pursuit. Similarly, Bolaño's Nazi writers think of themselves as literary geniuses when they are in fact nothing more than criminals.

Tracing its DNA to the ancient tradition of lives of famous men, as well as the Renaissance tradition of artists' lives, the modern fictional biography in the manner of Schwob claims the privilege of fiction by breaking free from the factual strictures of biography and history,[14] while also borrowing the art of brevity and striking detail from the late nineteenth-century genre of the prose poem. Such a mix would powerfully appeal to Borges and to his followers, among them Bolaño.

A Collection of Lives

Crusat hypothesizes that the foundational structure of Bolaño's novels is the collection of individual lives (257). In lieu of the more complex dramatic architecture on which nineteenth-century novels are built, the collection (or, later, the list) affords a simpler, looser pattern that sidesteps the requirement for a grand teleological construction or meaningful design. In this way, the longer texts of Bolaño would seem to solve two problems at once – on the one hand they allow him to write the novels required by the publishing world (Bolaño's rather flippant statement that he only

---

[12] Levine, "A universal tradition: the fictional biography," 24.
[13] Crusat quotes Bolaño's advice given in *Revista Quimera:* "lean a Marcel Schwob y de este pasen a Alfonso Reyes y de ahí a Borges" ("La tradición hispanoamericana de la 'vida imaginaria,'" 249).
[14] On the non-academic history of the genre, which both Borges and Bolaño would illustrate, see Crusat (2019, 248–249).

turned to writing novels in order to support his growing family),[15] but on the other hand, they also allow him to retain the compact, terse form of the short story, itself shot through with features of the prose poem, as has been observed. If the individual life story is the basic unit of the longer novel, it means that the structure can be of the simplest, most basic variety: the collection, or even less than the collection, the list of stories strung together.

Chris Andrews discusses the episodic feature at length in his study, connecting it among other things to the philosophical question of the meaning of life. Before returning to this key aspect of the episodic technique, it seems relevant to contextualize it within a French tradition honored by Bolaño, specifically, the works of Oulipian novelist Georges Perec (1936–1982). His best-known work, published shortly before his untimely death at the age of 45, is the large, heterogeneous, grab bag titled *Life, A User's Manual (La Vie mode d'emploi)*, subtitled "Romans" (novels), in plural. Perec remained a major figure in Bolaño's pantheon. The late collection of dream fragments mentioned earlier, *Un paseo por la literatura*, in which Schwob is seen passing in a coach, is framed by references to Perec in its opening and closing (first and fifty-seventh) fragments.

I will revisit the last dream later, since it speaks to key questions of writerly genealogy. First, I want to point out the connection that links Bolaño and Perec in terms of narrative structure. Perec's *Life, A User's Manual* speaks not only to Bolaño's preoccupation with the telling of lives, but also to the question of structuring a novel. Perec's "novels" center quite literally on a building (the fictional apartment building located at 11 rue Simon-Crubellier), with each of the chapters zeroing in on the inhabitants of the different apartments, their occupation at one precise point in time (June 23, 1975, shortly before 8 p.m.), their surroundings, their pasts, their stories. In this way, the book manages to be proliferating and infinite, yet also firmly anchored – or frozen – in one point both spatial and temporal. This principle of multiplicity-within-unity is also applied in a large number of the individual chapters where lists of things are numerous, from Madame Moreau's hardware catalogs to the recipes in her cookbook, the ports visited by the peripatetic Bartlebooth, the plagiarized bibliography produced by Dr. Lebran-Chastel, the luxury resorts designed by the tourist conglomerate Marvel Houses International, the junk accumulated in the Gratiolet basement over the years, the miniature scenes in the painter Valène's unfinished masterpiece, and so many more. The way in

---

[15] See Monroe (2020, 45) on Bolaño's bitterness at his lack of recognition as a poet.

which Bolaño's novel *2666* holds things together while allowing them also to fall apart is structurally analogous to Perec's apartment building solution. All the different lives narrated in the novel's "parts" converge on a geographical point, the fictional Mexican city of Santa Teresa. Bolaño's novels also make use of the list, a poetic device dear to Borges and Perec, as a way to suggest the infinite, unencompassable proliferation of life, for example the catalog of rebuses at the end of *The Savage Detectives*. Or the infinite proliferation of death, as the grisly "Part about the Crimes" chillingly reminds us.

Bolaño owes much to Perec, as his late text *Paseo* makes clear. Nevertheless, there are important differences between the two writers. Unlike Perec, Bolaño is not an Oulipian writer. Perec's sprawling narrative is held in place not just by the device of the single building and single point in time, but by an array of predetermined formal constraints ranging from the poetic (for example, each chapter must contain a specific number of items from 42 lists, such as a color, an activity, an emotion, painting, music, a literary quotation, etc., dictated by a mathematical algorithm) to the mathematical (for example, the sequencing of rooms-chapters is determined by a chess algorithm, the knight's tour, a formula that allows the knight to occupy all the squares in the chessboard only once). Perec's *Life* brings to a heightened level of complexity his earlier feat in *La Disparition (A Void)*, a novel entirely written without using the letter e. Naturally, characters in *Life* also live, create, and even die by the rule of formal constraint: Mme Moreau gives color-themed dinners, and the valet Smautf collects and arranges hotel labels, while his employer, the eccentric millionaire Percival Bartlebooth devotes his life to painting, then destroying his series of watercolor seascapes according to a monomaniacally precise prearranged plan.

However, contrary to Perec, for whom formal constraint is a major generating force of the creative process, and in whose narratives characters and episodes are not significant by themselves, but fit in a pre-arranged Oulipian structure that gives them meaning, Bolaño's individual lives are more haphazard, and their arrangement within the framework of the story more random. Despite his admiration for Perec, in his rewriting of Perec, Bolaño comes down strongly on the side of serendipity, and as such his world appears to be the product of a darker, more pessimistic outlook. And yet this too, perhaps, owes something to Perec, and to the inherent tension in Perec's fictional world between chance and constraint. Perec's own reflections on our attempts to order reality are developed in various essays, collected in *Penser/Classer, Espèces d'espaces,* or *Tentative d'épuisement d'un lieu parisien*: any organizational principle, ultimately, is as good as any other, suggesting the existential reversibility of order and disorder.[16] One character from *Life* sums up this tension particularly well: Smautf, Bartlebooth's valet, an obsessive collector of resort labels, who despairs of ever finding the perfect system for classifying his collection. Ultimately, any attempt to find order in the collection is deemed useless: "En laissant les étiquettes en vrac et en choisissant deux au hasard, on peut être sûr qu'elles auront toujours au moins trois points communs."[17] Constraint and chance, order and chaos, shape and shapelessness, meaning and meaninglessness, appear to be two sides of the same coin, set by Bolaño in Borgesian reversibility, albeit without Perec's signature playfulness.

Infra-ordinary and Visceral Realism

A combination of random occurrences, unexceptional lives and unremarkable narratives may not seem very promising from a literary point of view. Yet it links Bolaño to some of the most important contemporary French writers: in particular François Bon or Pierre Michon alongside Georges Perec. While these writers are formally and stylistically quite different from one another, they share an interest in the notion of the everyday, and the recording of daily activities: a certain take on the literary tradition of realistic fiction, on the reimagining of the notions of hero and the heroic, and on the place of documents in fiction. All these questions are refracted in turn in Bolaño's writing, anchoring it firmly in this widespread cultural trend.

Trained as a sociologist, Georges Perec, whose friendship with sociologist Henri Lefebvre was impactful in his early days as a writer, never lost his penchant for the recording of what he termed the "endotic" (the antonym of exotic) – or the "infra-ordinary" (the opposite of the extraordinary).[18] Chronicling in exhaustive detail the comings and goings of pedestrians, pigeons and vehicles and other micro-events on the Place Saint-Sulpice in central Paris, the short book *Tentative d'épuisement d'un lieu parisien* offers autobiographical evidence for such an interest in ordinariness for its own sake,[19] as does Perec's oddly impersonal memoir *Je me souviens* (I remember) with its focus on the shared and mundane memories, on the "petits morceaux de quotidien" (little pieces of everydayness: back cover) of a generation. Many of his fictional characters are similarly

---

[16] Alison James, *Constraining Chance*, 221–224.   [17] *La Vie mode d'emploi*, 56.
[18] Sheringham (2006, 250–251).   [19] Perec, *Tentative d'épuisement d'un lieu parisien*, 1995 [1975].

ordinary: the young couple, Jérôme and Sylvie, the unheroic heroes of his early novel *Les Choses,* hold degrees in sociology and land uneventful jobs polling consumers on their yoghurt preferences or their views on vacuum cleaners. Much of this infra-ordinary realism still informs the later novel *Life a User's Manual,* which can also be read as an example of "fictions of the daily" in seventies Paris. Perec's experimental interest in recording "ce qui se passe quand il ne se passe rien" (1995, 12), what goes on when there is nothing going on, carried over into the later novel *Life, A User's Manual.* Much of what goes on in the fictional building of the rue Simon-Crubellier is mundane, just as the lists of objects in the various rooms or found in the stairs over the years are ordinary, yet recorded in scrupulously exhaustive detail. Bolaño's "visceral realism" is close to this aesthetics of the everyday: the short story "Vagabond in France and Belgium" registers rundown hotels, small towns, the characters' clothes, a prostitute's wig, an old magazine, the young woman's apartment – all recorded by the eye of the passive yet meticulous protagonist, B.

Another representative of the factual turn in fiction is François Bon, whose narratives push against the boundary that traditionally separates fiction from reporting. Bon's texts – hybrids of journalism and novels – take to its limits the idea of literature as document. *Daewoo,* published in 2002, documents the closure of three Daewoo factories in the Lorraine region of Eastern France. The text combines elements of narrative, journalistic research, and actual or imagined interviews, that together testify to the real damage done to people caught in the multi-national economic squeeze. Much of the narrative is organized as a series of inquiries into the suicide of Sylvie, one of the factory workers left unemployed by the economic downturn. After the narrator visits her now-empty apartment, the book concludes with a re-affirmation of documentary transparency that takes precedence over the novelist's voice: "Et laisser toute question ouverte. Ne rien présenter que l'enquête" (and leave every question open. Present only the inquiry, nothing more).

Bolaño practiced a similar form of documentary writing in *2666:* his collaboration with journalist Sergio González Rodríguez,[20] whose inquiry into the serial femicides of Ciudad Juárez was published in 2002 as *Huesos en el desierto,* became the basis for the fourth section of the novel, "The Part about the Crimes," where the fictional account of the murders in Santa Teresa, except for changes in the names and a few particulars,

---

[20] See González Rodríguez's interview with Francesc Relea, "México se ha degradado completamente," *Babelia,* February 17, 2006.

follows very closely González Rodríguez's journalistic account, as Chris Andrews has demonstrated in his Appendix, which charts the real and fictional cases side by side.[21]

The stories of *Daewoo*, the female factory workers' broken lives, while they are heartbreakingly sad, are of course nowhere near the horrors endured by the Mexican factory workers, which are described with relentless brutality in Bolaño's *2666*. Yet they rely on a similar technique (the conflation of fiction and documentary nonfiction), and they raise similar questions, at the intersection of aesthetics and ethics. How engaged should the writer be? How should the account conclude? The formal question of the ending is intertwined with the ethical question of the writer's involvement. "This kind of story doesn't have an end," Bolaño's statement in his posthumous fragment "The Secret of Evil," reinforces the open-ended conclusion of the novel *2666*.[22] It also parallels François Bon's decision to leave questions open and let the inquiry speak for itself. At the end of *Daewoo*, we are not given a conclusion to the story of Sylvie, but we are left with another story: the discovery of celtic graves, exposed by construction of the TGV train tracks in the area, as if to put in very long perspective the story of human pain and death. A story that leaves a gap filled in part by another story: this is an apposite ending for a story without an ending, or a mystery without a solution, like the mystery of evil.

Minuscule Lives: The Biographical Imperative as Anti-teleology

The mundane life, the life lived by an unheroic, insignificant, unmemorable individual, is also the challenge taken up by Pierre Michon (born in 1945), another French writer admired by Bolaño.[23] Published in 1984, Michon's first novel, *Vies minuscules (Small Lives)*, propelled him to fame almost overnight, in ironic contradiction with the obscurity of the people his book attempted to resurrect. The gamble Michon set for himself was twofold: to write about his ancestors who had lived "small," inconsequential lives in an unremarkable area of rural France, and to redeem the insufficiency of those forgotten lives in his writing, precisely because they were so forgettable. The characters in *Small Lives* have little agency over their stories, which curtails opportunities and tethers them to an

---

[21] González Rodríguez is also a character in *2666*, further blending fiction and reality.
[22] Andrews (2014, 169–170).
[23] He refers to readers of Pierre Michon in *2666*, 136. The admiration was mutual: Michon praises Bolaño and Faulkner together: see Vila-Matas, "Decirlo Todo," *El País*, January 12, 2008.

unforgiving land and a stunted existence. Even those who try to leave fail: the opening story is devoted to André Dufourneau, whose attempt to seek fortune in colonial Africa ended in the void of an unexplained disappearance (although Michon chooses to go with the exotic fiction dreamed up by his grandmother, according to whom Dufourneau was murdered by angry Black employees.) Another son, in the third story, "Vies d'Eugène et de Clara," leaves the family home after a quarrel with his father and is never seen again, as wildly conflicting tales about his whereabouts and destiny, some infamous, others brilliant, all unverified, slowly eat away at his parents' sanity.

Bolaño's stories too are lost in the sand of forgetting, ignorance and indifference. People disappear never to be seen again, and in the case of the women of Santa Teresa, indifference to their fate is an active part of their inconsequential lives. Bleakness, smallness – both François Bon's unemployed factory workers and Pierre Michon's struggling farmers are one step beyond Georges Perec's infra-ordinary characters, and one step closer to the unrelenting sadness of Bolaño's life stories. What these stories have in common is a certain aimlessness, an anti-teleological principle undermining the storytelling. These lives, in their open-endedness, are non-destinies: in this too, Schwob provided a model, for alongside his famous poets and flamboyant pirates, he also made room for failed, minor lives, such as "Katherine la Dentellière" who falls into prostitution when lace-making can't support her, and ends up murdered in a ditch by a client.[24]

For all the resemblances, however, there are also key differences in the treatment of all these small lives. Michon's lyrical, glorious writing elevates his small people to a grand poetic level, sublimating their bleak lives by the beauty of poetry and the power of fiction that fills in the gaps of oblivion. Fabulation gives dignity, enhances the prosaic failures of these human lives, so much so that the book performs a grand ritual of anamnesis (Schwob 1993, 31).[25] In Perec's narratives, lives may be small or unaccomplished, but they are held together by the formal constraints that give them a place and a meaning in the novel's structure; Perec's empathetic, capacious fictional building, capable of accommodating "ordinary minds on an ordinary day,"[26] is itself a testimonial against destruction, oblivion, disappearance. And Bon's narrative, despite the serendipitous,

---

[24] Schwob, *Vies imaginaires*, 93.
[25] This is amplified even further in the almost mystical invocations at the book's conclusion (248–249).
[26] Virginia Woolf, "Modern Fiction," *The Common Reader*, 149.

unaccomplished character of life in *Daewoo*, emphasizes the human quality of the lives destroyed by the factory closure: the failure of these individual lives is entirely due to outside causes, not a tragic flaw or personal insufficiency. "Les visages et les voix [...] appellent le récit," Bon announces (*Daewoo*, 14): literature here works as a powerful symbolic compensation.

The theme of failure is potentially contained in the theme of small/ordinary lives. But Bolaño takes it to a brutal extreme. Deprived of aesthetic redemption, faced with a neutral, unemotional writing, a bluntly factual report of these small lives, the reader is unbuffered from the radical bitterness of Bolaño's world. In his characters' failure, there is no redeeming feature, just the unaccomplished potential of an existence losing itself in the sands of time. The mini-story of the nameless Salvadoran immigrant in *2666* is a case in point: he is entangled by chance in the series of femicides, wrongly jailed as a suspect, and his small life is destroyed in the process (392). In Bolaño's failed lives there is nothing exemplary, therefore no lesson to be learned. In contrast to what some critics (most recently Alexandre Gefen) have analyzed as a (conflicted) return to exemplarity in contemporary literature, Bolaño's characters seem rather buffeted by chance, their failures serendipitous and unredeemed: they are "personnages ballottés dans l'insignifiance,"[27] who could make theirs the nameless character's nihilistic self-assessment in Beckett's *Texts for Nothing*: "no need of a story, a story is not compulsory, just a life, that's the mistake I made, one of the mistakes, to have wanted a story for myself, whereas life alone is enough."[28]

Not a story, just a life: Chris Andrews has commented extensively on the aimlessness of so many of Bolaño's characters, on their drifting, unstructured lives. Bolaño's characters, he observes, "are rarely inclined to fashion selves through storytelling or to live their lives in a narrative mode" (Chris Andrews, *Roberto Bolaño's Fiction: An Expanding Universe*, 2014, 95), adding that "Bolaño has a marked preference for drifting, discontinuous, and inconclusive narrative forms" (100). Bolaño's short stories exacerbate the anti-teleological drift: "Anne Moore's Life" is an unfinished story about a woman who drifts aimlessly from one failed relationship to the next. The epitome of an episodic, deconstructed narrative, it is "deeply sad" (Andrews 2014, 104), "a way of living

---

[27] Catherine Grall, "Rhétorique des fictions brèves: quid de la tradition exemplaire?" in A. Gefen, ed., *Littérature et exemplarité*, 270.

[28] Beckett, *Stories and Texts for Nothing*, Text #4.

episodically that is intrinsically dysphoric" (105). "Mauricio ('The Eye') Silva" is similarly meandering, dysphoric and open-ended; Silva's wanderings through India and Europe, the death of his adopted children, leave him sobbing in the night, without providing him or us with any kind of closure, narrative or emotional. Similarly, the protagonist B's quest for the dead writer Henri Lefebvre in "Vagabond in France and Belgium" leads nowhere, and the story is suspended, not concluded. Bolaño's protagonists tend to grapple with failed quests, unresolved efforts, life in the margins; they seem metatextually to verify Lotte's description of her brother Archimboldi's writing: "The writing was clear and sometimes even transparent, but the way the stories followed one after another didn't lead anywhere" (*2666*, 887).

Sad Flesh

Amputated of their teleological energy, the stories are set adrift; whether that comes from Bolaño's rejection of a fictional convention or because the protagonists tend to be products of exile and rootlessness, rather like Bolaño himself (Andrews 2014, 100). Perhaps there is another cause: illness. Illness is the chance event that tends to cut short a life, providing an abrupt ending in lieu of a conclusion. It also opposes a brutal denial to the teleological attempt to fashion a story out of a life. With the exception of Michon and Bon, the French writers Bolaño admired and emulated (Baudelaire, Rimbaud, Schwob, Perec – along with Kafka and César Vallejo, of course)[29] were all affected by illness that brought them untimely death and consigned them to a posthumous destiny. Bolaño's deathbed essay, "Illness + Literature = Illness," engages deeply with French poets, beginning with Mallarmé's melancholy sonnet on the sadness of all flesh, which he interprets as a poem about illness ("Yo creo que Mallarmé está hablando de la enfermedad"). Meditating on Baudelaire's well-known poem "Le Voyage," which equates life with a voyage toward death, Bolaño adds a third term, illness.[30] As a third term, illness ensures the merging of life and writing: the essay ends with a meditative paragraph on Kafka, who understood when he began coughing blood that henceforth nothing separated him from his writing. This of course is even more

---

[29] See Monroe's chapter on "Poetry as Symptom and Cure" in *Framing Roberto Bolaño*, 36–49: *Monsieur Pain* is a pivotal novel in Bolaño's oeuvre; it focuses on the search for a dying César Vallejo in Paris, 1938, by a protagonist named "pain," who is ill himself.
[30] Baudelaire, "Le Voyage," *Les Fleurs du mal*, 169–177. The powerful line "Une oasis d'horreur dans un désert d'ennui" (section vii, p. 176) was used as an epigraph to *2666*.

applicable to Bolaño himself, whose literary output increased dramatically in the last ten years of his short life, when he knew he was racing against death, and the awareness of illness revealed the convergence of life and writing as the only road left to him.

Perhaps we could be justified in contextualizing Bolaño's work in the twenty-first-century literature that attempts to "heal the world," according to Alexandre Gefen, who mentions Pierre Michon and François Bon as examples of the "therapeutic paradigm" (spiritual as much as medical) of contemporary literature.[31] If Bolaño's fiction can be said to be healing, it is only with the understanding that it strips us from any complacency or delusion about its powers to heal or even to achieve teleological wholeness, instead offering harsh uncertainty, just as Monsieur Pain feels insecure about his ability to cure Vallejo, "the poet-patient whose illness can't be cured" (Monroe, *Framing Roberto Bolaño*, 2020, 47). Returning to Bolaño's *Paseo por la literatura*, we find that it ends as it began, with a dream encounter in which Bolaño, comforting a sobbing Perec, rewrites the dream-memory Perec recounts of himself at the age of three, in his autobiography *W ou le souvenir d'enfance*, surrounded by loving adults who praise him for having correctly identified a Hebrew letter in a newspaper.[32] No matter that it is most likely a fantasy or a fake memory, as Perec subsequently tells us: it is a myth of origin for the orphaned child of the Shoah, and a validation of his destiny as a writer. Reversing the genealogy and the direction of influence, Bolaño's dream makes him a "precursor," in a Borgesian sense, of Perec: vowing to protect him, to take him "home." And yet what begins as a scene of comfort and healing abandons the reader with a characteristically abrupt reversal that leaves us stranded in unknown territory – "¿Pero dónde estaba nuestra casa?" the final sentence asks; where are these two souls going, who have no more home?

How can writing heal anyone?[33] The essay's stark title (Illness + Literature = Illness) seems to eliminate literature from the equation and bluntly deny its healing powers. As we reread Bolaño, a sick writer, in the context of today's global pandemic, we may wish to revisit Alexander

---

[31] *Réparer le monde. La littérature française face au XXIe siècle* (Paris: Editions Corti, 2017).
[32] Perec (1975, 22–23).
[33] Perhaps Bolaño is torn between his belonging in a vast contemporary movement that aligns literature with a healing project, and his contrary allegiance to a more "ascetic" and "autotelic" paradigm inherited from Roland Barthes, one of Bolaño's most important formative influences: "savoir que l'écriture ne compense rien, ne sublime rien [...] c'est le commencement de l'écriture" (*Le Discours amoureux*, quoted by Gefen, *Réparer le monde*, 163.

Beecroft's "plot of globalization," born of 1989 (the end of the Cold War) and 9/11 (the iconic symptom of globalized terrorism.) Those were cardinal points in Bolaño's fictional world. It is tempting to wonder what the writer, whose life was cut short and whose work was shaped by disease, would have made of Covid-19, had he been fortunate to survive his liver disease and live until 2019, when a pandemic, born of a hyperglobalized world, put an end to our fluid, transnational, globalized life.

CHAPTER 14

German and Russian Precursors

Thomas O. Beebee

German and Russian authors both appear with regularity in the world literary constellations that form in the texts by Roberto Bolaño. There is, however a fundamental difference in the two repertoires: most Russian authors mentioned or alluded to in the work are recognized names in world literature read and appreciated by non-specialists, whereas his chosen German authors can be more recondite, i.e., confined to the knowledge of Germanists, and at times are even obscure within that field. Georg Trakl's role in *2666* is one example, as is the appearance of Thea von Harbou in *El espíritu de la ciencia-ficción*. A more extreme example is when Udo, the narrator of *El Tercer Reich*, discovers German literature through gaming and his friend Conrad, whose literary choices include Karl Bröger's *Soldaten der Erde* (Soldiers of the Earth) and *Bunker 17*, *Hammerschläge* (Hammer-Blows) and *Mensch im Eisen* (Men in Iron) by Heinrich Lersch, Max Barthel's *Das vergitterte Land* (Country Behind Bars), and Gerrit Engelke's *Rhythmus des neuen Europa* (Rhythm of the New Europe). Amazingly, these are all genuine authors active in the 1920s and 1930s, who came out of the working class, and their writing frequently involves experience of WWI. Conrad recites the names of 200 German authors from memory, and readers are left to imagine what other forgotten "gems" of German literature might lurk in his mind (*El Tercer Reich*, 48; *The Third Reich*, 30). Conrad especially likes Goethe and Ernst Jünger, the latter of whom makes an appearance as a character in *Nocturno de Chile* (see discussion below). Later, he makes a comparison between authors and generals: "Si el Quemado supiera y apreciara algo la literatura alemana de este siglo (y es probable que sepa y que la aprecie!) le diría que Manstein es comparable a Gunther Grass y que Rommel es comparable a ... Celan. De igual manera Paulus es comparable a Trakl y su predecessor, Reichenau, a Heinrich Hann [sic]. Guderian es el par de Jünger y Kluge de Böll. No lo entendería" ("If Quemado had the slightest knowledge or appreciation of twentieth-century German literature (and it's likely that he does!) – then

German and Russian Precursors 159

I would tell him that Manstein is like . . . Celan. And Paulus is like Trakl, and his predecessor, Reichenau, is like Heinrich Mann. Guderian is the equivalent of Jünger, and Kluge of Böll" [216]). It is not clear whether we understand it, either – or whether we accept the asymmetrical set of analogies – which have been altered somewhat in the published English translation. Later, Udo claims that if he came to know El Quemado's love for poetry, he would stop playing the war game with him. But El Quemado can't remember any verses. Udo confesses his fondness for Goethe (291).

In Bolaño's collection of short pieces *Between Parentheses*, the overwhelming number of mentions go to Spanish language authors. However, some comments on German and Russian writers are very powerful. He says of Lichtenberg that he is "our philosopher" (144–145). He writes admiringly of Günter Grass (169–170). Among the less obvious choices is Max Beerbohm (175). On the Russian side, a lesser-known novel by Turgenev provided an obsession through early adulthood (182–184). He confesses to wanting "to buy all the books by Tolstoy and Dostoevsky that I've read but don't own" and that while he has lost the copy of *Crime and Punishment* that he read as a teenager, "I couldn't lose Raskolnikov even if I wanted to" (238). And he ranks Chekhov with Raymond Carver as having written the best short stories of the twentieth century (351). We see that the Russian names all belong to the pantheon of world literature, as compared to a forgotten German author such as Beerbohm. The unevenness of selection concerning German authors exerts its influence on the structure and content of Bolaño's narratives, such as in the litany of obscure pre-1933 authors read by Udo in *El tercer Reich*, as mentioned above. Or, Thea von Harbou, author of the screenplay of Metropolis, appears in a dream to one of the protagonists of *El espíritu de la ciencia-ficción*, as though she were the muse of science fiction (*El espíritu*, 63–67). Yet she only inspires a retelling of the plot of a novel by Gene Wolfe. Harbou, who wrote the screenplay for *Metropolis* and other films by Fritz Lang, unlike her husband, remained in Germany after 1933 and joined the Nazi party. The section ends with a contra-historical account of tank commander Heinz Guderian taking Moscow instead of failing to, as of course happened in actuality. This links the novel with *The Third Reich*, where war games are the platforms for counter-narratives, and to *Nazi Literature in the Americas*.

There are, of course, examples of the tendency being reversed: the German-Czech Franz Kafka makes appearances throughout Bolaño's work; and the genuine Russian authors Vladimir Odoevsky (1803–1869) and Ivan Lazhechnikov (1792–1869) are cited as equal contributors to the science fiction of the invented author Efraim Ivanov in *2666* (711). Furthermore, the two literatures merge in the final chapter of *2666*, where a German, Hans Reiter, derives literary inspiration from the diary of a Russian Jew, Boris Abramovich Ansky. Furthermore, it is no accident that the German Reiter fulfills the function of an author of world literature, having been both personal and vicarious witness to and participant in the most terrible tragedies of the twentieth century.

In the last interview he gave in his life, Bolaño was asked by Monica Maristain to name the books that had "marked your life" (Maristain, 118). Along with works in Spanish, English, French, and Latin, he also named Franz Kafka's novels, the Aphorisms of Lichtenberg, and the *Tractatus* by Wittgenstein. This troika can be sighted throughout Bolaño's work. In his monograph on Bolaño, Alberto Bejarano supplements it with an imaginary library (Biblioteca Ideal), in which he includes Chekhov's *Cherry Orchard*, Kafka's *Amerika*, Friedrich Nietzsche's *Thus Spake Zarathustra*, and B. Traven's *The White Rose* (Bejarano, 2018, 210–211). Traven is perhaps the twentieth-century author about whom the least biographical information has been found, and given that the prevailing theory of his origins has him born in Germany, though he lived most of his life in Mexico, his reclusive profile is quite possibly a model for the character of Reiter.

Bolaño's admiration for Georg Christoph Lichtenberg (1742–1799) was deep-rooted. Eyewitness accounts of the former's visit to Göttingen report his running up to embrace the statue of the scientist-author in the main square. Undoubtedly, the quirkiness and undefinable nature of Lichtenberg's writings intrigued Bolaño. The former's *Sudelbücher* (Scrapbooks) alternate between philosophical, scientific, and moral topics. He is considered the founder of the German aphoristic tradition, and is famous for declaring that one should say "es denkt" (there is thinking going on) just as one says "es blitzt" (lightning is striking). He wrote humorous pieces such as a letter from the earth to the moon, and a speech by the number eight given before the Great Council of Numbers. But Bolaño devotes the most words to a relatively unknown retelling of a dream by the German, in which he finds himself at an inn where people are playing at dice, and he asks a woman whether anything is to be won at the game, and then whether anything can be lost. She answers both questions in the negative. "Dieses hielt ich für ein wichtiges Spiel" (*Gedanken*, 42; "This struck me as an important game"). Bolaño quotes in full the diary entry, the last made by Lichtenberg shortly before his death, and opines that it "foreshadows Kafka and much of twentieth-century literature. It also sums up the Enlightenment, and upon it a culture could be founded" (*Between Parentheses*, 145). Finally, Bolaño notes that when death had visited Lichtenberg a fortnight before his demise, he had responded with humor and curiosity. However, Bolaño may also have been attracted more to an aside by Lichtenberg in the middle of this dream, that no novelist would have come up with the idea that presented itself to him in his sleep. Kafka was the novelist who learned to write the way Lichtenberg dreamt. And the game of great importance, even though nothing can be either won or lost – or more precisely, *because* nothing can be either won or lost, can serve as analogy for Bolaño's view of literature as structured contingency.

I have been unable to discover how much Bolaño knew of so-called "Lichtenberg figures," which are forerunners of fractal geometry and hence, of chaos theory, but they could serve as maps of the structures for his longer narratives, that seem to be governed equally by a rigid determinism, say of the triumph of evil or of the rules of art, and by successive aleatory arrangements, such as the various alliances and rivalries of the four Archimboldi critics in *2666*, the successive geometrical arrangements of philosophers drawn by Amalfitano in the same novel, the cascade of witness statements on Arturo Belano in *The Savage Detectives*, or the order of entries in the encyclopedia-like *Nazi Literature in the Americas*.

Or also the connection that the Austrian poet Georg Trakl (1887–1914) provides between Amalfitano, the rector's son Marco Antonio Guerra, and the unnamed young pharmacist in Barcelona. Amalfitano asks both about their reading habits (*2666*, 288–290 [226–27]). Guerra responds that only poetry is worthwhile, and that Trakl is one of his favorites. This reminds Amalfitano of the time when he asked a young pharmacist in Barcelona what books he was reading, receiving the titles of four novellas as an answer: Kafka's *Metamorphosis*; Flaubert's *A Simple Heart*; Dickens' *Christmas Carol*; and Melville's *Bartleby the Scrivener*. Amalfitano senses this as a failing of the young man's going for the small but perfect as opposed to the volcanic, imperfect longer works of each author: Kafka's unfinished novel *The Trial* is mentioned. It could have been different, muses Amalfitano: "resultaba revelador el gusto de este joven farmacéutico ilustrado, que tal vez en otra vida fue Trakl o que tal vez en ésta aún le estaba deparado escribir poemas tan desesperados como su lejano colega austriaco, que prefería claramente, sin discusión, la obra menor a la obra mayor" (*2666*, 289; "there was something revelatory about the taste of this bookish young pharmacist, who in another life might have been Trakl or who in this life might still be writing poems as desperate as those of his distant Austrian counterpart, and who clearly and inarguably preferred minor works to major ones" [227]). Georg Trakl was trained as a pharmacist, which gave him easier access to the drugs that he became addicted to. His addiction and his suicide after witnessing the suffering of the wounded at the outbreak of WWI link him in turn to Guerra, who has connections to the drug cartels of Santa Teresa and who introduces Amalfitano to the mezcal Los Suicidas (The Suicides). A triangular relationship is established between minor-but-perfect prose works, major-but-flawed prose works, and the poetry of suicide. We will see that other combinations are possible as well, such as torrential works of imperfect masters (e.g., Ernst Jünger).

Kafka also figures prominently in the posthumous collection of Bolaño writings, *El gaucho insufrible* (*The Insufferable Gaucho*). The book's epigraph is taken from the Czech writer's last story, "Josefine die Sängerin" ("Josephine the Singer") which is also used as a prequel for one of the collection's longer stories, amplifying a bit of Kafka, much the way, for example, that the novella *Amuleto* expands a small portion of *Los detectives salvajes*. In the Lichtenberg-like pieces that comprise "The Myths of Cthulhu," Bolano writes: "when we talk about Kafka (may God forgive me), it's less about Kafka and the fire than a lady or a gentleman at a window" (*Insufferable*, 151).

As much as with Kafka, it is easy to see the necessity of Lev Tolstoy and Fyodor Dostoevsky as precursors for Bolaño's novelistic achievements – as they are for most of the great novelists of the past century, at least. One wonders about the absence of Nikolai Gogol, who contributed an oneiric, satirical prose style that is closer to the atmosphere of *2666* than is the deadly seriousness of *War and Peace* or *Crime and Punishment*. Indeed, readers might think of the listing of the murdered women in the fourth part of Bolaño's novel as an updated version of the list of deceased serfs acquired by Pavel Chichikov as he careens across Russia in Gogol's masterpiece, *Dead Souls*. However, there is no more fitting precedent for a narrative like *2666* that tells stories of geopolitics through the fates of individual characters, thus combining history with fiction, than Tolstoy's *War and Peace*. Dostoevsky, on the other hand, helped shape the polyphonic form wherein characters are vehicles for intense intellectual exchange and conflict, as seen in *2666*, *The Savage Detectives*, and other fiction by Bolaño.

Bolaño spends more words on Turgenev than on either Tolstoy or Dostoevsky, but his remarks in the piece titled "A Novel by Turgenev" in *Between Parentheses* simply give a plot summary of the former's first and least-read novel, *Rudin* (1856). While inferior in quality, the novel established Turgenev's repertoire of characters: the "blocked" intellectual protagonist loved by the impetuous, enlightened female. In the case of Rudin, the eponymous tutor turns down elopement with his pupil, the daughter of a landowner employer, then suffers psychologically from his choice, and finally expiates his failure to act by exposing himself to fatal gunfire on a Paris barricade in 1848. Bolaño's remark on the novel is that "Turgenev suggests to us that not only has [Rudin] found courage but also the burning bridge that links words and acts" (*Between Parentheses*, 184). Certainly, the linkage between words and acts, between literature and life – or the absence thereof – is one of the central themes in Bolaño's work.

"Police Rat" ("El policía de las ratas") one of the longer stories in the collection *The Insufferable Gaucho*, and the last story Bolaño wrote, is as mentioned explicitly indebted to one of Kafka's most famous stories, "Josefine die Sängerin" (Josephine the Singer). Whereas Kafka's story is relatively plotless, however, Bolaño adds to his sequel elements of the police procedural, derived mostly from the Anglo-American tradition. (Of course, Kafka's unfinished novel *The Trial* could be thought of as a similar deformation of the genre.) In choosing to parody "Josephine" rather than *The Trial*, Bolaño mimics the preferences of the young pharmacist in 2666, which Amalfitano judges harshly, as we have seen above. The story literalizes its metaphoric title: its first-person narrator is Pepe the Cop, who soon reveals himself to be a nephew of Kafka's character:

> One of [the rat community] at least, and maybe the others as well, already knew that I was one of Josephine the Singer's nephews, although they were careful not to go spreading it around. My brothers and cousins – the other nephews – were normal in every way, and happy. I was happy too, in my way, but it was obvious that I was related to Josephine, that I belonged to her line. (*The Insufferable Gaucho*, 46)

Pepe the Cop is a sewer rat, and the story follows him as he investigates the murder of an adult and tracks a missing child, finds the corpses in a dead sewer, and eventually determines that another rat is the killer, despite the widespread belief that "rats don't kill rats." He then personally confronts the murderer, Héctor, and kills him in hand-to-hand combat. The judge who investigates Pepe's culpability remarks that she, too, had once heard Josephine sing, before absolving the rat policeman of guilt.

Bolaño's story thus proves the truth of his epigraph for the collection that is drawn from the same story by Kafka, a sentence rendered in the

English translation as "So perhaps we shall not miss so much after all" (*Insufferable*, 2) a fairly close translation of Kafka's original German: "Vielleicht werden wir also gar nicht sehr viel entbehren." We need to understand "miss" as "do without" rather than as longing for an absent thing or person (nor as "missing the mark"). (The Spanish translation that serves as the epigraph to Bolaño's original uses the verb "perder," meaning "not much will be lost.") The phrase occurs almost at the end of Kafka's narrative, and the words are followed by an image of Josephine joining the gallery of mouse-heroes, who are consigned to being forgotten. As Bolaño noted, Josephine's singing – frequently interpreted as Kafka's metaphor for his own writing – is thus predicted by Lichtenberg's dream as a very important game where nothing can be either lost or won. Oddly, this is contradicted in Bolaño's story, where the memory of Josephine has been strongly preserved, giving truth to the epigraph that little has in fact gone missing. In Kafka's story, the phrase refers to the non-special qualities of the title figure's art. Indeed, the text begins by contradicting its own title: Josefine's performances can't be called singing, but piping (or whistling). Furthermore, piping requires no special effort for mice, but rather is something each of them can perform quite naturally. The text goes on to confirm its subtitle: "Or, the Mouse Folk." That is, Josefine's art is shown as a creation of her audience. The story may have thus inspired Bolaño's predilection for combining intense and thorough examination of authorial networks and political affiliations with complete non-disclosure of the works themselves. We never read a poem by Arturo Belano or an excerpt of one of Archimboldi's novels.

Brett Levinson locates the confluence of these two stories, of Josephine and Pepe, in the Heideggerian/Adornian reduction of language to "communication," i.e., of singing to piping, at which point a folk ceases to be a folk and becomes raw biological life:

> Pepe, the tyrant or *tira*, especially given the immunity that he receives, embodies the new sovereign: balance, evenness, not too much of anything. This is not the state sovereign, the sovereign of dictatorship. It is the sovereign of the market, of the neutral, of a piping that, as long as it remains, as long as it saves, represents, and polices natural life or biopolitical existence, cannot be judged, condemned, or touched. Without wrong, it is also without justice. (Levinson, 107–108)

In *2666* and other late work, Bolaño continues his theme of the political positioning of literature and the political responsibility of writers and intellectuals. The first chapter of *2666* focuses on the interactions of four literary critics, each from a different European nation, who are brought together by their passion for the writing of the reclusive German, Archimboldi. They fly to Mexico on the rumor that Archimboldi had traveled there, a hunch that turns out to be correct, though they miss meeting up with their literary idol. He had been in Mexico to help his nephew, who is imprisoned on suspicion of committing the femicides of Santa Teresa. This mass slaughter resonates symbolically with that of World Wars I and II that form the backdrop of the fifth chapter, Reiter's life story. Reiter is born to a father who lost his leg in the first war, and is drafted to fight in the second, where he encounters through another character's diary a Russian writer of science fiction, Efraim Ivanov, whose rise and fall seem a composite of writers and thinkers of these years. Ivanov is an enthusiastic communist, enjoys popular success, and then begins to fall out of favor with the regime, a decline ending with his imprisonment and execution. Reiter's trajectory is the opposite: writing seems to be an accident with him, one more attempt at useful employment, starting with rejections and gradually working up to a kind of cult popularity. Bolaño brings together two literary genres in this fictional biography: the European *Künstlerroman* (literally, "artist novel," a Bildungsroman focused on an artist, writer, or musician, as for example Thomas Mann's *Doktor Faustus* that centers on the composer Adrian Leverkühn); and the picaresque narrative, for which the best-known examples are from Spain and Spanish America, but for which German literature also furnishes examples, from Hans Jakob Grimmelshausen's *Der abenteuerliche Simplicissimus* (1689; Simplicius Simplicissimus) to Thomas Mann's *Bekenntnisse des Hochstaplers Felix Krull* (Confessions of the Confidence-Man Felix Krull), published posthumously in 1954.

As in Bolano's other work, very little actual content of Archimboldi's (or Ivanov's) writing is revealed, beyond the titles of their novels. The first and fifth chapters balance each other in interesting ways. For example, the complete lack of biographical detail that causes the four critics to go to extraordinary lengths to catch a glimpse of Archimboldi contrasts with the overabundance of it in the fifth chapter, which readers of 2666 are no doubt eager to apply to an interpretation of the works, whose content and texture are however kept from them. Indeed, the Hans Reiter chapter could be considered a parody of the *Künstlerroman*. We follow Reiter's entire life in some detail, including his favorite literary readings, the medieval epic *Parzifal* and the novels of Alfred Döblin (his taste for the latter providing a fortuitous link with Ansky, who reads the German author's works in a Moscow library). Yet ultimately, since the work itself remains hidden, we have nothing to connect those details to. The text we are asked to read is the life that encompasses the catastrophes of the twentieth century, and, as always in Bolaño, the position of the writer vis-à-vis other writers, his readership, and society in general. Juan Carlos Galdo suggests Günter Grass as the authorial model for Reiter, since Bolaño had specifically discussed a work of Grass' called *My Century*, published appropriately in 1999, the same year that Grass won the Nobel Prize. "Like the Nobel prizewinner, Archimboldi is a privileged eyewitness of his epoch and its horrors" (Galdo 2005, 32). Like Reiter, Grass fought in WWII. But as mentioned above, Reiter's reclusivity reminds us more of B. Traven. Certainly, Reiter is a composite figure with the traits of several authors. Since his novels lack popularity and are of interest to professional critics, we make certain assumptions about their relative difficulty and sophistication, but we can say nothing about their themes or genre. Conceivably, they could all be variants of the police procedural, as much of Bolaño's narrative work is. Above all, the degree to which aspects of Reiter's own biography appear in the fictions he writes remains unknown.

Reiter's influences are addressed specifically at one point. He divides literature into three "compartments": "in the first were the books he read and reread and considered magnificent and sometimes monstrous, like the fiction of Döblin, who was still one of his favorite authors, or Kafka's complete works. In the second compartment were the books of the epigones and authors he called the Horde, whom he essentially saw as his enemies. In the third compartment were his own books and his plans for future books, which he saw as a game and also a business, a game insofar as he derived pleasure from writing, a pleasure similar to that of the detective on the heels of the killer, and a business insofar as the publication of his books helped to augment, however modestly, his 'doorman's pay'" (*2666*, 817). Once again, Lichtenberg's game receives mention as the model for the literary enterprise in the twentieth century.

Soldier-author Ernst Jünger (1895–1998) also fought in WWII (and in WWI), and could also have contributed characteristics to the figure of Reiter. However, no work by Jünger is named by Bolaño as having been influential on his development as a writer, nor even as having engaged his emotions or interest. Indeed, Jünger appears in the novella *Nocturno de Chile* (By Night in Chile) as a kind of progenitor who allows the Nazi writers of America to flourish. The novel's protagonist and narrator, Urrutia Lacroix, a sympathizer with the dictatorship of Augusto Pinochet, has a vision of the German writer crashing in the Andes in a spaceship, and with his body preserved indefinitely by the snows à la

Lenin's Tomb, "que la escritura de los héroes y, por extension, los amanuenses de la escritura de los heroes, eran en sí mismos un canto, un canto de alabanza a Dios y la civilización" (*Nocturno de Chile*, 51; "the writings of the heroes together with the scribes who serve those writings would compose a hymn to the glory of God and civilization" [*By Night in Chile*, 38]). We can imagine that Bolaño encountered Jünger the same way that Urrutia does: through the praise of the German by Salvador Reyes Figueroa, author and Chilean consul in Paris during the German occupation: "don Salvador dijo que uno de los hombres más puros que había conocido en Europa era el escritor alemán Ernst Jünger" (*Nocturno de Chile*, 37; "Don Salvador said that one of the purest men he had met in Europe was the German writer Ernst Jünger" [*By Night in Chile*, 26]). "Pure" accords with a prevalent critical view of Jünger as well as with his self-assessment, as a writer who is scientific and who observes, without committing himself. While serving in Paris with the Wehrmacht, Jünger became acquainted with numerous literary figures, as detailed in his memoirs, titled *Strahlungen*, published in 1949. There, he mentions briefly but positively a novel by Salvador Reyes. So, there is a mutual admiration society and cabal between writers, both of whom use writing, as Urrutia does, as an ancillary to political power, and whose commitment to writing erases differences in language, culture, and politics. Urrutia happily joins the cabal, as he praises Reyes to the skies for being the only Chilean author thought by Jünger to be worthy of mention: "Not a single Chilean exists, as a human being or as the author of a book, in the dark, rich years of Jünger's chronicle, except for Don Salvador Reyes" (*By Night in Chile*, 38). His retelling of Salvador Reyes's account of an encounter in Paris between himself, a Guatemalan painter, and Jünger takes up considerable space in his memoir (25–39). Urrutia cries out in the Chilean wilderness, his screams directed at the uncultured readers of Chile, who are asked to improve themselves by assembling around them the art styles and artists of all ages, so that they may give names to them as Adam did to the beasts. Yet this look outward, this compiling of the monuments of world literature, directs the gaze away from what is right in front of everyone – or at least right beneath their feet in the torture dungeons of the Pinochet regime. The splendor of Urrutia's vision of world literature that he proclaims in the Chilean wilderness is produced out of his need to ignore the brutal reality of the dictatorship and the social inequalities it protects.

An interesting question with all the explicit references to German and Russian authors in Bolaño's work is whether they cover up deeper, unstated influences. Jonathan Monroe has argued that in its diary form, the novel *El tercer Reich*, for example, parodies *The Sorrows of Young Werther* (1774) by Johann Wolfgang von Goethe, with Udo Berger's enthusiasm for gaming replacing Werther's for nature and poetry (Monroe, 52). Bolaño explicitly mentions another Goethe novel, *The Elective Affinities*, as a kind of anti-story to the carnal love associated with prison or with illness (*Between Parentheses*, 128). There is evidence that Friedrich Nietzsche was not far from Bolaño's mind as he was writing *By Night in Chile*:

> In *By Night in Chile* what interested me was the Catholic priest's lack of guilt. The admirable aplomb of a man who due to his intellectual background ought to feel the burden of guilt. I believe that guilt, the feeling of guilt for the things one does, is one of the good aspects of the Catholic religion. I've always considered the idea of a man without guilt as a pseudo-Dionysian elucubration. In this sense, I am, of course, completely opposed to Nietzsche. (Aussenac, "Interview" 41)

Resistance is another form of influence, and the puffing of certain German and Russian writers by unsympathetic or ambiguous characters in Bolaño's work can implicitly function as critique, as is the case with Urrutia's enthusiasm for Ernst Jünger. On the other hand, however, the collaboration of Ansky and Reiter to create the "great writer" Archimboldi shows how seriously Bolaño took these two literary traditions.

CHAPTER 15

After the Two 9/11s: Santiago, 1973, New York, 2001

Nicholas Birns

Urrutia versus the Future

Whatever reasons the al-Qa'eda terrorists who attacked the World trade Center and the Pentagon on September 11, 2001 had for picking their date, we may plausibly exclude from consideration commemorating the anniversary of the overthrow of Chile's elected president, Salvador Allende Gossens, by an illegal military coup led by the general Allende had mistakenly trusted to respect democracy, Augusto Pinochet Ugarte.[1] Yet the coincidence between these two dates was almost immediately noted. Ariel Dorfman has wondered if "there is some sort of meaning hidden behind or inside the coincidence."[2] Dorfman stresses the contrast between an event in which the United States was the victim to one where it was a perpetrator. The Chilean novelist Carla Guelfenbein, in her 2013 novel *Nadar desnudas*, traces the fissures along the path from the creative optimism of the Allende era and the terror and warfare of the word in the early 2000s. But for Roberto Bolaño, the two 9/11s mark the boundaries of a career as a writer, and the political and temporal horizon in which he thought and worked.

Bolaño said that in 1973, "I lived through the Chilean 9/11, suffered through it, and, since I was twenty years old, enjoyed it, too," and in 2001, he was in Milan with his wife and children. And was reminded "of the images we had in the eighties of World War III" – of a war which never happened, but whose imagined violence was realized in a different, unforeseeable-from-then event.[3] Instead of the counterfactual wargame histories of World War II portrayed in *The Third Reich*, we have counterfactual wargame imaginings of a World War III between the US and the USSR

---

[1] This essay is dedicated to the memory of Gabriel Valdés Subercaseaux.
[2] Ariel Dorfman, "Epitaph for Another September 11," *The Nation*, September 10, 2011, 17–18.
[3] Quoted in Natasha Wimmer, "Introduction," Roberto Bolaño, *The Savage Detectives*, tr. Natasha WImmer (New York: Picador, 2008), xxi.

playing out in a different world, when the US, as hyperpower, is at war only with itself, with people who were living in America when they attacked it or with reverberations of American military strategy that bounced back against it in recursive irony.

The two 9/11s themselves are recursive. The trial of the now-aging and disempowered Pinochet in Spain for human rights abuses was heavily featured in world news in the first half of 2001, only to fade in the aftermath of the traumatic events of the second. The World Trade Center itself opened in April 1973, just five months before the coup. Its life and death dates, 1973–2001, encompass the two 9/11s.

Whether or not Roberto Bolaño in biographical terms was in Chile in September 1973 – and the language used of Arturo Belano in *The Savage Detectives*, "he had presented himself as a volunteer on September 11" is suggestive – his oeuvre takes place after that event (201). In a posthumously published interview, Bolaño says that at first he was disappointed by Allende, when he knew he was doomed, urging Chileans not to resist but to recognize the coup had happened, that his life was over, and to hope for a better future. At the time, he saw this gesture as defeatist and futile; by the end of his life, Bolaño respected Allende's altruism, his looking towards the future. Similarly, in the two Chilean novels Bolaño uses the *Nachträglichkeit* of the coup's trauma to actually augur for an implied, more positive future event, of a kind of traumatic coming-to-terms. In *By Night in Chile*, the general questions his half-willing intellectual cicerone, Sebastián Urrutia Lacroix, about whether Allende was an intellectual, evincing anxiety that if Allende was known as an intellectual, his reputation would survive posthumously. Telling Pinochet what the dictator wants to hear, Urrutia reassures him that all Allende read were "magazines" and "summaries of books," that Allende's predecessor Eduardo Frei Monatlva read nothing, and that his own predecessor Jorge Alessandri read romance novels.[4] Pinochet, on the other hand, sees himself as participating in the marketplace of ideas, perhaps even being a counterrevolutionary intellectual like Luiz Fontaine de Souza in *Nazi Literature in The Americas*. The narrative actually agrees with Pinochet's sense that the realm of ideas is where political victories are even semi-definitely gained. But Pinochet is not writing the narrative; Bolaño is, and he does so from the hidden point of view of the future. Bolaño is ironizing and mocking Pinochet even more decisively than the unelected Pinochet wishes to denigrate his elected predecessors. Yet Bolaño is skeptical that art can

---

[4] Roberto Bolaño, *By Night in Chile*, tr. Chris Andrews (New York: New Directions, 2003), 90.

redeem life. He has no more triumphalist an idea of aesthetics than he does of politics. All art can do is witness, and, for all his intertextual magic and cosmopolitan world-weariness, there is an aspect in Bolaño – seen most obviously in the oral history of *The Savage Detectives* – of *testimonio*.

Thus, Juan E. De Castro's contention that, despite its clear preference for Allende, Pinochet and Allende are structurally equivalent in Bolaño, may be too pessimistic.[5] This would be true if these events were definitively over for Bolaño. But his literary witnessing of the events puts their closed historical meaning in abeyance. But, just as the aftermath of the first avatar of visceral realism plays out in the second part of *The Savage Detectives*, the aftermath of the Second World War unfolds in the gaming of *The Third Reich* and the occulted violence of *2666*, the events of 1973 in Bolaño's work have a long aftermath, in which a normative leftist order may not be restored, but an emergent rightist order is not sanctioned.

Indeed – given that the vast majority of Bolaño's work was composed – although certainly not published – before 2001, the very possibility of including the second 9/11 in his field of vision is plausible because his work takes place as much in the future as in the past. The "spirit of science fiction" in Bolaño's works, a sense that the events he chronicles are seen from a vantage point perhaps as far as 2666, that two-thirds cutaway from the millennium, means that neo-fascist force can be opposed without assuming being nostalgic for the regimes that, had they won, "would have sent" intellectuals, as Bolaño observed in his 1999 Romulo Gallegos award acceptance speech in Caracas, "to labor camps."[6]

Bolaño, in the two short Chilean novels, establishes that Pinochet, not just in his repression but his neoliberal economic policies, was ushering in an era of randomness, in which the visible and purposeful evil of the dictators was being replaced by the slow violence of financialization. This is one of the effects of Bolaño's constant association of the aftermath of the coup with crisis in aesthetic representation, whether it is the airplane poetry of Carlos Wieder in *Distant Star* or the tormented philosophical ministrations of Urrutia in *By Night in Chile*. A group of concerned Americans, writing in the immediate aftermath of the coup, observed that

---

[5] Juan E. de Castro, "Politics and Ethics in Latin America: On Roberto Bolaño," in Juan E. de Castro and Nicholas Birns, eds., *Roberto Bolaño as World Literature* (New York: Bloomsbury, 2017), 72.
[6] Roberto Bolaño, *Between Parentheses: Essays, Articles, and Speeches, 1988–2001*, ed. Ignacio Echevarria, tr. Natasha Wimmer (New York: New Directions, 2011), 35.

"former members of the Allende government and many of its supporters are being brutally persecuted for their past political allegiances."[7] The idea of persecuting the past in the present easily morphs into the idea of the present trying to win the future against the past; thus as Urrutia instructs the dictator in Marxism so he can crush it, so Wieder uses the weapons of avant-garde experimentation against the freedom that had allowed it to creatively ferment; uses what was once the art of the future against human futurity as such.

The Pinochet coup disrupted Chilean democracy and buried progressive hopes. But it also upset the apple cart of history itself, making all politics aesthetic and all aesthetics up for grabs at the dictates of those who desire power. What David Harvey terms a "coup promoted by domestic business elites threatened by Allende's drive towards socialism" at once achieved its immediate objective, and was successful beyond its wildest dreams in advancing a philosophy of re-engineered and re-energized economic liberalism that would systematically discredit socialism.[8] Yet it was not in control of its own success, ricocheting into many different valences including the funding of the guerrilla wars in Africa observed by the exiled Arturo Belano (who may be said to be in permanent exile in the post-Pinochet Global South), among them the funding of Islamist militants in Afghanistan.

Pinochet's coup might be seen as the beginning of the twenty-first century in its combination of neoliberal economics and dark authoritarian forces. Eric Hobsbawm has argued that "the short twentieth century" ended in 1989 with the collapse of the Soviet bloc.[9] But one might argue that an even shorter twentieth century ended in 1973, with the Yom Kippur war and the consequent rise in oil prices, the looming impeachment crisis of Richard Nixon, and the Pinochet coup. This would mark the end of what Dominican poet Pedro Mir would call "mil novecientes neruda" – nineteen hundred Neruda.[10] That Neruda died shortly after the coup, and had his ideals utterly violated by it, was just one aspect of what Andreas Killen, speaking of 1973, has called the "nervous breakdown" of the twentieth-century consensus.[11] If, as Eli Jelly-Schapiro argues,

---

[7] Laurence Birns, Congressman Donald Fraser, and Michael Harrington, "The Chilean Tragedy," *New York Review of Books*, October 26, 1973.
[8] David Harvey, *A Brief History of Neoliberalism* (New York: Oxford University Press, 2020), 7.
[9] Eric Hobsbawm, *The Age of Extremes: The Short Twentieth Century, 1914–1991* (London: Michael Joseph, 1994).
[10] Pedro Mir, *Two Elegies of Hope*, tr. Jonathan Cohen (New York: Spuyten Duyvil, 2019), 47.
[11] Andreas Killen, *1973 Nervous Breakdown: Watergate, Warhol, and the Birth of Post-Sixties America* (New York: Bloomsbury, 2006).

Bolaño's fiction brings into conversation the interrelation of neoliberalism and colonial modernity, this conjunction, foregrounded in the Northern Hemisphere after 9/11/01, was already visible in the Global South after 9/11/73.[12] There is a sense in which the World Trade Center, an icon of capitalist power, was in another sense already made vestigial by the event of September 1973, redolent of an optimistic, technological modernity that had already begun to yield to an after-modernist world of force, and greed. "The victims of the femicides" chronicled in the fourth section of *2666*, "The Part about The Crimes," are akin to the victims of the terror attacks in Washington and New York in being killed in the course of life and work. These collective events represented different forms of violence entering the workplace, and a sense of the workplace as a public sphere that became, in Achille Mbembe's phrase, necropolitical.[13] The femicides also anticipate the deaths of migrant children on the border in the late 2010s by the way they comprise, in Giorgio Agamben's phrase, "bare life."[14] The femicide victims are expendable bodies whose lives do not matter to the mainstream. Their deaths would become anonymous, excepting inevitably half-futile gestures in the manner of the partial recognition afforded in *2666*. Though the subject matter is different, there is a direct line between both the witness to mass death of the border and the registering of Eurocentric violence in the American desert in *2666* and Valeria Luiselli's *Lost Children Archive*. Luiselli's book, in both being written in English (though the author's earlier books are in Spanish) and in its linkage of biopolitical crisis with a highbrow literary lineage, is inconceivable without Bolaño. *2666* heralds a border that is not only closed against intrusion, but which refracts violence back into the lands to the south. Far from a hope of proliferation, the border after the closing of America upon itself in the wake of 9/11 becomes itself an instrument of the terror against which its hardening was supposed to guard.

Abel Romero in Exile

In the light of all this, the implied politics of Roberto Bolaño are often presented as cynical, despairing, disillusioned, with only an ethical and aesthetic witness possible in the wake of the nightmare of the present and

---

[12] Eli Jelly-Schapiro, *Security and Terror* (Berkeley: University of California Press, 2018).
[13] Achille Mbembe, *Necropolitics*, tr. Steve Corcoran (Durham: Duke University Press, 2019).
[14] Giorgio Agamben, *Homo Sacer: Sovereign Power and Bare Life*, tr. Daniel Heller-Roazen (Stanford: Stanford University Press, 2008).

the future a nightmarish present increasingly seeks to abduct. But the specter of the two 9/11s in Bolaño's work presents, deeply occulted, a vision of resistance and even hope. There is an aspect of his narration that almost seems to be from the far-flung perspective of 2666, the year, a future *kairos* looking back at our own, crosscutting through time and giving us an unknowable, whispered assurance of balance and perspicuity. But even in the history that has actually occurred, futility and disaffection appear only on the surface.

The node where the connection between the two 9/11s emerge most crucially in Bolaño's fiction is in reference to a third 9/11, or at least a 9/11 that functions as a shadow of the first. In *The Savage Detectives*, Abel Romero, a character familiar from *Distant Star*, is interviewed in September 1989. Romero recounts the meeting in the Café Victor on Rue St. Sauveur in Paris of a group of "masochistic Chileans" on September 11, 1983 (373). Their atmosphere is one of futility, as they remember that "dismal day" and speak with melodramatic ineffectiveness about "enormous black wing" of evil. Romero meets Arturo Belano in this group, and lectures him that to oppose evil, one has to find out whether it was random or purposeful. If it is purposeful, it can be opposed meaningfully, but if random, there is basically no hope.

By 2001, it was clear that evil in the era of terror and neoliberalism was at once purposeful and random, as the attacks were concerted and formulated, yet were also reverberations of agencies which could not control any causative or consequential relations with the terrorist attacks themselves. But Romero's utterance, in a novel published in 1996, is really only about 9/11/1973, and sheds a different light on that event. A *coup d'état* seems consummately purposeful. And nothing could have been more targeted than the overthrow of Allende.

The Chilean exiles gather in Paris in 1983, unable to do anything to shake the preserved order in the county, almost with the sense that it would have been less injurious not to commemorate the event. But, in Chile itself, the months before the ten-year anniversary were dynamic ones. In August 1983, the Democratic Alliance, the first grouping of opposition parties since the coup, was formed. Prominent therein was Gabriel Valdés Subercaseaux, foreign minister under Frei, and the most radical figure in that administration. Though this proved a false dawn, and it was only the failure of the government's 1988 referendum that enabled the revival of Chilean democracy, that the Democratic Alliance existed at all was heartening. Labor unrest was also increasing in Chile in 1983, as the copper workers' union, La Confederación de Trabajadores del

Cobre, called protests beginning in May 1983 that continued through to the time of the anniversary.[15]

Though Seguel might not have been, as he was once heralded, the Chilean Lech Wałęsa, his labor movement also called for the reestablishment of political parties and provided a mass movement that correlated with their incipient reorganization. The Chile of 1983, though not yet finished with the Pinochet nightmare, was in a different state than that of the first post-coup referendum of 1980, so vividly described by Alberto Fuguet in *Mala onda*. In *Distant Star*, Abel Romero is described as in his fifties, a former "celebrity in the police force," perhaps a Southern Cone version of Mario Vargas Llosa's Lituma.[16] Romero exposes a staged kidnapping by a right-wing businessman and achieves celebrity in the Allende era. He is then forced into exile in Paris after being imprisoned under the junta. He and the narrator then embark on a thorough, but in the end futile, attempt to track down the rogue turncoat poet and filmmaker, Carlos Wieder. Romero is a figure associated with positive values, although he is sadly ineffective in implementing them. Jonathan Monroe observes that Romero is "the narrator's, and Bolaño's new alter-ego."[17]

And this is the position he occupies in the oral history of *The Savage Detectives* as well, as hero manqué, or a hero without the subtext of positive historical development that will accomodate his character. Though Abel Romero, Arturo Belano, and the exiles in Paris were inevitably somewhat removed from events at home – if it was any longer even their home – these events were in the newspapers at the time. Martín Prieto (1944–2019), the Chilean correspondent for *El Pais* and one of that newspaper's founders, did diligent reportage that inspired other foreign correspondents to cover these events as well.[18] But Bolaño did not mean to contrast the futility of the exiled literati with the valiant if, in the short term, also futile events in Chile. Futility, crucially, is an act of witness for Bolaño. What Carlos Burgos calls the "poor devils" in Bolaño may be

---

[15] Carlos Bungcam, *Sindicalismo chileno: Hechos y Documentos, 1973–1983* (Santiago: Circulo dos estudios Latinoamericanos, 1984), 237.
[16] Roberto Bolaño, *Distant Star*, tr. Chris Andrews (New York: New Directions, 2004), 112.
[17] Jonathan beck Monroe, *Framing Roberto Bolaño: Poetry, Fiction, Literary History, Politics* (Cambridge: Cambridge University Press, 2019), 99.
[18] Martín Prieto, "La liberación de Valdés, severo golpe para el régimen de Pinochet," *El Pais*, July 15, 1983, www.elpais.com/diario/1983/07/15/internacional/427068002_850215.html (accessed February 3, 2020).

losers, but they have integrity in their lack of success.[19] Against a neoliberalism that seeks a quantitative, calibrated and measurable idea of winning, that seeks to define humanity exclusively in terms of economic accumulation and justify that by a redefinition of special capital, Bolaño's little and big lumpen novelitas present people who do not so much fail to win but abstain from the very idea of winning as it has been distorted and disrupted from being anything remotely desirable.

That Bolaño eschews the left-wing rhetoric of calling out capitalist pigs and flailing away at the United States, that he does not demonize the right only to lionize the left, and that he does not seek to salvage a progressive center in Chilean politics as, in their very different ways, Isabel Allende, Antonio Skármeta, and even Guelfenbein all did, does not mean he does not oppose neoliberalism and its concomitant terrors. Indeed, futility may be the only stance that is capable of evading neoliberal scenarios. Importantly, the commemoration of 9/11/1973 occurs in *The Savage Detectives*, a work mainly concerned with Mexico and with the internecine activities of an obscure, definitionally minor, and endemically preposterous avant-garde poetry group, the Visceral Realists. If the Visceral Realists had taken the world by storm, in the mid-1970s, they would sooner or later have been appropriated by currents politically antithetical to them. Their failure, their ignominy, their obscurity are salvific. If not exactly losers who win, in the formulation made famous by Pierre Bourdieu – it is too modernist for them, although perhaps apt for the original visceral realism of Cesárea Tinajero – the later visceral realists are of a generation that realizes they cannot win creditably, even as creditably as did Octavio Paz, even before he was forgiven by Ulises Lima at Parque Hundido.

And yet Bolaño, who had been successful in Spanish before 2001, only emerged in the Anglophone market not only after 9/11 but because of 9/11. His own death, really just after he had become a name in the Anglophone literary world, further bound him with the literary necropolitics of the post-9/11 era in which premature authorial death conjured an apt spokesperson for the memory of violence. The unexpected and mostly accidental conjunction of 9/11/2001, Bolaño's international breakthrough, and his death – that these events were all more or less contemporaneous – adds a sort of biopolitical graphology to the mix. Bolaño's introduction to the world was followed hard by his obituary. His vision of Latin America tolled the bell of both death and rebirth for the Latin

---

[19] Carlos Burgos, "Roberto Bolaño," in Wilfrido Corral, Juan E. De Castro, and Nicholas Birns, eds., *The Contemporary Spanish American Novel* (New York: Bloomsbury, 2013), 305.

America of poverty and revolutions, marginality and genius the world had grown accustomed to. Bolaño, for the most part posthumously, was bringing news of a region. But he was doing so in a way very different from Neruda and Gabriel García Márquez, who were read as bringing news of a region where dire and drastic change was needed and underway, but in a way that was separate from the story of the rest of the world. Bolaño's oeuvre, in its registering of global trends such as a disillusionment with revolutionary movements, the persistence of a *sub rosa* fascism long after its extinction was officially pronounced, and the rising awareness that neoliberalism was not just a set of economic policies but a dominant worldview, was very much in sync with the times. Even such a committed leftist as John Beverley, in *Latin Americanism after 9/11*, called for an overhauling of views of Latin America from the ossified discourses of the twentieth century.[20] The arc of violence and terror in Bolaño's oeuvre from 1973 to 2001 provides a new eidolon of the region even as it resists its own potential for what Sarah Pollack called the "synecdoche of literary commodification."[21] The residue of 2001 excited Bolaño's success and provided an antidote to all the hype. In an atmosphere where Bolaño's impact outside of his work was measured only by his success, in terms of sales and prestige, it augured the inescapability of mass death, inside or outside of his oeuvre, in the femicides of Ciudad Juárez or the smoldering ruins of the World Trade Center, that had been completed when Salvador Allende was still the president of Chile and Augusto Pinochet his law-abiding appointed military commander. If, as De Castro puts it, Bolaño can be accused of concentrating on the "excessive" aspects of Latin America and not its "mundanity" – the mundanity – in the two senses of ordinariness and worldliness – is all in the narrative witness, a witness that traces the boundaries of a world where both purposeful and random evil were manifest, neither of which was easy to distinguish from the other.[22]

If Bolaño suggests that the politicization of aesthetics cannot proceed in the way the Latin American leftist intellectual mainstream had presumed throughout the short – or shorter – twentieth century, he more emphatically shows us that the aestheticization of politics is barbaric, and, in terms

---

[20] John Beverley, *Latin Americanism after 9/11* (Durham, NC: Duke University Press, 2011).

[21] Sarah Pollack, "After Bolaño: Rethinking the Politics of Latin American Literature in Translation," *PMLA* 128, no. 3 (May 2013).

[22] Juan E. De Castro, *Writing Revolution in Latin America: Form Marti to García Márquez to Bolaño* (Nashville: Vanderbilt University Press, 2019), 138.

of the Arcimboldi/femicides connection in *2666*, homicidal. Yet, in a twenty-first century ever more driven by ideology and zeal, and even further disillusioned by politics and aesthetics, the reader of Bolaño's work cannot entirely let go of, to quote *Distant Star*'s description of the Allende era, "the key that would open the door into a world of dreams, the only dreams worth living for" (3).

PART III
Genres, Discourses, Media

CHAPTER 16

Essays and Short Stories

José Luis Venegas

"Let's say that the story and the plot arise from chance, they belong in the realm of chance, that is chaos and disarray. ... Form, by contrast, is a choice ruled by intelligence, cunning, will, silence, the weapons that Ulysses uses to fight death. Form is artifice, the story the precipice."[1] Roberto Bolaño's explanation of his writing method seems to rest on the well-worn distinction between story and plot. In his classic study, *Aspects of the Novel* (1927), E. M. Forster claims that plot, which Bolaño calls "form," is what separates a sequence of random events from a logically organized string of causes and effects. "The king died, and then the queen died," Forster writes, is a story. "The king died, and then the queen died of grief," is a plot.[2] Plot is the device or "artifice" that sustains and shapes the story, keeping it from the "precipice" of futility and chaos. Bolaño's fiction certainly exemplifies this principle: characters and events are organized to create suspense and curiosity, often assembling detective plots, a narrative pattern that usually wrests necessity from arbitrariness. But if Bolaño deploys these formal resources, it is not to supply a unified and coherent narrative whole. His fictional universe is riddled with unanswered questions, puzzling enigmas without apparent solution, and clues that lead disoriented characters (and readers) nowhere. The result is not, however, a Dadaist joke or a celebration of absurdity. "The idea and the form," Henry James declared, "are the needle and the thread, and I never heard of a guild of tailors who recommend the use of the thread without the needle, or the needle without the thread."[3] Bolaño's short stories are a fitting example,

---

[1] Carmen Boullosa, "Carmen Boullosa entrevista a Roberto Bolaño," *Roberto Bolaño: La escritura como tauromaquia*, ed. Celina Manzoni (Buenos Aires: Ediciones Corregidor, 2002), 111. All translations are my own unless otherwise noted.
[2] E. M. Forster, *Aspects of the Novel* (New York: Harcourt, 1955), 86.
[3] Henry James, "The Art of Fiction," in *The Art of Criticism: Henry James on the Theory and the Practice of Fiction*, ed. William Veeder and Susan M. Griffin (Chicago: University of Chicago Press, 1986), 178.

though they involve a snarl of threads that tangle form and chaos, artifice and precipice. At the heart of this narrative process, and establishing a basic link between his fiction and non-fiction, is the notion of coincidence.

"Coincidence" is, as the *Oxford English Dictionary* defines it, "a notable concurrence of events and circumstances having no apparent causal connection." The word *apparent* opens the chilling possibility that random events might not be arbitrary after all. Like ripples in the fabric of experience, coincidences challenge our meaning-making mechanisms but do not abolish the possibility of meaning itself. Coincidences defy explanation, and yet constantly demand it. They point to what Borges called the "imminence of a revelation as yet unproduced."[4] This essential ambiguity is a recurrent trait of Bolaño's otherwise multifarious short story collections, none of which are organized along thematic or generic lines. In fact, the English translations of the twenty-seven stories in *Llamadas telefónicas* ("Phone Calls") (1997) and *Putas asesinas* ("Murderous Whores") (2001) were published in two volumes – *Last Evenings on Earth* (2006) and *The Return* (2010) – that disregard the order and chronology of the original. The posthumous collections *El gaucho insufrible* (2003) and *El secreto del mal* (2007) were translated as *The Insufferable Gaucho* (2010) and *The Secret of Evil* (2012). These stories take multiple narrative forms, including fragments of memoirs ("Sensini"), Kafkaesque fables ("Police Rat"), crime thrillers ("Two Catholic Tales"), and even Gothic stories ("The Return"). Sometimes they are hybrids: part-story and part-essay like "Literature + Illness = Illness" in *The Insufferable Gaucho*.

An autobiographical account of the day Bolaño receives a terminal diagnosis of his liver disease at a hospital in Barcelona, this text establishes chance and coincidence as a basic principle in Bolaño's work. Citing Mallarmé, he notes that "a roll of the dice will never abolish chance," the bleak implication being that our actions are pointless against the lack of certitude that rules the universe.[5] Bolaño offers no easy consolations, though he keeps rolling the dice in life and art. Every day since his fateful hospital visit, he holds his hands in front of him to check the irreversible progress of his disease – he would not be able to completely straighten up his fingers as his condition worsens – and he tirelessly writes stories that reveal rather than hide the horror of existence. Illness will prevail despite

---

[4] Jorge Luis Borges, "The Wall and the Books," in *Selected Non-Fictions*, ed. and trans. Eliot Weinberger (New York: Penguin, 1999), 346.
[5] Roberto Bolaño, "Literature + Illness = Illness," in *The Insufferable Gaucho*, trans. Chris Andrews (New York: New Directions, 2010), 143.

the daily tests. Literature will not offer a way out of the abyss of uncertainty. But Bolaño keeps plunging into the unknown, the unexpected, and the coincidental, curious to see how the dice will fall. With bracing courage, he eschews hope and despair as one and the same and accepts chance as the other side of fate – as a method that constantly renews the possibility of meaning and connection without the promise of redemption. As the painter Edwin Jones says in *2666*, coincidence is "total freedom, our natural destiny. Coincidence obeys no laws and if it does we don't know what they are. Coincidence," he concludes, "is like the manifestation of God at every moment on our planet."[6] Meaning, however unstable or fragmentary, rests on a principle of immanence, not transcendence.

In narrative terms, this principle translates into stories that unsettle causality and frustrate the reader's expectation of dénouement. The particular way in which Bolaño multiplies narrative threads and accumulates details that fail to form predictable or expected patterns can be observed in three stories: "The Outline of the Eye," "Buba," and "Dentist." Together they exemplify the push of Bolaño's storytelling toward the abrasive though infinitely productive threshold between randomness and causation. This emphasis on the aleatory spills over into his non-fiction, which extends its ethical and aesthetic implications into the realm of politics. Carrying the insights of his short fiction into his essays in *Between Parentheses* – particularly the "Caracas Address" that he delivered upon receiving the Rómulo Gallegos literary prize in 1999 – I will conclude by arguing that Bolaño uses chance and coincidence to challenge the bid for transcendence that often underlies reactionary politics and its adherence to nationalism and other totalizing doctrines and regulative concepts.

"Every Single Damn Thing Matters"

Collected in the original in *Cuentos completos* (2018) and still untranslated into English, "The Outline of the Eye" (1983), Bolaño's first published story, is the autobiographical account of Cheng Huo Deng, a war veteran and renowned author going into retirement to a remote Chinese village in 1980 to recover from a mental breakdown. His days are spent visiting with the locals (the doctor, the commissioner, the schoolteacher) and going for walks and bike rides in the countryside. He also collects newspaper clippings about random, sometimes bizarre and unexplainable events.

---

[6] Roberto Bolaño, *2666: A Novel*, trans. Natasha Wimmer (New York: Farrar, Straus and Giroux, 2008), 90.

Four of them stick in his mind like "red signs" that cannot be dismissed: the tragic death of three people at an overcrowded music festival in Beijing, sightings of a giant cow with a duck beak near the Korean border, the case of an eleven-year-old boy with X-ray vision, and the advice of a super-centenarian who attributes his longevity to optimism, physical exercise, and four to five hours of sleep a night in a sitting position. As he places the clippings on his desk, Cheng Huo Deng wonders: "What is the real meaning of all this?" and intimates that perhaps "behind the words there is something that can provoke an even higher emotion." Randomness is not enough of an explanation, and he keeps asking himself: "What do these news items have in common?"[7] The reader is thus primed for hidden links, connections, and even conspiracy.

Are these events in any way related to the mysterious actions that the narrator perceives in the village? The daily pilgrimage of the residents to a remote worksite beyond a line of cliffs; the fact that they wear gloves when they return; the cryptic reference to bacteriological weapons made by a young army officer – all these details join the newspaper clippings to form a vast and incomprehensible puzzle that Deng tries to solve in vain. A recovering mental patient, he wavers between the fear of a relapse and the conviction that he is on the "right track" to decipher a secret, perhaps a dark political secret linked to classified government operations. But the clues he sees remain suspended between chance and necessity, suggesting though never revealing an explanation for their synchronicity. Feeling as if he were trapped "in a forest of riddles," the narrator builds suspense but delivers no final answers (639, 644). The story ends with his suicide announcement, which significantly comes shortly after he decides to stop reading the newspaper and looking for connections among his clippings.

Deng's journal confirms Mallarmé's assertion that "a roll of the dice will never abolish chance." Chance cannot be overcome, but this is a limitation as well as a revelation. As Jacques Derrida explains in his essay, "My Chances," chance is the double rather than the antithesis of determination. When a pattern emerges, the scientific mind either dismisses it as meaningless chance or attributes it to an actual causal mechanism. But, as Derrida asks, "what is the difference between superstition and paranoia on the one hand, and science on the other, if they all mark a compulsive propensity to interpret random signs so as to restore to them meaning,

---

[7] Roberto Bolaño, "El contorno del ojo," in *Cuentos completos* (Barcelona: Alfaguara, 2018), 639, 641.

necessity, destination?"[8] What science presents as method is, Derrida writes, an arbitrarily isolated "context into which randomness no longer penetrates" yet always lurks: a fiction that suppresses but does not fully eliminate chance. In this respect, Deng's writing is a symptom not only of his mental illness but of a mysterious connecting principle that invites interpretation but ultimately eludes it. *Symptoma* is, as Derrida reminds us, the Greek word for "coincidence, fortuitous event, encounter," that which falls together (375, 350). Symptoms thus understood are the underlying element of Bolaño's formula, "Literature + Illness = Illness" and the object of continuous probing in his story collections.

Illness and literature meet again in "Dentist," included in *Last Evenings on Earth*. The story's narrator decides to take some time off to visit an old friend in the Mexican town of Irapuato, a dentist who is going through a difficult time: he feels guilty for the death of one his patients, an old Indian woman with gum cancer, and humiliated after an encounter with a painter he admires who called him a homosexual. Without apparent logic, the plot connects the woman's disease and death and the artist's homophobia to the dentist's relationship with a sixteen-year-old boy with a special literary talent. During a visit to the boy's shack on the destitute outskirts of the city, the narrator reads his writing and is struck by his ability to pack large amounts of narrative material in just a few pages. A tangle of disparate threads that do not coalesce in a single plotline, his stories mirror Bolaño's own short fiction. The boy's writing, like "Dentist" and other works by Bolaño, features diverse narrative strands that imply connections without ever spelling them out. Likewise, "Dentist" suggests links among art, poverty, race, and sexuality that cascade out of the basic association between literature and illness – between the Indian woman's gum cancer and the Indian boy's writing, both, along with the story itself, examples of what Mikhail Bakhtin calls the "grotesque body." Behaving like a tumor, but also like boundless writing open to the world's complexity, the grotesque body is not "a closed, completed unit; it is unfinished, outgrows itself, transgresses its own limits."[9] Isn't this an apt description of Bolaño's fictional world?

But there is in "Dentist" more than a paradigmatic example of Bolaño's peculiar brand of storytelling. There is also a reflection on the nature and

---

[8] Jacques Derrida, "My Chances/*Mes chances*: A Rendezvous with Some Epicurean Stereophonies," in *Psyche: Inventions of the Other*, vol. I, trans. Irene Harvey and Avital Ronell (Stanford: Stanford University Press, 2007), 364–365.
[9] Mikhail Bakhtin, *Rabelais and His World*, trans. Helene Iswolsky (Bloomington: Indiana University Press, 1984), 26.

function of literature and art that further highlights the centrality of chance and coincidence in his work. During one of their drunken conversations, the dentist tells the narrator that art and life are inextricable and that they both take the shape of "the secret story." By "secret story" he means "the one we'll never know, although we are living it from day to day."[10] Chris Andrews traces this concept back to Ricardo Piglia's "Theses on the Short Story," according to which "a short story always tells two stories": a "visible story" that hides "a secret tale, narrated in elliptical and fragmentary manner." Whereas the classic short story (Poe, Quiroga) produces surprise when the secret story – often a secret or enigma – "comes to the surface," the modern version (Chekhov, Joyce) "works on the tension between the two stories without ever resolving it."[11] Though closer to the second type, "Dentist," and by extension Bolaño's short fiction in general, belongs to a category of its own, where visible and secret stories collapse into each other. If, as Piglia points out, "the secret story is the key to the form of the short story" ("Theses," 64), then Bolaño's form is determined by a self-effacing yet ever-proliferating system of narrative causality in which, as the dentist puts it, "every single damn thing matters" ("Dentist," 192). This narrative procedure deflects straight plotlines and allows meaning to arise from the operations of chance as the random and contingent becomes indistinguishable from the necessary and predictable. In this fictional universe, where there are no final solutions, no straight paths leading to a predetermined goal, no uncovering of mysteries, analysis turns into paranoia, artifice into precipice, and like Bakhtin's grotesque body, narrative takes the shape of an "ever unfinished, ever creating" world where characters and readers become overinterpreters.

"Dentist" therefore exemplifies the process of overinterpretation that, according to Andrews, permeates Bolaño's fictional, and, I will argue, non-fictional writing. Bolaño's overinterpreters "make something out of nothing, or join too many dots" (Andrews 2014, 56). Some, like the narrators in stories that describe photographs of French writers ("Last Evenings on Earth," "Photos," and "Labyrinth") take the factual "merely as a springboard or launch pad" to draw conclusions based on fancy rather than logic (Andrews 2014, 66). Others are paranoid (e.g., Deng in "The Outline of the Eye" or the protagonist in "A Literary Adventure"). Still others are

---

[10] Roberto Bolaño, "Dentist," in *Last Evenings on Earth*, trans. Chris Andrews (New York: New Directions, 2006), 192.
[11] Ricardo Piglia, "Theses on the Short Story," *New Left Review* 70 (2011): 63–66. See Chris Andrews, *Roberto Bolaño's Fiction: An Expanding Universe* (New York: Columbia University Press, 2014), 74.

motivated by mysterious forces outside of causality. Such is the case of Acevedo, the narrator in "Buba" (*The Return*).

Shortly after his arrival in Barcelona to play for a professional soccer team, Acevedo, a young Chilean, is asked to share his apartment with Buba, a recruit from Africa. At the time, the team is going through a losing streak, which Buba offers to break by performing a ritual with the help of Acevedo and Herrera, another teammate. The ritual involves Buba's mixing a few drops of Acevedo's and Herrera's blood in a cup and disappearing with it into the bathroom, where he plays loud African tunes. The spell apparently works and the three players begin scoring goals that Acevedo deems inexplicable, even "miraculous," and contributing significantly to the national and international titles that the team wins that season and the next. Buba then leaves for Italy and, at the peak of his career, dies in a car accident. Is there any connection between this tragic event and the African player's success? Though Buba never admits to using magic, Acevedo becomes an overinterpreter after the first time the ritual is performed, attributing both the team's victories and his friend's sudden death to a secret order of things that defies predictability and logical explanation. Years later the mystery remains as a Brazilian singer who seems knowledgeable about voodoo and candomblé assures Acevedo and Herrera that Buba was simply crazy and that their wins happened "because they were good players."[12]

Rather than a supernatural power, magic in "Buba" is, like madness in "The Outline of the Eye," a catalyst to perceive the inherent strangeness of reality. For Bolaño, this questioning is invisible, silent work. He writes narrative like Acevedo plays soccer: accepting and respecting the rules of the game yet fully aware that all forms of play, like all experiences in life, are ultimately beyond formal control and open to blind chance. Instead of being dismissed as insignificant noise, however, chance is here a pervasive, unavoidable force suspended between truth and illusion – a sweeping force that endows randomness with absolute meaning while questioning our efforts to explain, represent, and categorize reality. Everywhere and nowhere, chance and coincidence are pure immanence always teetering on the verge of transcendence. They offer just a glimmering of a more encompassing order of things that is impossible to formulate. The nameless narrator in "Dentist" has this imponderable experience when he dreams of the young writer's ramshackle house and "for barely a second"

---

[12] Roberto Bolaño, "Buba," in *The Return*, trans. Chris Andrews (New York: New Directions, 212), 179.

understands "the mystery of art and its secret nature. But then somehow the corpse of the old Indian woman who had died of gum cancer came into the dream, and that is the last thing I can remember" (209).

History and Politics between Parenthesis

Bolaño's fiction mocks easy solutions to the enigma and drama of existence while at the same time multiplying the ways in which its significance might be experienced and understood. More a possibility than a problem, chance and coincidence offer an ethical, aesthetic, and even political alternative to unifying theories about life and literature. As Jean Franco points out, Bolaño's fiction might be seen as "an effort to redirect the whole literary enterprise ... in a moonscape of political and social disaster that encompasses post-coup Chile, the German retreat from Russia during the Second World War, Tlatelolco, Pinochet's Chile, the death cult in Ciudad Juárez and even the First Liberian War."[13] In this post-utopian, apocalyptic world ushered in by the defeat of communism, the erosion of the welfare state, and the triumph of market-driven neoliberalism, Bolaño abandons daydreams of salvation, fulfillment, and justice while embracing the political potential of arbitrariness and contingency.

Nowhere is this rejection of explicit political action more clearly stated than in his 1999 "Caracas Address," collected in *Between Parentheses: Essays, Articles and, Speeches, 1998–2003*. Here he states that the revolutionary ideals of the Latin American 1950s and 1960s "have been dead for more than fifty years." Had they triumphed, the outcome would have been no brighter than our neoliberal present: the leftist leaders would have sent the youth who blindly fought for them "straight to labor camps."[14] Disillusioned with the grand Cold War narratives, Bolaño places history and politics – to use the title of his book – between parentheses: within yet separate from specific social contexts and material conditions. The fictions we live by, he suggests, can no longer rely on absolute concepts of political subjectivity, nationality, and citizenship. His approach is not, however, to dismantle them and imagine better alternatives. Despite a life spent in exile, he states: "The truth is that I'm Chilean," but notes "and I'm also many other things" ("Caracas," 33).

---

[13] Jean Franco, "Questions for Bolaño," *Journal of Latin American Cultural Studies* 18, nos. 2–3 (2009): 207.
[14] Roberto Bolaño, "Caracas Address," in *Between Parentheses: Essays, Articles, and Speeches, 1998–2003*, ed. Ignacio Echevarría, trans. Natasha Wimmer (New York: New Directions, 2011), 35.

"Other" here means not additional or complementary, but unpredictable and unforeseen – an interruption rather than an extension of our political and cultural givens. Bolaño illustrates this process with a childhood memory. Left-footed but right-handed, he had trouble following the instructions of his soccer coach and often ended up kicking the ball or running in the opposite direction from which he intended. Bolaño's confusion of left and right is not devoid of a rather obvious metaphorical charge, but its political potential becomes apparent when he sees it as a symptom of his undiagnosed dyslexia. Somehow related to his inability to identify stable reference points in space, his dyslexia may also have something to do with the "verbal and alphabetical logic" whereby he always thought that the capital of Venezuela is Bogotá and the capital of Colombia is Caracas. Phonic resemblance redraws national boundaries and triggers other associations: Rómulo Gallegos's famous character Doña Bárbara, "with a *b*, sounds like Venezuela, and Bolívar sounds like Venezuela and Doña Bárbara, too, Bolívar and Bárbara, what a great pair they would have made." By the same token, other sound correspondences seem to signal the fact that Gallegos's novels *Cantaclaro* and *Canaima* "could have easily been Colombian" and that *La casa verde*, or *The Green House* by Peruvian Mario Vargas Llosa is "a Colombian-Venezuelan novel" ("Caracas," 31).

These meaningful yet apparently random connections suggest "a method hidden in [Bolaño's] dyslexia, a bastard semiotic or graphological or metasyntactic or phonemic method, or simply a poetic method." This method playfully reconfigures the arrangements of political, cultural, and literary history as well as those of fixed and predictable meaning-making mechanisms. Assuming the role of overinterpreter that many of his characters share, Bolaño tells his audience: "I've just been awarded the eleventh Rómulo Gallegos Prize. The 11th. My jersey number was 11. You'll think this is a coincidence, but it gives me the shivers. The 11 who didn't know how to tell left from right and who therefore mixed up Caracas with Bogotá has just won … the 11th Rómulo Gallegos Prize" ("Caracas," 31, 32). A chance occurrence? Maybe. Or maybe not.

A symptom both unnerving and liberating, coincidence suspends perceptual certainties and distorts lofty concepts like nation along with the narratives that sustain them. Looking for meaning in coincidences is risky business, potentially leading to blind fatalism, but so is literature, which, as Bolaño says, citing an unknown Andalusian folk singer "is danger" ("Caracas," 34). As his essays and short stories show, this is a risk worth taking. Here coincidence is not only a precipice, but an artifice to suspend authority – political or otherwise – and reconfigure the ways in which we feel and interpret the world. Isn't the endlessly renewed possibility of connection afforded by chance and coincidence the precondition of a radically democratic sense of community and a radically free sense of self? To find freedom in the unknown and meaning in the unexpected, Bolaño invites us to keep rolling the dice, even in the face of the abyss.

CHAPTER 17

Poetry I: The Ghost That Runs through the Writing
Rubén Medina

Bolaño as an Anomalous Writer

As Chris Andrews has explained, Roberto Bolaño is an anomalous case as a writer. He does not fit properly into the familiar paradigms of critics. Bolaño imposes himself masterfully as a writer following his own distinctive path characterized by atypical experiences. Such atypicality in him emerges in the mid 1970s shaped by the way he lived, embracing his own historical time. He suggests this in the poem "Vive tu tiempo," published in 1976, when he was still in Mexico. In "Live your time," his verses depict a generational condition common to his writing: social precariousness traversed by rebellious dreams, death, degraded love, and paradoxical perceptions: "but which is your time the time / of the cornered life by strange lights the / time of dreams full of adolescents / ... in the middle of which war of how many feelings in conflict" (Bolaño, *Pajaro de calor*, 1976). Ironically, the poem ends with the poetic subject telling his ex-lover to live instead in her own time, a time designed by the social denial of bourgeois "normalcy." As the poem reveals, from the start of his activity, writing is a way to deal with fear, failure, the horrors of the present life, and the questions and dilemmas that people – particularly those with privileges – tend to avoid. A posterior verse sums up the duty of elucidating and bearing witness to his historical time: "Wisdom is keeping your eyes open / during the fall" (Bolaño, *The Unknown University*, 213).

Bolaño is undoubtedly an anomalous writer. For Andrews, his anomaly lies in an unmistakable confluence of several attributes (Andrews, 2014). The first of these is of course that he is an exceptional writer – a fact which evolved quickly into a myth following his death in 2013 – that he is translatable into other languages, and because Bolaño has been read incorrectly. Bolaño's singular journey, Andrews points out, includes migration, his peculiar and significant break with the two dominant trends of poetry in Mexico (represented by Octavio Paz and the group *Espiga*

Amotinada, respectively), long periods of marginality (over two decades), late success (in the last five years of his life), and maintaining his critical attitude towards the literary institution (first articulated with his foundation of the Infrarealist movement, in conjunction with other young poets deeply dissatisfied with the current literary and artistic establishment).[1]

To that precise list of characteristics, however, other relevant features should be added. For example, Bolaño's own trajectory outside the institutions of higher education, the socioeconomic situation informing his marginality, his writing activity as a life project and (eventually) profession, and the fate of his work after his death. Indeed, Bolaño was self-taught. He attended only a brief part of high school in Mexico, bypassing both a university education and the way institutions discipline minds and impose hierarchies and conventions. His choice to drop out of school isn't superfluous, it attests to an enduring detachment from social normalcy. Bolaño comes from a lower class without pretext of social mobility unless through professional education or by the various paths of social corruption and opportunistic integration into the social networks (friendships) of Mexican society. In fact, by the beginning of the 1970s, higher education had become colossal, as migration from the countryside saturated major cities. The National Autonomous University of Mexico created many preparatory schools in the working-class neighborhoods of D.F. to accommodate such demand. Bolaño broke with this path for social mobility, what he often refers to as a "decent" life. His decision to subsist on low-wage jobs for most of his life illustrates the context of several of his poems in the *Unknown University* that refer to money and his attitude towards it –while acknowledging the intersection of material life, daily labor, and his identity as a poor writer. Early on, Bolaño opted to educate himself through plenty of readings, discussions and social interactions, and artistic and political experimentation – alone or with fellow Infrarealists. Later, Bolaño would refer to such a path as education in the "unknown university," the source of the title for the book in which he planned to house his entire poetic works – written from 1977 on, which would be posthumously published in 2007.

The fate of Bolaño's work after his death is important to take into account when analyzing his writing. Earlier novels he'd decided not to publish were edited according to marketing criteria, casting a shadow on

---

[1] For a critical account of Infrarealism, see Heriberto Yépez: "Historia de algunos infrarrealismos" in Alforja #38 (fall 2006), 132–153, and Rubén Medina, *Perros habitados por las voces del desierto*, 2nd ed. (México: Matadero, 2016).

his oeuvre.[2] In such marketing of Bolaño's work, his Mexican experience and Infrarealist activity are downplayed, reduced to passing mentions, or without considering the enduring traces of Infrarealism in his later poetics. One example is the publication of the novel *The Spirit of the Science Fiction*, whose prologue was written by Christopher Dominguez Michael. The prologue, as Heriberto Yépez notes, framing his argument within the context of the Mexican literary institution, is an act of the "colonization of Bolaño," an attempt to "co-opt him and neutralize him so that he becomes a 'high-brow' and domesticated author, whose work and orbit does not encourage others to reread Mexican literature as a right-wing hegemony" (Yépez, 2016). Yépez describes how the critic of *Letras Libres* disfigures and misrepresents Bolaño's background: "Dominguez does nothing more than mention Infrarealism ... there is also no mention of his violent opposition to Octavio Paz ... Nor does he mention Mario Santiago Papasquiaro, Bolaño's spiritual and literary companion" (Yépez, 2016). These new publications are frequently introduced by critics who are themselves members of the Mexican literary establishment which Bolaño's despised. It is highly ironic that an author who persistently criticized literary mafias with savage parody and description has been handed over to his enemies by his heirs.

The same strategy of obliteration can be seen in the prologue to *Poesía reunida* (2018), written by Manuel Vilas. *Poesía reunida* pretends to reunite in a single volume all the poetry written and published by Bolaño, yet many poems were excluded – particularly those published before 1980, which are essential to fully understand his poetics. The volume's poems do not follow a sequential order of date of publication or production. Readers are less able to see changes in Bolaño's poetry or links in later poems to his earlier Infrarealists poetics. Tellingly, those included poems written and published in Mexico, which do not appear until the third part of the volume in sections titled, "Other poems" and "Scattered poems." They are presented as oddities, as outliers in contrast to the rest of his work. Again, the prologue is full of sweeping and problematic statements which fail in effect and even intent to expound on Bolaño's poetry. For example, Vilas states that Parra "was his mentor, a poet who gave Bolaño a way of understanding poetry that was directly related to a

---

[2] See Rubén Ángel Arias's review of *Poesía reunida*, in the digital magazine: https://ctxt.es/es/20190320/Culturas/25150/roberto-bola%C3%B1o-universidad-desconocida-obra-inedita-ruben-angel-arias.htm; and Ignacio Echevarría, "Roberto Bolaño borrado," *El cultural*, September 23, 2016.

way of life. And that way of living pursued irreverence, iconoclasm, and mystery."³ Yet Vilas' prologue lacks depth or understanding of the historical context of Bolaño's poetics, since the author's relationship to Parra was not static. For now, it is sufficient to cite Bolaño's judgment of Parra in an article from 1977 – which will require us to trace such influence on him to either another poet or even to the Infrarealist movement itself.

> We do not follow Parra nor Neruda (neither do we ridicule those who, after having praised Parra as the renovator of Latin American poetry, now accuse him of being fascist and deny all his poetry. We believe that both Parra and those who excommunicate him today have been petty-bourgeois poets to the core who at the time did very important things, especially Nicanor). We pay more attention to Pablo de Rokha and Vicente Huidodro. (Bolaño, 1997. Translation is mine)

Bolaño as Poet

Another feature of Bolaño's atypicality as a writer is his poetic activity and the place of poetry in his oeuvre. His beginnings as a writer were in poetry, and he continued writing poetry until his death. Bolaño explained the following in an interview published posthumously: "At 20 years of age, more than writing poetry, because I also wrote poetry (actually I only wrote poetry) .... what I wanted was to live as a poet .... For me, being a poet was ... being a revolutionary ... open to everything ... it was universal brotherhood, something totally utopian" (Álvarez, 2006, 38. Translation is mine). A substantial part of Bolaño's writing is poetry, and he published several books of poetry during his lifetime: *Reinventing Love* (Mexico, 1976), *Naked Boys under the Rainbow of Fire* (an anthology of new Latin American poetry, Mexico, 1979), *Fragments of the Unknown University* (Spain, 1992), *Romantic Dogs* (Spain, 1994, 2000), *El último salvaje* (Mexico, 1995), and *Three* (Barcelona, 2000).

Scholars generally have dismissed Bolaño's poetry and studied his narrative, as the large number of articles and books published about precisely that in the last two decades can attest. Bolaño's poetry has been considered minor and secondary; many consider it a simple activity or a training through which the author had to journey in order to discover his extraordinary talents as narrator. In addition to this mischaracterization of his poetry, there is also a contempt for his activity as a poet, particularly from

---

³ Manuel Vilas, "La poesía de Roberto Bolaño," *Poesía reunida* (Alfaguara, 2017), 9.

some poets and novelists likely resentful of the global interest in Bolaño. Comments expressed by Raúl Zurita typify such scorn. Responding to a question by Chiara Bolognese on Bolaño's poetry, he said: "Bolaño's poetry, I mean the one that he or his publishers or his heirs qualify as such, is insufferable, but they are not worse than the poems of Faulkner, and Faulkner became Faulkner as Bolaño became Bolaño... They were extraordinary writers because they were horrifying poets" (Bolognese, 2010, 272. Translation is mine). Zurita's disdain for Bolaño is clear. Carefully chosen words extricate Bolaño from the relative context of all other poetry, positing his own sovereignty as a poet and allowing Zurita to assume the mantle as the most important Latin American poet. Unlike Bolaño, whose criticism was public and combative, Zurita waited many years after Bolaño's death and any possibility of response before leveling such criticism. These comments cannot go unnoticed for readers since Bolaño referred to him many times – even going so far as to parody his poetry in *Distant Star*.

There are, however, some key studies that consider Bolaño's poetry and tackle the relation between poetry and prose in his work. One such study is Chris Andrews' concise article considering the way poetry shapes Bolaño's prose. While analyzing the poetic elements that Bolaño uses in his prose, Andrews notes that "he does not write what is called a poetic or lyrical prose... Rather, in his case, poetic resources are at the service of the story, so that, along with surprising, the images also deepen the description of an environment or a character" (Andrews, 2003. Translation is mine). Andrews shows how images inform his narratives – noting also that dreams (so fundamental to all of Bolaño's poetry) are often also incorporated into narrative plot – and that the use of variations and enumerations about a topic are among other resources Bolaño employed in both poetry and narrative. In a later monograph, Andrews expands upon the significance of poetry in Bolaño's novels, particularly in *The Savage Detectives*: "In Bolaño's fiction, poetry stands synecdochally for what Giorgi Agamben, in *Idea of prose*, calls 'neotenic openness'... Neotenic openness, to allow the expression its broadest sense, is a youthful openness preserved beyond the age at which it is typically lost" (Andrews, 2014, 193–194). Andrews suggests that poetry in this novel is a manifestation of rebellious youth, nonconformity, and adventure that in Bolaño's case seems to continue until maturity, representing an active and stimulating openness to cultural expressions, artistic experimentation, and the ethical choices in life. What is striking in his discussion is that while Andrews makes a significant link between the poetic drive of Bolaño's narrative and the earlier poetics of the

Infrarrealist movement, he does not further explore either the relationship between narrative prose and poetry or the stubborn persistence of an Infrarrealist past that would have acknowledged the key presence and influence in Bolaño's writings of Mario Santiago Papasquiaro.

First published, like Andrews' *Roberto Bolaño's Fiction*, in 2014, one study that considers Bolaño's entire work – in both poetry and prose – is Nibaldo Acero's *La ruta de los niños rojos. La poética de Roberto Bolaño*. While Acero shares Andrews' sense that the poetry in Bolaño's novels represents a recurring refusal to abandon the "youthful openness" he acquired as an Infrarrealist, his study is based on two very different assumptions. It assumes, first, that the totality of Bolaño's work is multi-genre, made up of all the genres of the medium such as novels, short stories, poetry, articles, conferences, interviews. It also assumes, following Bruno Montané,[4] that Bolaño's poetry and prose emerge from the same understanding of writing, and that as such they're part of the same writing project. While Acero's understanding of Bolaño's work affirms in fundamental respects Andrew's metaphor of an "expanding universe," he considers it more literally, with respect to writing, as an integration of genres in which poetry, in particular, is fundamental.

Exploring the permanent tension of poetry and prose in Bolaño's work, and the figure of the poet in his writing, through an intertextual, transversal reading of his early poetry and late narrations, Acero shows the connections between his poem *Reinventing Love* (1976) and *2666* (2004) by analyzing the landscapes in both texts: in the former, the lyrical capacity of the poet to see and inscribe the present reality, and in the latter the horrific violence of a Santa Theresa where, as described by the narrator, people suffers from optophobia. Another connection exists in considering his first Infrarrealist manifesto "Leave It All, Once More" (1976) and *The Savage Detectives* (1998). Acero's procedure is quite productive, as it allows us to see the continuities and expansions of Bolaño's writing trajectory, and that which kept propelling it. Thus, adding to Acero's reading strategy, we can correlate Bolaño's article "La nueva poesía latinoamericana" from 1977 with the poem "La poesía latinoamericana," included in the first edition of *The Unknown University* (1992). In the latter, a virulent and blunt language emerges as the poetic subject describes Latin American poetry – a tone that is absent in the article of 1977. We can also compare the series of poems on the topic of "detectives" included in *The Unknown*

---

[4] Burno Montané, "Prefiguraciones de la Universidad Desconocida," in *Jornadas Homenaje–Roberto Bolaño (1953–2003)*, edited by Ramón González Ferriz (Barcelona: ICCI, 2005), 95–102.

University and *The Savage Detectives*, which presents an interesting insight since these poems predate the writing of the novel, and one must conclude that the poetry is the source for his narrative. The poem functioned as the script which the narrator-director relied upon to create his expansive and polyphonic film narrative.

Acero's main argument is that Bolaño's writing project is to be taken as a whole; that the poems of 1974–1977 present a specific view of the world with the realities of horror as primary theme and that this worldview appears as a coda twenty years later in *Nazi Literature in the Americas, Distant Star, The Savage Detectives,* and *Amulet.* Acero suggests that there is a deep and productive link between Bolaño's poetry and prose. Acero's intertextual procedure allows him to concurrently examine Bolaño's oeuvre in genealogical terms (a *Bildung* with temporal leaps and comparisons), and as a spiral that in its constant movement returns, retakes visions, and expands stories. In his analysis of Bolaño's key poems written over two and a half decades (he offers lengthy readings of "The years," "Roberto Bolaño's Devotion," "Lisa," "The Donkey," "Muse," among other less known poems), he notes that the figure of the oxymoron and the symbol of the ouroboro widely define his writing. Following Glissant, Acero understands the oxymoron as a convenient literary form to describe the chaos and unpredictability of human relationships. The figure of the ouroboro alludes to the cyclical flow (a snake biting its tail, which can refer to his constant imaginary return to México in fiction and poetry) that defines the nature of Bolaño's writing.

Approaching Bolaño's work in a way that is self-critical and dialogical, Acero places in conversation an important group of scholars who have written on Bolaño's poetry (Patricia Espinoza, José de Jesús Osorio, Rubén A. Arias, Andrés Ibañez, Andrea Cobas, José Promis, Miriam Pino, to name a few). Emphasizing, like Arias and Cobas, the expansion of the Infrarealist experience and writing throughout Bolaño's literary "career," and exploring in the process how later narratives echo some of his early texts, he identifies three stages of Bolaño's poetry: "the Infrarealist," "the deterritorialized author," and "that of the death." More than considering Bolaño as an Infrarealist poet and narrator, Acero tries to critically "auscultate those strands that more or less bind him to the tribe whether he wants it or not – and perhaps even to his own regret – because there are too many things that cannot be hidden within a discourse that only barely attempts to avoid minimally its history" (Acero, 2017, 77). The strands to which Acero refers includes Bolaño himself, who continually underscores his own distance and solitary path away from the Infrarealist stage.

In various interviews, Bolaño referred to Infrarealism as a movement that ended for him in 1977, upon his arrival in Barcelona. While critics have generally taken these commentaries at face value, José Jesús Osorio has called Bolaño's explanation into question: "he did not stop being an Infrarrealist as he imagines himself; although he no longer believes in the Revolution in his later days, he had not stopped equating aesthetics with ethics, as he did in his early writings expressed in the Infrarealist Manifesto: 'Our ethics are the Revolution, our Aesthetics, life: one-lone-thing'" (Osorio, 2013, 139). These approaches by Acero and Osorio have opened a fruitful field of analysis to be explored further.

Mario Santiago Papasquiaro

We know the following: poets are frequently characters in Bolaño's novels and short stories. Poets are depicted stubbornly surviving in low-paying jobs, going through the experience of exile, failure, marginality, loneliness, pursuing mysteries, and roaming the streets. In one of his major novels, *The Savage Detectives*, poets and poetry are at the center of a narrative that portrays a generation. Bolaño provides a fictionalized account of Infrarealism and one of the main co-protagonists – Ulyses Lima – is based on Mario Santiago Papasquiaro, who was as Yépez calls him Bolaño's "spiritual and literary companion." In the novel the protagonists seek the unification of poetry and life, a new ethics of writing, a rent with the traditional *modus operandi* of poets – as well as a nomadic existence. These principals fully represent the agenda of Infrarealism. The figure of the poet is central to Infrarealism's rebellion. For Infrarealists, poetry is not only a space for textual emancipation but a social practice of life; poetry resists being part of the market economy and can manage to have a full existence outside the literary establishment. The poet, and Mario Santiago-Ulyses Lima, therefore, fully embodies such rebellion and ethics.

Significantly, Santiago's presence in Bolaño's oeuvre also occurs in his poems. No other poet has been referenced or included as a character in Bolaño's poems as Mario Santiago has, including those poets that critics claim are major influences on Bolaño's work (such as Parra). In *The Unknown University* Bolaño references Santiago several times in his poems: "A sonnet," "Mario Santiago," "A FLY INSIDE A FLY / A THOUGHT INSIDE A THOUGHT / AND MARIO SANTIAGO INSIDE MARIO SANTIAGO," "The Worm," "Atole," "The Light," "The Donkey," "Roberto Bolaño's Devotion," and other untitled poems. In these poems Mario Santiago appears in different roles: his loyal partner of adventure, the guardian of the generation's dream, an indelible memory, and a poet victimized by the literary powers. In "The Donkey," Santiago is the poet who leads his friend toward the desert in the Mexico–US border to the world horrors at the end of twentieth century that Ciudad Juárez embodies.

While critics have acknowledged the existence of Mario Santiago when considering Bolaño's writing, the influence of his presence and crucial writing have been ignored. Yet as Miriam Pino rightly states, "Santiago led Bolaño through the meanders of another Mexican poetry, underground, that finds in *The Savage Detectives* perhaps the best and deepest tribute."[5] During his life Santiago published two poetry books, *Eternal Kiss* (1995) and *Swan's Howl* (1996), and two collections of his poems have been published posthumously, *Jeta de Santo* (2007), and *Art & Trash* (2012). Santiago is a decisive presence in Bolaño's life, epitomizing the poet's rebellion and ethics; his influence on Bolaño's poetics is palpable.

At the foundation of Infrarealism, two long poems articulated the group's poetics: *Reinventing Love* (1976) and *Advise from 1 Disciple of Marx to 1 Heidegger Fanatic* (1975) written by Bolaño and Mario Santiago, respectively. In both poems the poetic subject faces the fragmentation of reality and aims to undo such fragmentation by offering a larger, dialectical worldview. In his long poem *Reinventing Love*, the speaker wants to grasp social totality – make visible the dark holes of reality – through the many fragments that the lyrical subject observes in his surroundings: "All of a sudden everything exists beyond the startled eye ... All of a sudden everything weighs on the back ... All of a sudden everything exists between the vegetables and the flies on the market in ruins ... All of a sudden everything takes on substance and comes into view" (Bolaño, *Reiventing Love*, 1977). Within that observation, the poem discloses the intense, difficult relationship between lovers and social reality: "And if I don't love you why do I count the beds where we have formicated? / And love will come with Class Struggle at a decisive point / Bang! Bang! / We come from Infrareality. Where are we going?" (Bolaño, *Reiventing Love*, 24).

Written a year earlier, Santiago's *Advise from 1 Disciple of Marx to 1 Heidegger Fanatic* opens by explicitly naming reality's complex fragmentation: "The world gives you itself in fragments / in splinters: / in 1 melancholy face you glimpse 1 brushstroke by Dürer / in someone

---

[5] Miriam Pino, "Enigma de (Poe)sía: 'El burro' de Roberto Bolaño y 'Gas de los matrimonios' de Eduardo Espina," *Literatura y Lingüística* 19 (December 2007): 101–113; 104.

happy the grimace of 1 amateur clown" (Santiago, 2020, 19). While the poem describes a park in Mexico City, its images open onto a larger topography as the poetic subject elaborates from the many fragments a complex map of the world and poetry, and of the figure of the poet in his daily endeavors. The park thus acquires the sense of being a meeting place, a temporary retreat, as well as a crossroads of multiple historical and cultural realities, through which the young (Heideggerian and Marxist) poets traverse literally and metaphorically. Santiago thus juxtaposes images and attitudes opposing the bucolic and the urban, formal phrasing and verbal overflow, high and popular culture, daily anguish and complacency, writing and speech. The park – fragment and metaphor of the world – becomes one of the places where the subjectivity of the individual is constructed, including that of the poet. Santiago offered in his long poem a material and dialectical poetics, a way of dealing with poetic fragmentation through an unexpected flow of images between the local and the global material culture. Santiago makes clear this process in the poem: "The fragments the splinters from earlier / become in hands like Houdini's / 1 scream as solid & real / as 1 breast or 1 apple / or 1 desire that turns all bodies into 1 transparent prism" (49). While Bolaño in his poems depicted an autobiographical subject experiencing fragmentation – a poem can be seen as a microcosm – it was in the novels and short stories, following Santiago's poetics undoing fragmentation, where he fully explored the complex and horrific world of twentieth century.

CHAPTER 18

Poetry II: Parody and the Question of History
Sergio Villalobos-Ruminott

I

Roberto Bolaño has rapidly become a referential name in contemporary literature. His narrative work, prolifically translated into English and appreciated around the world, has been at the center of several debates concerning the status of Latin America's contemporary novel, global literature, "dirty" realism, and the transformations of the Latin American literary canon. His two main novels, *The Savage Detectives* and *2666*, along with a series of short novels revolving around the main ones as the Galilean moons around Jupiter, have informed if not defined the main lines of discussion around the relationship between literature and globalization, femicides, narco-narrative, torture and political violence, war and exile, and so on. However, we should keep in mind Bolaño's skeptical opinions about the mutations of the literary space precipitated by the ongoing process of transnational corporatization (Alfaguara, Planeta, Anagrama, among a few others). This is so since the corporatization of literature is affecting the Spanish American literary production and circulation *in toto*, at least from the Latin American Boom, redefining the whole tradition according to commercial imperatives.[1]

---

[1] See Roberto Bolaño, "Sevilla me mata." At: *Palabra de América* (Barcelona: Seis Barral, 2004), 17–21. The last part of his novel *The Savage Detectives* (Bolaño, Roberto, and Wimmer, Natasha Transl. *The Savage Detectives* [New York: Picador/Farrar, Straus and Giroux, 2008]), as well as "The Part of the Critics" in his novel *2666* (Roberto Bolaño and Natasha Wimmer, Transl. *2666* [New York: Farrar, Straus and Giroux, 2008]), are both thematizations of the crisis of the literary due to the constitution of transnational markets and the ongoing capture of literature by university experts. In fact, the replacement of the classical literary critic (who usually expressed his/her judgments through newspaper and public interventions) by the literary agent (who usually represents the interests of editorial corporations) and the university expert (who usually represents a "technical" approach to literature) implies the mutation of the standards that defined the quality of the literary "product," and the current predominance of easy-to-read, funny, and "digestible" texts as the ones that proliferate in airports and feed the reading diet of friendly and non-relevant reading clubs.

If this were not enough, a whole chapter could be written just on the impact Bolaño's work has had on Latin American studies in the North American universities, where along with several monographs and doctoral dissertations, one should add critical appraisals, compilations, and some relevant attempts to question his literary quality and his relevance in relation to the diversity and heterogeneity of Latin American literary production.[2] For better or for worse, Bolaño remains a central reference for current discussions on literature and his works still demand critical confrontation. By the same token, the obvious disparity between the reception of his narrative and his poetry not only reveals the priorities of the professional field, it also expresses the difference in the scope, quality, and relevance of his fiction and his poetry, or at least this seems to be the case. In fact, some critics consider his poetic work as notoriously less relevant, if not totally unexceptional, when compared to his novels and short stories, and some even claim that Bolaño's poetry is just an excuse for the fabrication of a fictional persona that, with all the autobiographical elements one can read in his literary alter egos, is instrumental for the invention of a literary myth.[3] It is in this context that the Chilean critic Matías Ayala insists on considering the relationship between Bolaño's poetry and narrative in the following terms: "As the work of Roberto Bolaño became well-known by the mid-nineties, his previous poetic work became part of the narrator's pre-history, despite the fact that he took part of that biographical material [which belonged to his poetry] for his fictional work. Thus, the poetry he wrote during all those years could be taken as a biographical-literary indication to retrospectively understand his creative process." (99) Following this line of argumentation, Arturo

---

[2] Héctor Hoyos, *Beyond Bolaño: The Global Latin American Novel* (New York: Columbia University Press, 2015). Hoyos attempts to break away from the monopoly Bolaño would have had in recent critical assessment of the regional literary production, trying to supplement this blind spot by referencing several contemporary Latin American writers (among them, César Aira, Fernando Vallejo, Diamela Eltit, and Mario Bellatin), which makes of his intervention not only a critique of Bolaño, but also an interrogation about the way his literature has been dealt with in US universities. In this sense, his study wants to think of the so-called global novel and the effect of globalization as it is thematized insistently by contemporary Latin American writers, however, what matters for me is precisely the singular status of this world literature and its conditions of possibilities in a post-literary world, a discussion that exceeds my current goal.

[3] Alejandro Palma Castro, "Un Poeta latinoamericano en el D.F.: irrupción poética de Roberto Bolaño," in *Roberto Bolaño: ruptura y violencia en la literatura finisecular*, ed. Felipe A. Ríos Baeza (Ciudad de México: Ediciones Eón, 2010), 89–105. See also, Matías Ayala, "Notas sobre la poesía de Roberto Bolaño," in *Bolaño Salvaje*, ed. Edmundo Paz Soldán, Gustavo Faverón Patriau, and Erik Haasnoot (Barcelona: Editorial Candaya, 2008), 91–101. Ayala even says: "Bolaño believes he is a bad poet and publishes to show and testify that he has failed" (100).

Belano, the young Viscerealist[4] poet who, along with Ulises Lima (Mario Santiago Papasquiaro), are the main characters of *The Savage Detectives*, would be not only a clear autobiographical reference, but also an embodiment of the literary strategy planned by Bolaño to overcome his frustrations as a poet and to introduce himself as a mythical persona within the literary market. Ayala emphasizes: "Being a mediocre poet grants him [Bolaño] authority to write about melancholic unexceptional poets, and about their arbitrary and humiliating destinies. Thus, poetry became an adjective qualifying his persona and his character Arturo Belano: narrator, reader, cultural animator, chronically ill, sometimes adventurous and sometimes a proletarian" (92).[5] With the 2007 publication of *La universidad desconocida*, however, a poetry book that gathers most of his early poetic work, a new image of the writer emerges.[6] Certainly, this publication made available for the first time poems that were published in unknown editorial houses and discontinued amateur journals. Thanks to this volume and its subsequent translation into English, the image of a failed poet, the one that deserted poetry to embrace narrative, is put in question, demanding a more sustained engagement with his creative process. This is the opinion that mobilizes the critical assessments of Patricia Spinoza and Adriana Castillo-Berchenko, who have emphasized some important characteristics of Bolaño's poetry: its conversational and quotidian use of language, the abundance of plain dialogues, humour and self-irony, the dream-like dimensions of its spaces, and the experimental character of his poetical topology in general.[7] They also emphasized the disparity and heterogeneity of Bolaño's *poemarios* (poem-books) according to different moments in the life of this itinerant writer, and the obvious influence of Nicanor Parra and Ernesto Cardenal. Nevertheless, Espinoza underlines the way in which Bolaño's poetry portrays the singularity of the isolated poet, his resistance to any sort of affiliation, and his critical understanding of Latin American history: "Roberto Bolaño's first three

---

[4] One should keep in mind that the Viscerealists are a literary representation, particularly in *The Savage Detectives*, of the actual Infrarealists, a group of poets founded in 1975 by Bolaño and Mario Santiago Papasquiaro.

[5] Ayala, nonetheless, pays attention to a very significant element, the transition from Bolaño's lyric discourse to a fictional one, which is triggered by the abandonment of the first person and the assumption of a fictional person that would be more adequate to his style.

[6] Robert Bolaño, *La universidad desconocida* (Barcelona: Anagrama, 2007). See also the English version: *The Unknown University*, translated by Laura Healy (New York: New Directions, 2011).

[7] Patricia Espinosa, "Tres libros de poesía del primer Bolaño: *Reiventar el amor, Fragmentos de la universidad desconocida y El último salvaje*," in *Roberto Bolaño: la experiencia del abismo*, edited by Fernando Moreno (Santiago: Ediciones Lastarria, 2011), 63–78. And Adriana Castillo-Berchenko, "Roberto Bolaño y la poesía del héroe desolado," in *Roberto Bolaño: la experiencia del abismo*, 79–88.

book of poetry, exposed us to a lyric inserted into the quotidian that belongs to an extremely solitary subject, but this lyric also contains a political vision, addressed to the Latin American collective, concerned with the constatation of the ruin, the loss, the failure of the revolutionary project" (78). Castillo-Berchenko insists for her part on Bolaño's ability to redefine the standards of Latin American poetry:

> Undisputed narrator, sagacious literary analyst, Roberto Bolaño is above everything else a poet. A gifted poet, authentic creator of a new tonality in Latin American and Hispanic poetry of the late 20th century. Atypical and touching at the same time, ironic and enigmatic, Bolaño's lyric discourse disturbs and surprises, dazzles and disarms the reader. Familiarized with it from his childhood, it is in his adolescence that poetry would have taken over the life of the artist. (80)

According to Espinosa and Castillo-Berchenko therefore, Bolaño is not only a creative, experimental, and natural poet, but one who is also concerned with the exhaustion of both the political and the aesthetic revolutionary project of his generation. However, to determine whether Bolaño is a great poet or instead his poetry is unexceptional and only represents a material to be recycled later by his narrative strategy is not relevant for my purpose here. My goal is not so much to comment on the quality of his poetry nor to evaluate his mythicizing strategy. I attempt to elaborate some indications regarding his poetic imagination. I understand poetic imagination as the complex system of ideas feeding his literary works, including his poems, novels, short stories, and his critical essays. In general terms, this poetic imagination is directly related to his self-representation as an exiled figure of Latin American literature, a "romantic dog" who, as a young writer, was politically committed but betrayed by the bureaucratic left and subsequently repressed by the right-wing regimes and their monopoly of cultural institutions. By the same token, I am not concerned with determining whether Bolaño was an active participant of the Chilean resistance to dictatorship, a political prisoner during the first days of the *coup d'état* of 1973, a defiant member of the post-68 Mexican youth, and a poor yet self-sufficient *émigré* in Mexico and Spain, or just a privileged witness to these brutal events, one who disguised his privileges by the invention of a romantic and long-suffering literary character. What concerns me the most is Bolaño's implicit elaboration of the historical processes that inform his literary works. In other words, more than poetry or narrative understood in conventional terms, what matters for me here is the way Bolaño grasps the transformation and possibilities of literature today, after the series of *coups d'état* and civil wars that devastated the continent in the last part of the twentieth century. It is not by chance that he positioned his work in direct yet oppositional relationship to those of the Latin American Boom and the Latin American long-poem – the highest achievements of twentieth century regional literature that shared a common conception about the potentiality of literature to fulfill the regional historical process, while believing in the power of language to capture and illustrate the distinctive characteristics of Latin American literature and culture.[8]

I contend that one can read in Bolaño's works a thematization of poetry and history as a parodical representation of the mythopoetic feeding the habitual canon of Latin American literature. At the same time, his sardonic approach to history interrupts the logic of history that co-belongs with the abovementioned mythopoetic, a logic of history oriented to and by an infinite process of liberation, which finds in the sociopolitical and literary revolutions its realization, and in the poetic and political avant-gardes, its main vehicles.

II

I take the notion of the mythopoetic from the French philosopher Philippe Lacoue-Labarthe, who, in several interventions regarding the mimetic tendency of Western literature and the ambiguous status of the "origin" in the philosophy of Martin Heidegger, interrogates the so-called singularity of the poetic experience and the construction, around the poem, of a particular myth (or myths), organized by the same principles defining Western metaphysics.[9] This mythopoetic would be particularly explicit (yet not privative) in the Romantics' reaction to modernity and would re-emerge in the German tradition as a sort of national aestheticism. According to Lacoue-Labarthe, what feeds Heidegger's political

---

[8] I am referring to the whole critical apparatus that has been predominant through the twentieth century, which reads and makes sense of Latin American literature by reducing it to the nation formation process, the process of transculturation, and the national liberation from imperialism. In this context, the classical examples of literary works already framed by this archeo-teleological mode of reading are Gabriel García Márquez's *One Hundred Year of Solitude* in narrative and, in poetry, Pablo Neruda's *Canto General*. Do these works demand a different reading? Yes, but the point here is that their "natural" inscription is within the hermeneutical horizon of the Cold War period. See Jean Franco, *The Decline and Fall of the Lettered City: Latin America in the Cold War* (Cambridge, MA: Harvard University Press, 2002).

[9] Philippe Lacoue-Labarthe, *Typography: Mimesis, Philosophy, Politics* (Cambridge, MA: Harvard University Press, 1989). See also his *Heidegger and the Politics of Poetry* (Urbana: University of Illinois Press, 2007).

involvement with the Nazi regime and its promises was precisely this national aestheticism. This is further supplemented by Jacques Derrida's analysis of Heidegger's interpretation of Georg Trakl's poetry, in his recently published *Geschlecht III*.[10] I won't elaborate further on this crucial topic here, but I will emphasize that there are many elements informing this mythopoetic that are relevant for us, among them: the self-appointed privileged position of German language and culture in relation to the classic world and its legacy; the exclusive ability of German poetry to capture human existence, dwelling, and thinking beyond the generalities of the Enlightenment; the correspondence of German poetry and its people (*Geschlecht*) to safeguard the meaning of idiomatic words before the babelic catastrophe of languages; and, of course, poetry's singular ability to deal with the question of the origin, national identity, and destiny. In fact, both Lacoue-Labarthe and Derrida criticized Heidegger's involvement with national-socialism by appealing not to the obvious and tiresome strategy that denounces his temporary membership in the NSDAP, his famous rectoral address of 1933, his antisemitism, and his silence regarding the Final Solution. They rather problematized Heidegger's shortcomings by inscribing them in this mythopoetic horizon that granted Germany a singular destiny, and to its poetry an exclusive access to history and thought.

What interests me the most from this deconstruction of the mythopoetic dimension of metaphysics is the privileged relationship between poetry and historical truth, or, alternatively, the relationship between the saying of the poets and the historicity of the people. Of course, I am not claiming that something similar might be said about Latin American literature, without considering several necessary mediations. I am using this deconstructive reading of the mythopoetic to formulate instead an interrogation about the Latin American literary tradition and the presumptions attached to it: the fact that we still speak about Latin American literature as a whole, that we assume it to be written "naturally" in Spanish, and that we still consider this literature as "equivalent" to the literary production of the West (our compensatory/symbolic access to modernity).[11] In this sense, both magical realism and the literary Boom as the highest moments in the region's literary history, as well as the poetical elaboration of this history by

---

[10] Jacques Derrida, *Geschlecht III: Sex, Race, Nation, Humanity* (Chicago: University of Chicago Press, 2020).
[11] See the incisive interrogation of these and other presumptions in Andrés Ajens, *Poetry after the Invention of América: Don't Light the Flower* (New York: Palgrave Macmillan, 2011).

a series of ambitious, comprehensive, and topologically rich poetic works I have called the Latin American long-poem – following the American long-poem, from Ezra Pound to Charles Olson, for example – shared the unproblematized assumption about the direct, self-evident, and transparent relationship between history and its literary representation. To be more precise, I am not only interested in questioning this isomorphic assumption (the so-called correspondence between the text and the historical context), but rather, I am more concerned with the very reduction of both history and the literary elaboration of it to a particular logic that determines this history and the meaning of literature according to an archeo-teleological, linear and progressive mechanism produced and reproduced by standard criticism.[12] Therefore, on one hand I am questioning the mimetic economy that reduces literary works to a particular logic of history, while on the other hand, and without renouncing a necessary complication of mimesis, I am questioning the very reduction of history to logic; a logic that manifests itself as a particular philosophy of history. This is so precisely because here we are dealing with a very persistent philosophy that organizes the history of the region according to an ongoing process of development and realization, a process that could be understood as leading towards a final access to modernity or, alternatively, towards a final liberation.[13]

To be clear, I am not attempting to read in Bolaño's works a simple allegorical representation of globalization and the exhaustion of the nation-state. Far from this, I am trying to read in Bolaño's poetical imagination a particular elaboration of the exhaustion and disarticulation affecting the mimetic economy that has fed standard criticism. Thus, to discard Bolaño in the name of a literary work committed to the fights against neoliberal globalization, for example, is to miss the point entirely. It would mean to reduce Bolaño's work to the historical and historicist frame that informs

---

[12] By standard criticism I mean the criticism that informs most of Latin American literary studies, a field that has produced the most relevant readings of this literature and, at the same time, has given the criteria and categories that organize the historicist disposition of this literature as a particular (identitarian and cultural) *myth and archive*. See the timely analysis of Brett Levinson, *The Ends of Literature: The Latin American "Boom" in the Neoliberal Marketplace* (Stanford: Stanford University Press, 2001).

[13] This philosophy of history is not restricted to the modern, bourgeois conception of history as progress and development, it is also central to the vulgar and schematic Marxist version of history related to the inevitability of the revolution as realization of history's laws. In other words, this archeo-teleological mechanism that organizes the meaning of history and literature according to the logic of liberation and realization expresses itself also through the historical sequence of Independence, nation formation, industrialization, modernization, and globalization, as different stages that define Latin America's painful and delayed access to modernity.

the mythopoetic of Latin American literary criticism and its particular version of history. I insist, Bolaño grants us access to the question of history without reinseminating the claims about a secret historicity that could only be disclosed through the careful reading of the "poem." Furthermore, the parodic aspects of his poetical imagination permit us to escape the isomorphic tendency that reads in literary work a direct, self-evident, and relatively transparent discourse on social reality, while also opening the question about the literary resources and skills needed to elaborate a thoughtful relation to history. From this perspective, it does not matter much if Bolaño is an exceptional or an unexceptional poet, or whether or not his literature is politically committed and, therefore, inserted within the hegemonic and sovereign frame that defined the mythopoetic of modern and contemporary literary criticism in Latin America. What matters is to determine to what degree does his work enable the question of history beyond any philosophical overdetermination.

III

There are many possibilities to corroborate Bolaño's parodic representation of history and literature, and to deal with his sardonic deconstruction of the logic of history and its archeo-teleological operations. We might refer to his short essays and public interventions to become acquainted with his particular detachment from the literary canon and its institutions,[14] or we might read his deconstructive strategy in his short stories and novels. For example, *By Night in Chile* could perfectly be interpreted as a deconstruction of the house as a central trope of Chilean literature (from Blest Gana and Eduardo Barrios to José Donoso) that now does not allegorize the conciliatory dynamics of the nation formation process, but the brutal secret of the co-belonging between literature and torture.[15] In a similar way, we can read Carlos Wieder, the pilot and poet who is the main character of *Distant Star*, as the allegory of the brutal co-belonging of

---

[14] "Sevilla me mata." See also Roberto Bolaño, *Entre paréntesis: ensayos, artículos y discursos (1998–2003)* (Barcelona: Editorial Anagrama, 2004).

[15] Roberto Bolaño, *By Night in Chile* (New York: New Directions Books, 2003). Let's recall that the house in question here is the place where María Canales (Mariana Callejas in real life) organized the late-night reunions with writers and artists during Pinochet's dictatorship, while her partner (Michael Townley in real life, an ex-CIA agent working for the dictatorship), tortured political prisoners in the basement. This curious architectural co-belonging of both scenes, the bohemian and the punitive one, is a clear allegory of the structural complicity between culture and power in those years, something that inevitably generated much critical reaction against Bolaño.

artistic and military avant-gardes and as a clear reference to the land art and sky poetry of Raúl Zurita (one of the greatest Chilean poets alive and the author of a one of the most impressive contemporary long-poems).[16] Wieder is also relevant beyond the local context in so far as he might be thought of as the literary re-enactment of Otto Dietrich zur Linde, the Nazi assassin and sophisticated official who is the main character of Borges's *Deutsches Requiem*, and who represents, as Wieder does, the unsuspected continuity between civilization and barbarism, between law and crime.[17] Finally, we might also follow the whereabouts of two central characters in Bolaño's literary universe, Oscar Amalfitano and Benno von Archimboldi, in as much as both, though in different circumstances, represent the complicated path of literature through the twentieth century. Amalfitano is a Chilean professor who first lived exiled in Spain, and then, moved to Santa Teresa (Ciudad Juárez), while Archimboldi, a German soldier in the Second World War, who fought on the Eastern front and later became an enigmatic writer, also ended up in the same northern city of México. Santa Teresa and the Sonoran Desert represent a sort of black hole towards which the plots and characters of Bolaño's literary universe are sucked in. Let's not forget that Cesárea Tinajero, the cult-like avant-gardist poet of the 1920 and crucial reference for Belano and Lima's search in *The Savages Detective*, is also hiding in the Sonoran Desert where Arturo Belano and Ulises Lima finally find her. Tinajero's uneventful deaths in the second part of the novel not only triggers the diaspora of the viscerealist in the last part of the novel, but also anticipates the series of deaths that constitute "The Part About the Crimes" in *2666*.

If this is the case, then Bolaño's work requires a certain consideration in order to grasp these internal and intertextual dynamics. At the same time, and this is my main suggestion – one that I can only adumbrate here since it demands further elaboration beyond the limits of this text – the main characters of *The Savage Detective* are neither Belano and Lima, nor the Viscerealists, but poetry and literature itself. That is to say, what the novel thematizes is the series of transformations affecting the status of poetry and literature in general after the brutal transformation of Latin America's historical reality thanks to the neoliberal globalization implemented from

---

[16] Raúl Zurita, *Anteparaíso* (Santiago de Chile: Editores Asociados, 1982). See also his *Purgatorio* (España: Visor Libros, 2010). And his *La Vida Nueva* (Santiago de Chile: Penguin Random House, 2018).
[17] Roberto Bolaño, *Distant Star* (New York: New Directions, 2004) and Jorge Luis Borges, "Deutsches Requiem," in *El Aleph* (Buenos Aires: Emecé Editores, 1968).

the 1970s onwards. To put it even more dramatically, what the novel thematizes is the final exhaustion of the long-poem's emancipatory aspirations, and the radical disarticulation of poetry and history that is at the core of Latin America's mythopoetic. The novel allows us to think through this disarticulation of history and poetry as an invitation to deal with the question of history beyond any overdetermination, any archeo-teleological organization, and beyond any principle of reason (*arche*) able to command and reinstitute the logic of history.

In an excellent approach to this topic, Andrea Cobas Carral and Verónica Garibotto understand Cesárea Tinajero as the allegory of this exhaustion: "The figure of Cesárea Tinajero condenses the failure of the modernization process undertaken by the avant-garde in 1920. With its passage from the dreamed modern metropolis to the Sonoran Desert, Cesárea breaks at the same time with the avant-garde and with the revolution" (167).[18] Since Cobas Carral and Garibotto are able to link the plot of the novel with the poetic imagination of Bolaño, therefore, their reading does not content itself with a mere description of the events, nor with a metaphorical emphasis on Bolaño's strategy of myth-production regarding his own *persona pública*. They read the poetic imagination at stake in the novel, a poetic imagination characterized by the exhaustion of former literary movements and their trust in literature's ability to change people's condition of life. The search for Cesárea Tinajero that mobilized the plot of the novel led Belano and Lima to the Sonora desert, only to find an unexceptional woman who suddenly dies a few moments after she is identified by them. The death of the poet is also the death of the investment in poetry's ability to make sense of history, representing not only an exhaustion of the poetic but also a disarticulation that sent both Belano and Lima on an erratic and infinite quest from which there is no return. This disarticulation implies, therefore, not only the separation of poetry and history, of language and historical destiny, but also the abrogation of the question of the origin and the end of history, its realization (the archeo-teleological dimension of mythopoetic), in a movement that destroys not only the utopic future but the aspiration of a clear origin, a home (*Heimat*) to which the poets could return. There is not gathering but proliferation, scattering fragments of the life of those who understood poetry as a way of looking at the reality without closing their

---

[18] Andrea Cobas Carral and Verónica Garibotto, "Un epitafio en el desierto: poesía y revolución en *Los detectives salvajes*," edited by Paz Soldán, Faverón Patriau, and Haasnoot, *Bolaño Salvaje*, 163–189.

eyes. Arturo Belano and Ulises Lima are not returning to Ithaca, they understand the world as an immense *Comala* – Rulfo's semi-fictional place – where, as in the Sonoran Desert, the living and the dead engage in a strange negative community that discloses the dark side of the former generations' revolutionary dreams:

> The failure of the avant-gardes' modernization process in the 1920s repeats itself in the 1970s, with the frustration of the cultural and political revolution for Latin America. The relationship between poetry and revolution is also present in the passage from the 1970s to the 1990s. If during the 1970s the promise of a Latin American revolution is part of the cultural climate from which Viscerealism emerges, [Ulises] Lima's experiences in Nicaragua and Belano's considerations before his departure to Africa unequivocally indicate the dramatic shipwreck of the revolutionary dream. If in the 1970s Viscerealists bet on an invisibility that put them away from the canonical circuits of literary consecration, in the 1990s the poetic paths of Lima and Belano ended up by radically separating from each other. (Cobas Carral and Garibotto 178–179)

The end of this story is Bolaño's paradoxical consecration, and his undesired centrality within Latin American literary studies. For better or for worse, his works are still alive and demanding a reading that does not content itself with easy identifications and subjective valuations. In short, we need a critical confrontation with Bolaño's works free from the mythopoetic frame that has informed conventional and professional criticism until today, a critical tradition that insists on reading literature in agreement with the imperatives of hegemonic thinking and calculative thought.

CHAPTER 19

The Novel and the Canon

Roberto González Echevarría

We suffer from nostalgia for the Boom. When will the next García Márquez emerge? Why has there not yet appeared a new Borges or Carpentier? We console or delude ourselves with the most recent novel by Vargas Llosa or Fuentes (now dead), or even the later novels of the author of *One Hundred Years of Solitude* (now also dead). We get excited about promising books by young authors. But it's not enough or the same. Those of us who had the joy of being shaped by the sixties in the past century remember an era in which new masterpieces appeared at vertiginous speed, with such unexpected classics as *Paradiso*, that extraordinary novel by a great writer (José Lezama Lima) we had barely heard of, and whom those who knew him considered to be a poet. In those same sixties a new generation burst on the scene in Latin America, with figures of the stature of Severo Sarduy and Manuel Puig, giving us the feeling that the party would never end. But that's not how it turned out. That new generation was decimated by AIDS, and the so-called post-boom (about which there are already various books) was a mute detonation. We continue waiting, like the Jews, for the Messiah to come. The Chilean Roberto Bolaño, who, with the tragic disposition to be the one, died young (at 50 years old, his dates 1953–2003), is the only recent Latin American narrator whose successes in our sphere and abroad recall those of the Boom, and announce perhaps the arrival of a splendid new era.

The irruption of Bolaño has led me to pose anew a problem that has continued to gnaw at me in recent years: How do we make judgments of literary value? According to what principles? And what are these principles based on? My obsession begins with reasons at once practical and theoretical. Many of us here are critics of contemporary literature, writing reviews for professional journals, deciding what should or should not appear in various publishing venues. In our daily routines as professors as well we are called upon, as Martí would say, to "exercise judgment," preparing reading lists for doctoral exams, or designing new courses on contemporary literature. In all these cases we have to decide, as the existentialists used to say, because we cannot accommodate everyone. It is true that sometimes ideologies or critical tendencies incline us in favor of this or that work, as if personal taste didn't intervene, but there is always an implicit judgment of value. What's more, and this is a theoretical matter albeit one based in practice, experience teaches us that however much we promote or disparage an author, there is a consensus developed over time that prevents anyone from daring to remove Neruda from the canon for having been a communist, or Borges for having been a conservative. And works that at one moment were acclaimed for political reasons, like *I, Rigoberta Menchu*, fall into the oblivion they deserve. There is, as it were, a general criterion, a kind of overall critical reason, I am alluding of course to Kant, surpassing that of each one of us, that settles at the base of many opinions and accumulated preferences. I am going to speak now of one of Bolaño's works, *By Night in Chile* (*Nocturno de Chile*), published in the year 2000, that has been received, as virtually all of his works have, with applause. I am using here the translation by Chris Matthews.

What does *By Night in Chile* consist of? It's the confession, through an entire night's fever, of a Chilean priest, literary critic, aspiring young poet and member of Opus Dei, that unfolds on the verge of death and recounts his life, in particular the years extending from before Pinochet's death through the arrival of democracy. Elbowed on the bed, Sebastián Urrutia Lacroix, those are his name and surname, recounts his religious and literary vocation, his European travels, but above all his relationship with an old and influential literary critic, whose pseudonym is Farewell, and who is his mentor, and with Chilean writers he has critiqued with whom he is friendly. Sebastián also dramatizes his tense and intense engagement with the "wizened youth," a character invented by him who represents his conscience, who frequently rebukes his behavior, and in response to whose accusations he offers his confession, which is the novel we read. This psychodrama leads to the story's culminating moment, the final anagnorisis with which this short 150-page novel closes.

In recent essays I have tried to determine criteria that help me, *a priori*, to evaluate a new work; new because the classics or those works that today we would say are canonical, come already endowed with a halo that interferes with the evaluation process.

To judge a work on the basis of these criteria is, for me, a Kantian gesture. I say gesture because it is not a question, not by a long shot, of the rigorous application of Kant's philosophy. While his critiques focus more on the question of knowledge than on aesthetic appreciation (though eventually it includes it), my concern is precisely that of judging the quality of the text and deciding if it does or does not merit being elevated to that canon whose existence we owe to Harold Bloom (1994). Such a judgment implies, of course, the knowledge of the text, but in the approach I propose, that knowledge is an integral part of the evaluation itself, it is inherent to it. The work considered valuable is made known because it exhibits qualities that meet my evaluative criteria. This is also part of the Kantian gesture I speak of, and part of the assumption that there is a general evaluative knowledge that surpasses my own critical experience and guides it in the practice of reading; it is about the consensus I was speaking of earlier that consolidates a canon we explicitly or tacitly accept and that contains the general values I apply to the new work. I am attracted to the balance Kant proposes between experience, practice and ideal categories. There is an apparent circularity in all this; this work is good because it is good. I say apparent because that virtual canon exists objectively before the appearance of the work we are preparing to evaluate and before my own evaluation. I desperately want to avoid the usual ideological determinisms without falling into pure impressionism or worse political propaganda.

I return now to what I said in some of those essays which I mentioned about my criteria for literary evaluation. These are contained principally in my *Oye mi son: ensayos y testimonios sobre literatura hispanoamericana*. I know that these may appear very personal, but my own person constitutes the limit of what I know as the sum of my readings and the subtraction of my deficiencies. This is a balance between my recollections, their shortcomings, and my life experience. They are also criteria that I suspect many, if not most critics, implicitly share, and that, despite their personal aspect, can thus serves as a first approximation. The personal, as common property rather than something exclusively one's own, can be and is sharable, and where it is not, it is likely to be corrected in dialogue with others; this is the pragmatic element that also leads us back to Kant. In my case, I would like to think that most of my judgments have been confirmed by others over time. Their acceptance is not due, of course, only to me, but to preferences that have been established by the continued circulation of works that I (and others) have deemed valuable, as well as by the disappearance of other works that have not withstood the test of time. For me, the paradigmatic cases have been Severo Sarduy and Reinaldo Arenas, who have imposed themselves as important writers despite the political, sexual, and aesthetic prejudices of the Cuban commissars and their acolytes. On the other side are not only the many mediocrities promoted by official Cuban criticism that have fallen into (deserved) oblivion, along with flashes in the pan such as the Nicaraguan poet Ernesto Cardenal, who has been fading as the political movement in whose reflection he once shone disappears. The already classic writers I have studied, such as Alejo Carpentier, have, of course, endured and will continue to do so, established in their appropriate place. But Carpentier's last novel, *The Rite of Spring* (*La consagración de la primavera*), which I considered deficient from the outset (I wasn't the only one), has had no resonance. On the other hand, I have been wrong about other "anointed ones." *Hopscotch* (*Rayuela*), for example, which at first dazzled me, today falls from my hands, and I suspect that Cortázar's legacy will be a handful of short stories, but nothing more. The silence that today hovers around his work corroborates, I think, that suspicion.

The five criteria I proposed in the aforementioned essays, and which I propose applying today to *By Night in Chile*, are as follows: First: the work must have elevation, height, in the sense Longinus gives to the term, in the issues that it addresses, which are the great ones of all time, and which seem banal when enumerated (but this is merely a rhetorical flaw): love, death, guilt, injustice, the desire for transcendence. This enumeration sounds hollow but only because what is decisive is how they take shape in the work. These issues are, in any case, the elements that give their works life and greatness, which, by the way, does not have to be matched by length. There are insufferable thousand-page, baggy-monster novels, and extraordinary ten-page stories.

Second: I prefer works that reveal their literary "warp," but with some discretion, like *One Hundred Years of Solitude*, and many good avant-garde novels, too. By warp I mean where irony resides, where the work and its author wink at us as readers reminding us that we are dealing with a work of fiction. This phenomenon is an important part of the work we are reading because, with it, the author reminds us of the imperfection of the human condition and our partial and very limited understanding of reality, writing and ourselves.

Third: the works that impress me always contain a certain secret that we are unable to decipher, even as they urge and provoke us to interpret it but which, in the end, nevertheless eludes us. That secret escapes as well, I believe, the consciousness of the writers themselves, who stand before it in a condition analogous to that of their readers. This secret unknowability is a residue, a supplement, in Derrida's sense, maybe the origin of the text itself, which presumes to be decisive, the opening or source in every sense. In trying to understand it, the writer's and reader's or critic's subconscious engage in dialogue with one other, and it is from this dialogue that the critic's text emanates, a text that tends at times to become enigmatic (*ma non troppo, per piacere*).

Fourth: important works transform the received tradition, but not uniquely at the local or national, but at the universal level. This is the hallmark of their originality, their brand, so to speak. I do not conceive of this relationship with tradition as an agonizing struggle between the new writer and his precursors, as in the theory of my great (late) friend Bloom, but rather as something more benign that may arise, on the contrary, from the new writer's desire to find protection in the shadow of a classic, but adding to it a personal touch that, in the best of cases, is transformed into something sublime in and of itself, not in relation to what precedes it. I think this is what happens with *One Hundred Years of Solitude*, in which we see echoes of Faulkner, of Carpentier, of Greek tragedy, of Cervantes, of Borges' short stories, and of many works that García Márquez himself mentions in the text. But the chronological frame of this great work, which indicates the presence of a carefully marked and fatal destiny, at once comic and tragic, is unique and all its own, also perfectly recognizable in any of its sentences, from the first to the last.

Fifth: the work must have a recognizable style of its own. There are writers without style, but we can at least characterize them as such. If we were radical materialists we would say that for us style depends on brain waves that determine periods of syntax and word order, as well as the placement of adjectives and use of verb tenses. The rhythm of a piece of prose or a poem consists of such choices, those that make up Proust's style, for example, incomparable and recognizable before we reach the end of the sentence which is, as we know, late to arrive.

To be sure, all these criteria refer to qualities simultaneously interwoven among them; the style has to be in tune with the theme, with the flirtation of that enigma that eludes us, with the elevation of the work, and so on. When this desired coherence does not take place, as occurs in works such as Joyce's *Ulysses*, and in those of such disciples of his as Guillermo Cabrera Infante, the resulting effect arises from the dissonance that then constitutes, paradoxically, a form of harmony.

First: *By Night in Chile* addresses transcendental themes, like death, to which the protagonist-narrator appears doomed, religious faith, the literary vocation, and the very nature of literature and criticism. It is saturated as well with guilt, the persistence of evil, and the complicity of writers and intellectuals with evil. In its very title, *By Night in Chile* announces a profound reflection, meticulous and sustained, about the nation. I say meticulous because the narrator's discourse includes a probing assessment of Chilean literature: several generations of modern writers are mentioned, some contemporary, and others from earlier periods, like Alberto Blest-Gana. There is a recapitulation of Chile's recent history and a considerable number of Chileanisms, almost as if it were a return to a nativist Chilean canon.[1] In the last analysis, the central theme of *By Night in Chile* is the essence of literature, and the spectacle of its being forged by a lucid consciousness saturated with literature, history, philosophy and theology. It is also fashioned by curiosity about the condition of that creative consciousness that manifests itself in the dramatic moment of its possible extinction: the narrator is about to die, and stages a psychodrama divided between the two previously mentioned characters: the protagonist-narrator and the "wizened youth," his conscience. The prostrated speaker identifies this as a purer, earlier self who has not yielded to the temptations and coercions of evil, and who questions him. In the end, in the anagnorisis that constitutes the novel's outcome, the narrator discovers that this "wizened youth" is still himself – that is to say, the one who has written the novel.

Regarding elevation, *By Night in Chile* not only achieves it for its transcendental themes, but plays with the Longinian concept itself, thus fulfilling the requirement to show its literary warp. I am referring to the series of scenes in which Sebastián is sent to Europe to study the preservation of medieval and renaissance churches. He discovers that their deterioration is due primarily to pigeon shit, and that the way to fight this scourge it through falconry, to hunt them with specially trained hawks. There is here a satirical element of nationalism, because the name of the guardian hawk of each church refers to some national characteristic, whether Italian, German, or Belgian. The Spanish hawk, which protects the cathedral of Burgos, is called, inevitably, "Rodrigo," and the French, "Ta Gueule" (the American version would be "Up yours," and the Cuban, "La tuya"). It seems to me that these falcons and their flights are an ironic allusion to Longinus and his theories of the "sublime," of elevation or height; those particular scenes display as well an accentuated literary tone, a rise in rhetorical tenor. I think I hear also in that "falconry of pigeons" a deformed echo of the mystic St. John of the Cross's "I flew so high, so high / that I caught my prey." All this is hilariously ironic because it is carried out to contain the rain of shit that the pigeons unload on the churches,

---

[1] Once, fundo, chupallas de paja, paltos, congrio, araucaria, eschumizado, chitas, roteque, guata, culear, picos, huevón, machas, micros, copuchentos, cartucho, etc.

which also announces the "shit storm" of the novel's final apocalyptic sentence. The relevance (pun intended) of these scenes increases if we take into account that the pigeon-cum-dove symbolizes the Holy Spirit in Roman Catholic doctrine. (There is an ample ornithological symbolism in *By Night in Chile* that I have no space to analyze here.) The Holy Spirit, and there is a white dove, shits on the Catholic church – literally on the Catholic churches – provoking their physical ruin. It is an eschatological prophecy in every sense, a brilliantly executed "fecal apocalypse," or a "scatological eschatology."

Second. For as much as it reveals its literary texture, and thus assumes a reflexive, ironic tone, *By Night in Chile* does so in a "natural" way, as if such a thing were possible, because it is the confession not only of a priest, but also that of a literary critic, very conscious of the elaboration of his discourse. In *By Night in Chile* there is no metatext, that is to say, there is nothing to clearly indicate what it is that we are reading. The illusion would be that it is a block of raw text, not subject to the rules of literature, not even to those of punctuation. But this in itself proves the contrary. We have already appreciated, in the scenes with the pigeons, a revelation of the literary aspect of the text. But, in addition, there is no doubt that what we read contains isolatable fragments, anthological, in some sublime cases, such as the vision, towards the end, of Father Antonio and Judas's Tree. The text is so literary and self-contained in its form because the protagonist-narrator is an immensely cultured individual. For example, the so-called "wizened youth" is an echo of the classic topos of the *puer senex* (the old man-child) studied by Ernst Robert Curtius (Sebastián is an assiduous reader of the Greek and Latin classics). But the literary warp manifests itself again in the narration of various histories, with characters drawn from real life, supposedly told by other characters, such as Farewell or Salvador Reyes, which are like passages from a novel in the making.

For example, in the story of the controversial author Ernst Jünger in German-occupied Paris, interwoven with that of the anorexic Guatemalan painter (no name given), the narrator enjoys an omniscience with respect to these characters as only a novelist using well-known literary license and resources could. The same is true in the dramatic final story, about the Chilean writer María Canales, in which the theme of the complicity between literature and evil reaches its apogee, and which we read knowing that it is like the draft of a novel or future story that the protagonist is preparing. The counterpoint between literature and immorality manifests itself in brilliant passages that alternate events in political life with the protagonist's readings, but which above all in this final story produce a kind of climactic transgression: the story of the literary meetings held in the mansion in which Canales, married to an American agent who turns out to be a collaborator with DINA (Pinochet's intelligence service), facilitates the persecution and torture of dissidents, actions that take place in the house's basement, sometimes even as these celebratory evenings are going on. When, with the fall of Pinochet, everything is discovered, many of the writers deny having attended the meetings. In this sense, *By Night in Chile* is itself as well a kind of political confession. In the end, the truth that emerges about all of this is not, of course, sharp and clear. It expresses itself rather in Canales' desolation and abandonment, once her complicity with the atrocities of the dictatorship is discovered. She is aware that it is in that situation of upheaval, complicity, consciousness of guilt, and the persistence of evil that literary creation takes place, that that creation is consubstantial with guilt. Sebastián abstains from judging her and, as priest, wants to absolve her. In the final instance this is the vision to which the protagonist has access in his night of nightmares and hallucinations as he sees himself, in his illness, on the verge of death. It is also, it seems to me, what gives the work its title. *By Night in Chile* alludes, of course, to the well-known poem "Night" ("Nocturno") by the Colombian poet José Asunción Silva, which Sebastián reads aloud to the delight of passengers and crew one night in the ship that transports him to Italy. This is also a nod to the complicit reader, presumably also imbued with literature. But "night" means here "Chile's nightmare," or "oneiric image of Chile."

Third. The secret a work keeps might be, it seems to me, that point at which my own ignorance manifests itself most clearly, or, to use the terminology of Paul de Man, my blindness, which I would like to see compensated for with some insight. This blindness can be congenital, innate ignorance, or a product of the defects of my upbringing and education, of the enormous cultural gaps we all have. But at times my incapacity opens a space for dialogue between my weak critical consciousness and Bolaño's powerful subconscious, with his literary critical persona as emblem or fetish of that shared practice. It will be by necessity a dialogue of the deaf, or a shared dark night, to the likely deception of which I give very conscious expression.

For me that blind spot is located in the fascist thematic suggested by the protagonist's belonging to Opus Dei. It is a story in which something like the origin of fascism seems to take shape, but which I can barely decipher. It is the account of an Austrian shoemaker (an allusion to Hitler?) who comes up with the idea of creating a park to honor national heroes whose monumental statues will be carved on the side of a mountain. But the shoemaker dies and the park falls into total neglect; it ends up being demolished by Soviet troops occupying the area during the Second World War. In the tale of the construction of the park (the opus) there is something like an oblique history of the creation of the literary work, with all its particulars and anxieties, which could be the story of how Bolaño conceives that process, including that of writing the very book we are reading:

> while the shoemaker lay exhausted, sprawled on the rumpled sheets, sometimes not even properly undressed, absorbed as he was in his obsessional dream, marching on through his nightmares, on the far side of which Heroes' Hill awaited him always, grave and quiet, dark and noble, his project, the work of which only fragments are known to us, the work we sometimes think we know but which in fact we hardly know at all, the mystery we carry in our hearts, and which, in a moment of rapture we set in the centre of a metal tray inscribed with Mycenaean characters, characters that stammer out our history and our hopes, but what they stammer out in fact is nothing more than our defeat, the joust in which we have fallen although we do not know it, and we have set our heart in the middle of that cold tray, our heart, our heart, and the shoemaker shivered in his bed ... (45–46)

> cuando el zapatero yacía rendido, enredado entre las sábanas, a veces sin siquiera desvestirse del todo entregado a su sueño obsesivo, marchando a través de sus pesadillas, al final de las cuales lo esperaba siempre la Colina de los Héroes, grave y quieta, oscura y noble, el proyecto, la obra de la que conocemos sólo fragmentos, la obra que a menudo creemos conocer pero que en realidad conocemos muy poco, el misterio que llevamos en el corazón y que en un momento de arrebato ponemos en el centro de una bandeja de metal labrada con caracteres micénicos, unos caracteres que balbucean nuestra derrota, la justa en donde hemos caído y no lo sabemos, y nosotros hemos puesto el corazón en medio de esa bandeja fría, el corazón, el corazón, y el zapatero se estremecía en el lecho. (59)

The switch from the first to the third person, from the discourse of the protagonist-narrator to that of the shoemaker, the position of the latter in bed, suggest a personal confession about literary creation, of the *work* – I italicize work to refer to Opus. The story of the shoemaker could be, in brief, an allegory of writing at the base of which there is a mixture of faith, dedication and praise of the nation and its traditions that approximates fascism. But I cannot understand the figure of the shoemaker: what has his profession to do with his desire to create the park, and how does all this tie in with the Chilean theme, although it could be a reflection about the Pinochet dictatorship, as it can also have parallels between the Paris occupied by the Nazis and Sebastián's Santiago, with its curfews during the dictatorship. This story is, for me, like a closed secret, but one that may contain the key to the very origin of *By Night in Chile*, which eludes me as it does possibly Bolaño as well, which is why he speaks "of the mystery we carry in our hearts."

Fourth. In *By Night in Chile* not only the national or the local, but the universal literary tradition is recycled or filtered. (I know "recycle" or "filter" are timeworn metaphors, maybe already useless, it would perhaps be better to say "consubstantial with received tradition"). I must say that, following the best conventions of Latin American literature – Garcilaso el Inca, Sigüenza y Gongora, Sor Juana, Bello, Martí, Carpentier, Neruda, Borges y Paz – Bolaño is a very learned writer, with all of Western culture in his head. The allusion to Silva's "Night" would come to represent the Latin American literature the narrator has absorbed; we must never forget that the protagonist is a literary critic with a vast erudition. But the novel is also a reflection on Chilean literature, from the most canonical to the most urgently contemporary. This Chilean literature passes through Sebastián's critical-creative consciousness to be reflected in the text he writes. Apart from Farewell, the old critic whom Sebastián the protagonist wants to see as his mentor, Chilean writers, from Neruda and Parra to Lafourcade and Lihn, all appear with their real names. *By Night in Chile* is not a *roman à clef*, but a settling of accounts of Chilean literature with itself, and its relationship to politics.

At the most abstract level, the novel reveals the complicity of literature with evil. For what besieges Sebastián is an acute sense of guilt, his own and that of other writers, palliated by his religious vocation, which inclines him toward mercy and forgiveness. This remorse is embodied in the figure of the "wizened youth," who would perhaps like to be the figure of Bolaño himself as novelist, a self-portrait. Regarding the history of Chile's relation to literature, specifically the era that extends from the electoral victory of Allende to the arrival of democracy after the defeat of Pinochet, the narrative is full of details about life in Santiago, and the protagonists, some of whom, like Pinochet and his Junta, are revealed to us in extraordinary conditions – they hire Sebastián to teach them a private course on Marxism! Here is the intellectual in the service of power.

As for Western literature, there is a strong presence of the *Confessions* of St. Augustine, justified by the fact that the protagonist-narrator is a priest who claims to have studied the saint at the seminary, among other fathers of the church. From the beginning we know that the supreme authority to whom he appeals in his confession is God himself, although he doesn't address himself to the deity directly as does St. Augustine: thus the dialogue remains instead within the drama of Sebastián´s own conscience. But, apart from the Augustinian religious theme (sin, guilt, patience, human inclination toward evil), the central issue is writing, as in the saint's *Confessions*. Here, and in his discourse, the narrator appeals to the Augustinian formula, adapted by Dante, of confession-conversion-poetry, except that here the conversion is at the very end of the text. That is to say, the conversion process would involve not only redeeming and reforming himself but also the practice of writing. Dante is present through the repeated mention of Sordello, a key character with whom the narrator seems to identify, whom he came to know only through Farewell, but who continues to resonate in his text in deformed versions as Sordel (this sounds in Spanish like "sórdido él," "sleazy him"). Sordello, who appears in Cantos VI and VII of *Purgatory*, was a troubadour born in Italy who wrote in Provençal and had a noteworthy political career (and love life, to be sure), to whom Dante concedes a place of honor in Purgatory like that of Farinata in *Inferno* and Cacciaguida in *Paradise*. The appearance of Sordello elicits a diatribe by the pilgrim-narrator about the *Comedy* and the political situation in the Italy of Dante's time. In *By Night in Chile*, Sordello seems to be a remote ancestor of the protagonist caught at a political and literary crossroads similar to his own – particularly in his relation to the Virgilian figure of Farewell. What this allusion to Dante suggests, evidently, is that the harangue against the Italian authorities could be made against the Chile of the 1970s and that *By Night in Chile* is, or could have been, that diatribe against Dante's Italy but in the present.

Fifth. The work must have style, *prosa* as we say in Spanish. I have already said several times that the protagonist-narrator, being a critic, a poet, and a man of culture, expresses himself in a polished, elevated, versatile style, with opportune allusions to art, philosophy and literature. I have mentioned as well that some of the stories he tells appear to be sketches of future stories or novels. I have referred, moreover, to sublime Longinian passages (we know that Longinus preferred the fragment) worthy of being anthologized. None is perhaps so playful, so full of rhetorical and poetic resources, so possessive of a syntactic, prosodic rhythm, attuned to what it narrates, as in this passage describing a ballroom dance:

> Dance, Father, I can't. I replied, it is contrary to my vows. With one hand I was holding a little notebook in which, with the other, I was drafting a book review. The book was called *As Time Goes By*. As time goes by, as time goes by, the whip-crack of the years, the precipice of illusions, the ravine that swallows up all human endeavour except the struggle to survive. The

syncopated serpent of the conga-line kept moving steadily towards my corner, lifting first its left legs all at once, then the right ones, and then I spotted Farewell among the dancers, Farewell with his hands on the hips of a woman who moved in the most exclusive circles of Chilean society at the time, a woman with a Basque surname, which unfortunately I had forgotten, while Farewell's hips in turn were gripped by an old man whose body was perilously frail, more dead than alive, but who beamed a smile at all and sundry and seemed to be having as much fun as anyone in the conga-line. (23)

Otras veces discernía a un grupo de figuras cogidas por la cintura, como si bailaran la conga, desplazarse a lo largo y ancho de un salón cuyas paredes estaban atiborradas de cuadros. Baile, padre, me decía alguien a quien yo no veía. No puedo, respondía, los votos no me lo permiten. Yo tenía un cuadernillo en una mano y con la otra escribía un esbozo de reseña literaria. El libro se llamaba *El paso del tiempo*. El paso del tiempo, el paso del tiempo, el crujidero de los años, el despeñadero de las ilusiones, la quebrada mortal de los afanes de todo tipo menos el afán de la supervivencia. La serpiente sincopada de la conga indefectiblemente se acercaba a mi rincón, moviendo y levantando al unísono primero la pierna izquierda, luego la derecha, luego la izquierda, luego la derecha, y entonces yo distinguía a Farewell que asía por la cintura a una señora de la mejor sociedad chilena de aquellos años, una señora de apellido vasco que desgraciadamente he olvidado, mientras él, a su vez, era asido por la cintura por un anciano cuyo cuerpo estaba a punto de desmoronarse, un viejo más muerto que vivo pero que sonreía a diestra y siniestra y que parecía disfrutar de la conga como el que más. (34–35)

Note that there is also an allusion, in this scene, to the medieval "dances of death." But the stylistic successes start from the first sentences, from the very opening of the novel itself: "I am dying now, but I still have many things to say" ["Ahora me muero, pero tengo muchas cosas que decir todavía" (1, 11)]. In that play of temporal adverbs – "now," "still" – the entire work is already contained.

At this stage, given such heights (pun, again, intended), it goes without saying that I believe *By Night in Chile* will, in fact, endure in the canon of Latin American, and of Western, literature. It is a little masterpiece at the level – and at times above the level – of the best that the canon's established novelists, those of the Boom, wrote. I think Bolaño is a better novelist than José Donoso, to place him in a strictly Chilean context. (My friend Pepe's ghost is going to come out tonight to pull my big toe). I declare myself an admirer of Bolaño, and I am delighted to be a student of his dense and enriching work.

CHAPTER 20

Detective Fiction
Pablo Piccato

In this chapter I propose to read Bolaño's most successful novels as works of crime fiction. The main aim is to offer another way to enjoy them, but also to reflect on the continuing relevance of his work to understand our present. There are two ways in which the lens of crime fiction helps us comprehend the narrative structure and the ethical content of *Los detectives salvajes* (*The Savage Detectives*) and *2666*.[1] The first one involves considering Bolaño's use of the conventions of the genre. The second concerns the central place that crime in contemporary Mexico plays in the construction of the vast landscape created by both novels. Recent studies have pointed at each of these aspects but not at the significance of their combination. It is as if the guilty pleasures of crime fiction (including here the detective and noir varieties) could not be reconciled with Bolaño's broad vision of violence in the twentieth century.[2] Rather than a dichotomy of form and meaning, genre and ideas, I intend to look simultaneously at Bolaño's narrative practices and at his construction of engaged, at times depressed but also playful and ironic, readers.

The two novels are quite long compared with the rest of Bolaño's books of prose, yet they are the most successful commercially. They form a clear unit in their Mexican setting and broad interest in literature and crime. *The Savage Detectives* is concerned with various forms of transgression that go from theft to homicide. *2666* contains different forms of violence, from the beating of a taxi driver by a couple of literary critics and the

---

[1] Roberto Bolaño, *The Savage Dectectives* (New York: Picador, 2007); Roberto Bolaño, *2666* (New York, Farrar, Straus and Giroux, 2008). Spanish editions in *Los detectives salvajes* (Barcelona: Editorial Anagrama, 1998); Roberto Bolaño, *2666* (Barcelona: Editorial Anagrama, 2004). This essay benefitted from the comments from Graciela Montaldo and Bruno Bosteels and other participants in the ILAS Faculty Seminar Series, Columbia University, October 2, 2020, as well as the timely assistance of Jay Pan.
[2] A summary on guilt and pleasure in the genre in critical insights on crime fiction in Rebecca Martin, ed., *Crime and Detective Fiction* (Ipswich, MA: Salem Press, 2013); on reading see Stephen Knight, *Form and Ideology in Crime Fiction* (London: Macmillan, 1980).

self-mutilation of a painter, to dismemberment, rape, torture, shootings and stabbings. *The Savage Detectives* frames multiple short testimonies with a first-person account. *2666*, which Bolaño conceived as one project that could be sold as five books, also disrupts the conventional structure of the novel in the service of a polyphonic capaciousness. In both, the plot is apparently open-ended and the exposition includes a lot of information (stories reported by characters, dreams, documents found in an abandoned house, invented or real books and movies) that would seem the antithesis of the narrative economy of crime fiction.

The chorus of voices and memories, and their omissions, folds and stretches time in both novels. Bolaño situated the stories in a broad temporal canvas extending into the past and the future. He talked about crime as a "symbol of the twentieth century," and suggested an apocalyptic vision of history.[3] Both novels refer to an unimaginably distant future: "Two thousand six hundred and something" in the futuristic speculations of poet Cesárea Tinajero, the object of the search in *The Savage Detectives* (633–634), or the eponymous 2666, a date that is not explained but echoes the prophecies of science fiction.

Despite this temporal ambition, Bolaño built each novel with a precise temporal structure. The first part of *The Savage Detectives* recounts, as the diary of budding poet Juan García Madero, the events of two months at the end of 1975. The second part is made of testimonies from more than fifty characters, dated from 1976 until 1996 but all circling around the events reported by García Madero. The testimonies are presented mostly in chronological order. The final section returns to the diary of García Madero and reveals important events, ignored by the witnesses of the second part, taking place in the first months of 1976. *2666* is divided into five parts that focus on a different but connected group of characters or events; each part follows a chronological order, although the five cover overlapping periods of time. Thus, for example, Part 4 is about murders that happen over five years in Santa Teresa between 1993 and 1997, while Part 5 is the life of Benno von Archimboldi from his birth in Prussia in 1920 to the present.

The methods of crime fiction were key to the production of both novels. Bolaño was intent on selling his books since the mid-1990s, as writing had become his sole source of income and he wanted to secure financial

---

[3] Ricardo Gutiérrez Mouat, *Understanding Roberto Bolaño* (Columbia: The University of South Carolina Press, 2016), 14; Roberto Bolaño, *Entre paréntesis: Ensayos, artículos y discursos (1998–2003)* (Barcelona: Editorial Anagrama, 2006), 215.

security for his children.[4] He declared in an interview that "there is nothing more profitable for an author than to track down a criminal or the victim of a disappearance" (Gutiérrez-Mouat 2016, 15).[5] The detective genre allowed for rapid production, suspense, readability; it attracted readers to a plot that offered comfort through enigma and resolution, and allowed the author to recycle stories and characters. Bolaño admitted, in a 2001 interview, that his choice was pragmatic, not determined by a belief in the aesthetic superiority of the genre.[6] As he explained to Carmen Boullosa, while the story was inevitable for him as a writer, a "precipice," the form and structure were the writer's free choice, complete "artifice."[7]

The conventions of the genre start with a puzzle that would engage the reader in a shared process of deduction. Both novels focus on the resolution of one or several enigmas. These were literary (where is Cesárea Tinajero, or who was Benno von Archimboldi, a famous but elusive German writer), or criminal (what happened to Tinajero when she was found, who was killing women in Santa Teresa).[8] The literary and the criminal converge as we learn in the third part of *The Savage Detectives* that Tinajero was killed in early 1976 by some *pistoleros*; in *2666* we eventually find Archimboldi in Mexico, where he has traveled to help his nephew, accused of the murders of Santa Teresa (872, 891–892). Bolaño, however, does not provide readers with the easy satisfaction of explanation or justice. None of the criminal enigmas are solved. The murders are committed by unknown men. The same with the literary puzzle: we know what happened to Tinajero but still cannot interpret the graphic poems she wrote, or know the contents of the notebooks she left.

A central convention of the detective genre is the role of the detective in providing an objective perspective and gathering the data needed to solve the case. The central characters in both novels are detectives of sorts,

---

[4] Jorge Herralde, *Para Roberto Bolaño, Lengua. Ensayo; Variation: Lengua; Ensayo* (Buenos Aires: Adriana Hidalgo Editora, 2005), 28; Jonathan Beck Monroe, *Framing Roberto Bolaño: Poetry, Fiction, Literary History, Politics* (New York: Cambridge University Press, 2020), 36, 32; Bolaño, *Entre paréntesis*, 343.

[5] For Ezequiel de Rosso, writing before the publication of *2666*, Bolaño did not write police novels because murder was not the central question in his works, except for *La pista de hielo* and *Estrella distante*. Ezequiel de Rosso. "Una lectura conjetural: Roberto Bolaño y el relato policial [2000]," in *Roberto Bolaño: La escritura como tauromaquia*, ed. Celia Manzoni (Buenos Aires: Corregidor, 2002), 135.

[6] Roberto Bolaño, "Sobre el juego y el olvido: Entrevista de Silvia Adela Kohan," *La Nación* (Buenos Aires), 25 April 2001.

[7] Carmen Boullosa, "Carmen Boullosa entrevista a Roberto Bolaño," [2002] in *Roberto Bolaño: La escritura como tauromaquia*, ed. Celia Manzoni (Buenos Aires: Corregidor, 2002), 111.

[8] The same combination of literary and police investigation in Simunovic Díaz, "Estrella distante."

although there is no omniscient narrator in any of them.⁹ In *The Savage Detectives* García Madero is confused and disoriented most of the time, and the accounts of Part 2 only offer partial views of Ulises Lima and Arturo Belano, the literary detectives who are trying to find Tinajero. Their voices are never heard, although they dutifully use their reason, look at documents, and enter dangerous situations in search of a revelation. When they find her, however, they botch the literary enterprise and get her killed. In *2666* the third person is used throughout but there is no mastermind. Bolaño left a note saying that Arturo Belano, one of the detectives in *The Savage Detectives* and his alter ego, is the narrator in *2666*, yet the detectives in the novel are various: the European literary critics who go to Santa Teresa to find Archimboldi, the American journalist who is compelled to understand the murders in that city, the Mexican cops who make a half-hearted attempt at breaking some cases. They all give up or fail, as did sheriff Harry Magaña, who comes from Arizona to solve the case of a disappeared American woman. He makes progress in his unofficial investigation, sometimes using torture to extract information, but apparently gets himself killed (411, 415, 449). Most often these investigators do not know exactly what they are looking for but in the process of detection get to face the depths of violence and silence.¹⁰ Bolaño often referred in his poems of the mid-nineties to Latin American detectives engaged in an aimless pursuit of truth, observers of a reality that refused to be explained away (Gutiérrez Mouat 2016, 15).¹¹ In the verse poem "Los detectives," included in *La universidad desconocida* and probably from the same years when he was writing *The Savage Detectives*, he presents an ethical type that will be filled in the two novels: "detectives ... utterly desperate" who nevertheless return to the crime scene.¹² In the prose poems of "Un paseo por la literatura" ("A Stroll through Literature"), he dreams of himself as an old detective facing "a damn tough case."¹³ Bolaño's imaginary detectives exist in a world of uncertainty but still think about the case.

---

⁹ For the varieties and functions of detectives, Luc Boltanski, *Enigmes et complots: Une enquête à propos d'enquêtes* (Paris: Gallimard, 2012), chs. 2 and 3. De Rosso admits that Bolaño does follow the "mecanismo hermenéutico del policial" in most of his novels, although leaving readers "en una situación de precariedad" relative to the facts. de Rosso, "Una lectura conjectural," 137.
¹⁰ Ricardo Piglia, *El último lector* (Barcelona: Editorial Anagrama, 2005), 77, 79.
¹¹ Diego Trelles Paz, "La novela policial alternativa en Hispanoamérica: Detectives perdidos, asesinos ausentes y enigmas sin respuesta" (Ph.D., Austin, TX, University of Texas at Austin, 2008), 241.
¹² Roberto Bolaño, *The Unknown University*, trans. Laura Healy (New York: New Directions, 2013), 605. Spanish edition in *La universidad desconocida* (Barcelona: Editorial Anagrama, 2007), 338.
¹³ Roberto Bolaño, *tres*, trans. Laura Healy (New York: New Directions, 2011), 151. Spanish edition in *Los perros románticos: Poemas 1980–1998* (Barcelona: Acantilado, 2006), 94.

Bolaño was more faithful to the model in another way: the engagement between writer, detective and reader in a game in which the smartest will have the pleasure of finding the solution to the puzzle.[14] This pact between reader and writer was a defining aspect of the mid-twentieth century emergence of the detective genre in Mexico. Without recognizing it, Bolaño belonged to this tradition because of a shared reality in which the official truth was evasive, requiring a new type of reader. The editors of popular detective magazines invited readers to play the game, a sport for smart and informed citizens – knowledgeable about the ways of delinquents, cops and judges, having what I elsewhere call *criminal literacy*.[15] During its golden age, crime fiction in Mexico lacked literary prestige but generated many one-time authors who understood the rules of the genre and tried their luck in pulpy magazines (Piccato 2017, chapter 6).[16] They were enticed with monetary prices and advice from editors Helú.[17] Bolaño continued with this impulse to make of the reader a detective and, more broadly, to create new readers (Trelles Paz 2008, 240, 272; de Rosso 2002, 142).[18]

In *Rayuela*, Julio Cortázar also invited the active participation of readers by altering the structure of the novel. A critic and inheritor of the Boom, Bolaño recentered the narrative into a plot without a linear structure, but disposed of the magic – which is incompatible with the detective genre. In *The Savage Detectives* the reader might change the order of the testimonies of the second part of the novel, yet they all look at a center that is evasive, the concentric enigmas of the origins of the *real visceralistas*, the events of

---

[14] Susanne Hartwig, "Jugar al detective: el desafío de Roberto Bolaño," *Iberoamericana (2001–)* 7, no. 28 (2007): 53–71; Trelles Paz, "La novela," 240. See also Bolaño, "Sobre el juego y el olvido," and *Entre paréntesis*, 191.

[15] Pablo Piccato, *A History of Infamy: Crime, Truth, and Justice in Mexico* (Berkeley: University of California Press, 2017), ch. 3.

[16] On rules and an economic interpretation of the emergence of the genre, Ernest Mandel, *Delightful Murder: A Social History of the Crime Story* (Minneapolis: University of Minnesota Press, 1984); overviews of the genre in Latin America and Mexico include Persephone Braham, *Crimes against the State, Crimes against Persons: Detective Fiction in Cuba and Mexico* (Minneapolis: University of Minnesota Press, 2004); Vicente Francisco Torres, *El Cuento policial mexicano* (Mexico City: Editorial Diógenes, 1982); Ilan Stavans, *Antiheroes* (Madison: Fairleigh Dickinson University Press, 1997). On literary prestige María Elvira Bermúdez, *Los mejores cuentos policíacos mexicanos* (Mexico City: Libro-Mex, 1955), 10–11. For a conventional formulation of detective rules S.S. Van Dine, *Twenty Rules for Writing Detective Stories* (Feedbooks, 1928).

[17] Carlos Monsiváis, "Prólogo," en *La obligación de asesinar: Novelas y cuentos policiacos* (Mexico City: M.A. Porrúa, 1998); Vicente Francisco Torres, *Muertos de papel: Un paseo por la narrativa policial mexicana* (Mexico City: CNCA/ Sello Bermejo, 2003).

[18] On police novel and creation of publics Umberto Eco, "El bautizo de la rosa," *Nexos*, October 1, 1984. Helú's work in *Selecciones Policiacas y de Misterio*, v. 2, November 15, 1946, p. 4; v. 4, no. 69, December 15, 1949.

early 1976, and the subsequent comings and goings of Lima and Belano (Trelles Paz, 2008, 274, 293). In *2666*, the whereabouts of Archimboldi and the murders of Santa Teresa also converge at a center that is not explicitly revealed but becomes increasingly clear as the story delves in the violence that runs through twentieth-century history. Bolaño extends the detective work of the reader beyond a single book: a good Bolaño reader needs to look at his "laboratory" and connect biographical reality, literary history, fiction and dreams.[19] The two novels are connected by parentage: the policeman Lalo Cura, who tries to solve the cases of Santa Teresa, the latest in a lineage of abandoned children, happens to be the child of either Ulises Lima or Arturo Belano, who knew María Expósito in January of 1976 (*2666*, 697).

Bolaño did not stick to the narrative economy and empiricism invented by Edgar Allan Poe and practiced by Agatha Christie. The testimonies in the second part of *The Savage Detectives* describe the lives of Lima, Belano and their friends. The repetitive descriptions of crime scenes in Part 4 of *2666* appear like a forensic trope but function also as a way to present the mounting scale of gender violence in Santa Teresa.[20] Poe may have been one of Bolaño's key authors in his embrace of nineteenth-century poetics, but offers limited guidance to understand his crime fiction.[21] The rationality of classic detective stories did not fit with the uncertainty of perception, motivation and the mystery itself in Bolaño's works. The nature of the puzzle to be solved by the amateur detectives in the two novels is never formulated. Bolaño was not interested in a narrow definition of the problem to be solved.[22] *Distant Star* and *2666* are closer to the idea of the detective and the pursuit of the truth found in the novels of Raymond Chandler or Dashiell Hammett – classics on their own right but also critics of the artificiality of conventional detective stories. Although Bolaño does not mention them in his own library of classics, he respected

---

[19] Diego Trelles, "El lector como detective en 'Los detectives salvajes' de Roberto Bolaño," *Hispamérica* 34, no. 100 (2005): 143.
[20] On cruelty, see Franklin Rodríguez, *Roberto Bolaño: El investigador desvelado* (Madrid: Editorial Verbum, 2015), p. 60 and ff.
[21] Monroe, *Framing Roberto Bolaño*, 29, 116; Hartwig, "Jugar al detective."
[22] See Mónica Maristain, *El hijo de Míster Playa: una semblanza de Roberto Bolaño* (Oaxaca: Editorial Almadía, 2012), 18, and Bolaño, *Entre paréntesis*, 343. On the identification of detective and writer in Bolaño see Rodríguez, *Roberto Bolaño*, 41, 85; see also Piglia, *Último lector*, 87. On homicide and authorship see Peter Elmore, "2666: La autoría en el tiempo del límite," in *Bolaño salvaje*, ed. Edmundo Paz Soldán, Gustavo Faverón Patriau, and Erik Haasnoot (Barcelona: Editorial Candaya, 2008), 259–292.

their craft.[23] Raymond Chandler's "The simple art of murder" [1950] contained the tenets of that critical version of the genre: the writer has the obligation to be "realistic," which in the case of detective stories implies acknowledging the basic "sociological implication" that murder is an act of cruelty. Realism is an ethical imperative but not a moral exercise. Reality is "a world in which gangsters can rule nations and almost rule cities." The redemption, if anything, resides in the detective: "He must be, to use a rather weathered phrase, a man of honor, by instinct, by inevitability, without thought of it, and certainly without saying it."[24] In his pursuit, the detective is bound to break the law, fight the police as well as the criminals, and get hurt in the process.[25]

The masculine sense of honor mentioned by Chandler moves Lima, Belano and others to save women from danger. In their conflicted feminism, they are incapable of fully separating their desire from their chivalrous impulses. Women are constantly being rescued: the scholar Liz Norton from a misogynistic taxi driver in London; young Rosa Amalfitano by African American journalist Oscar Fate, in *2666*; Lupe from her pimp, and Tinajero from oblivion, in *The Savage Detectives*. Fathers anguish over their daughters: Quim Font and Xosé Lendoiro in *The Savage Detectives* (451, 464), and Amalfitano in *2666* (198–199). It is never quite clear that any of those women need rescuing, but they provide a focus for the anxiety of detectives and author in front of widespread gender violence that is a synecdoche for other forms of evil in their century and country.

Bolaño knew that the detective genre in its pure form (objectivity, administration of clues, fair play toward the reader) was impossible when set in the Mexican context because institutions were not able to verify the truth.[26] That much had been observed by María Elvira Bermúdez and

---

[23] Trelles, "El lector como detective en 'Los detectives salvajes' de Roberto Bolaño," 141; Maristain, *El hijo de Míster Playa*, 73.

[24] Raymond Chandler, *The Simple Art of Murder* (New York: Vintage Books, 1988), 1, 2, 14, 16, 17, 18; Stephen Knight, "'A Hard Cheerfulness': An Introduction to Raymond Chandler," in *American Crime Fiction: Studies in the Genre*, ed. Brian Docherty (New York: St. Martin's Press, 1988), 71–87.

[25] See Catherine Nickerson, "Murder as Social Criticism," *American Literary History* 9, no. 4 (Winter 1997): 744–757.

[26] Gutiérrez Mouat, *Understanding Roberto Bolaño*, 15; Trelles Paz, "La novela," 3–6; Monroe, *Framing Roberto Bolaño*, 14; Simunovic Díaz, "Estrella distante"; John D. Dorst, "Neck-Riddle as a Dialogue Off Genres: Applying Bakhtin's Genre Theory," *The Journal of American Folklore* 96, no. 382 (October 1, 1983): 413–433. For a useful view of crime fiction as a "modo particular de narrar" rather than a genre in Latin America, see Brigitte Adriaensen and Valeria Grinberg Pla, "Introducción a cuatro manos," in *Narrativas del crimen en América Latina: transformaciones y transculturaciones del policial*, ed. Brigitte Adriaensen and Valeria Grinberg Pla (Berlin: Lit, 2012), 13.

other authors of the early period.[27] This did not mean, however, that his use of the genre was parodic (Monroe, 2020, 107), as it had been at the beginning of Mexican production in the 1940s. He wrote instead crime fiction that proposed a "novela policial alternativa," according to Diego Trelles Paz (2008, 6). In the dual perspective proposed in this chapter, Bolaño's crime fiction involved a subversive use of the trope of investigation, while also challenging the epistemological foundations of the genre. The truth that his detectives sought was not about the facts of the crime but involved a peek into the abyss of modern cruelty. This look at violence used Mexico as a window (as suggested in the literary puzzle that closes *The Savage Detectives*, 647–648) but also encompassed the legacies of fascism and racism in Europe and the United States.[28]

Crime fiction was useful for Bolaño as a way of seeing reality. Midcentury Mexican crime fiction had already established this function by offering readers a map of the new, aggressive urban life.[29] In the two novels, Bolaño embraced the disenchanted realism that Chandler proposed. *2666* is set on an imaginary map (Villaviciosa and Santa Teresa, Sonora; Huntsville, Arizona) populated with dreams, hallucinations, fragmentary forensic evidence that conveyed the effects of violence. Bolaño left Mexico in 1977. Although he traveled to the northern border in the seventies, he never visited Ciudad Juárez. While his research for *2666* was intense, he relied on friends and other authors like Sergio González Rodríguez.[30]

Bolaño also used the press as a source, probably through the internet (as Archimboldi did), but also because its fragmentary information best fit that fractured knowledge. In Mexican detective stories of the mid-century, crime news, or *nota roja*, was an unsparing source about the dangers of modern life, providing style, settings and characters. In a country where

---

[27] Miguel G. Rodríguez Lozano, *Pistas del relato policial en México: Somera expedición*, 1st ed., Colección de Bolsillo 35 (Mexico City: Universidad Nacional Autónoma de México, 2008); Bermúdez, *Los mejores cuentos policíacos mexicanos*, 16, 10.

[28] Oswaldo Zavala, *La modernidad insufrible: Roberto Bolaño en los límites de la literatura latinoamericana contemporánea* (Chapel Hill: U.N.C. Department of Romance Languages, University of North Carolina Press, 2015), 152. The connection between fascism and literature in Bolaño's *La literatura nazi en América* (Barcelona: Seix Barral, 1996). See also Julio Sebastián Figueroa Jofré, "Bolaño con Borges: Juegos con la infamia y el mal radical," in *Roberto Bolaño: ruptura y violencia en la literatura finisecular*, ed. Felipe Ríos Baeza, 1st ed. (Puebla de Zaragoza: Eón; Benemérita Universidad Autónoma de Puebla, 2010), 436–460.

[29] See Glen S. Close, *Contemporary Hispanic Crime Fiction: A Ttransatlantic Discourse on Urban Violence* (New York: Palgrave Macmillan, 2008); Boltanski, *Enigmes et complots*, 38.

[30] See Herralde, *Para Roberto Bolaño*, 27, 147; Maristain, *El hijo de Míster Playa*, 185–186, 299, 211; Trelles Paz, "La novela," 299.

the police and the judiciary could not be expected to bring out the truth, reporters and photographers played an essential role as investigators and but also instigators of public responses (Piccato 2017, chapter 2).[31] These diverse roles are illustrated when suspect Klaus Haas gives a press conference from jail to denounce others as the killers (*2666*, 489) – just as a real-life suspect did in Ciudad Juárez. Straying from his assignment for a New York magazine, Fate ends up discovering the sordid world of snuff movies, and rescues Amalfitano's daughter (*2666*, 535). González Rodríguez appears as a journalist in *2666*. In real life, he survived an assault for his journalistic work on the killings of Ciudad Juárez.[32] In the novel, his newspaper discourages him from pursuing the story, but he agrees to publish the results of investigations that a female politician had commissioned (629–632) – once again demonstrating the circuitous paths needed to get to reality in Mexico.

In a judicial model, this pursuit of the truth was destined to failure (Elmore 2008, 268).[33] In "The Part About the Crimes," Part 4 of *2666*, the corporal evidence is fragmentary, removed by the wind or the fauna (203, 206–207, 355–357). A few cases find a substitute for justice in the extrajudicial execution of the suspects (524, 626) but most are closed without legal results. Bolaño does not provide the reader with the solace of an overarching explanation. The women of Santa Teresa are killed by their boyfriends, their husbands, the police, the narcos, and the driver of a black car (f. ex., 359, 390, 450–451, 626, 524, 206–207, 529–530). The point of the investigation is precisely that it does not have an end point, and probably did not have a beginning (344–355).

In a broader, historical sense, Bolaño's research was more productive. Bolaño's detectives, like those of Chandler and other hard-boiled authors, in the words of Piglia, "not only decipher[s] the mysteries of the plot but also finds and uncovers, at every step, the determination of social relations." The two novels cover a period of Mexican history, from 1975 to the early years of the twenty-first century, characterized by economic crises,

---

[31] Piccato, *A History of Infamy*, ch. 2; Juan Carlos Ramírez-Pimienta and Juan Pablo Villalobos, "Detección Pública / Detección Privada: El periodista como detective en la narrativa policíaca norfronteriza," *Revista Iberoamericana* (June 2010).

[32] Bolaño, *Entre paréntesis*, 215; Herralde, *Para Roberto Bolaño*, 60, 65; Gutiérrez Mouat, *Understanding Roberto Bolaño*, 188.

[33] Elmore, "2666: La autoría," 268. On the limits of the judicial model see Carlo Ginzburg, *The Judge and the Historian: Marginal Notes on a Late-Twentieth-Century Miscarriage of Justice* (London: Verso, 1999).

impunity and growing violence.³⁴ Drug trafficking caused an increase in homicides since the 1990s in places like Ciudad Juárez. By the time of Bolaño's death in 2003 the worst spike in violence on the border was yet to arrive but the region, as well as other parts of the country, was already in the throes of a combination of increasingly powerful groups of organized crime and state agents that alternatively tolerated their business, stole from them, or did their dirty work. Police corruption and ineptitude can be traced back to the early post-revolutionary years, when *pistoleros* belonging to the police, or at least flashing a police badge, were involved in prostitution and other illegal businesses. Dirty policemen, *mordelones* in *2666* (554), profit from their expertise in violence and de facto immunity. They are involved in a broader range of crimes, including extortion, collaboration with narcos and the rape of female detainees (401).

More than a problem of rule of law, the dysfunctionality of Mexican police raised one of knowledge. Police flaws were integral to the fragmented epistemology of *2666*. Police agents torture suspects (537), carelessly let off their guns in night clubs (625), lose evidence, and drop cases without even identifying the victims (354). A couple of police investigators, Lalo Cura and Juan de Dios Martínez, try to take police methods seriously (437–438). Cura studies from police handbooks he finds abandoned at the police station, but his boss reminds him that "there is no such thing as modern criminal investigation" (527). Science offers no alternative. Professor Kessler, a famous criminologist, posits the existence of criminal archetypes, serial killers that can be studied without any reference to their context, yet he also admits the method does not work in Santa Teresa because the murders have multiple authors (470–478).

Unlike *neopoliciaco*, the Latin American version of noir that emerged in the 1970s, Bolaño did not get around the epistemological problem of inept cops by using conspiracy theories. Narcos are not prominent in *The Savage Detectives*, and in *2666* Bolaño does not give them the centrality that was often attributed to them as culprits of the Ciudad Juárez femicides. Perplexed characters speak of a "good drug lord" and a "bad drug lord" in the city (533). Both kinds are part of a large cast of actors, in novels and history, who played a role in the growth of violence and the expansion of impunity in the previous decades. The involvement of the police in illegal businesses was not a consequence of drug trafficking but a factor of the industry's transformation. Narcos used to bribe policemen or employed

---

[34] See Piglia, *Último lector*, 96, my translation. On impunity and narrative, Gabriel Trujillo Muñoz, *Testigos de cargo* (Mexico City: CONACULTA-CECUT, 2000).

them when they required security or the use of force against rivals. Things changed by the seventies: agencies like the Policía Judicial Federal and the Dirección Federal de Seguridad, true schools of *pistoleros*, shifted their use of torture and murder from the persecution of guerrillas to extortion; they began to compete with state cops for control of routes and cities. The US obsession with drugs funded their marauding. By the late nineties, powerful narco bosses began to take control over police agencies (like the municipal police of Ciudad Juárez) or create their private groups of enforcers. During the first decade of the twenty-first century the violence grew in pitched battles over territory fuelled by the government's deployment of soldiers. The result was not a weakening of the business but an unprecedented increase in the number of people killed and disappeared in Mexico.[35] In terms of the problem of truth about murder, narcos were a catalyst but not the cause of widespread impunity.

Bolaño was writing from a context in which violence had become a privilege of dirty cops and influential narcos, but not yet a generalized state of conflict. Rather than pinning the blame on narcos, he described an abyss of violence in which the murder of women was the darkest aspect of reality. He prefigured the nightmare of recent years because, from his desk in Blanes, he saw the lack of limits and the unspeakable effects of violence. Through his flawed detectives, he observed a reality that could only be fully narrated by crime fiction. Through irony, their investigation allows Bolaño to challenge the notion of an original Latin American violence.[36]

Bolaño linked crime and literature in multiple ways. He may have had problems with the law, and he admitted stealing books and selling drugs when need compelled him. Since his times as an *infrarrealista*, he believed that the writer had an obligation to place himself or herself in danger. Safety was the death of literature, while confrontation and marginality were essential to it. In *The Savage Detectives*, the real visceralistas plot literary crimes, like kidnapping Octavio Paz (175). It was their way to comment on the exclusion that defined twentieth-century Mexican literature and ignored Cesárea Tinajero.[37] Lima and Belano engage in violence to rescue women (Trelles Paz 2008, 290). Belano wanders into self-destructive pursuits in Africa, and Lima gets himself involved in petty

---

[35] See Ioan Grillo, *El Narco: Inside Mexico's Criminal Insurgency* (New York: Bloomsbury Press, 2011).
[36] Bruno Bosteels, "Critique of Originary Violence: Freud, Heidegger, Derrida," *The Undecidable Unconscious: A Journal of Deconstruction and Psychoanalysis* 4 (2017): 27–66.
[37] See Gutiérrez Mouat, *Understanding Roberto Bolaño*, 14.

crime and mingles with neofascists in Europe and Israel (*The Savage Detectives*, 346–347, 323, 325–329; Maristain 2012, 187).

A common way to interpret these novels proposes a solemn interpretation of Bolaño as the chronicler of the necropolitics of late capitalism or the deep conspiracy of silence in which an all-powerful Mexican state has surrounded the deaths of Ciudad Juárez.[38] He would offer a tragic paradigm of resistance to capitalism and western modernity (Zavala 2016, 150). In this perspective, the murder of women and the atrocities of WWII Europe would converge in the "absolute evil" at play in history.[39] This interpretation, however, neglects the weaknesses of cops and the entropic force of common crime (Zavala 2016, 85–87, 190, 192), and requires too heavy an imposition on texts that are driven, simultaneously, by irony and by the very capitalist pursuit of royalties. Bolaño writes to celebrate the civilized joy of reading, to paraphrase Borges, and to offer an alternative to the dangerous wish of purity in art (Jofré 2010, 456).[40] His is not a passive reading but is guided by "el placer no comprometido sino con el placer." Critics, sometimes the same that stress fear as the dominant tone in this literature of violence, also recognize that pleasure was at the heart of Bolaño's practice as a writer, just as it was for crime fiction in general (Muniz 2018, 568, 576). These two novels look into the abyss and bring out laughter, or at least an ironic smile. Most importantly, they activate the participation of the reader with the promise of a revelation that can be evasive in a literal sense (as the culprit of a crime or the whereabouts of an author) but points to a larger truth. Part of this is a game, as in the riddles of *The Savage Detectives* (Hartwig 2001, 53). As proposed by Chandler, the detective-writer of Bolaño's novels embraces a contract in which he commits to the honorable task of serving the customer-reader in the pursuit of the truth. Bolaño's rejection of ideology can thus be seen as complement to his ethical commitment, as detective-writer, to take risks. The heteroglossia of crime fiction is, to follow Bakhtin, democratic in the centrifugal

---

[38] Alice Driver, "More or Less Dead: Literary Representations of Feminicide in Juárez," in *More or Less Dead, Feminicide, Haunting, and the Ethics of Representation in Mexico* (Tucson: University of Arizona Press, 2015), 59–64.

[39] GaHartwig, "Jugar al detective," 53; Gabriela Muniz, "Nuevos miedos en la literatura policial de Chile y Argentina," *Revista Canadiense de Estudios Hispánicos* 42, no. 3 (2018): 572–573; Elmore, "2666: La autoría," 271.

[40] On irony used by Bolaño and others to challenge the exoticization of Latin American violence, see Adriaensen and Grinberg Pla, "Introducción a cuatro manos," 17–18. On irony and ideology see Bruno Bosteels, "La situación es catastrófica pero no es seria: Ironía, violencia y militancia en América Latina," in *Ironía y Violencia En La Literatura Latinoamericana Contemporánea*, ed. Brigitte Adriaensen and Carlos van Tongeren (Pittsburgh, PA: University of Pittsburgh, 2018), 41–57.

force of its challenge to the unity of nation and reason.[41] There is certainly a romantic streak in Bolaño's fictional detectives that is also explicit in his poetry.[42] But this is only part of an approach to the practice of writing and reading in which the pleasure of irony, the critique of nationalism, and the solution of puzzles were necessary for the construction of readers who could see the fiction behind realism and ideology.

[41] Monroe, *Framing Roberto Bolaño*, 3–4; M. M. Bakhtin, *The Dialogic Imagination: Four Essays* (Austin: University of Texas Press, 1981), 272. On police novel and democracy, Boltanski, *Enigmes et complots*, 46–51.

[42] Maristain, *El hijo de Míster Playa*, 76, 188, 215; "Ignacio Echavarría, Roberto Bolaño lector, el bibliotecario valiente," YouTube, www.youtube.com/watch?v=yhWyRKvEuAE (accessed June 12, 2020).

CHAPTER 21

Journalism, Media, Mass Culture

Tania Gentic

The first story Bolaño ever published begins with a newspaper clipping. "El contorno del ojo (Diario del oficial chino Chen Huo Deng, 1980)" ["The Contour of the Eye (Diary of the Chinese Official Chen Huo Deng, 1980)"] records the diary entries of a Chinese poet who cuts articles out of the newspapers delivered to him from military headquarters, intuiting that there is a connection between them but only able to deduce that "extraordinary things happen" (*Cuentos*, 2018, 643).[1] The newspapers repeatedly strain the presumption of verisimilitude expected of reportage, describing a child with X-ray vision, a man who is 142 years old, and sightings of a strange cow-like animal with a beak seen at the Korean border. In the end, the protagonist announces he is going to kill himself, but we do not know why: the reader, like Chen, can only try to make sense of the details, from the mundane to the extraordinary, he confronts in the text as he reads.[2] Bolaño's first published story, then, already toys with the overlap of fiction and nonfiction, and plays with confessional narrative and journalistic reportage, questioning the possibility of transparent language even as it seemingly engages in it. It also foreshadows the obsession with seeing that repeats in other Bolaño texts, as the poet either feels he is being spied on or himself seems to be spying on others. As in other Bolaño texts, this mix of personal and journalistic discourses performs what Ignacio Echevarría has called a "poetics of inconclusiveness," referencing a vast world while capturing it only in snippets that are episodic and fragmented.[3] Seen in retrospect, the story offers clues to understanding the spaces portrayed in

---

[1] Translations to English in this text are mine or those of the editor. For reasons of space, long quotes are given only in English.
[2] Christopher Andrews (2014) argues Bolaño's characters "seize on details, invest them with significance, and invent stories to connect and explain them" (xii). Structurally, the story reflects an idea presented in *Amberes (Antwerp)*: "la realidad me parece un enjambre de frases sueltas (reality seems to me a tangle of loose sentences)" (Bolaño, 2018, n.p.).
[3] Quoted in Andrews (2014, xiv).

Bolaño's writing not only as geographically expansive, but as shaped by newspapers and mass media that intertwine with both daily life and literature.

Bolaño's representation of the line between reality and fiction, seeing and perceiving, foreshadows the concerns about truth and fake news that have come to occupy discussions of journalism and mass media in the twenty-first century. But they also continue a tradition of what today, in the North, influenced by New Journalism, is called creative nonfiction; and the literary journalism that has long graced the pages of Latin American, and to a lesser degree Spanish, newspapers. The intense focus on seemingly minor details or artists in Bolaño's texts, and his characters' movement through urban and foreign spaces, do not just replicate the model of the detective novel or suggest a connection to investigative journalism, they draw our attention to the exilic condition of a journalistic art form known as the *crónica*, and Bolaño's repeated engagement with it.

To think about Roberto Bolaño in the context of journalism and mass culture is, then, to recognize how mainstays of globalized twentieth-century journalistic communication – photographic realism, reportage with a pretension of objectivity, investigative journalism – as well as discourses about literature, have circulated in different and transformative ways in Latin America, Europe, and the United States. As other articles in this volume explore, Bolaño lived in Chile, Mexico, and Spain, and had read literature from well beyond those places, leading him to affirm that all writers and readers are exiles, be it for years or for a weekend, because through literature one enters a strange land (Bolaño, *Entre paréntesis*, 51). The differing daily cultural and political contexts one confronts in the newspaper, though, produce a similarly exilic experience for the reader and are also present in Bolaño's work.

Once he had gained some notoriety, Bolaño published sketches, short essays, and travel writing in major newspapers such as *El País*, *El Mundo*, and *Clarín*, although he got his start with the smaller *Diari de Girona*, writing weekly or biweekly columns that were translated and published in Catalan, and later published in Spanish in *Las Últimas Noticias* (Chile). He also published in cultural supplements in *El Metropolitano* (Chile) and *unomásuno* (Mexico), as well as magazines like *Ajoblanco* (Barcelona), *Paula* (Chile), and *Cambio* (Mexico). Given the extensive geographic and literary scope of Bolaño's work, it is tempting to read his relationship to journalism as a global phenomenon that, in a formal sense, exists in strict opposition to Literature. In the United States, it took the New

Journalism of the late 1960s to discover that journalism could be literary; I will discuss the relationship of New Journalism to Bolaño below.[4]

But in Latin America and Spain, since the late nineteenth century, some of the greatest poets and novelists have simultaneously written for newspapers, creating a different relationship between literature, media, and the newspapers than existed in the North at the same time. The *crónica* has been a central part of newspaper culture, from Mariano José de Larra and Azorín, Rubén Darío and José Martí, to Carlos Monsiváis, Elena Poniatowska, Juan Villoro, and Pedro Lemebel. The *crónica* is a hybrid form that combines the short story, the essay, and reportage into reflections on contemporary society in which the writer is both intertwined with, and yet writing at a distance from, mass culture. It derives from both colonial travel narratives and nineteenth-century *folletines*, fusing literature with social commentary, and has been published in newspapers and magazines alongside news reports and editorials; until recently, women's *crónicas* often appeared in the so-called women's pages. In many cases, an author's *crónicas* were later collected and sold in book form.[5] If the Western, twentieth-century goal of reportage is to extract the narrator from the text, seemingly producing transparency in the process, *crónicas* and other literary journalism of their type use the figure of the narrator and other characters, some real, some fictional, to add authority, emotion, and other personal touches to their portrayal of culture and daily life. Through them, readers are offered the opportunity to travel to new places and societies or see their own in a new light.[6] José Martí walked through New York City and over the Brooklyn Bridge; Darío strolled through Madrid and Paris; Gutiérrez Nájera explored parts of Mexico City he had not visited before. Bolaño himself suggests that this kind of writing not only reflects the Latin American experience, it constructs the closest thing Latin America has to an epic: when the poet in *Estrella distante*, de Soto,

---

[4] As Tom Wolfe put it in 1972, "it was [now] possible in non-fiction, in journalism, to use any literary device, from the traditional dialogisms of the essay to stream-of-consciousness, and to use many different kinds simultaneously, or within a relatively short space ... to excite the reader both intellectually and emotionally" (Wolfe, 1972, n.p.).

[5] I use the term *crónica* because it is perhaps the broadest way to reference the kind of literary journalism to which I am referring, although in Spain one is likely to find reference also to *columnas* or, in the case of Juan José Millás, *articuentos*. The tradition is much more robust in Latin America than it is in Spain.

[6] Bolaño seems to value this kind of writing in comments he makes about reading. As the narrator puts it in *Los sinsabores del verdadero policía (Woes of the True Policeman)* (2016), "los estudiantes de Amalfitano 'comprendieron que ... lo más importante del mundo era leer y viajar, tal vez la misma cosa, sin detenerse nunca'" ("Amalfitano's students 'understood that ... the most important thing in the world was reading and traveling, maybe the same thing, without ever stopping'") (n.p.).

ends up in Perpignan, he is like all Latin American tourists and, especially, the most prolific *modernista* travel writer, Gómez Carrillo: "perplexed and desperate in equal measure (Gómez Carrillo is our Virgil)" (Bolaño, 1996, n.p.).

Generally associated with urban spaces and the *flâneur*, and cleaving neither to hard news nor the feature stories or human interest stories that constitute other typical newspaper modes of writing, as Puerto Rican *cronista* Edgardo Rodríguez Juliá (2003) has explained, the chronicle is "a promiscuous space, without canons, decodified, where the biographical sketch will coexist with reportage, where the essay would be animated with the tricks of narrative art, where the sketch, notes, the rapid reading of a vertiginous reality, should subvert the relaxed forms of short stories, long stories, the novel" (85). Gilda Waldman (2008) has written of the Chilean *crónica* in particular that in recent decades it has sought to "map the current ways of being that coexist in the city not only to interpret the culture and identity of the country, but to delve into them and contrast them with the idyllic vision that turns Chile into 'the happy copy of Eden'" (181).

Drawing attention to the hidden moments of urban life that are out of synch with a modernizing or globalizing project, the chronicle, which often focuses on seemingly minor details or moments of daily life, unearths that which is glossed over by dominant discourses – political, literary, and otherwise – often bringing ruins and moments of interiority to the forefront of public space, or presenting literature as a privileged escape from it. One need only think of Mariano José de Larra, whose "El día de difuntos de 1836" ("The Day of the Dead, 1836"), published under the pseudonym Fígaro, is an early example of the blending of subjectivity and space into social commentary. The narrator strolls through Madrid on the Day of the Dead, mapping the landmarks of the city as tombs in one big cemetery, not only because he is suffering from what at the time he called melancholy (Larra would kill himself a few months after publishing the text), but also because he was despondent about what he viewed as Spain's backward tendencies and need for modernization.

We might also consider Manuel Gutiérrez Nájera's "En la calle," first printed in 1882 in *El Nacional*, but published under a different title and with the pseudonym M. Can Can in *El Cronista de México* in 1883. The piece situates the first-person narrator as a *flâneur* moving through Mexico City "calle abajo, calle abajo" ("down the street, down the street," Gutiérrez Nájera, 1958, 131). Traveling to this remote part of the city, he describes a poor girl sick with tuberculosis sitting on a balcony, and her sister, eating truffles in a carriage. The sister's rich appearance confounds onlookers, who cannot tell whether she is a duchess or a prostitute. We can read this blurred line between duchess and prostitute as a metaphor for the *modernistas*, who had to publish *crónicas* in newspapers to survive economically, even as they would have preferred to write poetry for poetry's sake.[7] By presenting readers with a realist story that reveals the challenge of differentiating one social class from another, though, the text also addresses the distortion and deception of appearances in a rapidly modernizing world.

Texts like Larra's and Gutiérrez Nájera's, which today can be read as stories even though they once responded to contemporary political realities, are less shocking than the *crónica* that helped Bolaño describe the murders in *2666*, Sergio González Rodríguez's 2002 *Huesos en el desierto*.[8] González Rodríguez draws on another staple of Spanish and Latin American newspapers, a sensationalistic journalistic form known in different contexts as the *crónica negra, crónica roja*, or *nota roja*. Shadows of that form, which often takes a detectivesque approach to uncovering the forensic details of violent crimes (inspired by the likes of Rodolfo Walsh and Truman Capote), also abound in Bolaño's texts. The kind of writing Larra and Gutiérrez Nájera produce, though, sets the stage for the confluence of journalism and art, realism and metaphor, that has existed for over a century in the *crónica* and which is present in Bolaño's fiction and his newspaper articles.

Like Charles Baudelaire's "painter of modern life," the *cronistas modernistas* inaugurated a kind of writing in Spanish that captured in sketches the complex and fragmentary experience of daily life while also striving to elevate it through poetic language. Jonathan Monroe has argued that Bolaño seems to reflect Baudelaire and Rimbaud's bad boy poet style and search for modernity through language. But in doing so Bolaño also responds to the overlap between journalism and literature, between a Latin

---

[7] For Bolaño, the challenges of the market included a vast transatlantic publishing industry and the technological advances of film and television that diverted attention from literature's readers. When he goes to Chile and finds that even "Miss Chile o ... Miss Santiago o Miss Fundo en Llamas" considers herself a writer (without having written anything), his reply is both humorous and biting: "Nicanor Parra lo dijo: tal vez sería conveniente leer un poco más (Nicanor Parra said it: maybe it would be convenient to read a little more)" (Bolaño, 2004, *Entre*, 68–69).

[8] Bolaño wrote in *Entre paréntesis* that González Rodríguez's book is "no solo una fotografía imperfecta [...] del mal y de la corrupción, sino que se convierte en una metáfora de México y del pasado de México y del incierto futuro de toda Latinoamérica (not only an imperfect photograph ... of evil and corruption, but that it becomes a metphor of Mexico, and Mexico's past, and the uncertain future of all of Latin America)" (Bolaño, 2004, 215).

American sensibility and a world republic of letters, that drove the *modernistas'* cosmopolitan desire (also inspired by the likes of Baudelaire and Rimbaud) to escape what José Martí called the "tyranny" of a single literature in Spanish. This desire also led the Guatemalan foreign correspondent and *cronista* Gómez Carrillo to advocate making journalistic prose more poetic, and the Cuban Julián del Casal to reimagine Havana as Paris, in part by portraying women as sensual, exotic objects whose presence transformed a room just as *chinoiserie* and silk did. José Martí summarizes this revolutionary desire when he celebrates the global literary spirit of Oscar Wilde because, he writes, despite living under the tyranny of the normative, Wilde embodies a poetic fire: "Embellecer la vida es darle objeto" ("To beautify life is to give it an object").[9]

Although Bolaño tended to favor avant-garde and surrealist writers, the legacy of the journalistic *crónica* is reflected both in Bolaño's own newspaper sketches, and in the way in which his novels and short stories blur the line between reality and fiction even as they seem to capture a time and a place that strike the reader as real. In the sense that they reflect large-scale cultural phenomena by positing travel and the outside perspective of narrators or characters who immerse themselves in worlds that seem foreign and familiar at the same time, I would argue that it is possible to read *Los detectives salvajes*, *Estrella distante*, or even *2666* as *crónicas* as well as novels, as they portray deeply considered, yet fictionalized, reflections of specific cultural moments in the wider Atlantic world. Bolaño's engagement with the *crónica* also draws attention to the difficulty with which the contemporary writer can occupy the space of the observer and still maintain narrative authority, and in that sense his appreciation of the chronicle is distanced from its *modernista* precursors. In the apocalyptic era of global capitalism and violence, unlike a Darío or Martí who saw themselves as poetically translating foreign spaces for local readers, the wannabe *cronista* Oscar Fate in *2666* is unable to move beyond the overwhelming details of everyday engagement with violence and death, even though he knows there is more to them than what he perceives. In his paralysis, readers see something both more real and at the same time more estranged from the experience of contemporary reality informed by the media than investigative journalism or television can communicate.

The much-debated veracity of Bolaño's short piece "Playa" ("Beach") reflects this confusion of fact and fiction, which is not unique to Bolaño's

---

[9] As Sylvia Molloy (1992) has asserted, however, Martí actually found Wilde "Too Wilde for Comfort."

short stories or even a postmodern moment, as it also plays on the *crónica*'s tendency to reflect society by creating it in words, and taking poetic license while doing so. In the article, Bolaño reframes a short sketch, "Sol y calavera" ("Sun and Skull") he had published in the *Diari de Girona* ("Diary of Girona") in 1999 with a new opening line: "I stopped doing heroin and went back to my town and started the methadone treatment they gave me at the outpatient clinic" (*Entre*, 241). For those seeking to map autobiography onto literature, the debate that is raised is whether or not Bolaño is a drug addict. But if we read the piece as a *crónica*, this detail not only adds a thought-provoking depth that is evident in many of Bolaño's newspaper publications, it aligns with reflections he made in several texts that Blanes is a place of tolerance that admits all sorts. Gone are the days of Juan Marsé's social-realist *Últimas tardes con Teresa* (*Last Afternoons with Teresa*), he writes in "Beach," "La Selva Marítima" ("The Maritime Jungle"), and other *crónicas*, in which beachside towns are the paradisiacal purview of the Catalan bourgeois elite, and where the dark-skinned immigrant is an outsider. Now the beach is a place where the fat wife and her ill husband, whom Bolaño mistakes in "Sun and Skull" for a skeleton – that is to say, the living and the almost dead – come together publicly in near-nakedness. But in "Beach" it is also the place where, as the drug addict edges closer to life, he experiences and narrates society as an outsider, offering the reader a new perspective on the intermingling that takes place, often unseen and yet out in the open, in public spaces.

Whether or not the writer is actually a drug addict is irrelevant: the narrator draws our attention to a darker way of seeing a stereotyped beach scene, so important to Spain's image in the twentieth century, one which allows readers to recognize the superficial ideology of Spain's identity while also recognizing the interiority of the strangers around us. Bolaño opens the piece with a reference to heroin, but he ends by turning the camera back on the narrator, who knows that others on the beach probably find it strange to see "that young man who was crying silently, a young man of thirty-five who had nothing, but who was regaining his will and courage and who knew that he was still going to live a while longer" (*Entre*, 245). The narrator's sense of not belonging merely because of his humanity makes his *crónica* more effective in portraying society than strict reportage would be. For all the play with fiction and reality in which Bolaño engages throughout his texts, in "Beach" he evokes a sentiment about struggle that does not need to be factually correct to be true. In this sense, Bolaño's newspaper writing draws closer to memoir than to autobiography, *crónica* than to reportage.

In contrast, the reporters portrayed in the story "Putas asesinas" ("Killer Whores") who provide commentary as they watch shirtless men parade down the street after a sporting event, are described as vacuous, their words meaningless: "They are dancing, says his oafish voice, as if in our homes, in front of the television, we did not notice. Yes, they are having fun, says the other announcer. Another yokel" (301). The collapse of meaningful representation that has accompanied the rise of mass culture is often presented as a reflection, or source, of the emptiness that haunts Bolaño's characters. In *Una novelita lumpen (A Little Lumpen Novelita)*, for instance, the narrator watches television as a means of distracting herself from seeing her own terrible reality, even as the roommates who abuse her seem somehow legitimized in doing so by the pornographic films they watch. When Bolaño recounts how "the fat journalist" who interviews him in Chile complains that his job is boring, and that only those working the crime beat do anything interesting, he similarly critiques the journalists who think the horror of crime is merely entertainment (*Entre*, 66).

By questioning the possibility of the media and the elite that produce it to capture reality, Bolaño draws nearer to Carlos Monsiváis and Pedro Lemebel, perhaps the best-known *cronistas* during Bolaño's lifetime, than to the *modernistas*. Like Bolaño, Monsiváis suggests that interiority and beauty are impossible in the postmodern world. In his *crónicas*, Monsiváis created fictional characters who moved through Mexican society and allowed readers to participate vicariously in the emotions and experiences of the parties, rituals, and tragedies that affected large swaths of society. A mix of tourist and pseudo-anthropologist, Monsiváis' shapeshifting chronicler discusses popular culture like wrestling, religious processions, pop music, radio, and film. His texts present scenes similar to the one described in "Killer Whores," but rather than narrate the event, he imbues these scenes with humor and social critique that present a judgment of contemporary society, illustrating the constructed nature of national identity and social hierarchies, even as he is at times scathing in his representation of popular taste.

Linda Egan (2001) has suggested that Monsiváis' chronicles reflect the values of North American New Journalism, whose influential style upended the North American newspaper industry by revealing the underbelly of its sensationalizing and fearmongering headlines. Texts like Hunter S. Thompson's influential *Hell's Angels* challenged the high/popular culture divide, offering both the first deep look into the motorcycle gang and a critique of North American reportage in mainstays like *Time*, which came off sounding shallow, exaggerated, and inspired by

Hollywood. In an early article for the *Diari de Girona*, Bolaño recounts Thompson's portrayal of the Hells Angels in 1964, as well as Allen Ginsberg's "vain and naive attempts to ... ideologically redirect the soulless gang" (Bolaño, 2004, 130). Notably, perhaps reflecting the shift away from literature as a possibility in the contemporary mediatic world, Bolaño suggests that both Thompson's gritty description of gang rape and Ginsberg's beatnik poetry have become irrelevant, as the Hells Angels themselves are now only "another Hollywood *souvenir*" (*Entre*, 130).

Moreover, Bolaño goes a step further than Monsiváis or the New Journalism to question the line between fiction and reality by turning their own acerbic style against them. In *Los detectives salvajes* (*The Savage Detectives*), Bolaño presents Monsiváis as an aloof writer who looks down his nose at the young visceralist poets. The alleged encounter never actually appears in the text, though, and thus Monsiváis the chronicler becomes the center of a gossipy debate, even as the incident itself is only as real – or as fictional – as any of the reflections of Mexican society Monsiváis himself published.

Certain moments of Oscar Fate's experience at the boxing match in Santa Teresa in *2666* also recall the kinds of analysis Monsiváis performed in *Rituales del caos* (1995), as well as the New Journalism's approach to investigative reporting, which advocated that the journalist embed himself in the world about which he was writing, if only temporarily. Fate unwittingly engages in the kind of in-person investigative research that Tom Wolfe, Gay Talese, or Hunter S. Thompson brought to their works. Yet, as an outsider not only to the boxing world, but to Mexico, he cannot understand, much less write convincingly about, what he is experiencing in the way that Tom Wolfe or Monsiváis could. For Monsiváis (1995), México's greatest boxer, Julio César Chávez, is just one more spectacle that proves that "Si algo le queda al nacionalismo es su condición pop (If anything remains of nationalism, it is its pop condition)" (*Rituales*, n.p.) Describing the tricolor flags, commentators, flashing lights, and the boxing promoter Don King, who occupies the ring prior to the sporting event that is such a huge spectacle in Mexico, he laments that if boxing used to be "pure sport and pure psychology and pure sociology, the arena of poor young men with prospects," it is now nothing but corporate interests (Monsivaís, 1995, n.p.). And yet, in moments in which the *pueblo* participates in the rituals associated with sport, singing, waving flags, and the like, the group "is again, for an instant, the Nation" (n.p.).

The observations of the match attributed to Fate sound as though they could have been written by a Monsiváis who has lost his sense of humor: "Three thousand Mexicans perched in the gallery of the Arena Pavilion singing in unison the same song ... The tone of the voices, it seemed to him, was grave and defiant, a hymn of lost war interpreted in the dark" (*2666*, 390). Indeed, Fate exemplifies the disjunction, the out-of-placeness, of so many of Bolaño's characters, who cannot identify with the grand narratives that have created idealized understandings of community, be they local or exilic:

> Right at that moment, as if he'd had a revelation, Fate understood that almost everyone in the Arena Pavilion believed that Merolino Fernández was going to win the fight. What led them to such certainty? For a moment he thought he knew, but the idea escaped him like water through his hands. Better this way, he thought, for the elusive shadow and that idea (another silly idea) might be capable of destroying him with a single blow. (391)

The transcendent idea Monsiváis so easily and bitingly attributes to nation, or that Oscar Wilde would have turned into an object of beauty, is out of reach for Oscar Fate, even as it is compelling and disconcerting both for him and for the reader. Although we, like Fate, know there is more there than what we see, neither he nor we are able to comprehend the world that Fate perceives as unreal. If Fate is a *flâneur*, he is an unwitting and uncomfortable one.[10]

Just as Bolaño seems to invoke Monsiváis' humorous portrayals of society and postmodern style, he also reveres Pedro Lemebel, the Chilean *cronista* whose marginal background – as a lumpen, homosexual transvestite – brought extraordinary insights to contemporary Chilean culture. In *crónicas* like "Ronald Wood," "Las orquídeas negras de Mariana Callejas" ("The Black Orchids of Mariana Callejas"), and "La leva" ("The Pack") published in *La Nación* and *Página abierta* and also presented on *Radio Tierra*, Lemebel wrote vicious, yet elegant,

---

[10] Similarly, while in his hotel room in Detroit after interviewing a former Black Panther for a magazine article, Fate watches a television talk show, in which "una mujer obesa de unos cuarenta años tenía que soportar los insultos de su marido, un obeso de unos treintaicinco, y de su nueva novia, una semiobesa de unos treinta años" ("a fat woman of about forty years old had to put up with her husband's insults, an obese man of about thirty-five, and his new girlfriend, a somewhat obese woman of about thirty") (Bolaño, 2004, 327). After a long and detailed description of what each person on the program said about the other, Fate changes the channel. The straightforward narration of the events on a trash TV program, with its abrupt cut and subsequent disappearance from the novel, chronicles a common part of 1990s television culture in the United States, even as it signals the mundaneness of the melodramatic spectacle for Fate, who seems to perceive the sensationalistic programming as background noise. And, reflecting a latent sense of morality in Bolaño's writing, Fate falls asleep just as the programming turns for the first time to reports of the murders in Santa Teresa. Blending in with reality TV, today's serious news is just another spectacle to be ignored.

commentaries on the hypocrisy and tragedy of postdictatorship Chilean society. In "Fragmentos de un regreso al país natal" ("Fragments of a Return to the Native Land"), published in *Entre paréntesis* (2004), Bolaño alludes to the literariness of Lemebel's chronicles, spoken or written, when he writes, "Lemebel doesn't need to write poetry to be the best poet of my generation" (65). He also links the *cronista* to the *valentía* (bravery) he repeatedly associated with poetry: "And above all, as if that weren't enough, Lemebel is brave, that is, he knows how to open his eyes in the dark, in those territories where no one dares to enter" (*Entre*, 65). Here the *modernista* desire to fuse poetry and prose lives on in Lemebel's moving texts, even as his public performances mean he crosses the line from distant observer to transgender activist. What is revealed is not the authority of the intellectual elite, but the possibility of dismantling power through discourse. On more than one occasion, Bolaño wrote some version of this sentence: "the best tears are those that make us better, and [these are]... the ones that don't stray too far from laughter" (*Entre*, 217). If the tears provoked by Monsiváis come close to laughter, the tears provoked by Lemebel's nostalgic and thoughtful digging into the misogyny, homophobia, and even torture that is hidden by Chilean high society aspire to make us better people.

Stylistically and affectively, the journalistic chronicle seems to be reflected in Bolaño's fiction and reproduced in his own chronicles and essays. Yet he often portrays newspapers and mass media as mechanisms that are larger than the characters and fail to meet their claim to seeing or revealing truth. The investigative journalist digs deep so that others may see a darker side of reality. Yet in Bolaño's texts, seeing is occluded even as the *ojo* (eye) is ever-present. The eye is not just an aesthetic perspective that will transcend journalism, turning everyday life into art, as it was for the *modernistas*. It is not merely the power of the camera to capture a reality that itself evaporates, with the photograph preserving only a trace, as Bolaño describes in "Laberinto" ("Labyrinth").[11] Nor is it a mechanism for vigilance that can be studied and avoided, as Bolaño's son learns to do with the electronic "eyes" that control automatic doors opening and closing in "No sé leer" ("I Can't Read"). It is the name of a Chilean exile, "El Ojo Silva" ("Mauricio ('The Eye') Silva"), who becomes a photographer for a Mexican newspaper and who is sent to India on a photojournalism assignment, only to find himself confronted with a hidden violence, the castration of young boys who are later prostituted. Recognizing that

[11] All the short stories I cite are available in *Cuentos completos* (2018).

only a photograph can capture a hell that "Neither the victim, nor the executioners, nor the spectators" can imagine, he takes a photograph even as he realizes that, according to Indian superstition, he will be condemned for eternity for doing so (*Cuentos*, 221). And, as in many stories, the limitations of a photograph to encompass the violence and terror of human experience are symbolized by the end of the story, in which the man who embodies journalism's eye is reduced to weeping.

The dominant eye, like the dominant journalistic discourse, is masculine, and one could read Bolaño's steady portrayal of women's disempowerment as linked to the lack of interiority present in the social structures that are (re)produced in journalism. Women have long contributed to newspapers, from Alfonsina Storni to Clarice Lispector, to Elena Poniatowska, to María Moreno. But they have historically been relegated to the women's pages and, in turn, to relative anonymity, something which Bolaño recognizes in his portrayal of female reporters. In *2666*, Guadalupe Roncal is chosen by her editors to cover the crimes because she is unknown and because, as she recognizes, "we women cannot refuse a commission" (376). In the story "Crímenes" ("Crimes"), moreover, Bolaño asserts that male journalists perpetuate violence about women because they do not understand what they report: "The reporters who cover this kind of news are no different from the murderers" (*Cuentos*, 587). The story emphasizes the idea by focusing on a young female reporter who has interviewed a murderer and discusses the case with a sock salesman who comes into her office one night. The salesman has literally crossed an unspoken boundary, putting both the reporter and the reader in the position of imagining that he is going to kill her. The character's inability to read the woman's fear, combined with the reader's inability to know if he has harmful intentions, reveals the unspoken sense shared by women that they are always under threat. The inability of men to see, much less represent, women's felt reality, is encoded in the last lines of the discussion between the man and the female reporter: "Yes, says the sock salesman, now I see it clearly. No, you don't see anything clearly" (*Cuentos*, 590).

Mass media, moreover, exacerbates the limits of print journalism by falsely equating the visual with truth: "Television does not lie, that is its only virtue" (311), claims the woman in "Killer Whores" who has seduced, abducted, and tortured a man off the streets because "I saw you on TV, Max, and I told myself this is my type" (*Cuentos*, 300). Like women confronting the media image that represents them, the man she calls Max is not Max; he is doubled into himself and "your image, your other"

(*Cuentos*, 309). The objectifying and dehumanizing male gaze circulated via the media is not merely inverted in the story; rather, the interplay of image and reception provokes an almost justifiable use of violence as female empowerment, as any accepted moral code is diminished by the media's inability to enforce it through the superficiality of its reportage. The result is that the media, unlike the *crónica* that is so present in Bolaño's writing, negates any hierarchy of perceptions that could somehow validate one's interpretation of reality: "Keep your eyes open or close them," she tells not just the man who will surely die in her house of horrors, but the reader, "it's all the same" (*Cuentos*, 311).

CHAPTER 22

Literary Criticism and Literary History
Ana Del Sarto

Overture: "The Future Leaks Out"

After too many years of living a Bohemian life within literature, Roberto Bolaño decided to make a living out of it. Ironically, he transformed the source of his many torments into the wellspring of imaginary satisfaction. While plotting and writing his stories, Bolaño introduced many of his friends and foes as fictional characters into his narratives to create a heterogenous personal literary universe. That was his unique way to practice literary criticism while rewriting the literary history of Spanish letters. If given the chance to condense his activity in a specific dialectical image, as Walter Benjamin had done with Paul Klee's *Angelus Novus* (1920) like the angel of history, Bolaño would pick Félicien Rop's *Satan Sowing Tares* (*Satan semant d'ivraie*, 1882) to do the trick. Rop's engraving shows an elongated male figure walking over Paris, with big shoes crossing the Seine (Baudelaire's "Lethe"), throwing miniaturized human beings as seeds of joy and sorrow. The image is part of a series of five heliogravures on sex, death and religion, called *The Satanic Ones* (*Les Sataniques*, 1881–1882), which were banned because they "elicited from flesh on fire the sorrows of fever-stricken souls, and the joys of warped minds" (Huysmans, *The Lust for the Devil*, n.p.). In place of a storm blowing from Paradise ripping the beautiful Parisian arcades at the end of the nineteenth century, Bolaño deals with a cool, whispering breeze from Hell, rejuvenating the tunnels with streams of unmindful waters at the opening of the twenty-first century. Is he really offering us oblivion as the Real kernel of history? Sycorax, as usual, is absent, evicted; her howling remains unheard.

In any case, it takes courage, not passion, to confront sorrow, despair, and death: for Bolaño, that is poetry, because literature is equal to life (and politics for many critics). At the end of the millennium, poetry and poets, perhaps literature altogether, have been gusted out of sight by pixie dust:

"The dust cloud reduces everything to dust" ... and "it has no intention of moving" (*Amulet*, 13); "And then the storm of shit begins" (*Nocturno de Chile*, 150). Where would prophets and seers be found? Would delusional mirages and specters of young rebel poets be able to rekindle those oracular embers? According to Bolaño, we should revisit the forgotten graphic-poetry book, *Le pays où tout est permis* (1972) by Sophie Podolski, which borrows not only the title from William Burroughs's *Nova Express*, but also a dictum from his mysterious character, Hassan i Sabbah: "Nothing is True – Everything is Permitted." That is one of the twilight paths where Bolaño's ethical-aesthetic journey initiates: in Podolski's "Writing is a living thing."[1] Jonathan Monroe's *Framing Bolaño*'s hypotheses, especially those related to writing "fictive history and literary history by other means" in relation to "the history and legacy of the prose poem" (140 and 1) was indispensable for my personal journey into Bolaño's books. Monroe's book always reminded me that while Bolaño wrote literature, he wandered through several canons feeding eclectic libraries, and especially the Western literary canon and its many possible ramifications. Bolaño reorganized all of them in a more than personal literary history, according to a concrete and specific array of aesthetic principles: literature, literary criticism, and literary history, all interconnected but different, "experiences at full speed" outside of the constraining limits of disciplines and institutions.

Due to the colossal amount of critical work on both of his bestsellers, *The Savage Detectives* (1998) and *2666* (2004), the analysis here will be mapped through three novellas: *Amulet* (1999), *Distant Star* (1996), and *Monsieur Pain* (1999 [1981–1982]). If read in that precise order, these texts beckon a journey back to the beginnings of Bolaño's narrative project: Where is poetry? Where has it gone? What have we done to the world, to ourselves? At the same time, this reading exposes Bolaño's general poetics – What is the stuff of literature? What are its conditions of possibility? – in a fractal dimension: reading, writing, and the creative processes' sources –the precious souvenirs of the everyday struggles or the memorable experiences' residues of outcasts and losers. Following this itinerary, a complete circle of transformations could be unveiled, keeping his stories one inside the other like nesting dolls, by traversing back and

---

[1] Nicole Rudick. "Critical Eye: Woman with Powers." *Art in America*, June 1, 2019, www.artnews.com/art-in-america/features/sophie-podolski-le-pays-ou-tout-est-permis-critical-eye-63645/ Also see: Natasha Soobramenien, "Everything Is Permitted: Sophie Podolski's Poetic Exuberance." *Frieze* 194, February 15, 2018. www.frieze.com/article/everything-permitted-sophie-podolskis-poetic-exuberance

forth Bolaño's fantasies from a brave poet to a barbarian novelist. Was "the little hunchback the cop," Odradek, or the dwarf inside the puppet changing skin to "a slow and genius hunchback" after embodying Adorno's claim – "to write poetry after Auschwitz is barbaric" ("Cultural Criticism and Society," 34)? Or was Bolaño just a mundane mutation from a troublemaker and minor poet to the most prominent Latin American writer today?

"A Modest Proposal": Bolaño Superstar [Male, All Too Male!]

Bolaño's *oeuvre* was almost unknown until the mid- to late 1990s. There is something telling about his increasing popularity among global readers distractedly attracted to his books. Although several of them could be related to national, or even regional, contexts – for instance, *Distant Star* and *By Night in Chile* in relation to Chile; *Savage Detectives*, *Amulet*, and *2666*, to Mexico; *Monsieur Pain* to Paris; *Antwerp* to Barcelona and Costa Brava, etc. – Bolaño's Eurocentric *Weltliteratur* positioning is undeniable. During his last years in Mexico, before leaving for Spain in 1977, he was beginning to be recognized as a very young poet. He had published a book of poetry, *Reinventar el amor* (1976), and different poems had appeared in several anthologies, such as *Pájaro de calor. Ocho poetas infrarrealistas* (1976), *Muchachos desnudos bajo el arcoiris de fuego. Once jóvenes poetas latinoamericanos* (1979), and the Infrarealist manifesto, "Déjenlo todo, nuevamente" (1976), in order to be able to pay for his plane ticket to Europe. Perhaps as Boullosa quotes from an interview, he just wanted

> to live outside literature. In Mexico I lived a very literary life. I was surrounded by writers and moved in a world where everyone was either a writer or an artist. And in Barcelona I began to move in a world without writers. I had some writer friends, but gradually I made other sorts of friends. I did all sorts of jobs, of course. ("Bolaño in Mexico" 9)

Once in Catalonia, after years of menial jobs and scarcity, Bolaño deployed his mission to be a professional writer, wishing to make a living out of it. Its plotting took long decades of confabulating in his notebooks, submitting samples to Spanish province awards and prizes,[2] and too many "rejections from Anagrama, Grijalbo, Planeta, certainly also from Alfaguara,/ Mondadori. A no from Muchnik, Seix Barral, Destino ... All the

---

[2] His short story "Sensini," included in his first short story collection *Llamadas telefónicas* (1997), majestically exemplifies this situation.

publishers ... All the readers" ("My Literary Career," *The Unknown University*, vii). However, in 1984 two novels were published: one co-authored with Antoni Garcia Porta, *Consejos de un discípulo de Morrison a un fanático de Joyce*, and his awarded *La senda de los elefantes* (republished in 1999 as *Monsieur Pain*).

It was only in the mid-1990s that the intensity of Bolaño's meteoric rise to popularity unfolds in less than two decades through a variety of national, regional, and global geocultural spaces. His publications sometimes run parallel to each other, and sometimes spiraling concentric circles: from Spain, and published in Spanish, in three-year cycles: 1993, 1996, 1999; from the United States and translated to English, in 2003, 2007, 2009. In "Bolaño and the Canon," Gutiérrez Mouat argues that he was "a writer who labored in relative obscurity for over two decades before making his mark in the literary world. [...] Canonization in the Hispanic world was followed by canonization in the English-speaking world, where the Bolaño boom was, however, conditioned by the repackaging of his figure [a Kerouac and Che Guevara imbricated style (Gutiérrez Mouat, 2015)] for a US audience (Pollack)" (2014, 39). Evidently, his rapid success is the product of a carefully and jointly deliberate commercial strategy, the making of a superstar by several key actors, in addition to the writer himself, who sacrificing most of his teeth committed himself to finish a book every year from 1996 to the time of his death in 2003. First and foremost, Bolaño was supported by his editor Jorge Herralde, who was the founder-editor-owner of Anagrama until 2010, a prestigious and deep-pocketed Spanish publishing house, and with whom he developed a lasting friendship and working relationship. Then, Ignacio Echevarría, an established literary critic in Spain working at that time for *El País*, wrote initial reviews to promote Bolaño's outstanding novels.[3] Finally, marketing and advertisement artillerymen invested time and energy to design and implement the best way to build a literary celebrity. In the short span of three years, Bolaño won the Spanish Herralde Award in 1998; the Rómulo Gallegos Prize in 1999 (one of the most important prestigious awards in Latin America); and the Chilean National Council Book Award for *The Savage Detectives* (1998).[4] After this swift upsurge, slowly but steadily,

---

[3] After his untimely death, Echevarría will edit his unfinished manuscripts to publish them posthumously.
[4] Promoted as a detective, mystery, suspense, and crime thriller in the Anglo-Saxon world or as the best Wellesian thriller for the Spanish world, *The Savage Detectives* rapidly became the new anti-epic which, according to some critics, replaced those outdated Latin American Boom epics (M. Asturias, A. Carpentier, G. García Márquez, M. Vargas Llosa, and C. Fuentes).

academic scholars came on board, after the indispensable push by prominent critics, such as Susan Sontag, among others. This created a reticulated network of interpretations that led into the Bolañomania which, after his death, spread within the Western world of letters, and captured one of the most desired but reluctant markets, the United States. By the end of the first decade of the millennium, there was no Humanities scholar or student who had not read or written papers, even dissertations and books, on Bolaño's texts. *2666* ([2004] 2006), one of his glorious epic masterpieces, conquered the market. It became an international bestseller in just a few weeks. With all these successes, the cult of a male superstar literary idol began to take shape amid many cultural myths and autobiographical legends.

"Bolañismo or Bolañomania," as López-Calvo (2015a, 22; 2015b, 6) denominates this process, is definitively a publishing trademark, but the writer himself evidently had to be a wonderful storyteller: complex situations were wellsprings from which he discreetly dissected singular anecdotal details, the seeds for his golden purpose, the creation of a new story. Several critics claimed that since 1990, after the birth of his son Lautaro, Bolaño decided to leave poetry behind and devote himself entirely to fiction because, as he used to confirm, "that is what sells."[5] He definitively took advantage of this specific reading and profited out of it building one more myth. However, nothing was so far from his intention: Bolaño considered himself a poet, first and foremost, though he had always dabbled in other genres, such as theater, essay, and even, according to his sister, a novel as an adolescent in Mexico.[6] As his many publications corroborate, he ended up combining and mixing different genres in order to be faithful to one of his most cherished aesthetic principles: to make life a work of art by breaking all rules. If anything, he had always considered himself to be a revolutionary poet in the deepest Rimbaldian sense. Bolañomania, the myth-making construction of an ever-expanding universe of literary work, was definitively a joint business between the editorial industry and the institutionalized disciplinary academic apparatus – critics, intellectuals, scholars, graduate students – but also readers in general at the dawn of globalization, when the transnational power of capital materialized all over the Western world. Nevertheless, it was made possible because

---

[5] López-Calvo's tale of maturation goes from "a marginal, outcast poet into an iconic (iconoclast) novelist, a cult figure in the world republic of letters [... up to], the most influential Latin American writer of his generation" (2015a, 5). As much as I enjoyed reading López-Calvo's books on Bolaño, I find some disagreements related to minor details like this one.

[6] See Molina's somewhat personal interview.

Roberto Bolaño, Oh, "male, all too male," dedicated his life to write literature. His *oeuvre* – "masculine, all too masculine" – is so profuse and varied that it lends to a whole range of readings (from those that just scratch the surface to those that dig deep into structures), which simultaneously leads up to contradictory interpretations.

"The Snow-Novel," an Illusory Labyrinth or Eurydice's Call from Global Pop-culture?

If *Amulet* (1999), *Distant Star* (1996), and *Monsieur Pain* (1981–1982) are read together as prismatic refractions on the literary creative endeavor, readers end up with whispers, voices, affects, images, ideas – all of them fragments which might be reconstructed as possible topographies of Bolaño's own fertile imagination. If we follow this reading process forward, these novellas illustrate the author's migrant memories of his geocultural displacements: from Mexico (1968 to the late 1970s), to Chile (1973–1974), and Europe (France, Spain, during the 1980s and 1990s). If we reverse this movement and focus on the stories told within these texts, we can uncover how the unfolding and consolidation of Western civilization has been inherently distilling and disseminating the most hideous acts of barbarism: from Paris in 1938, the emergence of the Nazis and the occupation of France in the 1940s, to the 1973 Chilean military coup which overthrew the Socialist regime led by Salvador Allende, and the repression of the student movement in the 1968 Massacre of Tlatelolco, which paradoxly froze the Mexican Institutional Revolutionary Party in power. Ultimately, these texts show the underlying intense eroticism of power through violence, malice, horror, agony but also love, joy, generosity, tenderness; all of these are concocted in *jouissance* (pain in pleasure) or excess enjoyment. These affects uncover an arch of extremes and all its interior possible nuances, linking and contrasting the mighty and crushing repressive forces that structures of power can unleash when threatened to the shattering, disruptive, and pulverizing soothing power of poetry and literature. The triad proposed in this reading will allow us to deconstruct stagnant doubles and binary oppositions while revealing Bolaño's narrative plan: once in Europe, he transposed his practice of *poetic infrarealism* into the narratives of *real visceralism*, exposing the internal correspondences and the parallax gap of "the inhuman core of humans," the "banality of evil" and the triviality of good, the foolish and petty ways of being humans or "the gap between humanity and its own inhuman excess" (Zizek, *The Parallax View*, 5).

Poetry and poets are the surreptitious, furtive, and sneaky protagonists in these, and most, of Bolaño's books. For him, being a poet was a way of living through reading and writing as a constant adolescent rebel. That was the only worthy poetry for him, one that created life and at the same time expended it all in an instant. All of his books are populated by intense poets, writers, critics, scholars, academics, readers who are searching, in a detective-like manner, for the deep meanings of what really matters in life. They are all trying to decipher what is being written to make sense of what to write: Auxilio Lacouture (Alicia Soust Scaffo) in *Amulet*, Alberto Ruiz-Tagle (A.R.T.) – Carlos Wieder – Jules Defoe in *Distant Star*, and Pierre Pain in *Monsieur Pain* are second rate or minor poets who live intensively. They are all different kinds of wanderers, of outcasts, either weird, strange, or uncanny, marginalized, forgotten and forgettable poets, whose verses are seldom quoted.

Following a Lacanian topography, if *Amulet* presents the imaginary memories of reading poetry in a turbulent time, and *Distant Star* offers the overwhelming and unquestionable symbolic power of writing a foundational moment, *Monsieur Pain* allows us to nomadically traverse a fantasy to get to the bones of a Real/real. *Amulet* is elaborated from Auxilio's traumatized perspective, the archaic and imaginary "mother of all young Mexican poets," who is telling a horror story. "But it won't appear to be, for the simple reason that I am the teller. [...] Although, in fact, it's the story of a terrible crime" (*Amulet*, 1). Bolaño was a mere 15 years old in 1968, and it is possible that the military occupation of the National Autonomous University of Mexico and the slaughtering of the student movement might have left indelible traces in his memory. In that sense, *Amulet* is a tribute to the courage and tenacity of the students in Mexico during the late 60s as well as to the Republican resistance during the Spanish Civil War in the late 30s (represented by Pedro Garfias and Leon Felipe, two Spanish poets of the Generation of '27 exiled in Mexico City in 1938, when President Lázaro Cárdenas, a fervent supporter of the Republican cause, provided asylum for Republican intellectuals). Within the text, these two sociohistorical structures work parallelly and in coevalness with the actualization of several classical myths (among others Cassandra and Erigone), either observed through the voices coming out of the mouth of a vase or slipping down a delirious descent to the underworld (Fernández, 2012). Altogether they convey the life of horror and resistance under an authoritarian philanthropic ogre in Mexico as well as the dictatorial Fascist regime in Spain, while Auxilio keeps reading Pedro Garfias's book and writing evanescent poems on toilet paper.

In direct contrast, *Distant Star* is "a dreadful business": the story of a shadowy autodidactic poet, Alberto Ruiz-Tagle, who after the Pinochet's military coup becomes Carlos Wieder (aka "once more," "again," "a second time," "in Old German means against, contrary to" [DS 40/41]) an Air Force pilot. His oligarchic father is not only proud of him but enjoys his mischievous actions and feats. Wieder's mad skywriting verses,[7] which invigorated the new beginnings of the dictatorial regime, are recognized by the narrator, Arturo B., when he is arrested in a concentration camp in Concepción. In his later nomadic life in Spain, Arturo will disingenuously betray Wieder by deciphering his unforgettable aesthetic touches either in writing, photography, and even in pornographic films. Even though these parallel structures highly resemble the ones in *Amulet*, in *Distant Star* there is a clear instrumentalization of reason executed through deceits of infinite doubles and mirrors, *doppelganger* games across and through their constant recontextualization until they become "in itself, a mirror and an explosion" (*Distant Star*, initial page/n.p.). Like the hieroglyphs of "Rorschach stains" perceived through Borges' labyrinths, these reflections and refractions are the central artifices performed through an infinite and free falling abyss, even practiced over their selves and their multilayered others within: ART/Carlos Wieder and Lorenzo-Lorenza/Petra, Juan Stein and Diego Soto, the Garmendia twin sisters – Angélica and Verónica – Bibiano O'Reily and Arturo B., Ivan Chernyakhovsky and Abel Romero, up to the invented "barbaric writers," Raoul Delorme and Jules Defoe.

Monsieur Pain invites readers to enter the liquid portal of Pain's mind, his imagination of the future already gone, his world of dreams, nightmares, delusions, illusions, and fantasies.[8] Pierre Pain, a Great War (WWI) veteran, marginal poet with few publications, and mesmerist linked to many kinds of esoteric practices, is called out by his unrequited love, Madame Reynaud, to use his powers to try to save her friend's husband's life. No explanations are provided about who this person is. In fact, Pain never knows who César Vallejo is – a poor and unknown Peruvian poet – until the very end, when he learns from Blockman that "Aragon made a speech" at his burial and "now he'll become famous" (*Monsieur Pain*, 116).

---

[7] The parallel with Raúl Zurita's avant-gardist and transient tour de force would not need to be pointed out.
[8] According to Slavoj Zizek, "fantasy is the other side of reality, [...] it sustains the subject's 'sense of reality': when the phantasmatic frame disintegrates, the subject undergoes a 'loss of reality' and starts to perceive reality as an irreal nightmarish universe with no firm ontological foundation; this nightmarish universe is not 'pure fantasy' but, on the contrary, that which remains of reality after reality is deprived of its support in fantasy (Zizek, *The Plague of Fantasies*, 66).

Many critics have read this story as a mystery or enigmatic text (Franco); even as a detective story with an unknown crime at the center (Sepúlveda). According to Bolaño, its structure is unintelligible. It is true that there are open fragments, which do not play any purpose but to distract, and a few intentional mistakes to mislead the reader (for instance, Marcelle Reynaud's short bio at the end talks about "her second husband," when Blockman was her third [*Monsieur Pain*, 126]). However, its structure follows Pain's physical and oneiric wanderings, moving around Paris, from his apartment to several Cafés, from there to the movie theater and the Clinique Arago and to the catastrophic and ruinous environments of his dreams and daydreams of his imagination. At the same time, his whereabouts metacritically interact with *Actualité*, the film Pain watches in the theater. After the last page of the text, readers are left with a compulsion to start again: the narrative is short indeed, but chaotic, fragmentary, very theatrical, and confusing. There are many voices that are somewhat elucidated at the end in the "Epilogue for Voices: The Elephant Track" (*Monsieur Pain*, 117–134), where we learn there is an anonymous I (the narrator), who had been initiated by Pain, and there he was framing from the last two pages the first-person narrative voice, which predominates in the first part of the text. At the end, therefore, there are many associations and connections that remain unresolved, which only an incisive, somewhat obsessive, reader can grasp.

The Real Pierre Menard or How to Get "*Pennies from Heaven*"

The year 1968, in Mexico, is perceived through the heavy sediments of 1973, Chile, and interpreted from a huge backlash flourishing since 1938, Paris: the underground communicating vessels sketch today's blueprint of real power. Memories give accounts of the struggles; written texts trace indelible complicities; dreams and the imagination illuminate possible paths. 1968 is a crucial year to understand the configuration of contemporary Mexico. Cultural hegemony, carefully crafted from the institutionalized power structure since the Revolution, began its slow decay until its change in the mid-1980s. Women and youth, two emerging social subjects in the making, questioned fossilized political structures and mediated new cultural transformations. According to Elena Poniatowska, "from July to October 1968, Mexico was young and lived intensely" (*Fuerte es el silencio*, 48). Moreover, she notes

> in the years after the 1910 revolution and its million dead, the Mexican poor knew above all authoritarianism ... massacres ... were hushed. [...]

In 1968 a similar silence was ruling. Suddenly a dynamic, autonomous, somewhat maddening, movement broke out, [...] a movement for pure and untouched men [...] and thousands of young people united by an indissoluble bond: courage. (*Fuerte es el silencio* 34–35)

Roberto Bolaño moved to Mexico City early that year. "Since I was only fifteen years old, I quickly Mexicanized myself. I felt totally Mexican. I never felt like a stranger in Mexico" (Álvarez 2009, Kindle Loc 715). His mother was supposed to get a teaching position at the university, but social unrest changed the course of events and she could not. Only a few years before, during the early 1960s, Alcira Soust Scaffo,[9] the person on whose experience Bolaño built the main character of *Amulet*, Auxilio Lacouture, arrived in Mexico. She was a Uruguayan teacher and poet, who at that time barely made a living performing volunteer, and sometimes paid, work for the professors of Philosophy and Literature. On September 18, 1968, the UNAM premises were occupied by the Army. Many people were arrested during the raid. As the legend has it, Alcira played León Felipe's poems on the loudspeakers while helping people escape before hiding for almost two weeks in the fourth-floor women's bathroom. In *Amulet*, Auxilio also reads Pedro Garfias' book of poems and writes her own verses on toilet paper which she later has to eat to survive.

1973 is a fundamental year to grasp the power structure of contemporary Chile: on September 11, General Augusto Pinochet ousted President Salvador Allende's first democratically elected revolutionary government. At 8:42 a.m. "Cadena Democrática" radio broadcasted a military proclamation of the coup; at 9:55 a.m., military tanks unleashed fire in the streets around the government palace La Moneda; at 10:30 a.m., army tanks opened fired directly on La Moneda, while Allende and his close entourage resisted from the inside; at noon, the Chilean Air Force began a bombardment. Soon thereafter, Allende asked his men to surrender and committed suicide. The Popular Unity, with its radical and utopian optimism, did not have any "rational option." Its enemies, the military, neoliberal intellectuals and national and transnational companies with Washington's acquiescence, produced a new capitalist counterrevolution by merging the Law (normative and juridical power), terror (power over bodies), and knowledge (power over minds) (Moulian 1997, 22). Throughout the long twentieth century, Chile has been deeply and

---

[9] Alcira Soust Scaffo's first book, *Escribir poesía, ¿vivir dónde?* (2018), was posthumously published by the Museo Universitario Arte Contemporáneo (MUAC) from UNAM in Mexico. Many intellectuals, including Elena Poniatowska and José Revueltas, had publicly recognized her deed during the intervention of the university campus; but it was Bolaño's *Amulet* which paid homage by recreating her touching voice as the "friend of all Mexicans, [...] the mother of Mexican poetry" (*Amulet*, 1).

ideologically torn apart. Literature, music, theatre, performance, and the arts have been spaces of struggle, but its poetic tradition along with literary and cultural criticism have been fundamental to expose the contradictory complicities with power. Peculiarly and paradoxically, while the extreme right was gaining steam, Pablo Neruda was awarded the Nobel Prize for literature in 1971. Almost at the same time, many committed and engaged intellectuals signed a letter in support of Heberto Padilla against the Cuban Revolution. *Distant Star* (1996), as well as its companion *By Night in Chile* (1999), have been read as novels in which the crisis of signification befalls mourning. My interpretation moves away to other aspects, which do not cancel the previous readings, but dialectically set forth a different set of questions about the ambiguous sources of power and its contradictory and obscene underlying supplements: the constitutive complicity of opposed intellectual positions. Contradicting Adorno's maxim about the impossibility of poetry after Auschwitz, Bolaño places the source of the creative process directly in the kernel of suffering: the power of writing which comes from the impetus of limit-experiences of horror, such as kidnapping, disappearing, torturing, and killing.

1938 is a crucial year in Europe that illuminates the underlying foundations of Western culture and the gruesome barbarisms needed to endure its power. In 1938, Germany implemented the Aryan *Herrenvolk* (Master race) policy and began the persecution of Jews. On November 7, a young Polish Jew, Herschel Grynszpan, assassinated a German Diplomat, Ernst vom Rath in Paris, and Joseph Goebbels ordered retaliation: a pogrom against Jews. *Kristallnacht* ensued and inaugurated the modern era of massive extermination camps. Meanwhile, Adolf Hitler was declared Man of the Year by *Time* magazine. "Diabolical years they were, literally diabolical" (*Monsieur Pain*, 132): Pierre Pain was barely surviving, "shadows gliding through the Paris nights" (*Monsieur Pain*, 116), while nobody knew with certainty what was the cause of César Vallejo's death. The time span of *Monsieur Pain*'s major narrative goes from April 6, 1938 – when Pain receives Madame Reynaud's call – to April 20, 1938 – when Pain unexpectedly encounters Madame Reynaud with Monsieur Blockman strolling the streets of Paris. Vallejo had died on April 15 and his funeral was the day after. In the "Epilogue for Voices," all the voices, except for that of the narrator, are named and framed in a short bio, which considerably extends the text's temporality: from 1858 to 1985, a more-than-symbolic long century. Associating Bolaño's *Monsieur Pain* with Paul Valéry's *Monsieur Teste* (written in 1895–1896 and published in 1946) in enjambment with *Elephant Walk* (1953), a Hollywood movie based on a novel by Robert Standish and starring Elizabeth Taylor, offers us a unique dialogic possibility for contrasting the multiple perspectives on civilization and barbarism: how reason, intelligence, and even consciousness can become as barbarous as the blind animal instinct to get to the water through an obstructing luxurious mansion. Elephants do not forget: their savage fury will guide the way. In addition, Valéry created his fictional character, Monsieur Teste – his internal alter ego, "his cerebral conversation partner" (Bevan 1980, 15) – to test all his experiences. Although in Old French *teste* is head, in Latin *testis* means witness, and also testicle. This name allowed Valéry to set on trial everything related to mind and matter. Analogously, Bolaño used the name Monsieur Pain to penetrate what only poets can reach, since Bolaño, like Baudelaire as well as Rimbaud, believed that only true poets have access to that unbearable source of freedom. Fernando Iwasaki argues that "when Roberto Bolaño wrote *La senda de los elefantes* (*The Elephant Track*) in 1981 or 1982, Pierre Pain might have been his alter-ego. But when he published it in 1999 as *Monsieur Pain*, his definitive title, I believe Bolaño had already identified with César Vallejo" (Iwasaki 2008, 121). Iwasaki's conclusion (the last sentence of his text), with which I completely agree, advises us "not to look for Bolaño in Pierre Pain's dreams, but in the unfathomable pain of that poet who was agonizing in Paris while it was raining" (123).

Epitaphs for *Le voleur de feu* (1953–2003)

Roberto Bolaño is not the saint of my devotion. Nevertheless, his writing is extraordinary: amenable, understandable, accessible. The plasticity of the Spanish language was at the tip of his fingers. Like Benjamin's storyteller, he clearly embodied that talent. The sharp, at times too (melo)dramatic tone, his witty gallows humor and his – Mexican acquired – irony (a heterogenous blend of irony, satire and parody) are truly prodigious. Like Jonathan Swift (1667–1745), Bolaño would have liked to write his own epitaph – only true poets have access to that unbearable source of freedom, only true visionaries are fire stealers: Hic depositum est Corpus

[...]
Abi Viator
Et imitare, si poteris,
Strenuum pro virili
Libertatis Vindicatorem. [...][10]

---

[10] The prose translation of these lines would be the following: "Here is laid the body [...]. Go, traveler, and imitate if you can, this vigorous defender of human liberty [...]" (Allen 1981, 179).

The literariness of Bolano´s texts is not engrained so much in the questioning and the self-reflexivity of language, but in the invention of the stories, the artifice with structures vis-à-vis the corruption, subversion, and even the intertextuality amid traditional (classics and folk) literature with cinematic and popular genres. Although his fictional world is peopled by too many males, the witty new spin that Bolaño, absorbing Lautréamont's conception of plagiarism, creates from what Borges had done with Pierre Menard's original text and Surrealism,[11] is enthralling.

> Behind the misty fog, the specter of poetry
>   talking back
> In the middle of literature's whirlwind, a labyrinth of mirrors
> Haunted reminiscences, fractal versions through the abyss
>   rear window
> Saw it coming from afar   future
>   *nec spe nec metu*
> Loss and lost . . . ~~the losses and the lost~~

---

[11] See Delia Ungureanu's excellent 2016 article "Pierre Menard the *Sur*-realist."

PART IV

Aesthetics, Culture, and Politics

CHAPTER 23

The Abomination of Literature
Brett Levinson

I

No Latin American writer insists more doggedly on the relationship of literature and abomination than does Roberto Bolaño. In "Literature + Illness = Illness," Bolaño speaks directly to the issue. Via Baudelaire and Mallarmé, he first suggests that modern existence is monotonous and repetitive, and that means to transcend boredom themselves tend towards tedium. All that remains, then, is the oasis in the desert of ennui. Such an oasis is not an escape; escapes from ennui spell more ennui. The oasis is instead "horror, in other words, evil" (138). Literature is the overexposure of this evil.

The depiction of the interior of Carlos Wieder's apartment in *Distant Star*, offered by Bibiano, friend of the novel's nameless Chilean narrator-poet, supplies a glimpse into this last topos: "it was too empty, and there were spaces where things had obviously been removed . . .. as if the host had amputated parts of the interior" (7). Yet a living space is not like a living body that might be imagined as complete when possessing, say, four limbs, and incomplete when not. An "amputated" interior space is unimaginable. Wieder's "interior" is with a "without" that is not missing. Bibiano does not and cannot offer a sensible representation (amputated space) of a presence (the Idea of horror) that transcends words and the imagination but a linguistic figure of the not present elsewhere (elsewhere than language), which is not absent either, and which is the horror.

In the pivotal scene of the novel, the Pinochet henchman and Air Force lieutenant Wieder (Writer), in 1974, manifests his poetics through a skywritten "text." The select audience is then invited to Wieder's photo exhibition, a pageant of "the art of the future" (84) to which the skywriting also pertains. The portrait of the exposition seems to come third-hand: the narrator recounts the memory of the event as it is recollected two decades after the fact in the confessional self-denunciation of the former military personage Julio César Muñoz Cano. The narrator nonetheless sustains that his own rendering, via Muñoz Cano, is perfectly "accurate" (83). An Air Force lieutenant himself, Muñoz Cano is not an unlikely invitee and witness; and as repentant, his interest is to disclose ignominy truthfully. Nonetheless, the narrator's avowal of "accuracy" is something of a joke. Wieder's photos of "poor quality" (88) include a ceiling image of the cover of the *St. Petersburg Dialogues* by François-Xavier de Maistre, younger brother (so notes the novel) of Joseph de Maistre, anti-Enlightenment nationalist and founder of European conservatism. But François-Xavier was not Joseph's brother; he was his father. The brother is Xavier, a satirical writer who is cited by Borges (276) in "The Aleph." Yet neither François-Xavier nor Xavier is the author of *St. Petersburg Dialogues*; Joseph is. Perhaps the "moderately drunk" (83) lieutenant's "view" of the photo was impeded or cloudy; maybe his recall was off; or perchance the narrator's summary of the lieutenant's testimonial is flawed. Regardless, the account does not even feign "accuracy." Alongside the photo of the cover of *St. Petersberg Dialogues* is "the photo of that photo of a young blond woman who seems to be dissolving into the air" (89, translation modified) and one of a severed finger. The arrangement, then, could as well represent an avant-garde installation (two surrealist journalists attend the *soirée*), as the horridness of a Pinochet hitman, "accurately" captured.

Wieder's "rightwing" exhibition does represent some vision of a Nazi aesthetic. In fact, Wieder's artistic model, like that of the fictional Willy Schürlotz within Bolaño's *Nazi Literature in the Americas*, is the cofounder of the anti-Pinochet movement CADA ("Colectivo de Acciones de Arte"), Raúl Zurita (also a skywriter and, like Schürlotz, tiller of poetry in the Atacama desert).[1] In general, Wieder's artistic statements, traced over twenty-five years, sound as much like overenthusiastic treatises on a socialist art as they do like ones carving out the art of a military junta. Within Bolaño's ouevre, in fact, every right-wing artistic intervention is mirrored by a left-wing counterpart, and vice versa. If any poetry or literature is ignoble, for Bolaño all poetry and literature is. Horrible literature, like great literature, is hence without example. Bolaño therefore offers *no* passages from the innumerable histories of literature that he invents. *Nazi Literature* extends not one citation, nor any summary of passages that point up anything that is even *like* a Nazi literature,

---

[1] Zurita had his verses skywritten above New York City in 1982; in 1996 he had carved a couple of sentences into the Atacama desert.

just as Bolaño presents no extracts from Wieder's and Juan Stein's poetry in *Distant Star*, from the mythical Cesárea Tinajero in *The Savage Detectives*, or from the chief literary hero, Benno von Archimboldi, in *2666*.

At Wieder's exhibition the horror appears, not in the description of the photos, but in the vomiting of the one woman who witnesses them, the playing of Pink Floyd, and the persistent ringing of a wrong-number phone caller. These are not accurate or inaccurate representations, sensible appearances of an Idea. They are evocations of a mood of horror and incoherence which withdraws, for mood is the withdrawal from sense. By "mood" I refer to Martin Heidegger's *Stimmung*, mode and attunement as well as mood (172). What is the difference between a feeling and mood, sense and *Stimmung*? A *subject* feels, and does so before an object. In sensing the object, through this sensibility or intelligibility, the I affirms his presence. The object may impact or alter the I; yet it does not modify the fact that the I *is*. And if an I *feels* terror, the terror is not, since the "subjective feeling" sets up the I as the source of the terror, immutable ground, regardless of its encounters: sense is self-certainty and self-assurance. Conversely, *no one* is anxious – anxiety, for Heidegger, is the most fundamental mood – for anxiety does not appear before, but moves out the I, turning the I into the anxiety that overtakes it. Because no I is before anxiety, there is anxiety or mood, the withdrawal of self-representation.

Bolaño draws from his direct and indirect encounters with the Pinochet junta in order to cast mood in his manner, that is, as terror or horror. Agents of a dictatorship, after all, are not despotic individuals or sets of individuals whose sinister nature a potential victim might identify or objectify. In fact *anyone*, including one's best friend or spouse, may be terror's agent. And because anyone and any sign potentially represents the junta, no sign does. Terror is not marked. Nor does terror inject itself into the populace by virtue of the activities and/or beliefs, actual or imputed, of specific "victims," for example, leftists, students, the indigenous, workers, poets, or "subversives." Such "subversives" may well be the target of the terrorist state. But no person, regardless of his deeds, words, or past is certain, from the point of view of the regime, hence of any I, *not* to be one. In fact, among the individuals most likely to be posited as a "subversive" is one who witnesses or is thought to have witnessed a vile State act and who, as observer of a crime, must be eliminated because *now* a "subversive." There is terror, but no one is the terrorist, nor is any *subject* the victim of terror. Terror is ghostly; it is its return. In every sign dwells the possibility of terror's revisitation, yet no sign of terror appears. The terrorized are thereby attuned to terror at every instant, precisely because terror is no object – which is the terror.

Towards *Distant Star*'s conclusion, the Chilean ex-police detective Abel Romero and the writer-narrator receive considerable cash to "eliminate" Wieder, just outside of Barcelona, roughly a quarter-century after the Pinochet coup. The "disappearance" of Wieder, courtesy of Romero and the narrator, is therefore uncannily like that endured by many Chilean *subversivos*, erased from the earth or sentenced to death for unverified "offenses." Yet whereas Wieder is a soldier within a statist military regime Romero, no longer of the police, and the narrator-poet, are individual actors within a neoliberal, post-dictatorship universe who kill, not due to some perverse interest or enjoyment in law, order, or the State, but for the money that a wealthy donor has supplied. Though the writer accepts the bounty *sin ganas*, he accepts it, which acceptance cements his complicity.

The narrator plays his role in the murder for hire not by "pulling the trigger" (Romero apparently does that) but by reviewing creepy, fifth-rate contemporary literary journals and porno films, supplied by Romero. To the attuned-to-literature reader, namely, the writer-narrator, these will betray, Romero believes, Wieder's whereabouts in the late 1990s. They do: Romero then tracks down Wieder, who turns out to be a neighbor of the narrator. Romero had to have known, even before he consults the narrator in Barcelona, the general location (just as he had to have known the Wieder writing style that the narrator in theory identifies, else Romero could not have selected the revelatory journals) of Wieder. The narrator, then, adds *nothing* to Romero's investigation but the complicity of literature. When the narrator (who knows Wieder's general appearance from the Allende regime) identifies the villain – Wieder, like the narrator, is reading in a café – he actually identifies *himself*, as if all Writers were Wieders: "[f]or a nauseating moment I could see myself almost joined to him, like a Siamese twin, looking over the shoulder at the book he had opened" (144). The horror ("I realized, horrified" [146]) is not that the narrator helps murder Wieder. Horror is the iteration of the iniquitous Wieder in the writer-narrator, the writer's existence as Wieder's *prochain* or ghost, of the I as a programmed automaton who, not the source of himself but a repetition or return, is an assassin.

"Cat" names the "fluffy creature on the sofa" by virtue of iteration and convention. Yet "cat" never means "iteration" or makes iteration appear. Repetition retreats from the narrative, "cat," that it (repetition) renders. The iteration of Wieder's murders, executed by Romero and the narrator, is not shown in the novel, for iteration, like the act of Romero and narrator, is without mark or meaning. It is gratuitous. The narrator cannot narrate "accurately" his own abomination since, if he could, it would not be abominable. In the last lines of *Distant Star*, the narrator informs Romero that nothing like this has ever happened to him before. Romero replies, likely referring to the junta, that "[w]orse things have happened to us." Perhaps, the narrator retorts, but this business has been "particularly dreadful" (translation modified). Romero laughingly asks: "what else could it have been?" (149). Yet Romero has misunderstood the narrator, who has not marked the *dreadful* component of the Wieder affair but its *particularity*: "particularly dreadful." For Romero, in fact, neither Wieder nor his assassination is "particular." Monstrosities take place without particularity, one a copy of the next, with or without the input of an I, with or without consciousness, and will continue to do so. For the narrator, however, the same gratuitous mechanicity points up the *particularity* of evil. Evil, whose source is repetition, resists representation or narrative, surfacing therefore as singular, without sign, and hence as unfamiliar, not of the I who performs the evil act but of an actor and agent of an unidentifiable force, a kind of monster.

II

Bolaño's "The Insufferable Gaucho" represents a rewrite of Borges' "The South," as well as of other well-known texts within the Argentine literary tradition. The life of the protagonist, Manuel or Héctor Pereda, is pushed over the edge on which he teeters by the Argentine economic collapse that commences towards the end of 2001. Earlier the attorney Pereda, an irreproachable figure within the Buenos Aires community, chooses a judgeship over a candidacy within a political party. Disappointed by his judicial career after only three years, Pereda gives up "public life" (9). His adored wife dies when the couple's children, Cuca and Bebe, are five and seven. The retired "young widower" (10) cares punctiliously, indeed, too punctiliously for the children until Bebe leaves home about twenty years later. Bebe, an author, later returns to Buenos Aires; he vows to spend time with his father, who has prematurely aged. The two often sit at a café, chatting with Bebe's literary friends. When the conversation concerns literature, the well-read attorney is bored. Argentine letters, he sustains, include two great writers, Borges and his son, and all further discussion on the issue is so much claptrap. However, when dialogue turns to politics, Pereda – who has declined a political career – appears as if "under the effect of an electric current" (12). At this time Pereda lets his appearance go completely, not even wearing a tie in public. He commences resolutely to "look though the old books in his library, searching for something, though he couldn't have said what" (12). Suddenly, he announces that his treasured Buenos Aires, for him a combination of Paris and Berlin, or Prague and Lyon (10), is sinking. Days later the Argentine economy goes belly-up. Buenos Aires life shifts dramatically, which does not displease Pereda. Over a span of a few days three presidents preside, ironically rendering standard Argentine politics – revolution or military coup – improbable or unnecessary. At this precise juncture Pereda, like Borges' Juan Dahlmann, protagonist of "The South," decides to travel to the family ranch.

The train to the South, Pereda's stay in the pampas, and an eventual return to Buenos Aires overtly recall motifs from Borges' tales, the fact of which Pereda is quite aware: twice he notes the similarities between "The South" and his own experiences. Like Dahlmann, Pereda is not familiar with gaucho life, which he has eschewed as a man of culture (hence the reference to the tie and the various allusions to Pereda's library). His understanding of gaucho existence, also like Dahlmann's, is thereby mediated by literature. On the train, Pereda falls asleep; his "awaking" may form part of a dream sequence, or perhaps of a series of dreams within dreams, as in Dahlmann's case. Upon arrival, Pereda, like Dahlmann is greeted by someone who recognizes him (from childhood and as the Judge), but whom Pereda does not know or recall. Pereda's and Dahlmann's family ranches are similarly cast as shells or ruins. In the conclusion to Bolaño's tale, as in the closing to the "The South," a writerly personage faces a knife-wielding gaucho.

Yet the South does not correspond to Pereda's expectations, largely because it does not correspond to Dahlmann's, which form the basis of Pereda's own view. The gauchos play Monopoly and discuss the treatments offered by mental health clinics (a clinic plays a crucial role in "The South" as well). Almost all horses and cattle have disappeared, replaced by wild rabbits, which are not hunted but trapped. The inhabitants do not carry knives or recognize challenges to their honor. The latter is striking to Pereda: playing out a scene from Antonio Di Benedetto's "Aballay" and reversing one from "The South," the protagonist tries to lure the gauchos into acting according to codes concerning knife duels and honor. In "The South" Dahlmann, inside a general store, is spit at by some gaucho toughs, and is thereby compelled to defend his name in a fight to death. In a similar store, surrounded by gauchos, Pereda hocks a loogie, a "virulent gob of phlegm" (22), in order to gain recognition, but draws no response, as if the gauchos have not read their Borges scripts.

Buenos Aires, for Pereda, is a cultural rather than political center, set off from a barbarism that is represented not only by the gaucho but by this very politics. Barbarism, in Pereda's view, in fact does not exist apart from, but is a product of culture, which props itself by producing and reproducing the civilization/barbarism binary. Hence, in the story, politics is reduced to its mythical manifestations: military junta and leftist revolt, both embodied (for Pereda) by Perón, himself a literary topos. So is behavior: when in conversation with Pereda the gauchos do not talk like gauchos – like gauchos as the texts conceive them – Pereda requests their political opinions. The gauchos express nostalgia for Perón, at which point Pereda, as he will on various occasions, pulls "out his knife.... he thought that the gauchos would do the same and his destiny would be sealed that night, but the old guys recoiled in fear and asked what he was doing, for God's sake" (35). Pereda, in two manners (eliciting political views, initiating a skirmish) again strives to restore barbarism so as to refurbish simultaneously the domain of culture. And the desired barbarity is once more literary; Pereda's gestures, thoughts, and language in this scene are deliberately lifted from Borges. I mentioned above that, just before and in the wake of the 2001 *bancarrota*, "politics as usual" vanishes from the range of options due to the disarray into which the nation falls. So also, then, does the defense by culture against it, leaving Pereda in a helpless, anxious state. In the scene just described, he strives to recover politics (the political sympathies of the gauchos) in order to defeat it, an effort that belongs to Pereda's general strategy of rehabilitation: recreate barbarism so as to repair the cultured Buenos Aires so as to mend Argentina.

It is therefore noteworthy that the presumed "backwardness" of the gaucho is repeatedly presented as a matter of depression or psychological imbalance, and that an NGO shows up in the pampas in order to vaccinate the residents. These facts serve to disclose the possibility that the mixed-up existence (rabbits instead of cattle) that appears before Pereda in the South, and that seems to contradict the protagonist's expectancies, represents a dream or fantasy whose source is a wish-fulfillment: for, only if the gaucho universe is "sick" or "off" can Pereda realize his desire, which is to reset or "heal" the nation. Pereda holds "that nothing would ever be the same unless the cattle returned" (34); he informs others that "[w]e have fallen ... but we can pick ourselves up and go to our deaths like men" (28). In "The South," Dahlmann returns (without arriving) to a vacant home that was never his home in order to justify his lettered existence (Dahlmann, not unlike Pereda, is a librarian) through death. By perishing in a knife fight while safeguarding the import of the family name within history, Dahlmann would "excuse" or justify his literary being since, as it turns out, to suffer such a romantic end through action is itself a thing of a literature that is thusly saved. A life is never justified, and the attempt to justify it through arms plays out an aestheticized illusion in which the sword (knife) occupies the place of the pen, which illusion is the source of Dahlmann's anxiety in the first place.

Pereda is visited by Bebe, bearing gifts that include the son's most recent novel and a gun. Bebe, requiring some time to recognize a father who has completely "gone-gaucho," arrives with friends, one the publisher Ibarrola. When Bebe informs the father that his text was published in Spain, and that he is now known throughout Latin America, Pereda does not grasp what his son, the writer, is talking about. Publishing and commercial reception, on the one side, and literature on the other, represent for Pereda disconnected ambits. As to the gun, it is for Pereda equally incongruous. Pereda's wish to reconstitute the South can be realized solely with a blade. Ibarrola is bitten in the neck rather severely by a leaping rabbit, which wound Pereda cauterizes with a burning knife; Bebe's delegation believes incorrectly that Pereda has slit Ibarrola's throat. The episode prefigures the final one of the tale.

After three years on the ranch, Pereda is summoned to Buenos Aires for business reasons. Pereda imagines himself, on horse, entering into Buenos Aires like the Christ of James Ensor's painting, "Christ's Entry into Brussels in 1889": as the savior of the malnourished and dumbstruck metropolitan population that has by now returned to its routine, its deathly order. In fact, Pereda returns by train, hence is not even recognized (nor is Ensor's Christ). Alone and estranged, dressed as a cross between rabbit hunter and gaucho, as no figure but an old man on the brink of death, like Dahlmann, Pereda wanders toward the aforementioned café. He sees his son conversing with an elderly individual who reminds Pereda of himself. Another table is occupied by a group of writers, dressed as if advertising agents. Pereda stares down one of them, a man of fifty or sixty but with the look of a false adolescent; he is snorting cocaine. The cokehead holds court on world literature. The two gazes meet. The false adolescent steps out and demands to know just what the old man, Pereda, is eying. Pereda will later remember the look, full of terror and reproof, on the man's face, pleading for an explanation – "as if there were any way to explain fever and revulsion" (40) – as Pereda stabs him in the groin.

Pereda, in this scene, plays the role of the gaucho within Borges' "The South" who, from within the store, challenges Dahlmann to a duel. Yet the challenge in "The South" is effected according to protocols and cyphers, whereas Pereda lashes out at an unarmed person driven solely by nausea. Since the gaucho, in "The South," is a literary trope, it makes sense that Bolaño's artificial gaucho, Pereda, would circle back to his origin, "killing" the literature, now fallen into either world literature (as opposed to a national literature), a business enterprise, or the hands of cokeheads, that invents the gaucho. In fact, both the costumed Pereda and the equally costumed, middle-aged adolescent, represent the literary: that of the past (Pereda) and that of the present (the cokehead). Pereda cuts out his own displacement. The double of these doubles is Bebe who, like the false adolescent, engages an old man as well. Bebe, by now, is for Pereda also an embodiment of the unworthy "next" generation. A revision of *Facundo*, in which the barbarian Rosas arrogates Buenos Aires, this portion of "The Insufferable Gaucho" imagines an anarchism that returns to the center in order to mark the horror of the city's amputation, otherwise forgotten by those who have settled back into Buenos Aires's banal, neoliberal regularity. But the indicator of the blankness, the ghastly stabbing, is itself empty.

After the assault, Pereda wonders whether he should remain in Buenos Aires as a "champion of justice" (40) or return to the pampas. Previously he had told the gauchos that judges and police are contraries. Policemen are order, while judges are justice. Pereda does not elaborate. His definition of a judge, "we judges are justice" (23; translation modified), is at best redundant. And the "we," which is justice, is dubious: Pereda surrendered long ago the judgeship with which he identifies (but solely because, in the South, he has been *identified* as the Judge) due to his dissatisfaction with the profession, composed of "crooks and loudmouths" (26), at least within Buenos Aires. Justice, to be sure, is not order; an unjust state, indeed a police state, may in fact be quite orderly. Justice is at a minimum balance, which balancing may disturb order, for instance, the economic order. "The Insufferable Gaucho" thereby recalls "Literature + Illness = Illness," in which literature's addition to illness equals illness, as if literature were 0, "stabilizing" illness by neither adding to nor subtracting from it but by participating in it all the same. Pereda encounters throughout the course of the tale the fact that his novel eccentricities are but copies of old standards, hence that he is no one but the aged: neither father nor judge nor gaucho nor author. A duplicate of Dahlmann just as contemporary Latin American fiction, for Bolaño, stands as so many garbled reruns of Borges, Pereda fights off the non-being of himself and of civilization through the violence that would index his singularity, when the violence in fact is just the stupid completion of a canonized literary scene. The vanguardist and existentialist belief that the gratuitous deed disturbs is no less clichéd than the existence it would unsettle. Nothing attests to the bankruptcy of culture, a fact to which Pereda's "look though the old books in his library, searching for something" attests, for the times are a mood of revulsion for which no literary representation exists, as the condition of the marker is the repetition that annuls it. The "old books" return, as phantoms, in Pereda's meaningless and vengeful repeat of Dahlmann's homecoming, yet Pereda's gestures do not even signal his own meaninglessness. They supplement existence with a 0 that serves as the placeholder of a literature without whose insignificance and out-of-placeness neoliberal globalism would not stand as equal to itself, to wit, ill.

CHAPTER 24

Religion and Politics
Aníbal González

Roberto Bolaño's first major novel, *The Savage Detectives* (1998), begins with an epigraph from near the ending of Malcolm Lowry's *Under the Volcano* (1947) in which the doomed Consul who is the novel's main character hears two questions in Spanish enunciated during Mexico's counterrevolutionary *Cristero* uprising (1926–1929), and replies to both in the negative:

> Quiere usted la salvación de Méjico? ... Quiere usted que Cristo sea nuestro rey?
>
> No.
>
> ("Do you want Mexico to be saved? Do you want Christ to be our king?" "No.") (Lowry, 1994, 368)

As this epigraph suggests, Bolaño may justifiably be considered one of the least religious writers in the Spanish language, although not necessarily an antireligious one. At the same time, his areligious stance made it possible, and perhaps even necesssary, for him to write works in which the links between religion, literature, and Latin American culture are exposed and often subjected to scathing critique.

Although frequently compared with the novelists of the Latin American literary Boom, Bolaño rejected these authors' tendency to sacralize the novel and to incite in readers a more active and radical version of Coleridge's "poetic faith" in order to promote a feeling of pan–Latin American cultural and political unity (González, 2018, 181–182). As shown by Chris Andrews' insightful reading of "Bolaño's fiction-making system" (33–68), Bolaño's idea of the novel and of narrative in general is not based on theology but rather on cosmology.[1] Specifically, it derives from the scientifically accepted cosmological notion that the universe is

---

[1] It should be pointed out that Andrews does not develop in his text this metaphor of narrative as cosmology in Bolaño (doubtless to avoid distracting readers from the already complex discussion of

expanding after an initial Big Bang. Nevertheless, Bolaño is not interested in the universe's origins, but in the strategies needed to describe such an expanding universe. It is fundamentally a question of perspective. Bolaño's technique of "expansion," in which he re-elaborates and amplifies in subsequent texts previously undeveloped elements from his earlier works, is his way of urging readers to look more deeply and in greater detail at a segment of a more general panorama, which, by virtue of the universe's growth, offers new details, opens new perspectives.

Bolaño's most profound difference with the Boom's tradition lies in his post-national attitude, a view of Latin America devoid of essentialism and skeptical about fixed concepts of national and personal identity. His narrative also foregoes the use of religion as an artifice, as a "partial magic" or trick to sacralize both the novel and the nation (as the novel's ultimate subject) and endow them with a transcendent aura. His fiction could even be regarded as a successful example of narrating without religion at all, if religion is understood as the desire to reach a plenitude of meaning (Berger, 1967, 27–28).

However, as Rubén Medina cogently argues in a critique of Jean Franco's reading of Bolaño's politics, Bolaño's "romantic anarchism" (Franco, 2009, 208), with its apparent cynicism about politics and social reality in general, is counterbalanced by ethics (Medina, 2015, 168). Avoiding the tiresome penchant for blasphemy, for obsessively speaking about religion while trying to go beyond it, of authors such as the Colombian Fernando Vallejo, Bolaño's narrative questions religion's importance, seeking to follow non-transcendental coordinates by linking itself to ethics. Bolaño does not aim to assign meaning to the world, but instead to describe how human beings navigate (and sometimes sink) in a world without inherent meaning by forging often highly personal value systems to help them remain stable in their journey through life.

Furthermore, Bolaño's areligiosity does not imply an absence of religious symbols, characters, or issues in his narratives. Indeed, as will be evident in my brief discussion of *Nazi Literature in the Americas* (1996), *Amulet* (1999), *By Night in Chile* (2000), and *2666* (2004), religious elements are highly visible in Bolaño's narratives. Unlike the Boom novels, however, in Bolaño religion is neither a hidden key to the narratives' structure and meaning, nor the source of a numinous feeling – in Rudolf Otto's terminology – with which the Boom authors leavened their

---

Bolaño's narrative techniques), but the metaphor becomes quite visible in the book's subtitle: *An Expanding Universe*.

novels, but is instead represented matter-of-factly, with near-sociological detachment, as one of the various ways in which individuals articulate their relationship to their society as a whole. In turn, this predominantly sociocultural understanding of religion leads Bolaño to reflect about the links of religious feelings, institutions, and practices, with politics, as another salient way in which humans deal with each other.

Bolaño's reflections on religion and politics are explorations of the worldly (as opposed to the theological) aspect of religion, and of the related role of belief and credulity in politics, but they are also reflections on the dual religio-political aspect of literature itself, which is made particularly visible in and by the profession of literary criticism. In a way, Bolaño seems to accept the premise of the late nineteenth-century Spanish American *Modernistas* such as Rubén Darío and their European Symbolist colleagues such as Théophile Gautier and Oscar Wilde, that in the increasingly secularized world after the Industrial Revolution art had become an acceptable substitute for religion. However, in our postmodern age Bolaño goes one step further and suggests that even as art and religion merged in their discourses, there was a further merger of both art and religion with politics. Contemporary art (including literature, of course) is for Bolaño a potentially perverse fusion of religion's invocation of belief, politics' thirst for power, and art's own inherent powers of deceit and manipulation.[2]

Bolaño's first statement in narrative fiction about these matters is still his most explicit, and remains a touchstone of the narrative project in which he was engaged during the last decade of his too-short life: *Nazi Literature in the Americas*. The title says it all: much like Jorge Luis Borges' *A Universal History of Infamy* (1935), which is clearly its principal model, Bolaño's first successful narrative work presents itself as a pseudo-objective and ironic exposé of the unsuspected links of literature in both North and South America with Nazi ideology and its precursors on both sides of the Atlantic. Imitating the supposedly neutral style of a chronologically-organized biographical dictionary, Bolaño offers a rogues' gallery of apocryphal male and female writers of the Americas who at first seem to be merely inverted mirror images of their much better-known canonical counterparts (I use both terms, "apocryphal" and "canonical," advisedly, given that their usage in literary scholarship is notoriously derived from

---

[2] For a detailed account of the curiously antiliterary tendency common to most of the greatest writers of the modern Western tradition – from Cervantes to Borges – and its links to an "ethics of writing," see González, *Killer Books*.

religious discourse). The key to Bolaño's satire, however, lies in its parodic proximity to its canonical models; the names and personal traits of these fictional authors often have a familiar ring: the wealthy Argentine Edelmira Thompson de Mendiluce (*Nazi Literature*, 2008, 3–14) evokes a distorted right-wing image of her no-less wealthy and right-wing (but more successful) real-world compatriot, Victoria Ocampo; the bullying ultraconservative Cuban Ernesto Pérez Masón (54–58), who is said to hobnob with the real-world José Lezama Lima and other poets and essayists of the journal *Orígenes* until he has a falling out with Lezama, is a parody not only of the *Orígenes* writers but resembles other less bellicose, more respectable but no less conservative anti-Fidel Castro intellectual Cuban exiles such as the novelists and journalists Enrique Labrador Ruiz and Lino Novás Calvo.

Nazi Literature in the Americas juxtaposes the formulaic reverential treatment usually accorded authors in literary biographies, which harks back to the hagiographies or saints' lives of the Middle Ages, with the increasingly bizarre and ultimately brutal actions of the authors whose lives are being summarized. The book begins in the early twentieth century with a female author from the lettered, landowning elite of Argentina, but as the century advances the curriculum of its authors becomes increasingly dubious, visibly racist, and violent, culminating in the book's lengthiest biography, that of the Chilean poet and serial killer Carlos Ramírez Hoffman (179–204), whose double "career" reaches its zenith (or nadir) in the aftermath of the military *coup d'état* against Salvador Allende in 1973. Although appearing at first to be one of many scholarly texts through which literature "sacralizes" authors and authorship, *Nazi Literature in the Americas* soon shows itself to be an ethically-oriented desacralization and unmasking of literature's proximity to evil, a closeness often verging into outright complicity.

Reading Bolaño's works from the standpoint of ethics, it is not surprising that in his subsequent novels and stories he often distanced his authorial self from his texts through the invention of a literary alter-ego similar to Fernando Pessoa's "heteronyms" (Martínez 2020, 26), named Arturo Belano, perhaps in order to defuse potential ethical questioning of his own texts. Belano is one of the main characters in *The Savage Detectives*, which is loosely derived from Bolaño's youthful experiences in Mexico City as a leader of the "infrarealist" poets (the name is changed to "real visceralists" in the fiction). In this rambling novel (Bolaño's most extensive after *2666*), which has often been compared to Julio Cortázar's *Hopscotch* (1964), Bolaño offers not an homage but a parody of the *Boom* novels and of their various strategies to assimilate themselves to sacred texts: the narrative pattern of the quest; the use of prophetic discourse as protest or prognostication; the use of metanarrative to blur the borders between the inside and the outside of the text, and the evocation of eternity as a metaphor of totalization, be it through structural devices (a fragmented narrative similar to "chaotic enumeration") or of symbolic objects (such as Melquíades' manuscript in *One Hundred Years of Solitude*). *The Savage Detectives* derives from a "found manuscript" that is not produced by a wizard such as García Márquez's Melquíades, Cortázar's Morelli, or Lezama's Oppiano Licario, but is instead a fragment from the diary of one Juan García Madero, a seventeen-year-old aspiring poet, who is an absolute beginner in love as well as in life. Moreover, the diary does not encompass a whole epoch, nor anything resembling an eternity, but merely the experiences of Juan in Mexico City and in some cities and towns of the Mexican state of Sonora during a period of around three months, between November 2, 1975 and February 15, 1976.

The novel's longest segment "The Savage Detectives (1976–1996)" is divided into twenty-six chapters that constitute an expansion that projects into the past and into the future from the narrative's main plot line, which begins in "Mexicans Lost in Mexico (1975)" and ends in "The Deserts of Sonora (1976)." At first it would seem that, like many of the *Boom* novels, this one offers us the coexistence of past, present, and future in a single instant. However, this seeming imitation of eternity is undone not only by the exact dates it offers, but also by the fact that what we read are the first-person reminiscences, sometimes partial and prejudiced, filled with hypotheses and interpretations, of a whole cast of characters who interacted with Arturo Belano and Ulises Lima, the two characters "on a quest," the "savage detectives" of the novel's title, over the course of two decades, and that ultimately the story collectively told by all those narrators is an open and ill-defined one.

In contrast to *Hopscotch*, the two "detectives" who seem to repeat the wanderings of *Hopscotch*'s protagonist Horacio Oliveira are actually opposites of Horacio, about whom Cortázar offers abundant information regarding his life and opinions (particularly the latter), while readers rarely hear directly the voices of Arturo and Ulises, and what little they know about them comes through the impressions and hypotheses of other individuals. Horacio may not be able to understand himself, but Arturo and Ulises remain enigmatic for the readers throughout *The Savage Detectives*.

Unlike *Hopscotch*, with its multiple endings evocative of the overflowing time of eternity, the quest narrative in which Bolaño's enigmatic protagonists are involved in *The Savage Detectives* leads to death and banality. After searching for Cesárea Tinajero through the lonely villages of Sonora, she offers no illumination nor any link with poetic tradition. Although her obese body has a monumental quality ("she looked like a rock or an elephant," notes Juan [570]), Juan states: "Seen from behind, leaning over the trough, there was nothing poetic about her" (570). A short time later Cesárea dies heroically, although in confusing circumstances, while defending Ulises Lima from the corrupt policeman who, with Alberto, was trying to kidnap Lupe (572). Juan writes in his diary that he looked for and found Cesárea's poetry notebooks when he returned to her house in Villaviciosa (574), and later he claims to have read them, but he does not speak of their content, nor does he seem to give them any importance.

If *The Savage Detectives* seems to offer a dismantling through parody of the *Boom* novels' manipulation of sacredness, the short novel published soon afterwards, *Amulet*, which further develops the outlandish character of Auxilio Lacouture featured in Chapter 4 of "The Savage Detectives (1976–1996)," may also be read as a parody, specifically of Jorge Luis Borges' celebrated short story "The Aleph," which arguably served as a model of the *Boom* novels' strategic and secular evocation of theological concepts such as eternity and the sacred (González, 2018, 182). Based on the real-life Alcira Soust Scaffo (1924–1997), an eccentric Uruguayan expatriate poet who wandered around the campus of Mexico's National University (UNAM) in the 1970s and became notorious for having spent two weeks hidden in a bathroom in one of the university's buildings ("La UNAM recuerda"), Auxilio is a Quixotic, mentally unstable, and visionary character who in her rants calls herself "the mother of Mexican poetry" (*Amulet*, 1). Evocative of Sandra Gilbert and Susan Gubar's trope of "the madwoman in the attic," as well as a female version of the lovestruck, perplexed, and hyperrational male narrator of "The Aleph," Auxilio discovers her scatological version of the Aleph inside a toilet stall at the UNAM, while hiding from the Mexican military's occupation of the university during the 1968 antigovernment protests that led to the infamous Tlatelolco Massacre, where hundreds were machine-gunned in a public square by the army.

Despite her cartoonish appearance, Auxilio clearly functions in the novel as a Neo-Romantic poetic and prophetic figure, a *vates*, whose marginalized perspective, along with her wide-ranging culture and curiosity, allows her to glimpse the bitter truth about the fate of poetry and poets in contemporary Latin America. That truth, as the novel's ending makes clear, is that Latin American poets (a term which Bolaño seems to apply broadly, almost etymologically, to any Latin American endowed with creative talent), particularly of the younger generations, are doomed to be sacrificed again and again to the profoundly violent and conflictive forces of Latin American history and society, just as the rebellious Mexican youth was in 1968 and that of Chile in 1974 (the events of the coup against President Salvador Allende are also referenced in the text). In the novel's final lines, Auxilio describes "an interminable legion of young people . . . walking unstoppably toward the abyss." She continues:

> And I heard them sing. I hear them singing still, faintly . . . the prettiest children of Latin America, the ill-fed and the well-fed . . . such a beautiful song it is . . . and how beautiful they were . . . although they were swallowed by the abyss . . . And although the song that I heard was about war, about the heroic deeds of a whole generation of young Latin Americans led to sacrifice, I knew that above and beyond all, it was about courage and mirrors, desire and pleasure. / And that song is our amulet. (181–184)

An "amulet," in the usual dictionary definition, is "an ornament or small piece of jewelry thought to give protection against evil, danger, or disease" (*Oxford English Dictionary*). It is not so much a sacred object as one to which magical powers are attributed by superstition. As Sir James George Frazier argued, magic and its allied notion of superstition are at the antipodes of religion: magic is for Frazier a primitive form of rationalism that seeks regularities and principles in nature (Thrower, 1999, 102–103); superstition is in turn, from the standpoint of both religion and rationalism, a debased form of belief. In *Amulet* literature, as symbolized by Auxilio Lacouture the hallucinatory "mother of Mexican poetry," is viewed skeptically as a form of superstition, as irrational as the violent world of politics in which it seeks to intervene.

Perhaps the book by Bolaño most akin to the ferocious antireligious diatribes of Fernando Vallejo is *By Night in Chile*, which, if not for his friends' and editors' advice, Bolaño would have titled *The Shitstorm* (Maristáin, 2010, 36). This is undoubtedly one of Bolaño's most pugnacious texts. As in *Amulet*, the main character and narrator is based on a real-life person; this time, however, instead of an obscure though sympathetic individual like the Uruguayan Alcira Soust Scaffo, Bolaño chooses José Miguel Ibáñez Langlois (b.1936), a prominent poet and literary critic in Chile's main national newspaper, *El Mercurio* (from 1966 to 2014), who often published under the pseudonym "Ignacio Valente." Most importantly, Ibáñez Langlois is a Catholic priest and is said to belong to the prelature, or hierarchy, of the secretive, ultraconservative Opus Dei organization (*Memoria Chilena*). To prudently avoid accusations of libel, Bolaño renames his fictional poet-priest-literary critic Sebastián Urrutia Lacroix, and changes his pseudonym to "Ibacache" (a not-uncommon surname in Chile). However, the novel is otherwise explicit in its allusions to the military coup against Salvador Allende in 1973, its long repressive aftermath, and the collaborationist role played by the narrator along with other literary pretenders such as María Canales. In the figure of the hypocritical, self-serving, and sanctimonious Urrutia, Bolaño explicitly reunites and explores the sinister links among literature, religion, and politics suggested in his previous fictions.

By Night in Chile is structured as a self-justificatory monologue by Urrutia, who believes he is near death and wants to respond to "the slanderous rumours" spread by a "wizened youth ... in a single stormlit night to sully my name" (1). However, like its prototype in the anonymous Spanish Picaresque novel *Lazarillo de Tormes* (1554), the monologue leads to the narrator's self-incrimination, as he wonders in the final lines: "Am I that wizened youth?" (129). As Urrutia mentally reviews his life history, sinister and ironic elements and circumstances recur constantly: his evocation of his father's shadow "slipping from room to room in our house, as if it were the shadow of a weasel or an eel" (2); the meetings with his mentor, the arch-conservative literary critic of *El Mercurio* who writes under the pseudonym "Farewell" (a thinly-veiled portrayal of Hernán Díaz Arrieta [1881–1984], whose pseudonym was "Alone") and who was nevertheless a promoter of the great Chilean poet Pablo Neruda (*By Night*, 2003, 13–16), who was an avowed Communist, and the nearly-incredible literary *soirées* held during the Pinochet regime at the house of the well-heeled María Canales (whose real-world model was Mariana Callejas [1932–2016], *Memoria viva*) even as her husband (Michael Townley [b.1942] in historical reality, *Memoria viva*), a CIA operative, tortured prisoners in the basement (*By Night*, 2003, 120–126).

If Urrutia himself embodies the multisecular confluence and mixing of literature with politics and religion, three episodes in the novel highlight each of the three areas. The first addresses religion: narrated in a style appropriately filled with Medieval reminiscences and allegories, it tells of Urrutia's year-long trip to Europe to write a report on "the preservation of churches" underwritten by the Archiepiscopal College of Chile and managed by two mysterious characters, Raef and Etah (whose names are obvious anagrams of Fear and Hate, *By Night*, 2003, 65). Bolaño masterfully weaves through this narrative the striking image of a series of priests who have adopted falconry in order to be rid of the doves whose excrement fouls the ancient churches' structure. This outlandish image nevertheless effectively captures a vision of the Catholic Church as an isolated, archaic institution capable of resorting to violence to protect its privileges; the various priests' use of birds of prey evokes historical associations with the church's rapaciousness and thirst for power, and the avian image itself may arguably evoke the institution's manipulation of writing in the ancient use of quills as writing instruments.

The second episode, which happens when Urrutia has returned from Europe, shortly after the coup against Salvador Allende, is written in a darkly humorous key and shows Urrutia's face to face encounter with political power. In it, Urrutia recalls his brief nine-lesson stint as a tutor on Marxism to Pinochet and members of his junta (87–102), also managed by Raef and Etah. Urrutia's status as an Opus Dei priest guarantees that his lessons on Communism will be filtered through his sympathies toward the dictatorship. However, his literary, humanistic background, which includes a sense of irony, along with his awareness of Christian morality, allows Urrutia to observe in his monologue the crassness and vulgarity of the dictator and his henchmen and leads him to question the morality of what he has just done.

The novel's third and darkest episode, in which literature plays a central role, deals with the artistic gatherings during the dictatorship at María Canales' mansion. The brutal juxtaposition of prominent members of Chile's world of letters socializing right above a basement where prisoners were being tortured and disappeared, and the fact that not a few of Canales' guests were aware that something strange and terrible was going on in that house but chose to ignore it (*By Night*, 2003, 119), leads Urrutia to a crisis of conscience, and after the dictatorship's end, to be wracked by guilt and the fear of being brought to judgment for his complicity in Chile's oppression.

2666, the last and by far the longest and most ambitious of Bolaño's novels, is set in the globalized world of the early twenty-first century, where amidst the burgeoning international trade of a capitalism grown ever more unfettered after the Cold War's end, the city of Santa Teresa (a transparent version of Ciudad Juárez) on the US–Mexico border becomes the epicenter of widespread and almost incomprehensible gender violence against hundreds of women – many of them workers in the notorious *maquiladoras* – assassinated there. The number that is the novel's title seems to allude not just to a future date, but also to the "number of the Beast" in the Biblical Apocalypse (Revelation 13:18), and the text's renaming of Ciudad Juárez could refer to any of at least a half-dozen saints named Theresa from the Middle Ages to the nineteenth century (when Ciudad Juárez acquired its current designation). Analogously, the small group of literary scholars featured prominently at the beginning of the novel, all of whom are quasi-religious devotees of the mysterious German author Benno von Archimboldi, would seem to evoke literature's dependence on belief (or credulity) for its continued existence as well as the cult-like nature it has displayed throughout its history. Nevertheless, like its Ur-text *Nazi Literature in the Americas*, and unlike the Boom novels it resembles in its ambition, *2666* also takes place in a world where religions, political borders and the nation-states that sustain them, and the practice of literature itself, are being dissolved, bringing to the fore the need for renewed forms of aesthetic and ethical judgment.

CHAPTER 25

Gender and Sexuality

Ana Forcinito

"And although the song that I heard was about war, about the heroic deeds of a whole generation of Latin Americans led to sacrifice, I knew that above and beyond all, it was about courage and mirrors, desire and pleasure." As a distorting mirror of *Amulet's* very first words ("This will be a horror story" [1]), these final words can serve to condense Bolaño's literary world when thinking both about violence and gender. From *Nazi Literature in the Americas* (1996/2008) to *2666* (2004/2008), the mirrors that reflect the terror with which those "heroic deeds" of the past were defeated are intertwined with sexual desire – and, even more, with a pleasure associated with destruction and annihilation, and with narratives as a tool to either exhibit or hide such violence. The link between narrative and heroicness suggests that the dispute between masculinities is also a dispute for narrative authority. In Bolaño's novels, this fight between those who were defeated through atrocities and human rights violations in all Latin America in the 1970s and 1980s, and those who committed the crimes and even inscribed the history of horror in the Chilean sky (like Carlos Ramirez Hoffman in *Nazi Literature in the Americas* or Ruiz-Tagle/Carlos Wieder in *Distant Star*) continues in the present with new manifestations of war. The amulet of the heroic deeds of this "whole generation of Latin Americans" might reveal magic powers and alchemies of gender attributes (this generation might not explicitly endorse gender violence as the perpetrators did in the many clandestine detention centers) yet might still hide known and recurrent forms of violence. These amulets do not exclude the patriarchal (and violent) frameworks that they many times denounce. The transformations of masculinity, in Bolaño, are also caught between the two coordinates that feminist scholar Rita Segato has proposed in her study of gender violence: on the vertical coordinate, there is a message to the potential victims (and here the denigration and punishment of women take place). On the horizontal coordinate, there is a message to male peers, and it is in this coordinate that the negotiation for virility takes place

(2003, 185). In addition, the consideration of these competitive masculinities from a gender perspective brings to the forefront the inexorable link between masculinity and rape/femicide. And it is precisely within this link that literature plays such a central role, not only in the exposure of violence, but also in its normalization, and in a more silent (and hidden) consent to sexual violence and the killing of women. And this is what I would like to keep in mind in reading Bolaño from a gender perspective, because, as I hope to contend in these pages, it is precisely the horizontal coordinate that is at stake when thinking about gender violence and about the difficulty of representing it without falling, even unwillingly, into the consent of such violence.

Bolaño makes visible sexual violence and femicide as well as the transformation of landscapes of war in Latin America (and globally), including the gendered positions assigned throughout this transformation. Yet the failures of the past's heroic deeds are also intertwined with stories of desire and pleasure that indicate that we are still within a masculine paradigm (it is just that one model wins over the other). In these pages, I will discuss not only the most visible manifestations of violence but also the hidden and persistent violence that is imbricated in narratives that normalize rape and femicide.

Violence and Visibility

Horror becomes usually visible, in Bolaño, as an obscenity; and as Jean Franco has pointed out when discussing *By Night in Chile*, an obscenity that is simultaneously about atrocities and about "willed blindness" (116). Both "seeing" and "not-seeing" seem to be at the core of what becomes visible. This willed blindness is also an obscenity present in the literary practice: "it is as if the ivory tower depended on 'not seeing' the extermination camp" (Franco, 2013, 117).[1] Bolaño proposes an intimate relationship between literature (or art) and the exaltation of criminality. Even when art and literature expose violence, it is not enough to say that it attempts to undo the invisibility of violence but instead that constitutes a dispute to the previous visualization of atrocities. Yet, even within this new way of becoming visible, violence against women seems always trapped in between the claws of narratives of masculinity and their consent or normalization of criminality.

---

[1] For an excellent analysis of the space, and the architecture in which we can locate the masculinity represented in this novel, see Draper (2012, 125–151).

"The Part about the Crimes" in *2666* has been widely discussed as an attempt to make visible corpses and wounds and an exposure of sexual violence, as readers were presented with one femicide after another, confronting them with the details and names of more than one hundred murder victims.[2] It is difficult not to think of this exposure of naked bodies and the detailed information about sexual offenses as pornography, which is most clearly expressed in the exhibition of the mutilated bodies in *Distant Star* but can also be part of many of the *2666* references to sexual violence and femicide. In Bolaño, systematic violence becomes visible in conjunction with individual sexual desire and impulses, and therefore what is underlined is the pleasure taken in such destruction. And there, perhaps, is where the horror resides. Bolaño's work makes visible the connection between the dictatorship in Chile and the femicides in Mexico, and the many genocidal practices that seem to converge in Santa Teresa. And as Nicaraguan feminist scholar Ileana Rodríguez proposes in her study of sexual violence, it is impossible to approach the destruction of the other based on gender without a consideration of the pleasure taken in such destruction. Therefore, she suggests, we must study uncontainable, almost psychotic desires and impulses, because a study of deliberately executed annihilation omits the aspect of destruction that is visceral, uninhibited impulse, but is also associated with pleasure (2016, 193–194). Both dictatorships and democracies are conceived in Bolaño's texts within the framework of a patriarchal order in which sexual impulses and the pleasure in the mutilation of women and children are not only the legacy of the authoritarian abuses of dictatorships but also the very condition of the formation of the legal apparatuses of democratic states.

The portrait of aberrant excesses of the dictatorships and their systematic human rights abuses in Bolaño's narrative can be found at the intersection of democratic practices and the law's impotence for stopping systemic gender violence. In addition, it points to what Sergio Villalobos Ruminott called the "metamorphosis of violence." Santa Teresa signals this mutation and the conception of war and the globalized disposability of those bodies that seem not to matter. "No one pays attention to these killings, but the secret of the world is hidden in them" (348), we read in the third part of *2666*. Santa Teresa reveals the central place that rape and femicide hold in the new global landscapes. While from *Distant Star* to *2666* (or even from Benno von Archimboldi/Hans Reiter to "The Part about the Crimes") we seem to transit from genocide and enforced

---

[2] See for example, Pelaez (2014); Driver (2014); and Velazco and Schmidt (2014)

disappearance to sexual violence and serial killing, the numerous mirrors in Bolaño's narrative reveal a series of mutations within the foundational fabric of systematic/systemic gender violence and atrocities, be it through a terrorist state, a criminal organization, a serial killer, or a sexual partner.

The descriptions of the corpses in "The Part about the Crimes" make visible femicidal violence and provide the victims' names and some other information about their lives. Yet, the victims are still voiceless. The narrative is an exhibit of horror that offers the language that is used to frame the victims. I am not referring only to the detailed descriptions of misogynistic jokes, as the apparent component of such frame, but also to the forensic style used in the reports, which is supposedly "objective." Still, this style might be interpreted as an unconvincing pretension that covers sexist claims in a framework in which the victims' lives seem not to matter. Exposing the crimes and underlying the investigation around them does not necessarily imply a feminist reading of the relationship between gender and narration. And it is precisely this type of interrogation of the corpse that can lead us, as Catharine McKinnon suggested decades ago, to the understanding of the invisibility of gender even around the representation of femicide (including the masculine narratives in which such depiction is imprisoned).[3] Victims are exposed, counted, and even named in Bolaño. Yet, the lack of vulnerable voices traps this narrative in a visuality without a voice. Vulnerable women are "framed" as silent images, confined in inaudible visibility. We might be able to picture the bodies, but the voices we hear are still the masculine voices of the "objective" narrator in a distant forensic style that is reminiscent of the acquiescence of the law when it comes to gender violence.

Masculinities and Mutations

The mutation of violence that Bolaño represents both traces a connecting line between the killing of women in Santa Teresa and the atrocities of the dictatorships, and exposes the disjuncture between the two scenarios. In *Distant Star*, state terrorism, torture, and degrading treatments are part of a systematic plan with a common enemy (the left). In the fourth chapter of *2666*, the enemies are now vulnerable women and children. Following Rita Segato, we could refer to a transformation in the conceptualization of the enemy, from the enemy as "warrior" (the revolutionaries and guerrilla fighters in dictatorships) to a new enemy as "fragile bodies" (the women

---

[3] For an excellent discussion on masculinity and rape see Mardorossian (2014) and Rodríguez (2016).

in Santa Teresa). Within this new landscape of war, sexual violence is not a supplement of war or a collateral damage, but an act of writing on women's bodies documenting the victory of one dominant (masculine) group over the other within the context of permanent non-declared wars (Segato, 2014, 343). And while the dominant model of masculinity remains within the latitudes of criminality, the defeated model of masculinity shows a sense of failure and impotence that recycle the figure of a hero destined to be defeated one time after another. In that sense, while exposing the crimes of Santa Teresa, Bolaño makes visible the new failures of the defeated masculine model that survived the dictatorships of the Southern Cone and, simultaneously, the defeat of the law, or even worse, it shows the complicity between law and violence against women.

Many of the male characters in Bolaño's world attempt to save a victim, at one moment or another (Fate wants to rescue Rosa, Pelletier and Espinosa want to save Liz Norton). Yet their intervention is usually unsuccessful. This new model, the failed savior, also serves as the masculine paradigm to confront atrocities and crime and it seems like a recurrent reappearance of the masculine model defeated in the 1970s and 1980s. That is the case of Ojo Silva in *Putas asesinas*. Having experienced the dictatorship in Chile in the past, the photographer witnesses the castration of young boys in an initiation ceremony in India and their subsequent exploitation in prostitution. He, then, kidnaps two of those children and escapes with them. Even though this character "saves" them from the immediate situation, the two boys die at a young age.

This generation of defeated heroes is also a generation of survivors, not characterized necessarily through their heroic deeds, but through their failures. While they might well represent, as Franco suggested (2009), a generation "destitute of belief after the disasters of the Twentieth century [...] who have little less to amuse themselves besides occasional friendships and trivial pursuits including literature" (2009, 208), they are not completely "destitute of belief" or, if they are, it is because of the encounter of new disasters. In *The Savage Detectives*, (a novel that clearly exposes the link between poetry – and even marginalized artists – and desire, pleasure, and sexual impulses in the numerous sexual encounters and adventures of the protagonists) the search for Cesárea Tinajero initiated by Arturo Belano and Ulises Lima culminates with a violent episode and Cesárea's death. Here too, the dispute between masculinities generates a more feminized space (and I do not only refer to vulnerable women who become disposable, but also to the feminization of one of the masculine models in dispute). Almost as the reverse of the dominant and more violent model, this generation of survivors are defeated time after time, and with each failure, they increase the power of the dominant masculine model (and their violent manifestos written on women and children's bodies or corpses). The image that Bolaño uses to express the legacy of a violent past speaks eloquently of the (gendered) horrors of the present: "We are children trapped in the mansion of a pedophile. Some of you will say that it is better to be at the mercy of a pedophile. You are right. But our pedophiles are also killers" (*Between Parenthesis*, 339). The exploration of masculinities and their disputes within new paradigms of war seems to be one of the more visible aspects of Bolaño's reflection on gender and lays out a landscape in which to approach gender violence not only in consideration of the victims but also of the perpetrators or those who are trying to undo destruction but get caught in horrific mansions and masculine struggles for power.[4]

Trapped in Masculine Narratives

Even women who are strong and autonomous characters in Bolaño's literary world have been or will become the victims of gender violence, or at least, they have experienced firsthand the tentacles of the violence surrounding them. Moreover, being recognized and accepted as autonomous seems, nonetheless, to be conditional and, as in the case of Liz Norton in *2666*, occupies an ambiguous place in the patriarchal scenography. Consent to masculine norms is the condition for not posing a danger to patriarchal heteronormativity. Not surprisingly, the suspension of such consent seems to be the recipe for becoming dangerous. Norton is a strong and independent character, and although she shares an intellectual passion with her other European scholars (Pelletier, Espinoza, and Morini), she is presented as someone who is not quite intellectual. She shows her emotions ("when she suffered her pain was clearly visible, and when she was happy the happiness she felt was contagious," 8) and even more, she is described through a lack (she lacks the iron will that characterizes the other scholars). All these attributes already suggest the indelible marks of "femininity." In addition, she has consensual sexual relations with Morini, Pelletier, and Espinoza and, therefore is depicted as a woman with autonomy. However, at one point, she temporarily becomes "Medusa." That happens at the very moment of her non-consent to sexual intercourse,

---

[4] Many theoretical approaches dealt with the exploration of masculinities from a feminist perspective (for example Rita Segato [2014] or Sayak Valencia [2014]) after the publication of *2666*.

when she decides to stop or pause her sexual relations with Espinosa and Pelletier and finds another lover. The connection Liz-Medusa comes from her new lover Pritchard, in one of his encounters with Pelletier ("Be careful [...] of the Medusa," 69). Pelletier and Espinosa assume that if Liz is Medusa, Pritchard should be Perseus and he is probably planning to kill her. The scenography of the masculine dispute is set in motion. It shows a conditional existence of autonomous women on the verge of becoming monstrous and that such monstrosity (and the femicidal violence associated with it) is just one of the chapters in the narrative of male heroic deeds. Medusa here is relevant because this mythological character has become a symbol of many feminist readings that emphasize the normalization of violence against women through heroic narratives (and literature). This "becoming dangerous" of Norton, precisely at the moment of non-consenting to continue a sexual relationship with Espinosa and Pelletier, might serve to underline the place that consent has in Bolaño's narrative concerning violence. Liz is herself exposed to a series of violent interactions, when her colleagues struggle to exercise and exhibit male dominance and heroicness (both in the instance of the taxi driver and Liz's new sexual partner). Female characters, although many might be portrayed as strong, are not only reached by the tentacles of patriarchal violence, but also navigate between very fixed roles and positions (so they are allowed a certain autonomy and power, but conditioned to their acceptance of male desires).

Violence against women is exercised as a punishment or a threat in more subtle forms. Here literature shows that the tentacles of violence against women in Bolaño are rooted in language and narration. This trap is apparent in *Amulet*, a novel with a female character as narrator (Auxilio Lacouture, Uruguayan poet who resides in Mexico). Of course, that female narrator tells a different story and with different modulations than the narrator in *By Night in Chile*, for example, where Bolaño chooses a former priest and perpetrator to narrate another horror story. Auxilio is a female poet characterized as the "mother of Mexican poetry." Yet, she is surrounded by many male writers and artists (including Arturo Belano, alter ego of Bolaño) and performs many "feminine" roles, from cleaning to being the emotional caretaker and the narrative voice of the story of the poets, philosophers, and artists. Moreover, she is imprisoned in masculine visions and, like the muses, tells the story of patriarchal masculinity.

In this perhaps "minor" novel, this narrative voice bears witness of her own position as a victim of state repression. Auxilio resists during two weeks in a bathroom, while the military enters the university in 1968. The main narrative sequence is precisely about her survival (or a mirror of survivals). And while she constructs a story about a resistance that is unrelated to gender, towards the end she suggests that there is a gender component to her traumatic narrative, and her narration accounts for a traumatic narrative memory with fragments and reflections that point to sexual violence and the threat of femicide.[5]

The catalyst of this intromission of more invisible (yet effective forms) of gender violence in Auxilio's narrative is the story of Erigone, told by Carlos Coffeen Serpas. In the example that follows, it becomes apparent that women are trapped in male narratives that normalize more extreme forms of violence. This normalization of violence takes place when Carlos tells her the story of Erigone (the daughter of Clytemnestra and Aegisthus, and therefore Orestes and Electra's half-sister). After stating that Orestes rapes Erigone, the narration continues with references to Orestes being in love with Erigone and to additional "sexual encounters" between them through the expression "they made love" (142). Even when Orestes is planning to kill Erigone, Carlos's narrative voice continues, she "gives herself to Orestes without fear" (143). The sexual relation is normalized as consensual and the narration suggests that Erigone is more afraid of Electra than of Orestes, who has actually raped her. The narration has erased and normalized rape, and rape becomes consent, although with the cautionary note that Erigone "has quickly learned how to handle the new king's madness" (143). The narration then focuses on Orestes and Erigone spending all night as lovers as he convinces her to leave the city.

The story of Erigone as told by Carlos Coffeen Serpas is the myth that normalizes violence and rape, and points, as many other sequences in Bolaño's literary work, one more time to Santa Teresa. Even more, it reminds us of the extemporal order of the myth and the persistence of the complicity of language and gender violence. This story has a profound impact on Auxilio to the point that the narration/recollection (now Auxilio's) goes from the bathroom in the Facultad de Filosofia y Letras and the students of Tlatelolco to the feeling that she is herself Erigone and the image of Carlos Coffeen Serpas's eyes. We read the fear, and the hatred with which Auxilio reacts to such violence. In the midst of images that haunt Auxilio after she hears Erigone's story, we can read a fragmentary, traumatic, and hallucinatory chain of thoughts that contrast with Carlos' well-articulated narrative. Both the image of Orestes' eyes (as he sees Erigone leaving) and the story of Orestes' fame after Erigone's departure

---

[5] For an analysis of Auxilio from a gender perspective of horror, see Hoyos (2019).

(a narrative that erases Erigone's survival) are interrupted by this chaotic image that haunts Auxilio and allows readers to glimpse other shapes of the horror story. This example provides a new door to explore Bolaño's narrative in relation to gender, not now in terms of explicit forms of violence (as it might be the obvious way of approaching his novels and short stories), but instead in relation to the persistent complicities between narrative and sexual violence (or literature in general, another obsession in his work). The difference is that gender violence is not exposed but erased and normalized, in this case as love or attraction and most importantly, as consent.

This example brings us back to the violence in Santa Teresa, but nonetheless points to the empowerment of masculinity through narrative authority. And while many of Bolaño's female characters do not fit the passive or submissive woman category, they are still exposed to persistent narratives and interpretations that translate rape into consent, or that transform the affirmation of a lack of consent to a sexual relation into dangerous threats to masculinity.

Many of the approaches to gender in Bolaño have focused on the killing of women in Ciudad Juarez. What I tried to contend in these pages is that the normalization of violence against women or more subtle ways of erasing women's visions (in particular in relation to strong or independent women) is what most calls for a feminist reflection in Bolaño's world, because what is exposed is precisely the simultaneity of autonomy and vulnerability, and most importantly, the link between the heroic deeds that Auxilio's voice celebrates at the end of *Amuleto* and violence against women.[6] Here, the discussion moves away from violence as pornography, both on the part of the perpetrators and those who denounce it. Here the voiceless bodies of Saint Teresa acquire another reading: that of a writing that hides the marks of rape and even the stories of resistance and survival. This tension shows, as in many other parts of Bolaño's narrative, the inexorable link between literature and criminality, and most importantly for this chapter, between the struggles between masculinities and the patriarchal consent to sexual and femicidal violence.

---

[6] And not precisely in the way in which this continuity is usually articulated in the forensic or the judicial interpretations of situations of violence. In these cases, women in the most vulnerable situations are very conveniently granted the autonomy they are denied in more general terms, and that results in blaming women for the violence exercised against their bodies.

CHAPTER 26

Race and Ethnicity
Juan E. De Castro

As is the case with many modern Latin American novelists, issues related to race and ethnicity – such as cultural or linguistic identity, or racial or ethnic discrimination – are rarely obvert in Roberto Bolaño's narrative. Instead, his writing exhibits an awareness of the differences that originate in class origins, political sympathies, as well as in sexual identity and orientation, though without his texts ever threatening to become examples of thesis or social narrative.[1] This, of course, does not mean that the study of the manner in which race and/or ethnicity are depicted in his novels – when they are depicted – is without interest; in particular, since, as we will see, there are a few moments in his novels when Bolaño actually brings race and/or ethnicity to the foreground of the narrative.

I.

The explicit contrast between Farewell's elegant soirees at Là-bas, often with no less a figure than Neruda present, and the (perhaps funeral) peasant get-together in *By Night in Chile*,[2] or the story of Lorenzo/Lorenza/Petra, the poor, armless, boy who becomes a performance artist in *Distant Star*, his first narrative novel published by a major press, can serve as examples of how the impact of class and/or sexual orientation is often highlighted in Bolaño's writing. However, we are never told, for

---

[1] On the debated issue of the political valence see Nicholas Birns, "Valjean in the Age of Jouvert: Roberto Bolaño in the Era of Neoliberalism," in *Roberto Bolaño, A Less Distant Star*, ed. Ignacio López-Calvo (New York: Palgrave, 2015), 131–148; Wilfrido Corral, *Bolaño traducido. Nueva literatura mundial* (Madrid: Ediciones Escalera, 2011), 252–254; and Juan E De Castro, "Politics and Ethics in Latin America: On Roberto Bolaño," in *Roberto Bolaño as World Literature* (Bloomsbury: New York, 2017), 63–77.
[2] Roberto Bolaño, *By Night in Chile*, trans. Chris Andrews (New Directions: New York, 2003), 17–25.

instance, anything about Lorenzo/Lorenza's ethnicity or race. Instead, we read in *Distant Star*:

> Once upon a time in Chile there was a poor little boy ... I think the boy was called Lorenzo, I'm not sure ... One day he climbed up a pylon and got such a shock that he lost both his arms. They had to amputate them just below the shoulders. So Lorenzo grew up in Chile without arms, an unfortunate situation for any child, but he also grew up in Pinochet's Chile, which turned unfortunate situations into desperate ones, on top of which he soon discovered that he was homosexual, which made his already desperate situation inconceivable and indescribable.[3]

While one could easily surmise that Lorenzo/Lorenza is dark-skinned, that is not stated in the text and, one must note, not necessarily the case.

Even when Bolaño takes into account racial or ethnic differences, such as the cases of the Jewish Russian poet Juan Stein or the apparently indigenous poet Diego Soto, in *Distant Star*, his narrative rejects conventional identitarian ascriptions:

> If the sky over Chile had begun to crumble and fall, they would have gone on talking about poetry: the tall, fair-haired Stein and the short, dark Soto; one strong and well built, the other's fine-boned body hinting at future plumpness. Stein was mainly interested in Latin American poetry, while Soto was translating French poets who were at the time (and many of whom, I fear, still are) unknown in Chile and this, of course, infuriated a lot of people. How could that ugly little Indian presume to translate and correspond with Alain Jouffroy, Denis Roche and Marcelin Pleynet? Michel Bulteau, Mathieu Messagier, Claude Pelieu, Franck Venaille, Pierre Tilman, Daniel Biga ... who were these people, for God's sake? (65)

As Jonathan Monroe notes: "Forming a pair of perfect oxymorons, an embrace of contraries with and against type, Stein and Soto figure a schematic binary of contrastive, complementary, perhaps (ir)reconcilable choices facing aspiring poets at the time of the coup."[4]

In a characteristic irony, noted by Monroe, this schematic binary of contrastive choices includes Stein's and Soto's ethnicities, races, as well as literary preferences (87). Soto, the poet of indigenous origin, is obsessed with French poetry. Escaping from the coup, Soto ultimately chooses France, the capital of Western modernity for many twentieth-century Latin American writers, as his new home, marries a French woman, and

---

[3] Roberto Bolaño, *Distant Star*, trans. Chris Andrews (New Directions: New York, 2004), 72.
[4] Jonathan Beck Monroe, *Framing Roberto Bolaño: Poetry, Fiction, Literary History, Politics* (New York: Cambridge University Press, 2019), 87.

begins a successful academic career. The novel, without explicit irony, notes "it was not so much that Soto had become middle-class, he had never been anything else."[5] On the other hand, except for his admiration for the Jewish Soviet General Chernyakhovsky, Juan Stein seems uninterested in Russian or Jewish culture or literature but is instead fascinated by Latin American poetry. Rather than admiring Osip Maldestam or Vera Inber, "Parra, Lihn, and Teillier" (48), all Chilean poets, were the objects of his passion. In fact, freely borrowing from Jorge Luis Borges' "The Other Death" – Bolaño imagines two alternative post-coup lives for Stein: one as a free-roaming revolutionary, the other as a schoolteacher and mechanic.[6] While Soto's and Stein's artistic preferences can be explained in manners that are not inconsistent with discussions of identity – the indigenous Soto could give in to Eurocentric pleasures without feeling his Chileanness as undermined, or, perhaps, burned by Chilean racism, would have rejected the literature of the white establishment; while Stein could need to reaffirm his "Latin Americanness" precisely because he is of immigrant stock – Bolaño refuses to do so. It is left up to the reader to decide whether there is any relationship between their literary, as well as, after the coup, their political and ethical choices, and their ethnic origins.

One can also add the *visceral realist* "Piel Divina," literally "Divine Skin" (though called in the English-language translation "Luscious Skin") from *The Savage Detectives* to this group of characters whose ethnicity is deemphasized. There is a clear implication that he may be of indigenous ancestry: "Luscious Skin's father and mother were born in Oaxaca and, according to Luscious Skin himself, they starved to death."[7] Oaxaca is, of course, one of the states with large indigenous population, and the extreme poverty experienced by Luscious Skin's parents seems to tally with the poverty unfortunately often experienced with Mexico's autochthonous peoples. Luscious Skin's life is also characterized by a marginality that could be taken as reflective of his indigenous origins, as well as of the concomitant lack of access to higher education: "he told me that he'd come to Mexico City when he was eighteen, with no money, no clothes, no friends to turn to" (328). His ending is also reflective of his utter

---

[5] Walter Mignolo and Catherine Walsh, *On Decoloniality: Concepts, Analytics, Praxis* (Durham, NC: Duke University Press, 2018).

[6] Jorge Luis Borges, "The Other Death," *Collected Fictions*, trans. Andrew Hurley (New York: Penguin, 1998), 223–228; Roberto Bolaño, *Distant Star*, trans. Chris Andrews (New York: New Directions, 2004), 57–64.

[7] Roberto Bolaño, *The Savage Detectives*, trans. Natasha Wimmer (New York: Farrar, Straus & Giroux, 2007), 67.

marginality: "the police had killed him in a shootout in Tlalnepantla. The police were after some narcos, and they had the address of a boardinghouse on the way to Tlalnepantla. When they got there the people in the house put up a fight and the police killed all of them, including your friend" (342). However, characteristically, Bolaño does not mention his probable indigeneity.

Be that as it may, the character's sobriquet may itself be significant. According to Iván Degregori, having a light skin color is itself a kind of capital in Peru and, by extension, Latin America. Degregori calls this plus-value found in whiteness "Mercantilism of the skin": "this benefit that *criollos* in Peru still enjoy, where the fact of being white or light-skinned grants a kind of differential rent, that is gained only by showing one's face" (87–88).[8] However, as his "name" indicates, in the case of "Divine Skin," his skin, including his skin color, works in his favor. Rather than hindrance, it seems to be his only asset, as he becomes an irresistible object of desire for both female and male characters, who grant him not only affective but also economic and cultural support, even if his ultimate poverty and sad end stresses his marginality, be it based on his ethnic or class origin, or poverty.

Nevertheless, as we will see, there are several characters, including that of Amalia Maluenda, in *Distant Star*, or Oscar Fate, Barry Seaman, and Antonio Ulises Jones, in *2666*, that are described in ethnic and racial terms. These examples evidence a clear awareness not only of discrimination, but of discrimination's and racism's roots in political and social realities, including Latin America's colonial inheritance and the history of structural racism that began with slavery in the United States.

II.

For heuristic reasons, it may be of use to begin the examination of these latter characters with one of Bolaño's most enigmatic creations: El Quemado (the burnt one), found in *The Third Reich* (2010), one of the Chilean novelist's posthumous publications, but originally written in 1989. The novel has at its core the playing of the board game "The

---

[8] Carlos Iván Degregori, "El aprendiz de brujo y el curandero chino. Etnicidad, modernidad y ciudadanía," in *Elecciones 1990. Demonios y redentores en el nuevo Perú. Una tragedia en dos vueltas*, by Carlos Iván Degregori and Romeo Grompone (Lima: Instituto de Estudios Peruanos, 1991), 88–89. The full quotation in Spanish is as follows: "mercantilismo de la piel, ese beneficio del que gozan aún hoy los criollos en el Perú, donde todavía el hecho de ser blanco o de piel clara otorga una suerte de 'renta diferencial', que se gana con sólo mostrar la cara" (87–88).

Third Reich," which details the battles of the Second World War, between the German Udo Berger, a champion player vacationing in Spain's Costa Brava, and El Quemado, a burnt victim who rents pedal boats and lives on the beach. We are told "that El Quemado wasn't Spanish. Where was he from, then? South America; which country specifically, he didn't know."[9] We are also told that he was a victim of the Nazis:

> "The real Nazi soldiers on the loose around the world." Uh-huh, I said. . . . Then was it Nazis who were responsible for his burns, was that the story? And where had this happened, and when and why? The owner gave me a superior look before replying that El Quemado, in some hazy distant past, had been a soldier, "the kind of soldier who has to fight tooth and nail." Infantry, I deduced. Immediately, with a smile on my lips, I asked whether El Quemado was Jewish or Russian, but such subtleties were beyond the owner. (174)

One could, perhaps, come to Sharae Decker's conclusion that "El Quemado is a South American émigré, possibly Jewish, whose body visibly bears the scars of horrific torture."[10] However, given the qualifications made in the novel to these statements about El Quemado's background, one can see in him a stand-in, granted enigmatic, for the victimized "Other" of the different social and political catastrophes of the twentieth century unleashed by the "real Nazi soldiers on the loose around the world": in particular, Jews during the Second World War, and the victims of the South American dirty wars of the seventies.

But El Quemado can also be read as representing the indigenous populations of the Americas, the original "Others," victims of Western violence. Probably inspired by Ricardo Palma's description of Atahualpa as "after a couple of months being worthy of his teacher [Hernando de Soto], playing as an equal,"[11] the novel identifies El Quemado's exceptional ability at playing "The Third Reich" with the Inca captured by the conquistadors: "El Quemado has gone beyond my advice. In a way he reminds me of Atahualpa, the Inca prisoner of the Spaniards who learned to play chess in a single afternoon by watching how his captors moved the

---

[9] Roberto Bolaño, *The Third Reich*, trans. Natasha Wimmer (New York: Farrar, Straus & Girioux, 2011), 85.
[10] Sharae Decker, "Roberto Bolaño and the Remaking of World Literature," in *Roberto Bolaño and World Literature*, ed. Nicholas Birns and Juan E. De Castro (New York: Bloomsbury, 2017), 218.
[11] Ricardo Palma, "Los incas ajedrecistas," in *Tradiciones peruanas*, vol 2 (Madrid: Oceano, 2001), 1667. The full quotation in Spanish is: "Después de aquella tarde, y cediéndole siempre las piezas blancas, y al cabo de un par de meses el discípulo era ya digno del maestro. Jugaba de igual a igual" (1667).

pieces" (251). However, as Deckard points out, "unlike the captive emperor, who was eventually executed, Udo's opponent is not easily defeated, but rather enacts a triumphant reversal" (218).

In this manner, the character of El Quemado establishes connections between three of the key "Others" in Latin America and world history: indigenous populations of the Americas (during the conquest), European Jews (during the Nazi and other fascist regimes), and, in Bolaño's words from his "Caracas Address," "my own generation, those young people, those who ... died in Argentina or Peru, and those who survived went to die in Chile or Mexico, and who weren't killed there were killed later in Nicaragua, Colombia, or El Salvador."[12] But by linking the violence during the Spanish conquest (1492–1532 and beyond), the Fascist and Nazi Holocaust of the 1930s and 1940s, and Latin America in the 70s (and arguably earlier in the 60s), as well as, implicitly contemporary neo-Nazis, Bolaño insinuates a genealogy of violence that would have its origins precisely in Western colonialism.

Bolaño was well known for his distrust of academia, in general. As Wilfrido H. Corral notes: "The view he had of those intellectual exercises and of the career calculations that could be behind them annoyed him, and he does not try to be impartial."[13] Moreover, the Chilean novelist makes this antipathy explicit in "An Attempt at an Exhaustive Catalog of Patrons," where he levels his irony at Latin Americans ensconced in US academia:

> Most are on the left, politically speaking. To attend a dinner with them and their favorites is like gazing into a creepy diorama in which the chief of a clan of cavemen gnaws a leg while his acolytes nod and laugh. The patron-professor in Illinois or Iowa or South Carolina resembles Stalin and that's the strangest and most original thing about him.[14]

Moreover, any mentions of key theorists – Derrida, de Man, Foucault, Jameson, Said – are conspicuously absent from his collected non-fiction, as well as any reference to their Latin American peers, such as Ángel Rama or

---

[12] Roberto Bolaño, "Caracas Address," in *Between Parentheses: Essays, Articles, and Speeches*, ed. Ignacio Echevarría, trans. Natasha Wimmer (New York: New Directions, 2011), 35.
[13] Wilfrido H. Corral, "Bolaño, Ethics, and the Experts," in *Roberto Bolaño and World Literature*, ed. Nicholas Birns and Juan E. De Castro (New York: Bloomsbury, 2017), 107.
[14] Roberto Bolaño, "An Attempt at an Exhaustive Catalog of Patron," in *Between Parentheses: Essays, Articles, and Speeches*, ed. Ignacio Echevarría, trans. Natasha Wimmer (New York: New Directions, 2011), 209.

Antonio Cornejo Polar.[15] Instead, Harold Bloom is praised as being the "best literary essayist in our continent"![16]

However, whether by intuition or actual influence, through the figure of El Quemado, Bolaño insinuates ideas that have been proposed by anti-colonial, postcolonial, and decolonial scholars. For instance, Robin G. Kelley writes about Aimé Césaire's postcolonial theorizing: "its recasting of the history of Western Civilization helps us locate the origins of fascism within colonialism itself."[17] Probably reflecting his own personal experience, as well as his subjective location as a Chilean and South American, Bolaño complicates this trajectory of violence, not only by highlighting the Spanish conquest, rather than French or British colonialism, as the founding movement, but also by adding a third stage: the return of violence to the Americas by presenting the Pinochet regime as a revision of Nazism.

III.

It is precisely in *Distant Star*, his first mature novel, in which Bolaño returns to this (proto) postcolonial/decolonial reading of the violence that has unfortunately characterized the history of Western culture. However, reflecting his increased mastery as a novelist, Bolaño now manages to ground this view of history in a much more realistic and believable character: Amalia Maluenda, the Mapuche (indigenous) maid of the aunt of the Garmendia sisters, the only member of the household who escapes being murdered by Carlos Wieder, the poet, aviator, and fascist psycho-killer. Later, during Wieder's trial in absentia, "Amalia Maluenda, the Mapuche maid, made a surprise appearance in the witness box." Bolaño's brief description of her court testimony attempts to provide an indigenous, perhaps, decolonial view of the history of Chile and Latin America:

> Over the years her Spanish had dwindled. When she spoke in court, every second word was in Mapuche ... In her memory, the night of the crime was one episode in a long history of killing and injustice. Her account of the events was swept up in a cyclical, epic poem ... partly her story, the story of

---

[15] Roberto Bolaño, *A la intemperie. Colaboraciones periodísticas, intervenciones públicas y ensayos* (Madrid: Alfaguara, 2019), Kindle.

[16] Roberto Bolaño, "El libro que sobrevive," *A la intemperie. Colaboraciones periodísticas, intervenciones públicas y ensayos* (Madrid: Alfaguara, 2019), Kindle.

[17] Robin D. G. Kelley, "A Poetics of Anti-Colonialism," in *Discourse on Colonialism*, ed. Aimé Césaire (New York: Monthly Review P, n.d.), 10.

the Chilean citizen Amalia Maluenda ... and partly the story of the Chilean nation. A story of terror .... Remembering the black night of the crime, she said she had heard the music of the Spanish. When asked to clarify what she meant by "the music of the Spanish," she replied: "Rage, sir, sheer, futile rage." (110–111)

Amalia Maluenda is here seen as having gone through a process by means of which she has recovered her own indigenous knowledge and tradition, precisely as her ability in using Spanish has dwindled. As in the case of his description of El Quemado, in this passage Bolaño reflects – whether intuitively or consciously – a kind of decolonial thinking, now widespread among Latin Americanists, that not only proposes the foundational nature of colonial violence, and the colonial experience in the constitution of modernity, but also sees in indigenous traditions, histories, and modes of thinking, the roots of all anti-systemic resistance. As Walter Mignolo and Catherine Walsh note:

> Decoloniality has a history, *herstory*, and praxis of more than 500 years. From its beginnings in the Americas, decoloniality has been a component part of (trans)local struggles, movements, and Actions to resist and refuse the legacies and ongoing relations and patterns of power established by external and internal colonialism – what Silvia Rivera Cusicanqui calls colonialism's long duration and the global designs of the modern/colonial world. (99)[18]

Amalia Maluenda's herstory, which links colonial violence with that of Pinochet, is an example of decoloniality.

IV.

With the character of Oscar Fate – née Quincy Miller – an African-American journalist who has traveled to Santa Teresa to cover a boxing match, but ends up trying to investigate the femicides that plague the city, Bolaño expands his narrative world to include the United States and, in particular, the African-American experience. Much of "The Part About Fate," the third book of *2666*, amounts to an analepsis in which the Chilean novelists presents a condensed reflection on African-American life in the twentieth century: from the black church, to Black Communism, to the Black Panthers, to Hip Hop, seen as reflective of a deep cultural

---

[18] Walter Mignolo and Catherine Walsh, *On Decoloniality: Concepts, Analytics, Praxis* (Durham, NC: Duke University Press, 2018).

pessimism. Fate meets characters that can be seen as representative of black political activism: Antonio Ulises Jones, the last "member of the Communist Party in Brooklyn,"[19] a critical, but recalcitrant Marxist, and Harry Seaman, (fictional) founder of the Black Panthers (together with the also fictional Mike Newell), turned into a barbecued ribs expert (244). As Monroe has noted, in his description of Jones, but one can add that this reflection is also relevant to Seaman, Bolaño provides "a frame of reference where the ideological battles of the twentieth century give rise to those of race, ethnicity, gender, and technology that have increasingly come to define the twenty-first century" (182). However, one must also add that, despite the ironic portrayal of these failed twentieth-century revolutionaries, Bolaño correctly notes the manner that race and ethnicity have always been imbricated with Black Marxism. Seaman's party was, after all, called the Black Panthers, while Jones's nickname is Scottboro boy, given his frequent mention of the Scottsboro Boys, young African Americans falsely accused of rape in 1931. Moreover, when Fate looked at Jones's parting gift, "he saw with surprise that it wasn't the Manifesto but a fat volume titled *The Slave Trade* by someone called Hugh Thomas" (260).

Conclusion

As mentioned at the start of this article, it would be a mistake to see in Bolaño an author primarily concerned with issues of race. However, as this brief and incomplete overview has attempted to show, the Chilean novelist often took into account the effects of racism and discrimination as, in his fiction, he investigated the traumatic birth and rebirths of fascism (*Distant Star*, *2666*, or *Nazi Literature in the Americas*), or dealt with the horrors unleashed by neoliberalism (*2666*). Moreover, he did so in ways that, regardless of his own views on critical and literary theory, brought his novels into dialogue with some of the most important current theorizations of race and ethnicity. Underlying his novelistic practice is an acute awareness of the imbrication between fascism, contemporary violence and racism, and the processes of colonization that helped define Latin American cultures and societies.

---

[19] Roberto Bolaño, *2666: A Novel*, trans. Natasha Wimmer (New York: Farrar, Straus & Giroux), 261.

CHAPTER 27

Trauma and Collective Memory
Ryan F. Long

The novels Roberto Bolaño wrote about trauma and collective memory are often structured around dispersion. In *Distant Star* (1996) the hunt for a Chilean government torturer ends in Spain.[1] A Uruguayan navigates legacies of the Spanish Civil War and Tlatelolco in *Amulet* (1999). Scholars from England, France, and Italy travel to Mexico in search of a German author in *2666* (2004), a novel about the Holocaust and mass femicide. Óscar Amalfitano, a Chilean exile, moves to Mexico from Barcelona in *2666* and *Woes of the True Policeman* (2011). In *The Spirit of Science Fiction* (2016), Jan Schrella, a Chilean novelist shares a room in Mexico City with his friend Remo. Schrella writes letters to Science Fiction authors in the United States while Remo seeks poetry and affection.

By Night in Chile (2000) stands out from these texts because it features a nation-bound desire for narrative coherence. Sebastián Urrutia Lacroix, its narrator and protagonist, collaborated with Pinochet's regime, and before its violent interruption, his story thus appears capable of overlapping with official history. The novel consists entirely of Urrutia Lacroix's words, and its first paragraph spans 130 pages. Its second and final paragraph consists of seven words: "And then the storm of shit begins" (130). The tension released by this interruption has until then intensified in a suffocating display of a fragile narrative coherence whose fissures are visible from the beginning. Since page one, Urrutia Lacroix's monologue persists in the face of the enigmatic "wizened youth," who threatens narrative stability: "I used to be at peace with myself.... But it all blew up unexpectedly. That wizened youth is to blame" (1). That the unidentified youth may be Urrutia Lacroix's conscience only appears possible near the novel's end: "And little by little the truth begins to rise like a dead body.... Its shadow

---

[1] Dates of publication refer to the Spanish originals. The translations' dates are in the list of Works Cited.

rising as if it were climbing a hill on a fossil planet .... I see his face, his gentle face, and I ask myself: ... Is that the true, the supreme terror, to discover that I am the wizened youth whose cries no one can hear?" (129). A similarly divided but collective subjectivity appears a few pages earlier. Urrutia Lacroix visits María Canales at the mansion where during the dictatorship she hosted social events while her husband tortured and murdered political prisoners in the basement. Before leaving – and declining an invitation to see the basement – Urrutia Lacroix tries to comfort Canales by suggesting she pray. She responds enigmatically, "That's how literature is made in Chile" (126). Later Urrutia Lacroix considers Canales's observation: "I thought about what she had said. That is how literature is made in Chile, but not just in Chile, in Argentina and Mexico too, in Guatemala and Uruguay, in Spain and France and Germany, in green England and carefree Italy .... Or at least what we call literature, to keep ourselves from falling into the rubbish dump" (127). Driving away from a house that symbolizes the open secret of state terror, he conceives of literature as a way to avoid reckoning with his own criminal complicity, which fails.

I have begun with Urrutia Lacroix's last-ditch effort to make literature a shield in order to highlight three texts that openly refuse coherence: *Woes*, *Spirit*, and the poem "Visit to the Convalescent" (2000). They demonstrate that Bolaño's writing defines collective memory and trauma through a dynamic tension between totality and openness which moves across the boundaries of individual texts. My analysis of these processes focuses on narratives of concealment and complicity related to historical traumas, ghostly spaces, and the motifs of crying, holes, and storms. It aims to show that sustaining a critical perspective on Bolaño's treatment of trauma and collective memory demands a comparative approach that troubles if not rejects attributing a systematic coherence to Bolaño's texts.

In the final part of *Spirit* titled "Mexican Manifesto,"[2] historical trauma relates to the Conquest. An uncanny painting of Moctezuma at a bathhouse bearing his name portrays him in a pool surrounded by men and women bathing. Remo describes the mural: "Everyone seemed cheerful,

---

[2] The text's Spanish original, "Manifiesto mexicano," was published separately in the Spanish cultural magazine *Turia* in 2005 and then in *La universidad desconocida* (2007) before appearing in *El espíritu de la ciencia ficción*. Laura Healy's English translation of it as a separate text was published in the April 15, 2013 issue of the *New Yorker*. The facsimiles of Bolaño's notes in *Espíritu* show the ending of "Manifesto" as the final page of the manuscript of the novel, dated 1984. See Id. 137 on the seventeenth unnumbered page of the section at the end of *Espíritu* titled "Apuntes de Roberto Bolaño para la escritura de *El espíritu de la ciencia-ficción*."

except for the king, who stared out ... as if pursuing the unlikely spectator with wide, dark eyes in which many times I thought I glimpsed terror" (181). Remo returns to the mural at the novel's conclusion, recalling "Moctezuma's unreadable eyes," and the fact that those with the Aztec leader are "laughing and talking, trying with all their might to ignore whatever it is the emperor sees" (196). The contrast between Moctezuma's awareness of approaching danger and the others' illusory calm echoes the tension between consciousness and suppression that structures *By Night*.

Urrutia Lacroix's story attempts to suppress anguish. He associates the "supreme terror" of realizing he is his own nemesis with inaudible cries. The main characters in "Visit" – an unnamed narrator who resembles Bolaño, Mario Santiago, and Darío Galicia – hear crying from an unknown source. Both texts exemplify how sorrow spreads within a collective and establishes intersections with other texts. In *By Night* collective memory and trauma relate primarily to state terror in Chile. In "Visit," collective memory relates to Bolaño's years in Mexico, and trauma is related to a lost Revolution and to the character Galicia,[3] who suffers an aneurism and undergoes two trepanations, and whose queerness is something his father hopes will be forgotten: "They've trepanned Darío Galicia's skull. Twice! / And one of the aneurisms burst in the middle of the Dream .... / It's 1976 and it's Mexico and his friends say Darío has forgotten everything, including his own homosexuality. / And Darío's father says that all bad things happen for a reason" (104). First published in the second version of *Los perros románticos* (The Romantic Dogs) (2000), "Visit" recalls Bolaño's Infrarealist years in a way similar to Ignacio Bajter's defense of how Bolaño reimagines that era in *The Savage Detectives* (1998).[4] Bajter counters other Infrarealists' claims that Bolaño falsified their stories: "As if in order to be valid, memory, instead of presenting itself as an autobiographical tale [autofábula] that is also a reunion of ghosts, should opt for the English documentary" (2011/2012, 48).[5] The spectrality of Santiago's and Bolaño's encounter with Galicia in "Visit" manifests itself in different overlapping experiences, including the

---

[3] Darío Galicia is the historical counterpart to Ernesto San Epifanio, a character in *The Savage Detectives* who also undergoes brain surgery.
[4] *Los perros románticos* was published twice during Bolaño's lifetime, the first by the Fundación Social y Cultural Kutza, in 1994, and the second by Editorial Lumen, in 2000. A posthumous version published by Acantilado appeared in 2006.
[5] "Como si la memoria válida, en lugar de proponerse la autofábula como un reencuentro de fantasmas, debiera optar por el documentalismo inglés." Unless otherwise indicated, translations from the Spanish are my own.

mysterious crying: "For a moment we think [Darío is] going to cry. / But it isn't he who cries. / And it's not Mario or I. / Nevertheless somebody cries as darkness sets in with inaudible slowness" (105). Temporality in "Visit" is also spectrally layered. The first two lines read, "It's 1976 and the Revolution has been defeated/ but we've yet to find out" (104). Spectrality and suppression function together in the figure of a rainstorm that parallels the oblivion Galicia's father wishes for his son's queerness and makes visible a Mexican cinematic past. This past overlays the present, which is described from an unspecified future perspective: "And outside it's raining buckets: / in the tenement's courtyard rain sweeps the stairs / and hallways / and slips away through the faces of Tin Tan, Resortes, and Calambres, / which cloak, in semi-transparency, the year 1976" (104–105). Jumbled and overlapping sights, sounds, and moments structure "Visit." Their uneven layering resists the smoothness of suppression and oblivion.

"Visit" also challenges coherent narratives in the figure of the hole, associated early on with Galicia's trepanation and aneurism and near the poem's conclusion with "Mexican streets hanging in the abyss" and "a wormhole, the opening that appears where you least expect it" (106). The figure of the fissure that in *By Night* eventually splits Urrutia Lacroix's subjectivity and narrative coherence adopts several forms in "Visit." The hole reappears in *Woes*, when Amalfitano, at a dinner in Bologna, rejects the notion of a continuous and glorious past and enrages his right-wing interlocutors. For him, it is important to recognize that "history ... was rewritten daily, and, like a humble and virtuous seamstress, constantly stitched up any holes" (104). An awareness of the hole and further evidence of its power to connect Bolaño's texts appears in Remo's recollection of strangers he and his companion Laura encountered in bathhouses:

> The conversations seemed coded in a language I didn't know, certainly not the slang I spoke with my friends ... but a much more affectionate kind of talk in which each word and each sentence had a trace of burials and holes. (Once when Laura was there, Jan said that it might be Air Hole, one of the bizarre manifestations of the Immaculate Grave. Maybe, maybe not.) (187)

Gaps, sutures made visible, ghostly palimpsests, and a surprising association of affection with burials all inform Bolaño's critically constructed collective memory.

Álvaro Bisama shows how ghostly spaces and times informed Bolaño's approach to remembering Chile's trauma. Bolaño's early poem

"Bienvenida" (Welcome) (1978), writes Bisama, seeks a future, more apt moment for its reading. It allows "Bolaño to configure exile ... as a place from which the text aspires to be read, a type of coordinates that, in some way, define the reaches of his poetics" (2013, 45).[6] Bisama's research details Bolaño's participation in anthologies and magazines produced by exiled Chileans as a function of his "desire to establish connections with that ghostly country of the diaspora" (55). Bisama concludes that "Bolaño writes from there, thinks from there, a ghost nation, perhaps a possible country" (55).[7]

The collective memory of a "ghost nation" or "possible country" is different from the kind of literature Urrutia Lacroix tries to believe in. The predominantly national context of *By Night* expresses something similar to Aleida Assmann's appraisal of national narratives, which, "With respect to traumatic events ... provide effective protection shields against those events that a nation prefers to forget" (2014, 553). She juxtaposes national narratives to a transnational perspective that imagines nations differently, "as inherently and externally relational, embedded and contextualized, always implicated in and partaking of larger processes and changes" (547). Even in the ruptures that structure Urrutia Lacroix's perspective, Bolaño's texts return to traumatic national events from a position of exile which shares these traits of relationality.

Refusing to face up to state crimes committed during Pinochet's regime sustains a coherent narrative like Urrutia Lacroix's, one that, according to Nelly Richard, attempts to leave "submerged in the common grave of the neoliberal present ... all that the Transition has left unpublished: shattered biographies and wounded subjectivities, damaged bodies and broken affectivities" (Richard, 2019, 22). Richard relates the resurfacing of the "submerged" to memory's trace, "the ... mark that records memory, and ... the potential for reanimating the past that has been deposited in this reserve ... which keeps it prepared for any future advent of memory" (116). Memory and its futurity are functions of "an ambiguity toward times and modes (past-present, closeness-distance, disappearance-reappearance, original-copy) that causes traces of the past to oscillate between loss ... and restitution" (117). Richard continues by observing that restitution "can never assuage the sorrow of renunciation and loss

---

[6] "Bolaño configure al exilio ... como un lugar desde el que el texto aspira ser leído, una clase de coordenadas que, en cierto modo, definen los alcances de su poética."
[7] "deseo de establece lazos con ese país fantasmal que era el de la diáspora"; "Bolaño escribe desde ahí, se piensa desde ahí, una nación fantasma, acaso un país posible."

associated with the unrepeatability of the *already-was*" (117). Sorrow in Bolaño's texts appears against an ever-present and insurmountable background of loss. The repeatability of trauma and collective memory his writing enacts does not lead to restitution. Its critical engagement with collective memory relies instead on acknowledging the holes it must leave open.

In the texts I compare here, Bolaño's characters remain within the uneven and incomplete process of memory's trace by prefiguring or weathering storms. The shitstorm silences Urrutia Lacroix. Characters who outlast the storms grapple more actively with collective memory and trauma. The rain that eventually pours down in "Visit" is foreshadowed earlier in the poem by "storm clouds advancing slowly from the north" (104). Amalfitano writes of being with Edith Lieberman, his partner, in pre-coup Chile: "feeling her warm hand in mine, at peace, in love, while storms and hurricanes and great earthquakes of fate built up behind us" (*Woes*, 21). When asked whether the characters in his novel "dream about the Hurricane" (*Spirit*, 61), Schrella's answer describes a dream about a war with the United States, a catastrophe referred to repeatedly in *Spirit*.[8]

> [A] girl wakes with a fever. Her dreams were about a nuclear blast ... a Yankee battalion wiping out Los Ángeles [Chile] with a couple of neutron bombs. On the banks of the Bío-Bío is the Hurricane, and when the bombs explode, the Hurricane opens up like a giant cinema, and inside is a factory called Pompeya, where motorcycles are built. Benelli motorcycles. Soon a motorcycle emerges from the factory, and then another and another: a battalion of Komsomols from the south of Chile on its way to destroy or be destroyed by the Yankees. (62)

This revenge fantasy borrows details from later in *Spirit*, when the poet José Arco helps Remo acquire a Benelli motorcycle called the "Aztec Princess" (100). The Hurricane in Schrella's novel makes possible a scenario in which one of Moctezuma's daughters may provide a means of aiding hemispheric justice, redressing a history of grievances from the Conquest to twentieth-century U.S. military intervention.

Arco, a likely predecessor of a Visceral Realist from *Detectives*, reminds Bolaño's readers of the importance of poetry in his work. Amalfitano relates the love he feels before the "hurricanes" to poetry, which he teaches when he and Lieberman are in Chile together (*Woes*, 21). Decades later, in Santa Teresa, Amalfitano also teaches poetry, and the third-person

---

[8] See Gras Miravet for the way Bolaño writes about Science Fiction in order to highlight hemispheric tensions between Latin America and the United States (2016, 139, 144).

narrator of *Woes* asks, "So what did Amalfitano's students learn?" (102). In response, the narrator continues,

> They learned ... That all writing systems are frauds. That true poetry resides between the abyss and misfortune and that the grand highway of selfless acts, of the elegance of eyes and the fate of Marcabrú, passes near its abode. That the main lesson of literature was courage, a rare courage like a stone well in the middle of a lake district, like a whirlwind and a mirror. That reading wasn't more comfortable than writing. That by reading one learned to question and remember. That memory was love. (102)

This passage, which alludes to the abyss, a twelfth-century French troubadour, and a whirlwind, establishes connections among *Woes*, "Visit," and *Spirit* which recall the association of affection and burials in Remo's description of the bathhouse language because it associates falsity with a system – something akin to Urrutia Lacroix's desired coherence – and courage with approaching the abyss and storms. Teaching, reading, memory, and love remain as means of struggling against trauma in Amalfitano's exile.

Amalfitano knows that reading is a time-bound process. Asking himself why he hasn't read an important writer from his earlier adulthood, J. M. G. Arcimboldi,[9] for decades, he responds that it is "Life, of course, which puts the essential books under our noses only when they are strictly essential, or on some cosmic whim. Now that it was too late, he was going to read the rest of Arcimboldi's novels" (106). It's too late but he returns to Arcimboldi. In "Visit," recognizing the bravery of poets also appears to come too late. The Revolution has "been defeated" (104). On the other hand, the poets' courage – something Amalfitano taught his students – enables their legacy to travel through time and emerge from the abyss: "Like in a wormhole, the opening that appears where you least expect it,/ the metaphysical grave of gay adolescents who face up – bravest of all! – to poetry and adversity" ("Visit," 106).[10]

The necessarily belated responses to loss that structure Bolaño's writing make possible a future moment of reading, a moment of "essential books" or a "cosmic whim." *Woes* and *Spirit* were published posthumously, providing Bolaño's readers a vantage point he may never have imagined.

---

[9] Arcimboldi shares similarities with Benno von Archimboldi, of *2666*.
[10] This pairing of "wormholes" and "gay adolescents" suggests the importance of science fiction and queerness for Bolaño scholarship. For science fiction see: Bisama (2017); Dunia Gras (2017); Bizzarri (2017b); and Shames (2021). For queerness see: Amícola (2013); Bizzarri (2018, 2017a, 2020); and Long (2015, 2021).

Clues appear and suggest a tantalizing totality. For example, on a wall near the floor in the classroom where Remo attends a poetry workshop are the words "ALCIRA SOUST SCAFFO WAS HERE" (23). Soust Scaffo's fictional counterpart in *Amulet* and *Detectives*, novels Bolaño published during his lifetime, is Auxilio Lacouture. Remo shares with Bolaño's readers the urge to decipher this clue, and he emphasizes repetition: "Though at first glance the graffiti seemed completely innocent, after a few minutes of repeated reading it began to feel like a shout, an agonizing display" (23). Clues and decipherment appear elsewhere in *Spirit*, as in the case of Pedro Huachofeo's book, *The Paradoxical History of Latin America*, which, in Schrella's novel, an employee of the Unknown University's Potato Academy,[11] believes to consist of "signals in code" (35). The Academy's recording machines, Schrella explains, "work imperturbably, day and night, picking up curses and tantrums. The images begin to fall into place, each ready to be assigned its numbered spot on the map drawn with a firm hand and winged imagination by Dr. Huachofeo" (92). This parodical tone contrasts with the traumatic US invasion Schrella's novel also portrays. Parody takes on a critical edge upon considering that the Potato Academy's labor is akin to Amalfitano's fraudulent system. Clues and references that point beyond a system's boundaries include Soust Scaffo,[12] the Air Hole and Immaculate Grave, cited above, and the Hurricane, which for Schrella, like loss in Bolaño's writing, is assumed knowledge.

The collective memory Bolaño's texts continue to construct leads its characters and readers from clue to clue while refusing to be a system. It insists upon incompleteness, belatedness, palimpsests, and jarring shifts in tone. It is like the memory Assmann contrasts with *fama*: "While *fama* looks forward to future generations who will preserve forever an event deemed to be unforgettable, memory looks backward through the veil of oblivion into the past; it follows long faded, long forgotten tracks, and reconstructs those elements that are considered important for the present" (2011, 39). Bolaño's posthumous texts, the connections all his texts facilitate, and the focus on timely (even if belated) reading speak to the changing present and make space for what is still to come.

---

[11] The Unknown University refers to the Alfred Bester story from which Bolaño borrowed the name, "The Men Who Murdered Mohammed" (1958), and to Bolaño's poetry collections, which also bear the name, *Fragmentos de la universidad desconocida* (1993) and *La universidad desconocida*.

[12] See Bajter (2009).

The connections among Bolaño's texts present collective memory as a shifting surface that registers the sorrow that, as Richard notes, "cannot be assuaged." In a parodic shift in tone similar to the Potato Academy's serious association with US intervention, Schrella proposes in a letter to Philip José Farmer that the two of them work together on an anthology "titled something like *American Orgasms in Space* or *A Radiant Future*" (176–177). This comic pairing takes on a different valence in the Mexico City nightscape Remo traverses with Arco:

> The geometric landscape of the neighborhoods, even the colors, had a provisional look ... and if you sharpened your gaze and a certain latent madness, you could feel sadness in the form of flying sparks, Speedy Gonzales slipping along the great arteries of Mexico City for no reason at all or for some secret reason. Not a melancholy sadness but a devastating, paradoxical sadness that cried out for life, radiant life, wherever it might be. (161)

Heeding the cries of sorrow and vitality requires a "sharpened gaze" and a "certain madness," a shifted, provisional look, responding to and conditioned by trauma, a look that also responds to and is conditioned by repeated returns to and returns of Bolaño's writing.

CHAPTER 28

Fictions of the Avant-Gardes
Michelle Clayton

In the spring of 2007, while I was teaching a graduate seminar on Latin American avant-garde poetics, news began to circulate of a novel from 1998 about to appear in English translation, which everyone was therefore rushing to read in the original: Roberto Bolaño's *Los detectives salvajes*. There was particular excitement among the students in the seminar, because Bolaño's novel was itself about the avant-gardes: specifically, the neo-avant-gardes of the 1970s and their explorations into the historical avant-gardes of the 1920s. For a group studying the experiments of – among other movements – Mexican *estridentismo*, this was a sudden and startling encounter with a past yanked into the present; it was as though a ghost had taken a seat at our seminar table.[1]

The ghost of the avant-gardes has been going around Latin American literature for some time now: haunting the poetry of the 1970s, the novels of the 1990s, and the criticism of today. It does so trepidatiously, having to navigate various theoretical landmines, most of them planted by writings on the European avant-gardes. Peter Bürger's enormously influential *Theory of the Avant-Garde*, for instance, argued that the historical avant-gardes of the 1920s had failed in their dual mission of attacking the institution of art and revolutionizing the whole of life, and that any attempt on the part of the neo-avant-gardes of the 1970s to recover their legacy betrayed a misunderstanding of their mission, compounding their failure. Historians and theorists of the Latin American avant-gardes, however, have been careful to signal the importance of context for any understanding of the avant-gardes, treating these as strategic interventions in particular sociopolitical and economic environments; they argue in

---

[1] Derbyshire (2009) notes that the protagonists of *The Savage Detectives* are "ghosts in their own novel," and that the first diary entry is dated November 2, the day of the dead. There may also be an encrypted homage here to poem LXVI of César Vallejo's *Trilce* (1922), containing the line "dobla el dos de noviembre" and a reference to "encrucijadas."

particular that the Latin American avant-gardes of the 1920s were less invested in attacking institutions than in achieving contemporaneity with the West in terms of both infrastructure and aesthetics (Osorio, 1981; Unruh, 1994; Aguilar, 1996). Or as Amadeo Salvatierra puts it in *The Savage Detectives*, "Stridentism and visceral realism are just two masks to get us to where we really want to go [. . .] to modernity [. . .] to goddamned modernity" (488; henceforth *SD*). In more recent years, critics have revisited this question by reflecting on the uptake of the historical avant-gardes in the poetry and narrative of the 1970s and 1990s, inquiring into the reasons for these determined returns to experimental pasts, asking how they might avoid the failure to which Bürger condemns them (Bush and Castañeda, 2017; Tabarovsky, 2018; Kohan, 2021; Premat, 2021). As I will suggest, the self-given mission of the poets of the 1970s and the novelists of the 1990s – both represented by Bolaño – involves the recovery of understudied predecessors, the mapping out of contemporary paths and communities, the uncovering of absences and invisibilities, all in the context of an engagement with art conceived not as autonomous but as folded into life, laying the groundwork, crucially, for an ethics of care.

Focused on a mid-1970s Mexican neo-avant-garde group calling itself "visceral realism," and on its investigation of a Mexican avant-garde group from the 1920s, *The Savage Detectives* explores artistic movements in the making: it gives us glimpses behind the curtain into how experimental communities are created, how they hold together, how they fizzle and fall apart and can be made to flare up again. A narrative re-enactment of a poetic re-enactment, the novel specifically maps out how the neo-avant-gardes of mid-century and beyond recovered elements of and inspiration from the historical avant-gardes of the 1920s, trying to determine what in their legacy was or is still alive and useable even if neglected or forgotten. While the novel's protagonists investigate forgotten or unappreciated works from the past, they also form a community that produces works in the present tense, that aims to interrupt the production of what they see as unproductive forms and practices, and that reaches out to a much broader international horizon of experimental poetics, primarily Peru and France but also North America, Argentina, and Chile. While celebrating these legacies and affiliations, the novel surreptitiously points – elliptically and intermittently – to what is left out of even the most encompassing histories of the avant-gardes: namely, their female artists. As I will demonstrate in what follows, Bolaño draws upon modernist and avant-garde forms, and on real and fictional figures, to consider literature's ongoing possibilities, attending to its moment and conditions of production, and exploring its lingering legacies – which need to be actively inherited, as the novel emphasizes in a memorial at once self-satirizing and tender.[2]

The novel unfurls in an elongated present-tense, flowing from the 1970s to the 1990s between two "banks" of diary entries from late 1975 and early 1976 respectively. The diary entries are by Juan García Madero, a seventeen-year-old poet-in-training inducted into visceral realism by the movement's two leaders, Arturo Belano (a stand-in for Bolaño, familiar from other novels and stories) and Ulises Lima (based on Mario Santiago Papasquiaro, poet and friend of Bolaño in Mexico City in the 1970s), whom he eventually accompanies on their search for a missing poet in the Sonora desert. The long middle section is made up of interviews with characters who came into contact with Belano and/or Lima in the twenty years since the founding of visceral realism. As the novel moves forward in time, it keeps snapping us back to the past through the ongoing monologue of Amadeo Salvatierra, meted out in fragments.[3] A fictional adherent of the real Mexican *estridentista* movement of the 1920s, now eking out a living as a scribe, Salvatierra shares both his distant memories of the historical avant-garde of the 1920s, and his much more recent memories of a conversation over one long night in 1975 with Belano and Lima, who had been commissioned to interview the surviving members of the 1920s Mexican avant-garde for a literary magazine. Indeed, one of the surprising revelations of the novel is that the central *estridentistas* – Manuel Maples Arce (1900–1981), Arqueles Vela (1899–1977), and Germán List Arzubide (1898–1991) – were still alive in the mid-1970s, even if their works had long been forgotten. Belano and Lima show a marked lack of interest, however, in reactivating the legacy of these literary antecedents; after an initial interview, Maples Arce waits in vain for the two younger men to come back to visit him, dejectedly acknowledging that "these poets were meant to be orphans" (*SD*, 181). Their commitment, instead, is to rescuing the even-more-neglected (and like Salvatierra, fictional) female

---

[2] Critics have largely developed melancholy readings of the novel, focused on the disappearance of poetry (Derbyshire, 2009; Varón González, 2020); creative writers, however, continue to find in it inspiring depictions of local and transnational artistic communities and transhistorical literary experiment. Two of Bolaño's most active inheritors are Mexican Valeria Luiselli, whose 2011 novel *Los ingrávidos* has a female writer resuscitate an avant-garde figure from the 1920s (not an *estridentista* but a *contemporáneo*), and Chilean Alejandro Zambra, whose 2020 novel *Poeta chileno* replays characters and conflicts from *The Savage Detectives* to an uncanny degree.

[3] In a distribution that lays bare the novel's submerged structure – not to mention its investment in numbers and their symbolic associations – Amadeo's monologue is divided into thirteen parts, in a middle section comprising twenty-six chapters with monologues by fifty-two narrators.

poet Cesárea Tinajero, who before joining the *estridentistas* in the 1920s had founded her own movement titled *realismo visceral* – to which the movement of the 1970s is evidently paying homage. When the *realvisceralistas* of the 1970s track down this poet, missing for half a century, the discovery leads with savage irony to her death, and her recovered notebooks disappear for good in the hands of García Madero, who by the end of the novel has himself vanished from the historical record. As the scholarly expert on the visceral realists asserts with cruel confidence in the novel's penultimate monologue, "No, the name [Juan García Madero] doesn't ring a bell. He never belonged to the group" (*SD*, 585).

To give form to his narrative revisiting of the historical and neo-avant-gardes, Bolaño draws on the genre of the *roman-fleuve*, a series of novels featuring common characters or settings (such as Balzac's *Human Comedy*), compressed here to a single novel dispersed across multiple settings; he also joked that *The Savage Detectives* was his *Huckleberry Finn*, carrying his central characters down a metaphorical Mississippi in its mid-section (Bolaño, 2011, 353). But the tripartite structure of the novel is built on a much more solid modernist edifice, that of Joyce's 1922 novel *Ulysses*. Part I, "Mexicans Lost in Mexico (1975)," offers a portrait of the artist as a young man, replacing Stephen Dedalus with García Madero, a figure of disarming innocence and vampiric enthusiasms whose vision sharpens and darkens as the novel progresses. The lengthy Part II, titled "The Savage Detectives (1976–1996)," narrates the wanderings of a dual protagonist, swapping out the singular Leopold Bloom for Belano and Lima: the former a grown-up version of Stephen Dedalus, the latter an updated Odysseus, named not for Mexico City or Santiago de Chile but for a city located between the two. The novel's third and final section, "The Sonora Desert (1976)," reunites the figures of Ulises/Belano and García Madero and takes them on a quest for the Molly Bloom/Penelope character, Cesárea Tinajero.[4]

Ostensibly missing from this reading is the central figure of *Ulysses*: the *paterfamilias*, husband, and advertising agent Leopold Bloom, elbowed out of view by this novel's focus on younger actors, the natural protagonists of the avant-gardes. But we glimpse him in the figure of Quim Font: father to the sisters María and Angélica, lover of Lupe, protector of García Madero,

---

[4] We also catch glimpses and echoes of other figures from *Ulysses*: Joyce's sirens become barmaids; the Pirate of chapter 8 recalls the yarn-spinning sailor DB Murphy; Heimito Künst recalls the violent rhetoric and threatening corporeality of Joyce's Citizen. And María Font, an unimpressed Penelope/Molly, acidly rejects the stories Ulises brings back from his travels as having "too much literature" in the telling (*SD*, 335).

who Bloom-like notes that "there's room for a lot of memories in a twenty-four-hour day" (*SD*, 222). Architect by training and patron by choice to the experimental young poets who cross his horizon, Quim seems at once a figure for fluidity (his Catalan surname "Font," meaning fountain) and for fixity ("font" as typography). He uses his training as an architect to design magazines for the emerging neo-avant-garde: 2D spaces for their battles. His first effort, the magazine *Lee Harvey Oswald* (1973), was admired – María tells García Madero – for Quim's design more than for its contents; and significantly, when sketching out plans for a new magazine, Quim leaves space on the page for the poetry to come: "Those jackasses will learn what the avant-garde is now, won't they? And that's even without the poems, see? This is where all of your poems will go" (*Savage Detectives*, 77). This might suggest that poetry is the least important component of this avant-garde machine – or more damningly, that the poetry worthy of filling its assigned role has not yet been written – but it also points to a different understanding of the avant-garde: not explosive, as commonly understood (Walter Benjamin's notion of the "infernal machines" built between 1865 and 1875, primed to explode forty years later; 1929, 214) but coolly strategic, its mission residing in determining what remained to be done. As Angelo Guglielmi put it of the neo-avant-gardes, the experimental poet is no longer the soldier but the specialist, going into a space filled with mines, identifying and picking his way through the blank spots (cited in Calinescu, 1987, 122–123).

But what does the avant-garde, as presented in *The Savage Detectives*, look like? Bolaño gives us multiple narrow apertures onto his fictionalized version of the 1970s movement, and the effect is of watching visceral realism play out in a zoetrope or a Kaiserpanorama: catching tiny slivers of its liveliness, we "look in from the outside" (*SD*, 45) as if through the gaps in the frame of the window that closes the book.[5] Our first impression, nonetheless, is of full immersion; we experience the movement via the hapless García Madero, who under the sporadic tutelage of Belano and Lima learns to steal books, joins a ragtag community of writers, and throws himself with gusto into writing, alternating between diary entries and poetry. The tenets of the movement remain blurry to him, beyond the hilariously vague "complete agreement that Mexican poetry must be

---

[5] This window is one among many references to Julio Cortázar's *Rayuela* (1963), itself a novel engaged with the historical avant-gardes and their legacies, and which ends (at least in one reading) with its protagonist falling through a window. Cortázar's Horacio Oliveira is Stephen Dedalus and Leopold Bloom rolled into one, with all the awkwardness that results from having a forty-something-year old protagonist still preoccupied by aesthetic/existential questions better suited to one's twenties.

transformed. Our situation (as far as I could understand) is unsustainable, trapped as we are between the reign of Paz and the reign of Neruda" (*SD*, 21). What he finds galvanizing, though, in his encounter with visceral realism is the sense of participating in a community –a community of frenetically active writers[6] – and of finding an audience for his work: an entanglement of literary and sentimental educations which explains the kinesthetic intensity of his approach to both reading and writing. More than producing poetry for a movement, García Madero is moved to produce poetry; and as he throws himself into frenetic production, he embodies the spirit spelled out in a manifesto Bolaño himself had written in 1976, "poetry producing poets producing poems producing poetry."

That manifesto, "Leave Everything, Again," borrowed its title from the 1922 poem "Leave Everything" by French surrealist André Breton. We never hear any reference to it in this novel, but it laid out a blueprint for Infrarealism, the neo-avant-garde movement helmed by Bolaño and Papasquiaro in Mexico City in the mid-1970s, which loudly proclaimed its affiliation with contemporary movements from Latin America (especially Peru's Hora Zero), the United States (primarily the Beats), and France (the Electric Poetry movement). In their manifestoes and poems, Infrarealism's participants mapped out a canon of lodestars, from Rimbaud, Baudelaire, and Lautréamont to the historical avant-gardes proper: cubism and futurism (taken up in Mexican *estridentismo* and Argentinean *ultraísmo*); individual innovators such as Blaise Cendrars (Switzerland),[7] Vicente Huidobro (Chile), César Vallejo (Peru); and the European movements of Dada and surrealism – Dada's anarchic enthusiasms lending energy to neo-avant-garde experiments throughout the continent, and surrealism unleashing its image bank into the visual arts, magical realist narrative, and poetry. Infrarealism aligned most directly with Dada's anti-establishment stance and its focus on improvisational, ephemeral aesthetics; while reading omnivorously and producing a whirl of

---

[6] Even if we do not see the poetry that is produced (in tune with the poets' own refusal to publish), there can no doubt about the group members' productivity. The diary sections and later interviews are filled with references to poetry being written, beginning in the heady days of 1975–1976 (on December 28, for instance, García Madero tallies his output at 55 poems over 76 pages totaling 2453 lines; *SD*, 121).

[7] Bolaño's poems "The Romantic Dogs" and "Self-Portrait at Twenty" make clear his debt to Cendrars, who had also appeared in Maples Arce's Stridentist Manifesto. Like Cendrars (who in his 1917 *Prose of the Transsiberian* worried about "so many associations images I can't get into my poem"), Bolaño declares himself to be "a really bad poet." Papasquiaro dedicated the poem "Adolescencia bisiesta" to Cendrars, and the novel's Lupe might be seen as an avatar of the *Transsiberian*'s "Jeanne de France."

poetry shared amongst themselves, the Infrarealists largely avoided publishing their own work, adopting what poet and critic Rubén Medina has dubbed an "ethics of strategic marginality" (2017, 22).[8] Indeed in its moment, Infrarealism was best known for its disruptive activities, and Bolaño gives us some sense of this in *The Savage Detectives* (interruptions of workshops; anti-interviews with establishment figures), but he places more emphasis, curiously, on its constructive activities: producing a magazine, organizing an anthology, spurring one another to constant experiment within the bounds of a group. And their artistic activities are sporadic, folded into life; Bolaño relentlessly insists on his characters' readings and writings as stitched into a broader canvas of daily activities, from making a living to family dynamics to love-affairs to acts of camaraderie.

There are two key moments, however, when the novel opens an organized window onto the avant-gardes – from the 1920s and from the 1970s – and significantly, they both appear in the same chapter, the middle section's Chapter 6. They appear in reverse order. In May 1976, Rafael Barrios rattles off the activities of the remaining visceral realists in the year since Belano and Lima decamped to Europe (*SD*, 221). The list format inevitably renders this tumult of activities as parody, but it features a remarkable range of experiments and alignments: from early French surrealist practices – "automatic writing, exquisite corpses" – through the neo-avant-gardes of the 1950s and 60s, featuring conceptual art ("performances with no spectators"), recalibrations of the lyric ("conversational poetry, antipoetry, Brazilian concrete poetry"), Oulipo-like constraint poetics ("sonnets always ending with the same word"), experiments within and across genres ("poems in hard-boiled prose," haikus, madrigals, beat poetry, lettrist poetry), work with and on the body ("masturbatory writing"), up to the collective transnational projects of the 1970s (mail-poetry) and finally coming to rest among homegrown movements: Colombian Nadaístas, Peruvian Horazerianos, Uruguayan Catalepticos, Ecuadorian Tzantzicos, Brazilian cannibals. The list's form, petering out in ellipses ("we kept moving ...") may be melancholy, but its contents are anything but: what we witness in this madcap recap of the mice's activities while the cats are away is a yes to experiment, a yes to experience, a Molly

---

[8] Medina (Rafael Barrios in the novel) has in recent years dedicated himself to gathering Infrarealist productions and practices, e.g., in the anthology *Perros habitados por las voces del desierto*, or a 2017 issue of *The Chicago Review* devoted to Infrarealism, containing Medina's lucid summary of the movement's relationship to the historical and neo-avant-gardes, manifestoes by Papasquiaro and Bolaño, and a selection of poems.

Bloom–like yes to art enfolded in life. This is less an investment in repeating techniques than a trying out of ways of connecting to a contemporary horizon; as Argentinean novelist César Aira succinctly put it in his own take on literary experimentalism (Aira, 2013), "the avant-garde [...] is an attempt to recuperate the amateur gesture, and to place it on a higher level of historical synthesis."

Later in the same chapter (*SD*, 224–228) we encounter the list's historical parallel, the *Actual #1* manifesto from late 1921. In this high-speed, high-stakes, high-pitched manifesto, pasted on the walls of downtown Mexico City, Maples Arce opens up a time and space for the exchange of ideas within a globalizing avant-garde – connected not actually but virtually, not continuously but intermittently.[9] Building through a gleeful concatenation of adjectives and insults, exhortations and images, the manifesto ends with an international "Avant-Garde Directory" listing some two hundred figures from the Iberian, Latin American, North American, French, Italian, German, and Soviet avant-gardes (writers, painters, film-makers, dramatists, theorists): names drawn from circulating journals which the non-traveling Maples Arce must have been ingesting in a frenzy. With his brazenly imaginary directory of adherents, he inscribes his movement in a worldwide burst of creativity, although in tune with what Esther Gabara calls the "errancy of modernism" in Latin America, the list contains plenty of mistakes – a fact played up by the "performance" of the manifesto in Bolaño's novel, as Amadeo and his visitors pore over the list for figures they recognize, raising eyebrows at dropped first names, giggling over errors ("Kokodika" almost certainly points to Oscar Kokoschka, as they note, while "Sontine" masks Chaim Soutine).[10] But more crucial than accuracy or actual contact, in the 1970s as in the 1920s, was the feeling of belonging to an international community of artists, with a supportive grounding in the local. Maples Arce, like the visceral realists who come after him, approaches the contemporary horizon as an "amateur," an "aficionado," wanting above all to belong to a group, to attach to the present.

But how long does the present last? In a monologue spliced between the two lists analysed above, Quim Font reflects from a mental health clinic on the limited duration of joy. Where García Madero had worried about the

---

[9] Flores (2013, 17–48) analyzes the manifesto and its context in relation to Bürger's theory of the avant-garde and Latin American recalibrations.

[10] Plenty of mistakes are nonetheless missed by the latter-day commentators: Walter Conrad Arensberg, patron of New York Dada, apparently not known to the trio, is misspelled as Bonrad; Charles-Édouard Jeanneret (the future Le Corbusier) passes unnoticed under the name Jeauneiet.

number of his and his partner's orgasms – here as elsewhere, putting quantity over quality – a younger Quim was taught by a girlfriend to focus instead on timing his pleasure, counting it out in Mississippis (*SD*, 222). The same reservoir of affective energy, the novel seems to suggest, is tapped for erotics as for aesthetics, and vast amounts of energy are required to produce the kind of improvisational work that characterized Zurich Dada as much as Mexico City Infrarealism. Hence the novel's association of experimental poetry with youth. *The Savage Detectives* abounds with references to poets who died young – Rimbaud, Lautréamont, and his virtual homonym, Laura Damián – while those who live longer seem to gravitate away from poetry over the course of their lifetime. This is not, however, a sign of poetry's failure. What the novel performs, rather, is the principle of the historical avant-gardes: the sublation of poetry into life, the building of an ethics upon it.

This is emblematized in the novel's handling of female characters, who may seem to be placed in an auxiliary role to their productive male friends and colleagues, but whose activities are far more interesting and consequential than their elliptical referral might suggest. For a novel infamously filled with male writers, there are a surprising number of female figures threaded through the narrative, acquaintances and artists pursing their own projects, who do not fit neatly into the account or the characteristics of a movement.[11] The most salient is Cesárea Tinajero, around whom the novel is built, not just associated with *estridentismo* but shown to be the founder of her own movement of *realismo visceral*. While the tenets of that movement are withheld from the men of the novel (and hence too from its reader), Amadeo underlines her talent for multitasking ("The talent of that woman, boys. [... To] be talking about politics, for example, and at the same time writing a little article on gardening or spondaic hexameters"; *SD*, 312) – an ability to handle several different modes and requirements simultaneously which speaks to the multipronged demands on women's attention, but which also points to Cesárea's resistance to categorization. Something similar strikes García Madero in his first encounter with María

---

[11] This parallels the disciplinary trajectories of literature and art history, which have allowed their narratives to be determined by the movements announced by male actors; it is only in recent years that histories of the avant-gardes have begun to pay proper attention to, for instance, Sonia Delaunay and Sophie Taeuber-Arp in the visual arts, Alice Guy-Blaché and Germaine Dulac in film, the Baroness Elsa and Mina Loy in literature, or the female-led discipline of dance (well-represented in the novel at hand; Clayton, 2022). In the Latin American context we might point to Magda Portal, Blanca Luz Brum, or Hilda Mundy in poetry, Silvina Ocampo and Leonora Carrington in narrative, or visual and plastic artists such as Norah Borges and Elena Izcue, Kati Horna, Grete Stern, and Remedios Varo.

Font, whom he finds "standing in the middle of the room, practicing dance steps, reading Sor Juana Inés de la Cruz, listening to a Billie Holiday record, and absentmindedly painting a watercolor of two women holding hands at the foot of a volcano, surrounded by streams of lava" (SD, 26). Both women develop a flexible artistry which cuts across bounds of medium and matter, blending the visual with the textual, the physical with the cerebral, the mundane with the visionary – cross-pollinations which require that criticism adopt an equal mobility to be able to follow them in their movements.

These artists appear to produce solitary movements, but they develop their practices within relations of female friendship. What motivates Cesárea's exit from the *estridentista* movement is her male colleagues' dismissal of her friend Encarnación Guzmán Arredondo, silenced for her opinions, her poetry, the timbre of her voice; what rekindles her productivity is a friendship with a teacher. María Font falls into a desultory affair with Xóchitl García's husband Jacinto Requena, but when it dissolves and a female friendship takes its place, the two women are bemused and amused to find themselves writing poetry, visceral realist poetry no less: as though what were needed to unleash their creativity and friendship were for the male soldiers to abandon the besieged town.

This is equally palpable in the eviscerating account of the movement from one of its early female participants, Laura Jáuregui, who has good reason to be scornful about the supposed inclusiveness of the enterprise. Involved in the planning of the magazine *Lee Harvey Oswald*, its published version struck a double blow: not only did it not carry any of her poetry (the second issue had promised to include her poem "Lilith," named for a female demon associated with eschewing male domination) but the poem by César Arriaga whose title paid homage to her, "Laura y César," was modified by Ulises Lima, its typography changed to "Laura & César."[12] A tender relationship with Belano is overtaken by what she reads as male peacocking (SD, 172) after the movement's official founding, and knocked off-kilter by an unsettling physical altercation with Belano prior to his departure from Paris (SD, 218). The aggression – a slap in the face – seems out of keeping with Belano's gentleness, but it may have been intended as

---

[12] The title of the poem recalls the collection Mexican poet Ulises Carrión published in English in 1973, *Arguments*, each of whose poems consists of columns of names in juxtaposition, occasionally joined by an ampersand, e.g., "John & Mary / Lawrence / John & Mary / John & Mary & Lawrence." What in Spanish would be a question of "plot" (*argumentos*) in translation becomes a source of tension. We might say the same for Ulises' reworking of César's poem, where the formal "Laura and César" is made a more casual coupling, "&."

a clumsy caress, an inept scrambling of lovers' discourses, borrowing a gesture learned from Simone Darrieux, a Frenchwoman who introduced Belano (and others) to sadomasochistic practices during several months spend studying anthropology in Mexico City (*SD*, 233–235). Intriguingly, Simone has another, more encrypted role to play in the novel. As Chris Andrews notes (2014, 47), there is evidence to suggest that this same Simone is the wife of Argentinean Jacobo Urenda, who encounters an ailing Belano during his final months in Africa; thus the person who introduced Belano to the loving possibilities of violence is also the person who makes sure he is cared for toward the end of his life. Intimacy here, with a grounding in what we might call avant-garde practices, elongates into friendship – the same friendship that leads so many characters to set up care systems across periods and continents over the novel.[13]

This is one of the most surprising aspects of the novel: the transmutation of avant-garde aesthetics into an ethics of community and female-driven care. Notably, this lives on beyond the novel. Bolaño gives the final word not to Amadeo, not to Belano or Lima, not to García Madero, but to Auxilio Lacouture, tender to poets young and old; he does so by giving her another novel, the 1998 *Amulet*. In this new vessel, Auxilio's voice will ring out with an ongoing message: singing a song of memory, war, and love on the edge of an abyss.

---

[13] The novel has a vanishing point in the figure of Claudia, an Argentine exile in Mexico and later transplant to Israel; her real-life counterpart, Claudia Kerik, is an academic fittingly specializing in Walter Benjamin, poetry, and modernity. Glimpsed only through momentary mentions, Claudia nonetheless exerts a magnetic force on Ulises and serves to link others (Belano and Edith Oster, for instance), suggesting that she is a key part of the novel's connective tissue.

CHAPTER 29

Love and Friendship

Ignacio López-Calvo

That friendship was crucial in Bolaño's life and is one of the main leitmotivs in his oeuvre is apparent in his last interview, conducted with Mónica Maristain for the magazine *Playboy México* in 2003. When asked about his trailblazing books, he modestly answers that, besides providing money for his family, they are useful for "making friends who are very generous and nice."[1] In this same interview, he does not hesitate to name his best friend: Mario Santiago Papasquiaro (pen name of José Alfredo Zendejas Pined, 1953–1998), the Mexican poet and cofounder of the Infrarealist poetry movement who died in 1998 in a car accident. Known for his love of lists for everything, he adds that, at the moment, his best friends are Ignacio Echevarría (1960–), editor, one of Spain's most prominent literary critics, and sometimes mistakenly considered Bolaño's literary executor; the Argentine fiction writer Rodrigo Fresán (1963–); and A. G. Porta (1954–), who co-wrote with Bolaño the novel *Consejos de un discípulo de Morrison a un fanático de Joyce* (*Advice from a Morrison Disciple to a Joyce*, 1984; Bolaño's first published novel) and the short story "Diario de bar" (Bar Diary).

Many people, and writers in particular, saw Bolaño as a close friend as well. This was evident at his Barcelona funeral, where they bid him farewell before his ashes were dropped in the Mediterranean Sea by the town of Blanes, his place of residence for the last two decades of his life. His friends Rodrigo Fresán, Ignacio Echevarría, and Jorge Herralde, the editor and founder of the publishing house Anagrama, where Bolaño published most of his works during his life, all said kind words about the Chilean (or Latin American, since, according to his last interview, he considered himself Latin American rather than just Chilean) author. So moved was Herralde that, after describing Bolaño as a "trapeze artist without a net," explaining that he placed "literature above anything else,"

---

[1] "Para hacer amigos que son muy generosos y simpáticos" (2003, 8).

and confessing that Bolaño's and the Spanish writer Carmen Martín Gaite's (1925–2000) deaths had been "his two great pains as an editor," Echevarría had to finish reading his speech. Tellingly, when Maristain asked Bolaño about his rapport with his editor, Herralde, the Chilean answered: "Quite well. Herralde is an intelligent and often charming person. Maybe it would be better for me if he weren't so charming. The truth is that I have known him for eight years and, at least as far as I'm concerned, the affection does nothing but grow, as a bolero says. Although maybe I shouldn't love him so much."[2] In 2005, Herralde put together some of his speeches, chronicles, and interviews about his friend Bolaño in his book *Para Roberto Bolaño*.

For his part, Fresán recalled in his speech how Bolaño had recently participated in a symposium of Latin American authors in Seville, Spain, where younger writers had anointed him as a sort of "totem" for their generation. Fresán reminisced about the way in which Bolaño would repeat time and again the same joke, but using different variations, which the Argentine saw as the best kind of literary workshop. He also mentioned how Bolaño would suddenly appear by his house, looking like a dandy and a freak, to ask him questions or tell him stories (how humankind's next evolutionary step would be artificial, rather than natural, for example).

At a conference in Incheon, South Korea, in 2013, the late Mexican writer Ignacio Padilla (1968–2016) described to me, with equal admiration for the Chilean, the same anecdote about his retelling of the same joke in different styles. I later asked him to put those impressions in writing and the outcome was his essay "Homo Bolañus: Missing Link or the Last Dodo," which I published a year before Padilla's passing in an edited volume. Padilla's impression of that evening is summarized in the opening sentence, which I translated thus in the volume: "If it were possible (it is not) to establish a central date to understand Latin American literature, I would choose June 17, 2003. And if it were indispensable – which, luckily, it is not – I would specify that it happened between midnight and one in the morning" (235). The Mexican writer conceived of this moment as the discovery of Bolaño, the last Latin American writer as well as the missing link between Borges and their admired Boom writers on the one hand, and his generation of authors in their thirties on the other:

---

[2] "Bastante bien. Herralde es una persona inteligente y a menudo encantadora. Tal vez a mí me convendría más que no fuera tan encantador. Lo cierto es que ya hace ocho años que lo conozco y, al menos de mi parte, el cariño no hace más que crecer, como dice un bolero. Aunque tal vez me convendría no quererlo tanto" (2003, 9).

Only then, when we found out that Roberto Bolaño had left us, did we understand the true dimension of that crucial moment, the moment when Roberto, spontaneously, tequila in hand, decided to embark on the task of telling, in all the possible literary versions, a bad joke. He would laugh, he would have fun, he varied the joke without noting the silence, without realizing that we, a collective of supposedly Latin American writers, were experiencing an epiphany: the expression of a native-born author, of a classic. (235–236)

Besides Padilla and Fresán, other then young Latin American writers present at that symposium, such as the Bolivian Edmundo Paz Soldán (1967–), the Peruvian Fernando Iwasaki (1961–), and the Mexican Jorge Volpi (1968–) have described the scene with equal wonder and have considered him a leader, which is indicative of the effect Bolaño would have on people around him.

The Catalan editor Andreu Jaume and the team of Anagrama publishing house were also present at Bolaño's funeral, as were other writers, including the Mexican Juan Villoro (1956–), the Cuban Rolando Sánchez Mejías (1959–), and the Spaniards Javier Cercas (1962–) and Antoni García "A. G." Porta.[3] In Bolaño's posthumous novel *Los sinsabores del verdadero policía* (*Woes of the True Policeman*, 2011), his dear friend Porta appears fictionalized as a character. Earlier, he had turned other friends into characters in his fiction, including Mario Santiago, who becomes Ulises Lima in *Los detectives salvajes*, and Bruno Montané, who was the inspiration behind the character Felipe Müller in the same novel. Returning the favor, Bolaño has been fictionalized in his friend Javier Cercas's (1962–) novel *Soldados de Salamina* (*Soldiers of Salamis*, 2001) and Jorge Volpi (1968–) also pays homage to him in his novel *El fin de la locura* (*The End of Madness*, 2003).

Porta's note about his friend's passing, titled "Disculpen lo personal" (Sorry about How Personal This Is) and published by the Spanish newspaper *El País* on July 16, 2003, opens and closes by emphasizing what a great friend Bolaño was: "A friend has died. For you all, one of the greats in literature has died, but for me one of the best friends I've ever had is gone... But you can believe me if I tell you that I admired him because he

---

[3] Among the friends who could not attend the funeral because they were traveling, were the Spanish writer Enrique Vila-Matas (1948–), the editor of his poetry Jaume Vallcorba (1949–2014), and the editor Claudio López Lamadrid (1960–2019).

was a great friend of his friends."[4] Then, in an interview in March 2013, coinciding with the launching of the Archivo Bolaño 1977–2003 (Bolaño Archive, 1977–2003), Porta remembers how, when they were in their twenties in 1977, he and Bolaño would meet in the latter's apartment to talk about literature and their respective projects and, after a few hours, they would go downstairs to drink coffee and tea. Other times, they walked around, played foosball, or went to the movies. Porta also recalls that Bolaño, for whom literature was his life, could become combative when talking about other writers' literature, being often ironical or even corrosive. He speculates that the reason for this occasional cruelty was that the Chilean knew he was a better writer than most, even though he had not yet managed to publish (by the time Bolaño finally published with an important publisher, he was already forty-three years old).

Other friends of Bolaño's, such as the Chileans Jorge Morales and Bruno Montané (1957, cofounder of the Infrarrealista [Infrarealist] movement; the "realvisceralistas" in *Los detectives salvajes* [*The Savage Detectives*, 1998]), have also given speeches in his honor at different events. Regarding his friendship with Montané, in Soledad Bianchi's anthology *Entre la lluvia y el arcoíris* (Between the Rain and the Rainbow, 1983), Bolaño states: "I have learned poetry, as well, and daily camaraderie from Bruno Montané, who came to my house in Mexico in 1974, when he was 17 and I was 21, and from then on, how many adventures, recitals, loans, SOS, conversations at the bottom of the Gilette."[5]

Juan Villoro, who met Bolaño in Mexico City in 1976, opens his note "Roberto Bolaño: mito literario a su pesar" (Roberto Bolaño: Literary Myth in Spite of Himself) by describing him as an "irreplaceable friend"[6] and by acknowledging that his friends now feel a bit ashamed of "having failed to find out what he thought about the great questions of human existence" (n.p.).[7] Without questioning his charisma, Villoro adds, they loved him, joked and exchanged views with him, but did not see him as a historical figure or know that he would become a myth. Like many of Bolaño's friends, Villoro recalls his long phone calls:

---

[4] "Ha muerto un amigo. Para ustedes ha muerto uno de los grandes de la literatura, pero para mí se ha ido uno de los mejores amigos que he tenido ... Pero pueden creerme si les digo que le admiraba porque fue un gran amigo de sus amigos" (n.p.).

[5] "He aprendido poesía, también, y camaradería cotidiana, de Bruno Montané, quien llegó a mi casa en México, en 1974, cuando tenía 17 años y yo 21, y de allí en adelante cuántas aventuras, recitales, préstamos, S.O.S., conversaciones en el fondo de la Gillette" (n.p.).

[6] "Amigo imprescindible" (n.p.).

[7] "Ahora nos sentimos un poco avergonzados de carecer de información sobre lo que él pensaba sobre los grandes temas de la humanidad" (n.p.).

> Roberto kept the working hours of a vampire. He would wake up in the afternoon and, to get warmed up, he would call his friends ... He might talk about an actress he liked, recount a dream, describe a military maneuver at the battle of Borodino, or just ask how my little girl was doing. Then he would hang up and start his night's work.[8]

In Mónica Maristain's 2014 *Bolaño: A Biography in Conversations*, the Chilean's friends describe him as a kind man, who was generous with younger writers, and loved phone conversations and discussing literature. In 2019, the Chilean writer Roberto Brodsky (1957–) compiled, in *Adiós a Bolaño* (Farewell to Bolaño), texts about his friend and his oeuvre read at different events, including at the 1999 Rómulo Gallegos Award, which he attended at the invitation of Bolaño. Likewise, in Brodsky's 2012 novel *Veneno* (Poison), dedicated to Bolaño's memory and friendship, he pays homage to the latter, who is, along with Diamela Eltit (1947–), the only writer mentioned by name. In my personal correspondence with Brodsky, he kindly described Bolaño as a friend in the following terms:

> I can tell you that, in matters of friendship, Bolaño was very direct and open to new encounters, new readings, new survivals and ways of conceiving of literature. And this was not because of philanthropy or literary priesthood, but because his literature was made of authors, as you already know: dead or alive, famous or sunk in anonymity, refugees in the academy or walking out in the open, Latin Americans or Spanish, Nazis or humanists. This characteristic, in addition, marked the different forms of friendship for him: in a group, personal, old, new, of total trust or of growing suspicion ... If you were a writer, there were only two options with Bolaño: you either were his friend no matter what, or you were his enemy whenever it was your turn.[9]

"Roberto Brodsky," one of the articles included in *Entre paréntesis* (*Between Parenthesis*, 2004), is a positive review Brodsky's first novel, *El peor de los heroes* (The Worst of Heroes). In it, Bolaño calls Brodsky his friend and describes his family's visit to his house in Blanes, and their

---

[8] "Roberto tenía el horario laboral de un vampiro. Despertaba en la tarde y, para entrar en calor, llamaba a sus amigos ... De pronto hablaba de una actriz que le gustaba, contaba un sueño, describía un movimiento militar en la batalla de Borodino o se interesaba en saber cómo estaba mi pequeña hija. Luego colgaba para adentrarse en su noche de escritura."

[9] "Te puedo decir que en cuestiones de amistad Bolaño era muy directo y abierto a nuevos encuentros, nuevas lecturas, nuevas sobrevivencias y modos de llevar la literatura. Y esto no era por filantropía o sacerdocio literario, sino porque su literatura estaba hecha de autores, como ya sabes: vivos o muertos, célebres o hundidos en el anonimato, refugiados en la academia o caminando a la intemperie, latinoamericanos o españoles, nazis o humanistas. Esta característica, además, marcaba las formas distintas que asumía la amistad con él: de grupo, personal, antigua, nueva, de confianza total o de sospecha creciente ... Si eras escritor, solo había dos opciones con Bolaño: o eras su amigo para estar en todas, o eras su enemigo donde te tocara."

conversations about laughter, likely and unlikely adventures, and about sadness and bravery, two constants in Brodsky's novel.

The former infrarrealista Rubén Medina (1955–) coincides with Brodsky in his assessment of what Bolaño found more attractive in people: "Roberto became interested in people – the ones he knew, the ones he didn't know, those he intuited – but he was even more interested in their writing, in their literary adventure."[10] In our personal correspondence, Medina described Bolaño, as a friend, as "supportive, loyal, and also a little distant," as well as "critical, and nothing stopped him from telling you what he thought."[11] After mentioning the different friendships Bolaño kept in Mexico City with the Chilean writers Poli Délano (1936–2017) and Hernán Lavín Cerda (1939–), as well as with the Mexican poet Efraín Huerta (1914–1982), Medina states that "out of all that variety of friends, he managed to have a close, intimate, more personal friendship only with very few of them."[12] Among the infrarrealistas, Medina lists Bruno Montané, Mara Larrosa, and Mario Santiago as Bolaño's only close friends.

Regarding the presence of love in his private life, it was Carmen Pérez de Vega, Bolaño's partner during his last six years, who took him to the hospital in Barcelona before his passing. One day before being interned in the hospital, Bolaño visited his editor Jorge Herralde at the office of the Anagrama publishing house to give him the manuscript of his short story collection *El gaucho insufrible* (*The Insufferable Gaucho*, 2003) and to talk about *2666* (2004), the novel that he had been frantically writing for months. Bolaño's idea was to publish it in five separate volumes in order to leave a larger inheritance for his wife and beloved children, the thirteen-year-old Lautaro and the two-year-old Alexandra. In his testament, Bolaño left the rights of his entire oeuvre to his wife, Carolina López, and children.

Carolina López and Bolaño met in Girona in 1981 (Bolaño was twenty-eight and López, twenty) and three years later, they began to live together. They married in 1985 and moved to Blanes, where Bolaño worked at his mother's bijouterie shop. In his last interview with Maristain, Bolaño states that it was always Carolina López, his wife, who was the first to read all his books, and then Herralde; this reveals his profound respect for her as a reader. For her part, in an interview with Josep Massot for the Catalan

---

[10] "Roberto se interesaba en la gente – la conocida, la desconocida, la que intuía –, pero se interesaba más en su escritura, en su aventura literaria."
[11] "Solidario, leal, y también un poco distante"; "Crítico, y no se detenía a decirte lo que pensaba."
[12] "De toda esa variedad de amigos con muy pocos lograba tener una amistad cercana, íntima, más personal."

newspaper *La Vanguardia,* Carolina López describes Bolaño's attitude toward love: "As his attitude toward games, literature, love, friendship or enmity, in reality toward life, he had a completely excessive vital attitude, which made our live together very fun but also very complicated."[13] Regarding his love for his children, it can be summarized in the answer he gave in his last interview when Maristain asked him what "fatherland" meant for him: "My only homeland is my two children, Lautaro and Alexandra. And maybe, but in the background, some moments, some streets, some faces or scenes or books that are inside me and that one day I will forget, which is the best thing you can do with your homeland."[14] And when Maristain asks him what things amuse him, he answers: looking at his daughter Alexandra play.

The fact that love and friendship were central concerns in Bolaño's life is unmistakably reflected in his oeuvre. Friendship is often a key topic, if not the main one, and at times it is the engine that moves the action in the plot. For instance, in "La parte de los críticos" ("The Part about the Critics"), the opening section in his novel *2666*, love and friendship famously intervene and interrupt the search for clues about the elusive, German author Benno Von Archimboldi, when three European critics roam around in the Northern Mexican city of Santa Teresa (supposedly Ciudad Juárez) and in the Sonora desert. Eventually, the interpersonal relationships between four academic friends – the male literary critics Spaniard Manuel Espinoza, Italian Piero Morini, and Frenchman Jean Claude Pelletier, and the English female literary critic Liz Norton – gradually encroach into their professional research. After Norton has a romance with each of them (and a *ménage à trois* with Espinoza and Pelletier), interactions become more tense and awkward – at one point, Espinoza and Pelletier, rejected by Norton, actually become closer. Eventually, Norton begins a love relationship with Morini. As Felipe Adrián Ríos Baeza explains:

> The understanding of rupture, of the uselessness of efforts, that the private will always envelop the public. This, then, is the radical politics of friendship, which almost ties in with another of Derrida's concepts: that of hospitality ... Without achieving the conceptual or emotional

---

[13] "Como en el juego, en la literatura, en el amor, en la amistad o enemistad, en realidad ante la vida, tenía una actitud vital completamente desmesurada y esto hacía muy divertida e interesante la vida en común, también muy complicada" (n.p.).

[14] "Mi única patria son mis dos hijos, Lautaro y Alexandra. Y tal vez, pero en segundo plano, algunos instantes, algunas calles, algunos rostros o escenas o libros que están dentro de mí y que algún día olvidaré, que es lo mejor que uno puede hacer con la patria" (2003, 2).

apprehension, the critics have glimpsed a quite palpable edge of the human condition: in any type of search, there is a risk of being invaded by the other, the enemy, the hostile, the person whom one was trying so hard to hold off.[15]

The academic clique is disbanded after friendship turns into love and sexual attraction. According to Ríos Baeza, their friendship, physical attraction, and love ends up "eclipsing" their academic and professional concerns about consecrating Archimboldi. In fact, the nature of their friendship becomes diffuse and contradictory as it includes in it the very notion of enemy (blackmail, repression, postponement of desire, exclusion of the other, according to Derrida).

Likewise, José Ramón Ruisánchez Serra, who claims that the heart of Bolaño's opus is not violence or evil but the constant exploration of friendship and fraternity, has considered "La parte de los críticos" a novel about friendship:

> It can be read as an adventure of the friendship between two men who want the same woman, are her lovers simultaneously, and finally lose her. Two men who despite these adventures do not stop being friends. Be it as the novel of a woman who is capable of being the lover of her friends, while still being their friend or rather, that of four critics who are friends because they admire the same writer whom they have never seen.[16]

Elsewhere, Ruisánchez Serra praises the fact that Bolaño was capable of elevating the novel of friendship to the time-tested level of the horror novel or the love novel:

> Because what interests me when proposing the friendship novel and tensing it with the two other thematic models with older lineage is to underscore Roberto Bolaño's enormous achievement in making the slow processes of friendship (and not only of the friendship that begins but, above all, of the

---

[15] "La comprensión de la ruptura, de la inutilidad de los esfuerzos, de que lo privado envolverá siempre lo público. Ésta es, pues, la radical política de la amistad, que casi empata con otro concepto de Derrida: el de hospitalidad ... Sin conseguir la aprehensión conceptual ni emocional, los críticos han entrevisto una arista bastante palpable de la condición humana: en la búsqueda de cualquier clase se corre el riesgo de ser invadido por el otro, el enemigo, el hostil, al que tanto se procuraba mantener a distancia" (37).

[16] "Puede ser leída como una aventura de la amistad de dos hombres que desean a la misma mujer, son amantes de manera simultánea y finalmente la pierden. Dos hombres que a pesar de estas peripecias no dejan de ser amigos. Ya sea como la novela de una mujer que es capaz de ser amante de sus amigos, sin dejar de ser su amiga. O bien de cuatro críticos que son amigos porque admiran al mismo escritor que nunca han visto" (Ruisánchez Serra, 2019, 16).

friendship that continues, the one that overcomes its impossibilities) not only narrative but also effectively thrilling.[17]

Friendships such as the one between Ulises Lima and Arturo Belano (Bolaño's alter ego) are also central in *Los detectives salvajes*. It is based on the real-life friendship that united the young Infrarrealistas (Mario Santiago, Bruno Montané, Rubén Medina, and others) with whom Bolaño founded a minor literary group named Infrarrealismo in 1975 in Mexico City. Villoro coincides with this assessment when he explains that "*The Savage Detectives* is a curious *Bildungsroman*, a 'sentimental education.' Like Jack Kerouac's *On the Road*, it tells the story of two buddies searching for the meaning of existence on a car trip."[18] Along these lines, many of Bolaño's drifting characters in *Consejos de un discípulo de Morrison a un fanático de Joyce*, *La senda de los elefantes* (*Monsieur Pain*, 1994), *La literatura nazi en América* (*Nazi Literature in the Americas*, 1996), *Estrella distante* (*Distant Star*, 1996), *Los detectives salvajes*, *Amuleto* (*Amulet*, 1999), *Nocturno de Chile* (*By Night in Chile*, 2000), *Amberes* (*Antwerp*, 2002), *El Tercer Reich* (*The Third Reich*, 2010), *Los sinsabores del verdadero policía* (*Woes of the True Policeman*, 2011), and *El espíritu de la ciencia ficción* (*The Spirit of Science Fiction*, 2016), along with several of his short stories, have long lost their hope in utopian political projects and now they only find solace in true friendships.

Regarding the topic of friendship in *La literatura nazi en América* and *Estrella distante*, Gareth Williams argues that these two novels are marked by Bolaño's apparent "inability to contemplate the political from a place other than the friend/enemy divide" (129). Bolaño, according to Williams, displaces the Left–Right political divide into paranoid friend–enemy hostilities, as Carl Schmitt's notion of the friend/enemy divide guides his understanding of sovereignty and the political: "One of his many concerns, to which he returned on numerous occasions, was the question of enemy recognition in the relation between avant-garde poetics, history and the political. As a result, he was also concerned with the status of the friend in the historical context of state brutality against its enemies" (Williams,

---

[17] "Porque lo que me interesa al proponer la novela de amistad y tensarla con estos otros dos modelos temáticos de mayor prosapia es subrayar el enorme logro de Roberto Bolaño al volver no sólo narrativos, sino efectivamente emocionantes los lentos procesos de la amistad y no sólo de la que comienza sino, sobre todo, los de la amistad que continúa, de la que supera sus imposibilidades" (Ruisánchez Serra, 2010, 47).

[18] "'¿Los detectives salvajes' es una curiosa 'bildungsroman' o novela de educación sentimental. Como 'En el camino', de Jack Kerouac, narra la historia de dos compinches que peregrinan en un auto buscando el sentido de la existencia" (n.p.).

2009, 125). By contrast, Cory Stockwell argues that the problem is actually the narrator's despair upon realizing his uncanny proximity to Wieder: "he would like nothing more than to declare Wieder a simple enemy, clearly distinct from him, but he knows that this is impossible" (2016, 259 n. 31). In turn, Rory O'Bryen adds that Bolaño's play on the heteronym "adds greater depth to Bolaño's deconstruction of the friend/enemy opposition and opens up the novel's melancholic ending to a reflection on the failure of justice postdictatorship – the failure, among other things, to rid the future of the hostilities that organized the past and continue to haunt the present – as well as to a more progressive deconstruction of justice as that which is still, necessarily, to come, à venir" (2015, 28). In reality, one of the ways in which Weider is demonized in *Estrella distante* is precisely by exposing his betrayal of people who were supposed to be his friends, such as the Garmendia sisters.

The *axis mundi* in the plot of other works, such as the short novel *Amuleto* or the short story "Sensini," included in *Llamadas telefónicas* (*Last Evenings on Earth*, 1997), is also the resilient friendship among the protagonists. In *Amuleto*, the relationship between Auxilio Lacouture, the Uruguayan poet, narrator, and self-appointed "mother of the new Mexican poetry" (37),[19] and a host of young Latin American writers and artists, including Arturo Belano (Bolaño's alter ego), determines the rest of the action. The same happens with the epistolary friendship between the unnamed narrator and the older Argentine writer Luis Antonio Sensini in "Sensini," even though they stop writing letters to each other after Sensini returns to Argentina. Thus, recognizing the importance of this friendship, Sensini's daughter, Miranda, will visit the narrator after her father's death. Overall, therefore, the significance of love and friendship in both Bolaño's life and oeuvre cannot be overstated.

---

[19] "Madre de la poesía joven de México" (38).

CHAPTER 30

World Literature: Twenty-First-Century Legacies
Héctor Hoyos

Tel Avivians raise their eyebrows upon discovering that *The Savage Detectives* misrepresents the urban layout of their city. After a lively dinner party, the wandering bohemian poet Ulises Lima and his friends walk a literally impossible path. Lest anyone suspect their own geography, Hebrew cotranslators Moshe Ron and Adam Blumenthal add a pithy footnote: "it is hard to see why or from where would one return to one's house in Hashomer street in Tel Aviv, which is near the Carmel Market, through Arlozorov Street. Here, and in the rest of this chapter, it seems that the sites in Bolaño's Israel are rooted in the writer's imagination."[1] In other words: dear reader, we too get it that this is all wrong, but let's carry on.

Roberto Bolaño's work, as several studies have shown, comments on interminable global war;[2] fictionalizes globalization;[3] occupies a place in World Literature;[4] disrupts transnational cultural prestige;[5] among others.

While all claims and mistakes are very much my own, this article could not have been written without generous interlocutors who went out of their way to liaise or to provide factual and anecdotal evidence. For reasons of space, I have omitted many of their findings. I am indebted to Ariel Horowitz, Sergio Parra, Zhao Deming, Nan Zheng, Zhen Daqian, Elhabib Louai, Delia Ungureanu, Rafael Reyes-Ruiz, Chang Liu, Yurim Kim, Kyoeng-Min Lee, Woo Suk-Kyun, Kenji Matsumoto, Alexander Key, Jay Corwin, Katia De La Cruz, Takaatsu Yanagihara, Melissa Hosek, Evan Alterman, Michael Lavery, Shadi Rohana, Alexander Erokhin, Aleksandr Skidan, Alexandra Semenova, Alissa De Carbonel, Alexandra Ortiz Wallner, Youssef Rakha, Billy Kahora, Magalí Armillas-Tiseyra, Gilad Shiram, Fatoumata Seck, and Nicolás Rodríguez Galvis. Joseph Wager and Sanjana Friedman kindly provided editorial assistance.

[1] Roberto Bolaño, הפרא בלשי, trans. by Moshe Ron and Adam Blumenthal (Tel Aviv: Am Oved, 2011), 648.

[2] Eli Jelly-Schapiro, "'This Is Our Threnody': Roberto Bolaño and the History of the Present," *Critique: Studies in Contemporary Fiction* 56, no. 1 (January 2015): 77–93.

[3] Héctor Hoyos, *Beyond Bolaño: The Global Latin American Novel* (New York: Columbia University Press, 2015).

[4] Nicholas Birns and Juan E. De Castro, eds. *Roberto Bolaño as World Literature* (New York: Bloomsbury Academic, 2017).

[5] Héctor Hoyos, *Things with a History: Transcultural Materialism and the Literatures of Extraction in Contemporary Latin America* (New York: Columbia University Press, 2019).

But how can any author do all this if he, in a sense, gets the world wrong? The Tel Aviv referential faux pas serves as a vivid reminder that negativity is key for understanding both the world depicted in Bolaño and his legacy for a potentially global readership. Simply put, gaps and missed connections matter. The present speculative essay explores the limits of Bolaño's worlding in light of Asian and African contexts. With a caveat: cosmopolitanism is not an all-or-nothing proposition. Someone can be eminently worldly in some ways and parochial in others. Provided the world is big enough, anyone's parochialism will shine through. Bolaño and the undersigned are no exception.

Israel, at the crossroads of Africa, Asia, and Europe, is the first of several locations visited by Bolaño's characters beyond Europe and the Americas. This expansion of narrative space knew but two obstacles: verisimilitude and the author's untimely death, aged fifty. But the tendency was there. In *The Savage Detectives*, Arturo Belano's travels will take him on a cross-continental tour of sub-Saharan Africa. In *2666*, Archimboldi's travels shall be wide-ranging; the Black Panther-inspired character Barry Seaman (what's in a name?) will visit China and Algeria; Stevenson's grave in Samoa gets a conspicuous nod. Picture Bolaño, ever the agonistic Latin American exile, looking for excuses to reverse-colonize the Global North, first, and take it from there. This is a complex, contradictory, and unfinished operation. Adventure novelists like Emilio Salgari or Karl May orientalize to assert, wittingly or not, the superiority of Western civilization. Readers suspicious of Bolaño could see him as enacting a two-part movement: first, situate himself within the West, grudgingly but unequivocally; then, become the West. However, the adventurism espoused by Bolaño is more erratic than programmatic, and his literary politics are firmly rooted in vitalism and solidarity, rather than empire.

Because a literary life for Bolaño is always a voluptuous affair, it is fitting that unrequited love takes Lima to Tel Aviv. Israel loves Bolaño back, as it turns out. Am Oved Press's successful print runs and critically acclaimed translations bear this out, despite the compromises made along the way. At moments such as the above, the galloping enthusiasm of *real visceralismo*, the avant-gardist fleshy ethos that arguably underwrites the entirety of Bolaño's writing, stumbles, and the literariness of it all sinks in. In some ways, translators vie for invisibility. By making their presence felt, they expose the artifice in World Literature, the friction in what is supposed to be a fluid medium. Beyond brokerage revealed, there is the suspicion that Israelis were never an intended audience, or at least not one worth fact-checking for in an otherwise verisimilar body of realist writing.

In fact, the Hebrew edition has a whopping twelve pages of footnotes, typically elucidations of the real-life characters alluded to in the novel. They cement the impression that Bolaño is important, serious literature that indexes a wide world of mostly foreign references (and botched local markers). Other languages follow suit: Chinese translations are rather systematic in this regard; the Korean translation of the relatively short *The Insufferable Gaucho* has 135 footnotes. Japanese translations prefer other paratexts and in-text parenthetical explanation over footnotes, and are more economical, but ultimately seek the same effect. Following local custom, epilogues by one of the six translators into Japanese and by a local author or critic are common: nineteen pages for *The Insufferable Gaucho*, sixteen for *Distant Star*, eighteen for *The Third Reich*, and so on. The irony here is that the Spanish originals lack such signposts, however readers could use them all the same. The encyclopedic ambition of Bolaño's semifictional libraries confound anyone – Bolaño included, surely. This happens by design. How else would one convey the sense that the world is incommensurably vast or that literature is infinitely rich and variegated? Channeling Mao, one could say that, in Bolaño, literature is the spark that can light a prairie fire, except the prairie grows and grows.

And yet the institution of literature prevails, for better *and* for worse. Compare this paratextual anxiety to the famous family tree in Gabriel García Márquez's *One Hundred Years of Solitude*, which Spanish editions lack, but other languages can't seem to do without. "The point is getting lost" does not fly as a valid explanation when legibility and book circulation is at stake. Bolaño translations came to light already halfway on the path to a critical edition, as of yet, unavailable in Spanish. (Given Bolaño's suspicion toward the institution of literature, the contributions of such an edition, would be, in turn, suspect.)

Does this wider world reinforce the tokenization of contemporary Latin American literature that Bolaño, posthumously and unwittingly, participates in? In the English language, Bolaño opens doors for his contemporaries. Those he lived to read get blurbs in re-editions, including authors whose aesthetic ambition and accomplishment are on a par, such as the Argentine César Aira, or those he at one point endorsed as emerging figures, such as the Peruvian Fernando Iwasaki. The late Mexican Mario Santiago Papasquiaro, the inspiration for Ulises Lima, got an English translation of his poetry thanks to his association with Bolaño. Meanwhile, a postscript in the Japanese edition of *Distant Star* acknowledges Raúl Zurita as the inspiration for Carlos Wieder, the pilot poet character, citing the original air verses that Wieder distorts. One can only be hopeful that a new Japanese translation of Zurita might come under its wings and, moreover, that the trend towards an expansive understanding of Latin American literature and culture will continue. But this is uncertain. According to Kenji Matsumoto, the Japanese market for Latin American literature in translation is so small, and the available translators so few, that this wouldn't be possible "without the support of an embassy."[6] That said, he estimates that Bolaño's Japanese standing is comparable to that of Michel Houellebecq, Kashuo Ishiguro, or Karl Ove Knausgaard, all at a far remove from local darling Haruki Murakami. Takaatsu Yanagihara, from University of Tokyo, notes that besides a few works by Aira, Alejandro Zambra, Eduardo Halfon, Fernando Vallejo, and Juan Gabriel Vásquez, contemporary Latin American literature is absent from bookstores. (Mario Bellatin and Diamela Eltit are notable lacunae.) However, Bolaño transcended an initial circulation within the "Ex Libris" series at Hakusuisha Press, devoted to World Literature, to having his own "Colección Bolaño" series, also known as ボラーニョ・コレクション.

Market forces conspire for Bolaño to register either by himself or among World Literature greats. Intertextual winks to other Latin American figures offer a modicum of resistance. The net effect remains a decontextualization from Latin America and a recontextualization into hypercanonicity. There is also an anachronistic communion of Bolaño and the Latin American literary Boom. Disturbingly, it is almost as if the Chilean were a late coda to that big event, with little happening in the interim. Between Natalia Bogomolova and Valentin Kapanadze, two of Bolaño's translators into Russian, they are also responsible for translations of Borges, Bioy Casares, Vargas Llosa, Cortázar, Fuentes, and Arreola.

Meanwhile, the Bolaño master's thesis seems by now a well-established genre the world over. China, where rigorous academic milestones are the norm, provides many examples, including Shi Shaojie's *Sobre la desfamiliarización en la novela panorámica 2666 de Roberto Bolaño* (2018), written in Spanish at Dalian University of Foreign Languages. As Chinese scholarship becomes every day more in sync with the West – a process long since foreshadowed by supply chains – master's theses on Bolaño, though almost always written in Mandarin, often include abstracts in English. (The fact that the opposite is not the case speaks volumes.) They cover topics such as exile, space, and civilization versus barbarism,

---

[6] Kenji Matsumoto, "Kenji Matsumoto: De Bolaño al 'Canto General,'" Interview by Pablo Guerrero, *El Mercurio*, May 6, 2018.

hailing from institutions such as Zhejiang Gongshang University, Nanjing Normal University, or Sichuan Normal University, by way of a partial overview. Some of these emerging critics seem to repeat the arguments formulated by Patricia Espinosa and others in the late nineties, that is, to rediscover the *roman à clef* when the key had already been found elsewhere. Regardless, they clearly contribute to robust local scholarly exchange.

Master's theses have the salutary aspect of serving as a capstone for initiatory reading, something that Bolaño's countercultural appeal, like that of the Beatniks before him, seems especially well poised to do. (Reportedly, five young readers of Bolaño opened a short-lived bookstore in Shanghai called "2666.") On the other hand, it is unclear how the master's credential might transform literary institutions predominantly oriented toward the local and the historical, rather than the worldly and the contemporary. One wonders what will become of these young readers as their aesthetic choices determine whether they advance in the profession of literature or they join the precariat that Bolaño romanticizes. Thanks to its foreignness, the rebelliousness that Bolaño espouses flies under the radar. In literary milieux that place a premium on propriety, to put the matter delicately, it would be more challenging for local authors to deploy a similar aesthetic. Reading about the breach of university autonomy and the suppression of student movements in Mexico City in 1968, the plot of *Amulet*, is one thing. But no one could set that story in Beijing in 1989 without ruffling feathers.

This may be one of the reasons for Bolaño's notoriety in China. Fueled by prompt translations that Horizon Media and Shanghai People Press entrusted to several different translators, Bolañomania rages on. Still, readership is niche: as of 2019, editor Wang Ling estimates that the loyal core of Bolaño readers numbers no more than 10,000.[7] That number is but a drop in the bucket for the Chinese literary market, much as it would sustain a midlist literary career in Chile. There were compromises here, too. *The Savage Detectives* was translated from English; a volume under the title *The Unknown University* (未知大学) binds together Bolaño's poetry, but also short stories and a novella. Master's theses aside, more advanced Chinese research on Bolaño includes a 2015 dissertation at Beijing Foreign Studies University by Yan Bo, who will go on to produce peer-reviewed articles for *Foreign Literature* (外国文学). These pieces are conversant with bibliographies from several Latin American nations, Spain, and the United States. The opposite trajectory, where scholars from Europe and

---

[7] Wang Ling, "Interview with the Editor of Bolaño." Zhen Daqian, September 29, 2019.

the Americas engage more fully with their Chinese counterparts, cannot be long in the making.

Yet transactions of cultural prestige are hard to predict. San Francisco–based Lebanese-American writer Rabih Alameddine structures his 2013 English language novel *An Unnecessary Woman* around the title character, Aaliya Saleh, and her attempt to translate *2666* from English or French into Arabic. The Beirut introvert faces a late-life crisis, and ultimately founders: "The novel *2666*, incomplete though it may be, is too big. [...] Can I risk missing the rite of beginning a translation on the first of January?"[8] Saleh never publishes her translations. To boot, her translation of the unfinished novel is, well, unfinished. That Alameddine's novel's unity of action should hinge upon this quixotic task may speak to a number of things: Bolaño's star power, which already merits name-dropping; affinity between the experience of Lebanon's civil war and violence in Latin America (though at one point the protagonist muses that García Márquez's Macondo is more predictable than the Middle East); sympathy for the Chilean's frustration vis-à-vis literature's meager capacity to effect justice in the world; happenstance. Digressive and writerly, but also jittery and superficial in its engagement with numerous intertexts, Alameddine's fiction illustrates how Bolaño has become an emblem for dislocation.

Note that what makes its premise implausible is not that the translation in question should be done from English. This happens in real life, as in China, above, but also in Persian with *By Night in Chile*.[9] The improbability lies in that no literary agents or book fairs are involved. Mediation is the fact, immediacy the fantasy. In the actual Arabic translation of *The Savage Detectives*, Shadi Rohana reports, transliteration renders Mexican names with the peninsular Spanish lisp, Juan GarTHía Madero (مادرو غارثيّا خوان). In an unfortunate turn, the idiomatic warning "¡aguas!," uttered during a noted bathroom-stall *fellatio interrupta*, is rendered literally as the plural of water (miyāh).[10]

Such gaffes notwithstanding, the Chilean author seems to speak directly to local issues in unexpected places. Egyptian novelist Youssef Rakha, whose 2013 *The Crocodiles* (التماسيح) tells the exploits of a secret society of poets in Cairo, finds that *2666* "covered enough of the world, and

---

[8] Rabih, Alameddine, *An Unnecessary Woman* (New York: Grove Press, 2013), 261–262.
[9] "Works by Bolaño, Otsuka Released in Persian," Iran's Book News Agency, February 17, 2014, www.ibna.ir/en/naghli/194547/works-by-bola%C3%B1o-otsuka-released-in-persian
[10] Shadi Rohana, email interview with the author, December 21, 2020.

stressed enough of the third (or non-Western) world to feel like a kind of millennial Old Testament."¹¹ For the author, Bolaño illustrates how to engage with politics without flattening literature into mere propaganda.

For his part, scholar and translator Woo Suk-kyun demonstrates in a scintillating piece how Koreans read Bolaño through a pre-existing identification.¹² The military junta that ruled the country from 1961 to 1963, forceful neoliberalization, and anticommunism primed Bolaño's Korean readers to understand the poignancy of a novel like *By Night in Chile*. Kyeong-Min Lee, who edited a collection of articles by (mostly) Korean scholars on the author (로베르토 볼라뇨, or *Roberto Bolaño*, which came out in 2018) mentions a revealing incident. When former president Park Geun-hye was removed from office amid a corruption scandal, novelist Jang Jung-il used the occasion of a Bolaño review to criticize the role of Korean intellectuals in buttressing an illegitimate regime (182).¹³ Per Lee, Bolaño opened his readers' eyes to the disquieting links between inexcusable politicians and their ghost writers, unethical intellectuals the lot of them. The most striking legacy of Bolaño in Korea is through its young authors, notably Jeong Jidon and Oh Han-ki, who in 2012 founded an Analrealist movement inspired by *The Savage Detectives*. Their goal was to inject new energy into the country's stale, similarly corrupt literary establishment. A major case of plagiarism by a bestselling novelist had recently led to a reckoning, practically setting up the mood for Bolaño's perverse poet pilots.

Meanwhile, Roanne Kantor has traced how Indian novelists, banking on a South–South dialogue that goes back to Neruda, look to Latin American literature to unsettle their own site of enunciation within World Literature, specifically the Anglophone sphere.¹⁴ She goes on to note that Karan Mahajan, who grew up in New Delhi and relocated to the United States for college, finds in Bolaño an example of unapologetic writing that does not have to explain itself, but proudly seems "*addressed* to another audience."¹⁵ The literary politics of this statement are fascinatingly

---

[11] Youssef Rakha, email interview with the author, November 4, 2020.
[12] Suk-kyun Woo, "Reception of Chilean Literature and South Korean Intellectual Genealogy," in Axel Gasquet and Gorica Majstorovic, eds., *Cultural and Literary Dialogues Between Asia and Latin America* (New York: Palgrave Macmillan, 2021), 103–117.
[13] Kyeong-Min Lee, "Recepción de la literatura de Roberto Bolaño en Corea," *Hispania* 102, no. 2 (2019): 182.
[14] Roanne Kantor, "South Asian Writers, Latin American Literature, and the Rise of Global English" (unpublished manuscript), PDF.
[15] Karan Mahajan, "Karan Mahajan on the Inner Lives of Terrorists & Victims in Today's India," Interview by Megha Majumdar, *Electric Lit*, March 22, 2016.

complicated, as Kantor expounds. Suffice it to say here that Bolaño is caught between registers of Spanish (Chilean, Peninsular, Mexican) much in the way that Mahajan is between two very distinct languages (Hindi and English). For a certain parochial mainstream readership, both their oeuvres may somehow "feel translated" – a form of dislocation that Mahajan comes to value. Gurgaon-based novelist Tanuj Solanki takes the Bolaño forebear motif one step further, as Kantor also examines. In a dreamlike short story, he imagines a park bench conversation between the Punjabi writer Saadat Hasan Manto (1912–1955) and a mysterious figure. It dawns upon the narrator, while examining the man with round glasses, thin curly hair, dirty jeans, and long slender fingers, that "this man is Roberto Bolaño, no fucking doubt." This Bolaño quotes in Urdu, conjures Third World solidarity, but also puts literary geopolitics in suspense: "There were enough like [Manto] in Latin America. Or maybe I should say the West. But then it's not The Third World I'm talking about any more."[16] Manto, a rebellious writer accused of obscenity, a stark opponent of the partition of India and Pakistan, meets an author whose heroism lies in crafting a politically charged oeuvre against the backdrop of looming liver failure. They both "skirt the abyss" in Solanki's tale, which speaks to the transnational generative power of Bolaño's literary politics.

One angle Kantor does not explore is Bolaño's own engagement with India. His own park bench fable, the short story "Mauricio, 'The Eye' Silva" features a middle-aged Bolaño alter ego and an old acquaintance, a fellow Chilean exile who reminisce about their youth in Mexico City and about the title character's traumatic sojourn in the subcontinent. The bench in question is located in a park in Berlin, in the dead of night. Silva is a photographer. In a purposefully long *mise en abyme*, we learn that a young Silva had remarked casually that only certain Indians don't like to be photographed, and the narrator's mother thought he referred to the Mapuche.[17] The slippage foretells the horror that – carefully, paratactically, in ways too subtle to do justice to here – "the Eye" witnessed ritual mutilation in the subcontinent. The castration of boy prostitutes to be exact. Boys he eventually fathered, or mothered as he puts it, until, matter-of-factly, a disease comes to the village and the boys die.

Bolaño writes in sfumato, blurring referential markers. The city with brothels could have been Bombay [*sic*], Calcutta, Benares, or Madras; the

---

[16] Tanuj Solanki, "The Geometry of the Gaze," *Litro Live*, July 28, 2013.
[17] Roberto Bolaño, "Mauricio 'The Eye' Silva,'" in *Last Evenings on Earth*, trans. Chris Andrews (New York: New Directions, 2006), 108.

village goes unnamed. Bolaño walks a very fine line here between parodying a heart-of-darkness mode of writing, where unspeakable evil lurches in faraway lands, and participating in it. Solanki gets the subtlety, and is willing to engage with Bolaño's symbolic bridge between Chile's disappeared and India's undercaste. "[R]eal violence is unavoidable," muses the narrator, "at least for those of us who were about twenty years old at the time of Salvador Allende's death" ("Mauricio," 106). The rewriting suspends the "at least." The affordance here is universal solidarity with the mangled body. The pitfall, unspecificity. This leads Mariano Siskind to posit, in a perceptive reading that sees the story as an emblem of a cosmopolitanism of loss and orphanhood, that "the fact that India is not actually India precludes the possibility of reading 'El ojo Silva' in relation to the concepts of Global South and South-South forms of solidarity."[18] Here we reach aporia: either Solanki proves Siskind's assessment wrong or Siskind undermines Solanki's story.

Bolaño's engagement with Africa is more suspect. In *The Savage Detectives*, the Catalan Susana Puig wonders why her former lover, Arturo Belano, despite his frail health, is heading to Africa:

> So what about Africa? I said. Africa comes afterward, he said (his voice sounded the same as it always did, a tiny bit ironic, but not the least bit insane), it's the future. The future? Nice future. And what do you plan to do there? I said. His answer was vague, as always. Things, assignments, the usual, is what I think he said, or something like that.[19]

The passage collapses narrative levels, nodding at once to the time of the plot and to historical teleology. There is a whiff of Leonard Cohen here: "I've seen the future, baby/ it is murder"[20] – or suicide, or both. As if Belano's existence were not precarious enough, Puig seems to think, with undertones of Eurocentrism. Readers are invited to read between the lines and wonder whether Belano is being earnest, which would somehow render Africa as the lost land of Mexican poetry. The dizzying hermeneutical cue pits the noble savage against the savage *tout court*, death drive against vitalism. But in the final analysis, does *The Savage Detectives*, and Bolaño's oeuvre, ultimately side with Susana Puig? The compromising

---

[18] Mariano Siskind, "Towards a Cosmopolitanism of Loss: An Essay about the End of the World," in Gesine Müller and Mariano Siskind, eds., *World Literature: Cosmopolitanism, Globality: Beyond, Against, Post, Otherwise* (Berlin: De Gruyter, 2019), 221.
[19] Roberto Bolaño, *The Savage Detectives*, trans. Natasha Wimmer (New York: Farrar, Straus and Giroux, 2007), 434.
[20] Leonard Cohen, "The Future," track 1 on *The Future*, Columbia 1992, compact disc.

answer is yes, but not for lack of trying: they expose an internal limit of the Western imagination.

In this spirit, Belano's African travels test the pact of verisimilitude. The penniless poet crosses the continent from East to West, from Dar Es Salaam to Monrovia. Never mind that through much of his journey he would have been regarded as Mzungu, colloquial Bantu for White man or foreigner, roughly equivalent to "gringo." Alternatively affectionate or derogatory, the term also signifies a wanderer, which is fitting, but more importantly speaks to the unlikelihood of the journey. Here, the menial jobs that sustain wandering Latin Americans in Europe are already taken, access to pharmaceuticals is spotty. At this point, readers are familiar with the increasingly unlikely exploits of traveling *real visceralistas* through more or less unreliable witnesses. Belano's journeys are seen through the eyes of one such witness, Jacobo Urenda, an Argentine-born European correspondent who runs into the poet in Luanda, Kigali, and rural Liberia. After the first two encounters, he sends him medicine from Paris, thus becoming his lifeline. The third encounter ends with a chirpy Belano walking into all but certain death, as ethnic civil war rages somewhere in the vicinity of Brownsville and Black Creek. These names have an allegorical rather than a geographical function, gesturing ambiguously at either Black and Brown solidarity or enmity. The whole approach to this heart of Black and Brownness is gothic and suspenseful, arguably because Urenda is a swaggering adventurer eager to be back among the comforts of Europe

The Kenyan writer Billy Kahora observes that Bolaño "gets a pass" on the referential blunders thanks to his experimentalism.[21] After all, the depiction of Africa does not come from a cavalier omniscient narrator with claims to firsthand knowledge, but from a cadre of unreliable character-narrators. Kahora, whose aesthetic affinities with Bolaño are evident in the short story "The Gorilla's Apprentice" – "we are in the abyss and the abyss is us," he writes – is also an advocate of pan-African literary fiction via the Kwani Trust writer network. In that capacity, he admires how Bolaño teaches "to talk about your place and get recognition, without compromising [...] breaking rules on how to publish internationally." Compromises may be unavoidable, as the present essay suggests, but Bolaño remains an inspiration among the younger African literary intelligentsia. One shouldn't wait standing up for translations into Swahili, Hausa, or Yoruba – English, French, and Arabic reach this readership. Kahora has to "switch off [his] literal brain" when reading the sub-Saharan

---

[21] Billy Kahora, Zoom interview with the author, February 25, 2021.

travel bits, playing along with Bolaño because he grasps that, unlike the Polish journalist poet Ryszard Kapuściński, the Chilean novelist is no fabulist of Africa. Still, *The Savage Detectives* hits a wall of the imagination: known places are places, distant locales are but figures of speech.

The epitome of this nonchalance comes in *2666*, voiced through one Lothar Junge, a high priest of German-language literary criticism. Archimboldi, an emerging writer at the time, is at the mercy of his whims. An eager editor asks Junge for his opinion, and although it is unclear whether the critic has actually read the author or not, he remarks that Archimboldi does not quite read like a European author, or even an American one:

> "[M]ore like African," said Junge, and he made more faces under the tree branches. "Or rather: Asian," murmured the critic.
>
> "From what part of Asia?" Bubis asked.
>
> "Who knows?" said Junge. "Indochina, Malaya, at his best he seems Persian."
>
> "Ah, the literature of Persia," said Bubis, who in fact knew nothing about Persian literature.
>
> "Malayan, Malayan," said Junge.[22]

The racist flattening of several continents should not surprise. After all, nationalism and Nazism shape Archimboldi's life and milieu. The pointing fingers at the literary institution – always caricaturized, always extreme – poses *via negativa* an antagonism between Latin American literature and academia. How so? The only excluded major region of the world in Junge's sweeping digression is the region we've come to associate with Bolaño. Perhaps the missing simile for Archimboldi's oddity is, precisely, that of a Latin American author writing in German. Always the punster, Bolaño iterates the Spanish demonym for Malaysian, "malayo," homophonous to "mal hayo" as in "this escapes me," "I find this lousy," or even "I see evil." As a just-so comparison escapes Junge, the first reading is clear. Meanwhile, the editor's startling retelling of the episode bears out the second reading, for he says that the critic did not like the author, as if anything un-German is already at a disadvantage. But it is the third reading that brings us closer to the generative power of Bolaño's writing, for here the author teasingly connects the lurking evil of the unknown

---

[22] Roberto Bolaño, *2666*, trans. Natasha Wimmer (New York: Farrar, Straus and Giroux, 2008), 841–842.

world with the insinuation that there is a form of literary knowledge, an unspoken secret, that exceeds academic rationalization and geopolitics.

Junge's xenophobia may very well be a distorted mirror to Bolaño's philoxenia, but they both share the same frame: a Hegelian teleology of history, whose inexorable march to progress and (White, European) rationality Junge perverts, Bolaño subverts.[23] Both are defined by it. (Rakha disagrees: "[Bolaño] manages to talk about the world that 'Westerners' talk about without being Western."[24]) In the proverbial dialectical inversion, there is a Spirit that gradually seizes the world in Bolaño's fiction, but that Spirit is the bodily. The search for lost bodies that underlies much of Bolaño's fiction – loved ones, matron poets, *desaparecidos*, German novelists, femicide victims – is a constitutive element of his worlding. David Kurnick situates this search: "the crucial point about Bolaño's work is not its totalizing vision but its grounding of this vision at the border of north and south."[25] If we look at Bolaño's totality from the outside in, so to speak, it turns out that the emphasis on the North–South axis ends up imposing itself on an East–West understanding of the world. Unwittingly, Bolaño reveals the internal consistency of the West. A freerider of the Anglophone publishing industry, he taps onto the broad English language readership in regions such as the Persian Gulf or the Indian subcontinent, as well as countries such as Singapore and Kenya. The case to translate his work into the non-Western languages spoken in these locales resembles that of translating rock and roll music: to what extent is it necessary, viable, or profitable, given the self-selected audience? If on one level Bolaño denounces the Americanization of the world, on another level he may participate in this process. Other forms of Western brokerage are more subtle: Dar Al Jamal, the one-man press behind the timely but flawed Arabic translations above, is based in Germany.

Trajectories cannot be scripted, however. As this chapter goes to press, 31-year-old Senegalese writer Mohamed Mbougar Sarr receives the über prestigious Prix Goncourt, where he joins the ranks of Marcel Proust, Simone de Beauvoir, and Marguerite Duras, for a heavily Bolaño-inflected

---

[23] Cf. "Africa proper, as far back as History goes, has remained – for all purposes of connection with the rest of the World – shut up; it is the Goldland compressed within itself – the land of childhood, which, lying beyond the day of self-conscious history, is enveloped in the dark mantle of Night." Georg Wilhelm Friedrich Hegel, *The Philosophy of History*, trans. J. Sibree (New York: Dover Publications, 1956), 91.

[24] Youssef Rakha, email interview with the author, November 4, 2020.

[25] David Kurnick, "Comparison, Allegory, and the Address of 'Global' Realism (The Part about Bolaño)," *boundary 2*, no. 42 (January 2015): 124.

novel, *La plus secrète mémoire des hommes* (2021). Traveling writers, their love life and a lengthy epigraph from *The Savage Detectives* feature prominently, suggesting the Chilean writer's unexpected remediation of *Francophonie*. Ironically perhaps, as the Bolaño archive in France changes hands from Christian Bourgois éditeur to Éditions de L'Olivier, the new cover of the urtext sports an unabashedly exoticizing drawing of a hat-clad Latin lover in a broad-shouldered suit with more resemblance to Dick Tracy than to anything happening in the novel.

My own critical gesture, as a Latin American scholar based in a Californian research university, participates in this knot of contradiction. I have leveraged scholarly networks to piece together this exploration. Others may expand upon it. The Bolaño World could be at the cusp of losing its totality – about to be consumed by specialized local criticism, for better or for worse. There is a certain kind of professionalization that sits ill at ease with Bolaño's vindication of amateurism. US academia has an outsize role in global literary consecration, commensurate with the country's geopolitical standing. Though arguably less hegemonic now than in the immediate post-1989 world Bolaño writes about, the latter is gargantuan, still. And yet *2666* dismisses the academic powerhouse in passing, as the "critic" antiheroes of the eponymous Part learn about a "very strange" literary conference to be held at the University of Minnesota, "supposedly to be attended by five hundred professors, translators, and German literature specialists, though Morini had reason to believe the whole thing was a hoax [un bulo]" (19). Through the eyes of these very flawed, but also very distinct and passionate *críticos*, American Heartland scholars are a massive, cold, and specialized crowd, for whom the stakes of German literature do not transcend their métier. And yet, the very strange word here is "bulo," a seldom-used term, possibly of Roma origin, for either a flop or for false news propagated with an obscure end. So, there could be an inversion here. The scholar characters in question, even the relatively sensible Morini, are far from being role models. One could hypothesize that US professional readers, merely hinted at here, are a beacon of light in the somber landscape of Archimboldiana. Or perhaps they (we?) are condemned all the same: safe from perversity, prey to inanity.

A key takeaway from this exercise in self-reflection is that Bolaño's worlding, a compulsive *ars combinatoria*, will continue to produce contradiction. Take the term "critic" in "The Part about the Critics." In Spanish, it was already something of a misnomer, because critics write for newspapers and not for journals. Morini, Norton et al. would be called *catedráticos* or possibly *académicos*. The original coinage is already a white-glove attack.

The English translation gets it, as does the Hebrew, using a context-dependent noun whose ambiguous meaning ranges from visitor to literary critic to ticket collector (מבקרים).²⁶ Things can get wildly interesting across translations. In Korean, 비평가들 sounds judgmental, closer to criticizing than to critiquing; other languages connote specialists, intellectuals, mandarins, commentators. *Real visceralismo* remains a Shibboleth. This brings to mind George Steiner's observations about the range of translatability, from the naturalization and at-homeness ascribed to the Bible to the "permanent strangeness" of Nabokov's *Onegin*.²⁷ The genius of Bolaño lies in his layered approach, captured in the final *ars poetica* of the Fürst Pückler, the thick German desert alluded to in the waning pages of *2666*. Borrowing Walkowitz's felicitous phrase, one could say that the "born translated"²⁸ elements in his writing are but the icing on the cake.

---

[26] Shoshana Kordova, "Word of the Day: Mevaker," *Haaretz*, October 27, 2012.
[27] George Steiner, *After Babel: Aspects of Language and Translation* (New York: Oxford University Press, 1975), 158.
[28] Rebecca L. Walkowitz, *Born Translated: The Contemporary Novel in an Age of World Literature* (New York: Columbia University Press 2015).

Further Reading

Acero, Nibaldo. *La ruta de los niños. La poética de Roberto Bolaño.* Mexico City: Matadero, 2017.
"Bolaño: elegía y alegría." *Revista Mensaje* 494 (November 2003): 35–36.
Adorno, Theodor. "Cultural Criticism and Society." *Prisms.* Translated by Samuel and Shierry Weber. Cambridge, MA: MIT Press, 1983, 17–34.
Adriaensen, Brigitte, and Valeria Grinberg Pla. "Introducción a cuatro manos." *Narrativas del crimen en América Latina: transformaciones y transculturaciones del policial.* Edited by Brigitte Adriaensen and Valeria Grinberg Pla. Berlin: Lit, 2012.
Agamben, Giorgio. *Homo Sacer: Sovereign Power and Bare Life.* Translated by Daniel Heller-Roazen. Stanford: Stanford University Press, 2008.
"What Is a Destituent Power?" Translated by Stephanie Wakefield. *Environment and Planning D: Society and Space* 32 (2014).
Aguilar, Gonzalo. "El lugar de Latinoamérica en la teoría de la vanguardia." *Fronteras literarias en la literatura latinoamericana.* Buenos Aires: Instituto de Literatura Hispanoamericana, 1996, 111–120.
Aguilar, Paula. "*Monsieur Pain* y los comienzos de un escritor melancólico." *Revista iberoamericana* 80, no. 247 (2014): 493–510.
Ajens, Andrés. *Poetry after the Invention of América: Don't Light the Flower.* New York: Palgrave Macmillan, 2011.
Alameddine, Rabih. *An Unnecessary Woman.* New York: Grove Press, 2013.
Alexander, Robert J. *Communism in Latin America.* New Brunswick, NJ: Rutgers University Press, 1957.
Allard, Sergio. *50 años después. Inicio en Chile de la Reforma Universitaria de 1967.* Valparaíso, Chile: Ediciones Universitarias de Valparaíso, 2017.
Allen, James Lovic. "'Imitate Him If You Dare': Relationships between the Epitaphs of Swift and Yeats." *Studies: An Irish Quarterly Review* 70, no. 278–279 (1981): 177–186.
Álvarez, Eliseo. "Las posturas son las posturas y el sexo es el sexo." *Bolaño por sí mismo. Entrevistas escogidas.* Edited by Andrés Braithwaite. Santiago, Chile: Ediciones Universidad Diego Portales, 2006, 34–45.
"Positions Are Positions and Sex Is Sex." Interview. In *Roberto Bolaño: The Last Inteview and Other Conversations.* Brooklyn, NY: Melville House, 2009 (Kindle).

Amar Sánchez, Ana María. *Instrucciones para la derrota. Narrativas éticas y políticas de perdedores*. Barcelona: Anthropos, 2010.
Amícola, José. "Roberto Bolaño o los sinsabores de la razón queer." *Léctures du genre* 10 (2013): 5–10.
Anderson, Benedict. *Imagined Communities: Reflections on the Rise and Spread of Nationalism*. London: Verso, 1991.
Assmann, Aleida. "Transnational Memories." *European Review* 22, no. 4 (2014): 546–556.
Andrews, Chris. *Bolaño's Fiction: An Expanding Universe*. New York: Columbia University Press, 2014.
Arias, Rubén Angel. "La Universidad desconocida abre una sucursal." *Contexto y acción* (ctxt), digital magazine, March 22, 2019.
Ault, Ann Warner. *Masked Men: Staging Identity in Mexican Experimental Prose, 1921–1929*. Dissertation, New York: Columbia University, 2007.
Aussenac, Dominique. "Interview with Roberto Bolaño." *Le Matricule des Anges* 40 (2002): 40–41.
Avelar, Idelber. *The Untimely Present: Postdictatorial Latin American Fiction and the Task of Mourning*, vols. 45, 44. Durham, NC: Duke University Press, 1999.
Ayala, Matías. "Notas sobre la poesía de Roberto Bolaño." *Bolaño Salvaje*. Edited by Edmundo Paz Soldán, Gustavo Faverón Patriau, and Erik Haasnoot. Barcelona: Editorial Candaya, 2008.
Bajter, Ignacio. "Soles Negros en el Cielo Mexicano: (Infrarrealismo 1974–...)." *Nuevo Texto Crítico* 24–25, no. 47–48 (2011/2012): 47–59.
"Tras las huellas de Alcira Soust: Poeta vagabunda y bellamente desolada." *La Lupa, Brecha* (January 9, 2009): I–III.
Bakhtin, Mikhail. *The Dialogic Imagination: Four Essays*. Edited by Michael Holquist and Caryl Emerson. Austin: University of Texas Press, 1981.
Rabelais and His World. Translated by Helene Iswolsky. Bloomington: Indiana University Press, 1984.
Baldez, Lisa. *Why Women Protest. Women's Movements in Chile*. Cambridge: Cambridge University Press, 2002.
Balibar, Étienne. "What Is a Border." *Politics and the Other Scene*. London: Verso, 2002.
Barrientos Arellano, Ramón. "Los Bolaño, especie angelina." *Revista Ateneo*, no. 22 (2003): 39–42. www.bibliotecanacionaldigital.gob.cl/colecciones/BND/00/RC/RC0232248.pdf
Barnard, Andrew. *Chile in Latin America between the Second World War and the Cold War, 1944–1948*. Edited by Leslie Bethell and Ian Roxborough. Cambridge: Cambridge University Press, 1992.
Barnhisel, Greg. *Cold War Modernists: Art, Literature, and American Cultural Diplomacy*. New York: Columbia University Press, 2015.
Barthes, Roland. "The Death of the Author." *Image, Music, Text*. Translated by Stephen Heath. New York: Hill & Wang, 1977.

"The Reality Effect." *The Rustle of Language*. Translated by Richard Howard. New York: Hill & Wang, 1986, 141–148.

S/Z. Translated by Richard Miller. New York: Noonday Press, 1988.

Bateson, Mary Catherine. *Composing a Life*. New York: Grove Press, 1989.

Bautista, Virginia. "Evocan al infrarrealista imprescindible: Roberto Bolaño (1953–2003)." *Excelsior* (July 15, 2013).

Baudelaire, Charles. "À Arsène Houssaye." *Oeuvres completes*, vol. 1. Edited by Claude Pichois. Paris: Gallimard, 1976, 275–276.

Les Fleurs du mal. Paris: Livre de Poche, 1972.

Petits poèmes en prose. Paris: Gallimard, collection Poésie, 1973.

Le Spleen de Paris. Paris: Gallimard, 2010.

Bauman, Zygmunt. *Globalization: The Human Consequences*. New York: Columbia University Press, 1998.

Beckett, Samuel. *Stories and Texts for Nothing*. New York: Grove Press, 1967.

Beecroft, Alexander. *An Ecology of World Literature, from Antiquity to the Present Day*, London; New York: Verso, 2015.

Bejarano, Alberto. *Ficción e historia en Roberto Bolaño: buscar puentes sobre los abismos*. Bogotá: Instituto Caro y Cuervo, 2018.

Benjamin, Walter. *The Arcades Project*. Translated by Howard Eiland and Kevin McLaughlin, edited by Rolf Tiedemann. Cambridge, MA: Belknap Press of Harvard University Press, 1999.

Illuminations. New York: Schocken Books, 1979.

Reflections. New York: Schocken Books, 1986.

"Surrealism: The Last Snapshot of the European Intelligentsia" (1929). *Selected Writings*, vol. 2. Cambridge, MA: Harvard University Press, 1999, 207–221.

Berger, Peter. *The Sacred Canopy: Elements of a Sociological Theory of Religion*. Doubleday, 1967.

Bermúdez, María Elvira. *Los mejores cuentos policíacos mexicanos*. Mexico City: Libro-Mex, 1955.

Bethell, Leslie, and Ian Roxborough. *Latin America between the Second World War and the Cold War, 1944–1948*. Cambridge; New York: Cambridge University Press, 1992.

Bevan Jr., Ernest. "Dialogue with the Self: Paul Valéry and Monsieur Teste." *Twentieth Century Literature* 26, no. 1 (1980): 15–26.

Beverley, John. *Latin Americanism After 9/11*. Durham, NC: Duke University Press, 2011.

Bianchi, Soledad. Conversatorio con Soledad Bianchi. "El escritor joven y la crítica, muestras del epistolario Bianchi / Bolaño." Facilitator: Álvaro Bisama. Universidad Diego Portales. July 6, 2017. www.youtube.com/watch?v=pdynBVUFc1A

https://comunicacionyletras.udp.cl/2017/12/13/donacion-de-cartas-y-postales-de-roberto-bolano-refuerzan-archivos-udp/

"De qué hablamos cuando decimos 'nueva narrativa chilena.'" 1997. https://web.uchile.cl/publicaciones/cyber/07/de_que_hablamos.htm#1 Inc. August 8, 2020.

Birns, Laurence, Congressman Donald Fraser, and Michael Harrington. "The Chilean Tragedy." *New York Review of Books*, October 26, 1973.

Birns, Nicholas. "Valjean in the Age of Jouvert: Roberto Bolaño in the Era of Neoliberalism." *Roberto Bolaño, a Less Distant Star: Critical Essays*. Edited by Ignacio López-Calvo. New York: Palgrave, 2015.

Birns, Nicholas, and Juan E. De Castro, eds. *Roberto Bolaño as World Literature*. New York: Bloomsbury Academic, 2017.

Bisama, Álvaro. "Nuevos mapas del infierno: Una lectura sobre Bolaño y la ciencia ficción." *Orillas* 6 (2017): 7–17.

"Un país posible: Roberto Bolaño y el exilio." *Mitologías hoy* 7 (2013): 41–56.

Bizzarri, Gabriele. "La 'Alita Rota' del discurso latinoamericanista: Estrategias *queer* en Roberto Bolaño, Diamela Eltit y Pedro Lemebel." *Anales de Literatura Chilena* 19, no. 29 (2018): 53–68.

"Hacia una des-categorización de la 'identidad hispanoamericana': estrategias queer en Roberto Bolaño y Pedro Lemebel." *Rivista di studi letterari y culturari* 17 (2017a): 19–29.

"Lo propio y lo alienígena: Ciencia ficción e identidad en la construcción imaginaria de Santa Teresa." *Orillas* 6 (2017b): 171–183.

"Santa Teresa out of the Closet: Queer Intertextuality and the Performance of Latin American Identity in Roberto Bolaño's 'Amalfitano Cycle.'" *Whatever* 3 (2020): 401–418.

The Spirit of Science Fiction. Translated by Natasha Wimmer. New York: Penguin, 2019.

"Visit to the Convalescent." Translated by Laura Healy. *Poetry* 193, no. 2 (2008): 104–107.

Bloom, Harold. 1994. *The Western Canon: The Books and School of the Ages*. New York: Harcourt Brace.

Bolaño, Roberto. *A la intemperie. Colaboraciones periodísticas, intervenciones públicas y ensayos*. Madrid: Alfaguara, 2019.

"An Attempt at an Exhaustive Catalog of Patron." *Between Parentheses: Essays, Articles, and Speeches*. Edited by Ignacio Echevarría. Translated by Natasha Wimmer. New York: New Directions, 2011.

A Little Lumpen Novelita. Translated by Natasha Wimmer. New York: New Directions, 2014.

Amberes. Madrid: Alfaguara, 2018.

Amulet. New York: New Directions, 2008.

Amuleto. Barcelona: Anagrama, 1999.

Antwerp. Translated by Natasha Wimmer. New York: New Directions, 2010.

"Beach." *Between Parenthesis: Essays, Articles and Speeches (1998–2003)*. Translated by Natasha Wimmer. New York: New Directions, 2011.

Between Parenthesis. Translated by Natasha Wimmer. New York: New Directions, 2011.

"Buba." *The Return*. Translated by Chris Andrews. New York: New Directions, 2012.

By Night in Chile. 2000. Translated by Chris Andrews. New York: New Directions, 2003.
"Caracas Address." *Between Parentheses: Essays, Articles, and Speeches.* Edited by Ignacio Echevarría. Translated by Natasha Wimmer. New York: New Directions, 2011.
"The Caracas Speech." www.canopycanopycanopy.com/contents/the_caracas_speech
"Cartas de Roberto Bolaño a sus padres desde Chile y España." www.catedraabierta.udp.cl/cartas-de-roberto-bolano/
"Colonia Lindavista." *The Secret of Evil.* www.google.com/books/edition/The_Secret_of_Evil/TZ-MCsCHMYgC?hl=en&gbpv=0
"La colonia Lindavista." *El secreto del mal.* Anagrama 2013, 15–22.
Consejos de un discípulo de Morrison a un fanático de Joyce. Diario de bar, co-written with A.G. Porta. Madrid: Penguin Random House, 2016.
Cuentos Completos. Prologue by Lina Meruane. New York: Vintage, Penguin Random House, 2018.
"Déjenlo todo, nuevamente." Primer Manifiesto Infrarrealista. Appendix to *Bolaño infra, 1975–1977: Los años que inspiraron* Los detectives salvajes, by Monserrat Madariaga Caro, Ril Editores, 2010, 143–52; Mexico City, 1976. *Archivo Bolaño*, martes 7 de agosto 2007. https://garciamadero.blogspot.com/2007/08/djenlo-todo-nuevamente-primer.html
"Dentist." *Cuentos completos.* Translated by Chris Andrews. New York: New Directions, 2006.
"Detectives." *Llamadas telefónicas.* Barcelona: Anagrama, 1997, 114–133.
"Detectives." *The Return.* Translated by Chris Andrews. New York: New Directions, 2010.
Los detectives salvajes. Barcelona: Anagrama, 1998.
בלשי הפרא (*Los detectives salvajes*). Translated by משה רון and עם בלומנטל. עם עובד, 2011.
Distant Star. 1996. Translated by Chris Andrews. New York: New Directions, 2004.
2666. Barcelona: Anagrama, 2004.
Entre paréntesis. Ensayos, artículos y discursos (1998–2003). Edited by Ignacio Echevarría. 2004. 3rd ed., 2008.
El espíritu de la ciencia-ficción. Barcelona: Alfaguara, 2016.
Estrella distante. 1996. Madrid: Alfaguara, 2016.
"El gaucho insufrible." *El gaucho insufrible.* Barcelona: Anagrama, 2003, 15–51.
El gaucho insufrible. Barcelona: Anagrama, 2003.
"I Can't Read." *Harper's Magazine.* Translated by Chris Andrews. April 2012. https://harpers.org/archive/2012/04/i-cant-read/
"The Insufferable Gaucho." Translated by Chris Andrews. *The Insufferable Gaucho.* New York: New Directions, 2010, 9–41.
"Labyrinth." *The Secret of Evil.* Translated by Chris Andrews and Natasha Wimmer. New York: New Directions, 2012.

"Last Evenings on Earth." Translated by Chris Andrews. *The New Yorker*, December 19, 2005. https://newyorker.com/magazine/2005/last-evenings-on-earth
Last Evenings on Earth. Translated by Chris Andrews. New York: New Directions, 2006.
The Last Interview. Translated by Sybil Perez. New York: Melville House, 2009.
"El libro que sobrevive." *A la intemperie. Colaboraciones periodísticas, intervenciones públicas y ensayos*. Madrid: Alfaguara, 2019.
"Literature + Illness = Illness." Translated by Chris Andrews. *The Insufferable Gaucho*. New York: New Directions, 2010, 121–144.
"Literatura + enfermedad = enfermedad." *Cuentos*, 2003, 2018, 515–533.
La literatura nazi en América. Barcelona: Seix Barral, 1996.
Llamadas telefónicas. Barcelona: Anagrama, 1997.
"Mauricio 'The Eye' Silva.'" *Last Evenings on Earth*. Translated by Chris Andrews. New York: New Directions, 2006.
Monsieur Pain. Vintage Español, 1999.
Muchachos desnudos bajo el arcoíris de fuego. Once jóvenes poetas latinoamericanos. Mexico City: Extemporáneos, 1979.
Nazi Literature in the Americas. 1996. Translated by Chris Andrews. New York: New Directions, 2008.
Nocturno de Chile. Barcelona: Anagrama, 2000. Translated by Chris Andrews. *By Night in Chile*. New York: New Directions, 2003.
"No sé leer." *El secreto del mal*. Anagrama 2013, 113–122.
"La nueva poesía latinoamericana. ¿Crisis o renacimiento?" *Plural* 68. Mexico City, May 1977, 44–46.
"The Part of the Critics." *2666*. New York: Farrar, Straus and Giroux, 2008.
"Paseo por la literatura." *Tres*. Barcelona: Acantilado, 2000. www.letras.mysite.com/rb150304.htm
Perfiles de dos continentes: Una mirada crítica. Booby Grise. www.youtube.com/watch?v=XUXA6qH7asI
Los perros románticos: poemas 1980–1998. Barcelona: Acantilado, 2006.
Putas asesinas. New York: Penguin Random House, [2001] 2017.
Reinventar el amor: Punto de Partida. Mexico City: UNAM, 1977, 51–52.
"Roberto Brodsky." *Between Parentheses: Essays, Articles, and Speeches (1998–2003)*. Edited by Ignacio Echevarría. Translated by Natasha Wimmer. New York: New Directions, 2004, 132–133.
"Roberto Brodsky." *Entre paréntesis: Ensayos, artículos y discursos (1998–2003)*. Edited by Ignacio Echevarría. Barcelona: Anagrama, 2004, 123–124.
The Romantic Dogs. Translated by Laura Healy. New York: New Directions, 2008.
The Savage Detectives. Translated by Natasha Wimmer. New York: Picador/Farrar, Straus and Giroux, 2010.

"Secret of Evil." Translated by Chris Andrews and Natasha Wimmer. New York: New Directions, 2012, 11–13.
La senda de los elefantes. Ayuntamiento de Toledo, Concejalía del Area de Cultura, 1994.
"Sensini." *Cuentos. Llamadas telefónicas. Putas asesinas. El gaucho insufrible*. Barcelona: Anagrama, 2010, 17–33.
"Sevilla me mata." *Palabra de América*, 17–21. Barcelona: Seis Barral, 2004.
Los sinsabores del verdadero policía. Barcelona: Anagrama, 2011.
The Skating Rink. Translated by Chris Andrews and Natasha Wimmer. New York: Picador, 2011.
"Sobre el juego y el olvido: Entrevista de Silvia Adela Kohan." *La Nación*, April 25, 2001.
El Tercer Reich. Barcelona: Anagrama, 2010. Translated by Natasha Wimmer. *The Third Reich*. New York: Picador, 2014.
The Third Reich. Translated by Natasha Wimmer. New York: Farrar, Straus & Giroux, 2011.
"Town Crier of Blanes." *Between Parenthesis: Essays, Articles and Speeches (1998–2003)*. Translated by Natasha Wimmer. New York: New Directions, 2011, 249–250.
Tres. Translated by Laura Healy. New York: New Directions, 2011.
2666. Translated by Natasha Wimmer. New York: Farrar, Strauss & Giroux, 2008.
El último salvaje. Mexico City: Al este del paraiso, 1995.
"Últimos atardeceres en la tierra." *Cuentos completos*. New York: Vintage Penguin Random House, 2018, 235–258.
Una novelita lumpen. Madrid: Alfaguara, 2016.
La universidad desconocida. Barcelona: Anagrama, 2007.
The Unknown University. Translated by Laura Healy. New York: New Directions, 2013.
"Vive tu tiempo." *Pájaro de calor. Ocho poetas infrarrealistas*. Mexico City, 1976.
Woes of the True Policeman. Translated by Natasha Wimmer. New York: Farrar, Straus and Giroux, 2011.
Bolaño, Roberto and Antoni García (A. G.) Porta. *Consejos de un discípulo de Morrison a un fanático de Joyce*. Barcelona: Anthropos, 1984.
Consejos de un discípulo de Morrison a un fanático de Joyce and Diario de bar. Barcelona: Acantilado, 2006.
Bolaño, Roberto, Antoni García (A. G.) Porta, Andrés Braithwaite, and Juan Villoro, eds. "Bolaño por sí mismo: Entrevistas escogidas." *Revisada, Colección Huellas*. Santiago, Chile: Ediciones Universidad Diego Portales, 2011, 2, 37–38, 105–107.
Bolaño, Roberto, Antoni García (A. G.) Porta, and Homi K. Bhabha. "By Night in Chile." *The Location of Culture*. Translated by Chris Andrews. London: Harvill Press, 2003, 128–130.

Bolognese, Chiara. "Roberto Bolaño y Raúl Zurita: referencias cruzadas." *Anales de Literatura Chilena* 14 (December 2010): 259–272.
Boltanski, Luc. *Enigmes et complots: Une enquête à propos d'enquêtes*, vols. 2 and 3. Paris: Gallimard, 2012.
Bon, François, *Daewoo*. Paris: Fayard, 2004.
Borges, Jorge Luis. *Collected Fictions*. Translated by Andrew Hurley. New York: Penguin, 1998.
  "Deutsches Requiem." *El Aleph*. Buenos Aires: Emecé Editores, 1968.
  "El escritor argentino y la tradición." *Sur*, no. 232 (1955): 128–137.
  "The Other Death." *Collected Fictions*. Translated by Andrew Hurley. New York: Penguin, 1998, 223–228.
  "The Wall and the Books." *Selected Non-Fictions*. Translated by Eliot Weinberger. New York: Penguin, 1999.
Bosteels, Bruno. "Critique of Originary Violence: Freud, Heidegger, Derrida." *The Undecidable Unconscious: A Journal of Deconstruction and Psychoanalysis* 4 (2017): 27–66.
  "La situación es catastrófica pero no es seria: Ironía, violencia y militancia en América Latina." *Ironía y Violencia En La Literatura Latinoamericana Contemporánea*. Edited by Brigitte Adriaensen and Carlos. Van Tongeren. Pittsburgh, PA: University of Pittsburgh, 2018, 41–57.
Boullosa, Carmen. "Carmen Boullosa entrevista a Roberto Bolaño." *Roberto Bolaño: La escritura como tauromaquia*. Edited by Celina Manzoni. Buenos Aires: Ediciones Corregidor, 2002.
  "Bolaño in Mexico." *The Nation*. June 29, 2015, www.thenation.com/article/archive/bolantildeo-mexico/.
Braham, Persephone. *Crimes against the State, Crimes against Persons: Detective Fiction in Cuba and Mexico*. Minneapolis: University of Minnesota Press, 2004.
Braidotti, Rosi. *Nomadic Subjects. Embodiment and Sexual Difference in Contemporary Feminist Theory*. 2nd ed. Columbia University Press, 2011.
Braithwaite, Andrés, ed. *Bolaño por sí mismo. Entrevistas escogidas*. Ediciones Universidad Diego Portales, 2006.
Brands, Hal. *Latin America's Cold War*. Cambridge, MA: Harvard University Press, 2010.
Brodsky, Roberto. *El peor de los héroes*. Alfaguara, 1999.
Bungcam, Carlos. *SIndicalismo chileno: Hechos y Documentos, 1973–1983*. Santiago: Circulo dos estudios Latinoamericanos, 1984.
Burgos, Carlos. "Roberto Bolaño." *The Contemporary Spanish American Novel*. Edited by Wilfrido Corral, Juan E. De Castro, and Nicholas Birns. New York: Bloomsbury, 2013.
Burgos-Debray, Elisabeth. 1983. *Me llamo Rigoberta Menchú y así me nació la conciencia*. La Habana: Casa de las Américas.
Bürger, Peter. *Theory of the Avant-Garde*. Minneapolis: University of Minnesota, 1984.
Burroughs, William. *Nova Express*. Barcelona: Bruguera, 1980.

Bush, Matthew and Luis Castañeda. *Un asombro renovado: vanguardias contemporáneas en América Latina*. Iberoamericana/Vervuert, 2017.
Caballero, Manuel. *Latin America and the Comintern, 1919–1943*. Cambridge; New York: Cambridge University Press, 1986.
Calasso, Roberto. *La folie Baudelaire*. London: Penguin, 2008.
Calinescu, Matei. *Five Faces of Modernity*. Durham, NC: Duke University Press, 1987.
Candia Cáceres, Alexis. "La Universidad (des)conocida de Roberto Bolaño." *Mitologías Hoy* 7, no. 1 (2013): 19–28.
Cárdenas, Lázaro. *Apuntes*. Mexico City: Universidad Nacional Autónoma de México, 1957.
Carpentier, Alejo. 1978. *La consagración de la primavera*. Mexico City: Siglo Veintiuno.
Carvajal, Alfonso. "Diario." *El Tiempo*. Bogotá, January 3, 2003.
Casal, Julián. *Poesía completa y prosa selecta*. Edited by Álvaro Salvador. Madrid: Verbum, 2001.
Castro, Alejandro Palma. *Un Poeta latinoamericano en el D.F.: irrupción poética de Roberto Bolaño." Roberto Bolaño: ruptura y violencia en la literatura finisecular*. Edited by Felipe A. Ríos Baeza. Ciudad de México: Ediciones Eón, 2010.
Castro, Juan E. "Politics and Ethics in Latin America: On Roberto Bolaño." *Roberto Bolaño as World Literature*. Edited by Juan E. de Castro and Nicholas Birns. New York: Bloomsbury, 2017.
Castro-Klarén, Sara, Sylvia Molloy, Beatriz Sarlo. Gabriela Mistral, "Land of Absence." Translation by Doris Dana. *Women's Writing in Latin America: An Anthology*. Westview P, 1991, 129.
Cercas, Javier. "Print the legend!" Madrid: *El País* (Babelia, Aorul 14, 2007). *Soldados de Salamina*. Barcelona: TusQuets, 2001.
Chandler, Raymond. *The Simple Art of Murder*. New York: Vintage Books, 1988.
Cinzano, Martín. "Exilio distante: Roberto Bolaño y el exilio en México." Carcaj. cl, 02.09.2018. https://garciamadero.blogspot.com/2019/06/exilio-distante-roberto-bolano-y-el.html
Clayton, Michelle. *Poetry in Pieces: César Vallejo and Lyric Modernity*. Berkeley: University of California Press, 2011.
"Tracking Dance in Latin American Literature." *The Routledge Companion to Twentieth and Twenty-First Century Latin American Literary and Cultural Forms*. Edited by Guillermina De Ferrari and Mariano Siskind. London: Routledge, 2022.
Close, Glen S. *Contemporary Hispanic Crime Fiction: A Transatlantic Discourse on Urban Violence*. New York: Palgrave Macmillan, 2008.
Cobas Carral, Andrea. "Marginalidad y derrota: La poesía infrarrealista de Roberto Bolaño." *Actas del II Congreso International – Transformaciones culturales. Debates de la teoría, la crítica y la lingüística*. Universidad de Buenos Aires, Buenos Aires, 2008.
Cobas Carral, Andrea, and Verónica Garibotto. "Un epitafio en el desierto: poesía y revolución en *Los detectives salvajes*." Edited by Edmundo Paz Soldán, and

Gustavo Faverón. *Bolaño salvaje.* 2008. 2nd amplified ed. Barcelona: Candaya, 2013, 160–186.
Cohen, Leonard, "The Future." 1992, track 1 on *The Future.* Columbia, 1992, compact disc.
Collier, Simon and William F. Sater. *A History of Chile, 1808–2002.* 2nd ed. Cambridge: Cambridge University Press, 2004.
Córboba, Antonio. "(De)Mythologizing the Disabled. Chilean Freaks in Roberto Bolaño's 'El Tercer Reich' and 'Estrella distante.'" *Hispanic Issues Online* 20 (2018): 77–96.
Corral, Wilfrido H. "Bolaño, Ethics, and the Experts." *Roberto Bolaño and World Literature.* Edited by Nicholas Birns and Juan E. De Castro. New York: Bloomsbury, 2017.
Corral, Will H. *Bolaño traducido: Nueva Literatura Mundial.* Madrid: Escalera, 2011.
Corral, Will H., Nicholas Birns, and Juan E. De Castro, eds. *The Contemporary Spanish-American Novel: Bolaño and After.* London and New York: Bloomsbury, 2013.
Cortázar, Julio. 1963. *Rayuela.* Buenos Aires: Sudamericana.
Crusat, Cristian. "La tradición hispanoamericana de la "vida imaginaria": una antología inminente desde Alfonso Reyes a Roberto Bolaño (y un decadente francés)." *Taller de Letras N° 64* (2019): 247–262.
Cruzcamarillo, Orlando. "Descifrando a Bolaño." *Confabulario. El Universal,* Mexico City. October 24, 2015. https://confabulario.eluniversal.com.mx/descifrando-a-bolano/
De Castro, Juan E. *Writing Revolution in Latin America: Form Marti to García Márquez to Bolaño.* Nashville, TN: Vanderbilt University Press, 2019.
Dechêne, Antoine. *Detective Fiction and the Problem of Knowledge: Perspectives on the Metacognitive Mystery Tale.* London and New York: Palgrave, 2019.
Decker, Sharae. "Roberto Bolaño and the Remaking of World Literature." *Roberto Bolaño and World Literature.* Edited by Nicholas Birns and Juan E. De Castro. New York: Bloomsbury, 2017.
Degregori, Carlos Iván. *El aprendiz de brujo y el curandero chino. Etnicidad, modernidad y ciudadanía.* Lima: Instituto de Estudios Peruanos, 1990.
"Peripheral Realism, Millennial Capitalism, and Roberto Bolaño's 2666." *Modern Language Quarterly* 73, no. 3 (2012): 351–372.
"Déclaration." *Tel Quel* 1, 1960.
Deleuze, Gilles, and Félix Guattari. *A Thousand Plateaus: Capitalism and Schizophrenia.* 1987. Translated by Brian Massumi. Minneapolis: University of Minnesota Press, 1987.
de Man, Paul. "Autobiography as Defacement." *MLN* 94, no. 5 (1979): 919–930.
Derbyshire, Philip. "*Los Detectives Salvajes*: Line, Loss and the Political'." *Journal of Latin American Cultural Studies* 18, no. 2 (2009): 167–176.
Derrida, Jacques. *Geschlecht III: Sex, Race, Nation, Humanity.* Chicago: University of Chicago Press, 2020.
"My Chances/Mes Chances: A Rendezvous with Some Epicurean Stereophonies." *Psyche: Inventions of the Other.* Translated by Irene Harvey and Avital Ronell, vol. I. Stanford: Stanford University Press, 2007.

Dés, Mihály. "Entrevista a Roberto Bolaño" (February 17, 1998). *Lateral*, no. 4, April 1998. https://desmihaly.wordpress.com/1998/02/17/entrevista-a-roberto-bolano/
Dews, Peter. *The Idea of Evil*. Hoboken: Wiley-Blackwell, 2012.
Díaz Klaassen, Francisco. *Bolaño histórico: Chile, neoliberalismo, obsolescencia*. Ph.D. dissertation, Cornell University, 2020.
Di Benedetto, Antonio. "Aballay." *Nest in the Bones*. Translated by Martina Broner. Brooklyn, NY: Archipelago Books, 2017, 133–160.
Dine, S. S. Van. *Twenty Rules for Writing Detective Stories*. Paris, France: Feedbooks, 1928.
Dinges, John. *The Condor Years: How Pinochet and His Allies Brought Terrorism to Three Continents*. New York: New Press, 2004.
Domínguez, Christopher Michael. "El arcón de Roberto Bolaño. Prólogo." *El espíritu de la ciencia-ficción*. Madrid and New York: Alfaguara, 2016, 9–16.
Donoso, José. "El tiempo perdido." *Cuatro para Delfina*, 150–209. Barcelona: Seix Barral, Biblioteca Breve, 1982.
Dorfman, Ariel. "Epitaph for Another September 11." *The Nation*, September 10, 2011, 17–18.
Dorst, John D. "Neck-Riddle as a Dialogue off Genres: Applying Bakhtin's Genre Theory." *The Journal of American Folklore* 96, no. 382 (October 1, 1983): 413–433.
Dove, Patrick. "The Night of the Senses: Literary (Dis)Orders in Nocturno de Chile." *Journal of Latin American Cultural Studies* 18, no. 2 (2009): 141–154.
Draper, Susana. "Fragmentos de futuro en los abismos del pasado, *Amuleto*, 1968–1998." *Fuera de quicio: Bolaño en el tiempo de sus espectros*. Edited by Raúl Rodríguez Freire. Santiago: Ripio Ediciones, 2012, 53–76.
Driver, Alice Laurel. "Más o Menos Muerto: Bare Life in Roberto Bolaño's 2666." *Journal of Latin American Cultural Studies* 23 (2014): 51–64.
  "More or Less Dead: Literary Representations of Feminicide in Juárez." *More or Less Dead, Feminicide, Haunting, and the Ethics of Representation in Mexico*. Tucson: University of Arizona Press, 2015.
Echevarría, Ignacio. "Nota preliminar." *El secreto del mal*. Anagrama 2013, 7–11.
  Roberto Bolaño lector, el bibliotecario valiente, n.d. www.youtube.com/watch?v=yhWyRKvEuAE.
Eco, Umberto. "El bautizo de la rosa." *Nexos*, October 1, 1984.
Egurbide, Peru. "Sánchez Ferlosio ve en los fastos del V Centenario un 'marketing' de Estado." *El País*, April 9, 1992.
Elmore, Peter. "2666: La autoría en el tiempo del límite." *Bolaño salvaje*. Edited by Edmundo Paz Soldán, Gustavo Faverón Patriau, and Erik Haasnoot. Barcelona: Editorial Candaya, 2008.
  "2666: La autoría." *On the Limits of the Judicial Model See Carlo Ginzburg, the Judge and the Historian: Marginal Notes on a Late-Twentieth-Century Miscarriage of Justice*. London: Verso, 1999.
Emerson, Camilla. "Doubles, Doubles Everywhere: The Uncanny in Roberto Bolaño's *Monsieur Pain*." *From the Supernatural to the Uncanny*. Edited by

Stephen M. Hart and Zoltán Biedermann. Newcastle upon Tyne, UK: Cambridge Scholars, 2017, 204–225.
Felski, Rita. "Context Stinks." *New Literary History* 42, no. 4 (2011): 573–591.
Fernández, Nona. *Space*. Alquimia Ediciones, 2013.
Fernández, Tomás. "Bolaño y los clásicos." *VIII Congreso Internacional Orbis Tertius de Teoría y Crítica Literaria*. Mayo 2012. http://sedici.unlp.edu.ar/handle/10915/29793
Finchelstein, Federico. *A Brief History of Fascist Lies*. Berkeley: University of California Press, 2020.
  "On Fascism, History, and Evil in Roberto Bolaño." *Roberto Bolaño as World Literature*. Edited by Nicholas Birns and Juan E. de Castro. London and New York: Bloomsbury Academic, 2017, 23–40.
Flores, Tatiana. *Mexico's Revolutionary Avant-Gardes: From Estridentismo to ¡30–30!* New Haven, CT: Yale University Press, 2013.
Forster, E. M. *Aspects of the Novel*. New York: Harcourt, 1955.
Foucault, Michel. "Preface." *Anti-Oedipus: Capitalism and Schizophrenia*. 1972. Edited by Gilles Deleuze and Félix Guattari. Translated by Robert Hurley, Mark Seem, and Helen R. Lane. Minneapolis: University of Minnesota Press, 1983.
  What Is an Author? Language, Counter-Memory, Practice: Selected Essays and Interviews. Ithaca, NY: Cornell University Press, 1977.
Franco, Jean. *Cruel Modernity*. Durham, NC: Duke University Press, 2013.
  The Decline and Fall of the Lettered City: Latin America and the Cold War. Cambridge, MA: Harvard University Press, 2002.
  "Questions for Bolaño." *Journal of Latin American Cultural Studies* 18, no. 2 (2009): 207–217.
Franco, Sergio R. "*Monseur Pain* o la crítica de la razón instrumental." *Revista de Estudios Hispánicos* 48, no. 3 (2014): 471–492.
Franz, Carlos. "'Una tristeza insoportable'. Ocho hipótesis sobre la Mela-Cholé de B." *Bolaño salvaje*. 2nd ed. Edited by Edmundo Paz Soldán and Gustavo Faverón Patriau. Barcelona: Editorial Candaya, 2013, 99–111.
Freud, Sigmund. *Civilization and Its Discontents*. London: Vintage, 2010.
Gabara, Esther. *Errant Modernism*. Durham, NC: Duke University Press, 2008.
Galdo, Juan Carlos. "Fronteras del mal / genealogías del horror: *2666* de Roberto Bolaño." *Hipertexto 2* (Summer 2005): 23–34.
Gallo, Rubén. "Severo Sarduy, Jacques Lacan y el psicoanálisis: entrevista con François Wahl." *Revista Hispánica Moderna* 59, no. 1–2 (2006): 51–60.
García, Luis. Revista *El Péndulo*. Bogotá, January 3, 2003.
García-Huidobro, Paz Balmaceda. "La violencia del norte: Dos aproximaciones a las muertas sin fin." *Roberto Bolaño: ruptura y violencia en la literatura finisecular*. Edited by Felipe Ríos Baeza. Puebla: Eón, Benemérita Universidad Autónoma de Puebla, 2010, 327–342.
García Márquez, Gabriel. *Cien años de soledad*. Buenos Aires: Buenos Aires Sudamericana, 1967.
Gefen, Alexandre. *Réparer le monde. La littérature française face au XXIe siècle*. Paris: Editions Corti, 2017.

Gefen, Alexandre, Emmanuel Bouju, Marielle Macé, and Guiomar Hautcœur, eds. *Littérature et Exemplarité*. Rennes, France: Presses Universitaires De Rennes, 2007.
Gleijeses, Piero. *Shattered Hope: The Guatemalan Revolution and the United States, 1944–1954*. Princeton, NJ: Princeton University Press, 1991.
Goldman, Francisco. "The Great Bolaño." *The New York Review of Books*, July 19, 2007.
Gómez Bravo, Andrés. "La historia no contada de León Bolaño." *La Tercera, Cultura*, October 7, 2006. www.letras.mysite.com/rb150108.html
González, Aníbal. *In Search of the Sacred Book: Religion and the Contemporary Latin American Novel*. Pittsburgh, PA: Pittsburgh University Press, 2018.
  Killer Books: Writing, Violence, and Ethics in Modern Spanish American Narrative. Austin, TX: University of Texas Press, 2001.
González Echevarría, Roberto. 2008. *Oye mi son: ensayos y testimonios sobre literatura hispanoamericana*. Sevilla: Renacimiento.
González Rodríguez, Sergio. *Huesos en el desierto*. Barcelona: Anagrama, 2002.
Gould, Jeffrey L. and Aldo Lauria-Santiago. *To Rise in Darkness: Revolution, Repression, and Memory in El Salvador, 1920–1932*. Durham, NC: Duke University Press, 2008.
Grandin, Greg. *The Last Colonial Massacre: Latin America in the Cold War*. Chicago: University of Chicago Press, 2004.
Grau, Anna. "*2666* en EE.UU.: La cara y la cruz de Roberto Bolaño." *ABC*, March 2, 2009. Abc.es/.../2666-cara-cruz-roberto-200
Gras Miravet, Dunia. "La literatura nazi en América (1996), veinte años después: Una lectura hemisférica compartida por El espíritu de la ciencia-ficción (2016)." *Roberto Bolaño: Estrella distante*. Edited by Juan Antonio González Fuentes and Dámaso López García. Sevilla: Editorial Renacimiento, 2017, 129–164.
Grillo, Ioan. *El Narco: Inside Mexico's Criminal Insurgency*. New York: Bloomsbury, 2011.
Grossberg, Lawrence. *Cultural Studies in the Future Tense*. Durham, NC: Duke University Press, 2010.
Gutiérrez-Mouat, Ricardo. "Bolaño and the Canon." *New Trends in Contemporary Latin American Narratives*. Edited by Timothy R. Robbins and José Eduardo González. New York: Palgrave MacMillan, 2014, 39–54.
  Understanding Roberto Bolaño. Columbia: University of South Carolina Press, 2016.
  "Vallejo en Bolaño." *Academia.edu*. Web. August 24, 2020.
Gutiérrez Nájera, Manuel. *Cuentos completos y otras narraciones*. Mexico City: Fondo de Cultura Económica, 1958.
Harmer, Tanya. *Allende's Chile and the Inter-American Cold War*. Chapel Hill: University of North Carolina Press, 2011.
Hart, Stephen M. *César Vallejo: A Literary Biography*. Tamesis, 2013.
Hartwig, Susanne. "Jugar al detective: el desafío de Roberto Bolaño." *Iberoamericana* 7, no. 28 (2001): 53–71.
Harvey, David. *A Brief History of Neoliberalism*. New York: Oxford University Press, 2020.

Heidegger, Martin. *Being and Time.* Translated by John Macquarrie and Edward Robinson. New York: Harper & Row, 1962.
Hegel, Georg Wilhelm Friedrich. *The Philosophy of History.* Translated by J. Sibree. New York: Dover, 1956.
Helú, *Selecciones Policiacas and Misterio,* vol 4. Edited by Helú. 1946.
Hernández, Sonia, and Marta Puig. "Conclusión: una entrevista inédita. Entrañable huraño." Edited by Edmundo Paz Soldán and Patriau Gustavo. *Bolaño salvaje.* 2nd ed. Editorial Candaya, 2013, 509–512.
Herralde, Jorge. *Para Roberto Bolaño.* Catalonia, 2005.
    Para Roberto Bolaño, Lengua. Ensayo; Variation: Lengua; Ensayo. Buenos Aires: Adriana Hidalgo Editora, 2005.
Hobsbawm, Eric. *The Age of Extremes: The Short Twentieth Century, 1914–1991.* London: Michael Joseph, 1994.
House, Ricardo. *Roberto Bolaño. La batalla futura.* Vimeo 64 min. Chile, Mexico City, Spain. 2016.
Hoyos, Héctor. *Beyond Bolaño: The Global Latin American Novel.* New York: Columbia University Press, 2015.
    "Corpse Narratives as Literary History." *Things with a History: Transcultural Materialism and the Literatures of Extraction in Contemporary Latin America.* New York: Columbia University Press, 2019, 105–140.
    In things with a History: Transcultural Materialism and the Literatures of Extraction in Contemporary Latin America. New York: Columbia University Press, 2019.
Huneeus, Carlos. *The Pinochet Regime.* Translated by Lake Sagaris. Boulder, CO: Lynne Rienner, 2007.
Hurst, Steven. *Cold War US Foreign Policy: Key Perspectives.* Edinburgh: Edinburgh University Press, 2005.
Iber, Patrick. *Neither Peace nor Freedom: The Cultural Cold War in Latin America.* Cambridge, MA: Harvard University Press, 2015.
    "The Cultural Cold War." *Oxford Research Encyclopedia of American History,* n.d. https://doi.org/10.1093/acrefore/9780199329175.013.760
Illas, Edgar. *Thinking Barcelona: Ideologies of a Global City.* Liverpool: Liverpool University Press, 2012.
Iran's Book News Agency. "Works by Bolaño, Otsuka Released in Persian." February 17, 2014. www.ibna.ir/en/naghli/194547/works-by-bola%C3%B10-otsuka-released-in-persian
Iwasaki, Fernando. "Roberto Bolaño, Monsieur Pain." *Bolaño salvaje.* Edited by Edmundo Paz Soldán and Gustavo Faverón Patriau. Barcelona: Editorial Candaya, 2008, 117–123.
James, Alison Siân. *Constraining Chance: Georges Perec and the Oulipo.* Evanston, IL: Northwestern University Press, 2009.
    "Thinking the Everyday: Genre, Form, Fiction." *L'Esprit Créateur* 54, no. 3 (2014): 78–91.
James, Henry. "The Art of Fiction." *The Art of Criticism: Henry James on the Theory and the Practice of Fiction.* Edited by William Veeder and Susan M. Griffin. Chicago: University of Chicago Press, 1986.

Jelly-Schapiro, Eli. *Security and Terror*. Berkeley: University of California Press, 2018.

"'This Is Our Threnody': Roberto Bolaño and the History of the Present." *Critique: Studies in Contemporary Fiction* 56, no. 1 (January 2015): 77–93.

Jofré, Julio Sebastián Figueroa. "Bolaño con Borges: Juegos con la infamia y el mal radical." *Roberto Bolaño: ruptura y violencia en la literatura finisecular*. Edited by Felipe Ríos Baeza. Puebla de Zaragoza: Eón; Benemérita Universidad Autónoma de Puebla, 2010, 1, 436–460.

Keller, Renata. *Mexico's Cold War: Cuba, the United States, and the Legacy of the Mexican Revolution*. New York: Cambridge University Press, 2015.

Kelley, Robin D. G. "A Poetics of Anti-Colonialism." *Aimé Césaire, Discourse on Colonialism*. New York: Monthly Review P, n.d.

Killen, Andreas. *Nervous Breakdown: Watergate, Warhol, and the Birth of Post-Sixties America*. New York: Bloomsbury, 1973.

Kirk, John M., and Leonardo Padura Fuentes. *Culture and the Cuban Revolution: Conversations in Havana*. Gainsville: University Press of Florida, 2001.

Klein, Marcus. *Easterns, Westerns, and Private Eyes: American Matters, 1870–1900*. Madison: University of Wisconsin Press, 1994.

Knight, Stephen. "'A Hard Cheerfulness': An Introduction to Raymond Chandler." *American Crime Fiction: Studies in the Genre*. Edited by Brian Docherty. New York: St. Martin's Press, 1988.

'*Form and Ideology in Crime Fiction*. London: Macmillan, 1980.

Kohan, Martín. *La vanguardia permanente*. Paidós, 2021.

Kordova, Shoshana. "Word of the Day: Mevaker." *Haaretz*, October 27, 2012.

Kurnick, David. "Comparison, Allegory, and the Address of 'Global' Realism (The Part about Bolaño)." *boundary 2* 42, no. 2 (January 2015): 105–134.

Lacan, Jacques. "The Signification of the Phallus." *Écrits*. Translated by Bruce Fink. New York: WW Norton, 2006, 575–584.

Lacoue-Labarthe, Philippe. *Heidegger and the Politics of Poetry*. Urbana: University of Illinois Press, 2007.

Typography: Mimesis, Philosophy, Politics. Cambridge, MA: Harvard University Press, 1989.

Latour, Bruno. *Pandora's Hope: Essays on the Reality of Science Studies*. Cambridge, MA: Harvard University Press, 1999.

"La UNAM recuerda a la poeta Alcira Soust y su paso por el movimiento estudiantil del 1968." www.proceso.com.mx/546383/la-unam-recuerda-a-la-poeta-uruguaya-alcira-soust-y-su-paso-por-el-movimiento-estudiantil-del-68 (accessed July 3, 2020)

Lawrence, Jeffrey. *Anxieties of Experience: The Literatures of the Americas from Whitman to Bolaño*. Oxford and New York: Oxford University Press, 2018.

Lazzara, Michael. *Civil Obedience: Complicity and Complacency in Chile since Pinochet*. Madison: University of Wisconsin Press, 2018.

Lee, Kyeong-Min. "Recepción de la literatura de Roberto Bolaño en Corea." *Hispania* 102, no. 2 (2019): 179–190.
Lemebel, Pedro. *De perlas y cicatrices*. 4th ed. Santiago: Editorial Planeta Chilena, 2015.
Leonart, Marcelo, Ximena Carrera, and Nona Fernández, eds. "Carlos Iturra Fictionalized the Case of Callejas and Townley in His Short Story "'Caída en desgracia.'" *Crimen y perdón: Cuentos*. Santiago de Chile: Catalonia, 2008, 183–219.
Levine, Suzanne Jill. "A Universal Tradition: The Fictional Biography." *Review: Literature and Arts of the Americas* 7, no. 8 (1973): 24–28.
Levinson, Brett. "Case Closed: Madness and Dissociation in *2666*." *Journal of Latin American Cultural Studies* 18, no. 2–3 (2009): 177–191.
  The Ends of Literature: The Latin American "Boom" in the Neoliberal Marketplace. Stanford: Stanford University Press, 2001.
  "Of Rats and Men: Bolaño Meets Kafka." *Centennial Review* 14, no.3 (2014): 93–109.
Lezama Lima, José. 1967. *Paradiso*. Havana: Ediciones Unión.
Lichtenberg, Georg Christoph. *Gedanken, Satiren, Fragmente*. Edited by Wilhelm Herzog. Jena: E. Diederichs, 1907.
Long, Ryan. "Roberto Bolaño's Queer Poetics." *Critical Insights: Roberto Bolaño*. Edited by Ignacio López-Calvo. Amenia, NY: Grey House, 2015, 150–166.
  Queer Exposures: Sexuality and Photography in Roberto Bolaño's Fiction and Poetry. Pittsburgh, PA: University of Pittsburgh Press, 2021.
  "Traumatic Time in Roberto Bolaño's *Amuleto* and the Archive of 1968." *Bulletin of Latin American Research* 29, no. 1 (2010): 128–143.
López, Emmanuel Rodríguez. *Por qué fracasó la democracia en España. La Transición y el régimen del'78*. Madrid: Traficantes de Sueños, 2015.
López-Calvo, Ignacio, ed. *Critical Insights: Roberto Bolaño*. New York: Grey House, 2015a.
  ed. *Roberto Bolaño, a Less Distant Star: Critical Essays*. New York: Palgrave/Macmillan, 2015b.
  ed. *Roberto Bolaño's Flower War: Memory, Melancholy, and Pierre Menard*. New York: Palgrave Macmillan, 2015.
  ed. "The Violence of Writing: Literature and Discontent in Roberto Bolaño's 'Chilean' Novels.'" *Journal of Latin American Cultural Studies* 18, no. 2 (2009): 155–166.
  ed. "World Literature and the Marketing of Roberto Bolaño's Posthumous Works." *Critical Insights: Contemporary Latin American Fiction*. Edited by Ignacio López-Calvo. New York: Salem Press, 2017, 26–41.
López-Vicuña, Ignacio. "The Part of the Exile: Displacement and Belonging in Bolaño's *Putas asesinas*." *Hispanófila* 164 (January 2012): 81–93.
Lowry, Malcolm. *The 1940 Under the Volcano*. Edited by Paul Tiessen and Miguel Mota with the assistance of Frederick Asals; introd. Frederick Asals; assistant editor: Deborah Harmon. MLR Editions Canada, 1994.

Lozano, Miguel G. Rodríguez. *Pistas del relato policial en México: Somera expedición, 1a ed, Colección de Bolsillo 35*. Mexico City: Universidad Nacional Autónoma de México, 2008.
Luis, Julio García. *Cuban Revolution Reader: A Documentary History of 40 Key Moments of the Cuban Revolution*. Melbourne; New York: Ocean Press, 2001.
Luiselli, Valeria. *Los ingrávidos*. Sexto Piso, 2011.
Mahajan, Karan. "Karan Mahajan on the Inner Lives of Terrorists & Victims in Today's India." Interview by Megha Majumdar. *Electric Lit*, March 22, 2016.
Mallarmé, Stéphane. *Collected Poems and Other Verse*. Translated by E.H. and A.M. Blackmore. New York: Oxford University Press, 2006.
Mandel, Ernest. *Delightful Murder: A Social History of the Crime Story*. Minneapolis: University of Minnesota Press, 1984.
Manzoni, Celia. "Ciencia, superchería y complot en Monsieur Pain." *Roberto Bolaño: la experiencia del abismo*. Edited by Fernando Moreno and Ediciones Lastarria, 2011, 107–117.
Mardorossian, Carine M. *Framing the Rape Victim: Gender and Agency Reconsidered*. New Brunswick, NJ: Rutgers University Press, 2014.
Marinescu, Andreea. "*Testimonio* in the Lettered City: Literature and Witnessing in Bolaño's *Amuleto*." *Chasqui* 42, no.1 (2013) Brooklyn and London: 134–146.
Maristain, Monica. *Bolaño: A Biography in Conversations*. Translated by Kit Maude. Brooklyn and London: Melville House, 2012.
 El hijo de Míster Playa. Una semblanza biográfica de Roberto Bolaño. Alquimia Ediciones. Kindle Edition, 2017.
Maristain, Monica, and Roberto Bolaño. "The Last Interview." *Roberto Bolaño: The Last Interview & Other Conversations*. Edited by Marcela Valdes, translated by Sybil Perez. New York: Melville House, 2009, 93–123.
 "La última entrevista de Roberto Bolaño: Estrella distante." *Playboy México*, July 23, 2003 www.astro.puc.cl/~rparra/tools/ROCK_EDITIONS/entrevista_con_roberto_bolano.pdf (accessed July 3, 2020).
 La última entrevista a Roberto Bolaño y otras entrevistas a grandes escritores. Axial, 2010.
Martin, Rebecca, ed. *Crime and Detective Fiction*. Ipswich, MA: Salem Press, 2013.
Martínez, José Darío. *Valga la redundancia: repetición y creación en los ciclos narrativos de Gabriel García Márquez, Roberto Bolaño y Juan Carlos Onetti*. Ph.D. dissertation, Yale University, 2020.
Massot, Josep. Interview: "La viuda del escritor, Carolina López: 'Roberto Bolaño tuvo tiempo de disfrutar el reconocimiento.'" *La Vanguardia*, December 19, 2019. www.lavanguardia.com/cultura/20101219/54091163845/la-viuda-del-escritor-carolina-lopez-roberto-bolano-tuvo-tiempo-de-disfrutar-el-reconocimiento.html (accessed July 3, 2020).
Matsumoto, Kenji. "Kenji Matsumoto: De Bolaño al 'Canto General.'" Interview by Pablo Guerrero. *El Mercurio*, May 6, 2018.
Mbembe, Achille. *Necropolitics*. Translated by Steve Corcoran. Durham, NC: Duke University Press, 2019.

Mbougar Sarr, Mohamed. *La plus secrète mémoire des hommes.* Paris: Philippe Rey/ Jimsaan, 2021.
Medina, Alberto. "Arts of Homelessness: Roberto Bolaño or the Commodification of Exile." *Novel: A Forum on Fiction.* 43, no. 2 (2009): 546–554.
Medina, Rubén. "Bolaño and Infrarealism, or Ethics as Politics." *Roberto Bolaño.* Edited and introduced by Ignacio López-Calvo. New York: Salem Press, Grey House, 2015.
  "Infrarealism: A Latin American Neo-Avant-Garde." *Chicago Review* 60, no. 3 (2017). www.chicagoreview.org/issues/issue-6003-2/ (accessed June 22, 2021).
  ed. *Perros habitados por las voces del desierto: poesía infrarrealista entre dos siglos, Segunda edición.* Ciudad de México: Matadero, 2016.
  Personal correspondence. July 7, 2020.
Memoria chilena: Biblioteca Digital Nacional de Chile. "José Miguel Ibáñez Langlois (Ignacio Valente)." www.memoriachilena.gob.cl/602/w3-printer-93098.html (Accessed July 3, 2020).
Memoria viva. www.memoriaviva.com/criminales/criminales_c/callejas_mariana.htm (Accessed July 3, 2020).
Meo Zilio, Giovanni. "El lenguaje poético de César Vallejo desde *Los heraldos negros* hasta *España, aparta de mí este cáliz*, visto a la luz de los resultados computacionales." *Obra poética* by César Vallejo. Edited by Américo Ferrari. Archivos, 1988, 621–660.
Meruane, Lina. "Nunca más volvió a verlo." *Roberto Bolaño. Cuentos Completos.* Vintage, New York and Miami: Penguin Random House, 2018, 9–21.
  Revista *Caras.* February 20 1998. *Bolaño por sí mismo. Entrevistas escogidas.* Edited by Andrés Braithwaite. Ediciones Universidad Diego Portales, 2006, 111.
Michon, Pierre. *Vies minuscules.* Paris: Gallimard, "Folio," 1984.
Mignolo, Walter, and Catherine Walsh. *On Decoloniality: Concepts, Analytics, Praxis.* Durham, NC: Duke University Press, 2018.
Mir, Pedro. *Two Elegies of Hope.* Translated by Jonathan Cohen. New York: Spuyten Duyvil, 2019.
Molina, Ignacio. "Hermana de Roberto Bolaño sobre Carolina López: 'Mi mamá sufrió mucho por esa mujer.'" Interview to María Salomé Bolaño. *Paniko.cl*, November 2016. https://paniko.cl/maria-salome-bolano-carolina-lopez-ha-sido-como-las-clasicas-viudas-de-escritores/
Molloy, Sylvia. "Too Wilde for Comfort: Desire and Ideology in Fin-De-Siecle Spanish America." *Social Text*, 31/32 (1992): 187–201.
Montaldo Graciela and Bruno Bosteels . . . the ILAS Faculty Seminar Series. New York: Columbia University, 2020.
Monroe, Jonathan B. *Framing Roberto Bolaño: Poetry, Fiction, Literary History, Politics.* Cambridge: Cambridge University Press, 2019.
  "Los amores y juegos del joven Berger." Edited by Edmundo Paz Soldán and Gustavo Faverón Patriau. *Bolaño salvaje.* 2nd ed. Editorial Candaya, 2013, 487–506.

A Poverty of Objects: The Prose Poem and the Politics of Genre. Ithaca: Cornell University Press, 1987.
Monsiváis, Carlos. "Prólogo." *La obligación de asesinar: Novelas y cuentos policiacos*. Mexico City: M.A. Porrúa, 1998.
Montesinos, Elisa. "Roberto Bolaño: el peligro de la escritura." Proyecto patrimonio. Roberto Bolaño. www.letras.mysite.com/robbolano1508.html
Moreiras, Alberto. "Postdictadura y reforma del pensamiento." *Revista de Crítica Cultural* 7 (November 1993): 27.
Morley, Jefferson. *Our Man in Mexico: Winston Scott and the Hidden History of the CIA*. Lawrence: University Press of Kansas, 2008.
Morton, Timothy. "Deconstruction and/as Ecology.'" *The Oxford Handbook of Ecocriticism*. Edited by Greg Garrard. Oxford: Oxford University Press, 2014, 291–304.
Moulian, Tomás. *Chile actual: anatomía de un mito*. Santiago de Chile: LOM / ARCIS, 1997.
Müller, Gesine and Mariano Siskind, eds. *World Literature, Cosmopolitanism, Globality*. Berlin/Munich/Boston: de Gruyter, 2019.
Muniz, Gabriela. "Nuevos miedos en la literatura policial de Chile y Argentina." *Revista Canadiense de Estudios Hispánicos* 42, no. 3 (n.d.).
Muñoz, Gabriel Trujillo. *Testigos de cargo*. Mexico City: CONACULTA-CECUT, 2000.
Neruda, Pablo. *Canto General*. Translated by Jack Schmitt. Berkeley: University of California Press, 1991.
Nickerson, Catherine. "Murder as Social Criticism." *American Literary History* 9, no. 4 (1997): 744–757.
O'Bryen, Rory. "Memory, Melancholia and Political Transition in *Amuleto* and *Nocturno de Chile* by Roberto Bolaño." *Bulletin of Latin American Research* 30, no. 4 (2011): 473–487.
"Writing with the Ghost of Pierre Menard: Authorship, Responsibility, and Justice in Roberto Bolaño's *Distant Star*." *Roberto Bolaño, a Less Distant Star: Critical Essays*. Edited by Ignacio López-Calvo. London and New York: Palgrave Macmillan, 2015, 17–34.
Ortega Parada, Hernán. "Roberto Bolaño: algunas precisiones biográficas." https://garciamadero.blogspot.com/2017/10/roberto-bolano-algunas-precisiones.html
Osorio, Juan José. "La poesía de Roberto Bolaño: Tópicos y ensueños." *Revista de Humanidades* 27 (January–June 2013): 123–156.
Osorio, Nelson. "Para una caracterización histórica del vanguardismo literario hispanoamericano." *Revista iberoamericana* XLVII, nos. 114–115 (1981): 227–254.
Otto, Rudolf. *The Idea of the Holy. An Inquiry into the Non-rational Factor in the Idea of the Divine and Its Relation to the Rational*. 2nd ed. Translated by John W. Harvey. Oxford, UK: Oxford University Press, 1958.
Oviedo, José Miguel. "*La literatura nazi en América*, de Roberto Bolaño." *Revista Letras Libres* (November 30, 2005). www.letraslibres.com/mexico/libros/la-literatura-nazi-en-america-roberto-bolano

Padilla, Ignacio. "Homo Bolañus: Missing Link or the Last Dodo." *Critical Insights*. Edited by Ignacio López-Calvo. Salem Press, 2015, 235–240.
Palma, Ricardo. "Los incas ajedrecistas." in *Tradiciones peruanas*, vol. 2. Madrid: Oceano, 2001.
Paz, Octavio. *Itinerario*. Mexico City: Fondo de Cultura Económica, 1993.
Paz Soldán, Edmundo, and Gustavo Faverón Patriau, eds. *Bolaño salvaje*. 2nd ed. Barcelona: Editorial Candaya, 2013.
Peláez, Sol. "Counting Violence: Roberto Bolaño and 2666." *Chasqui* 43, no. 2 (2014): 30–47.
Perec, Georges. *La Vie mode d'emploi*. Paris: Hachette, 1978.
Tentative d'épuisement d'un lieu parisien. Christian Bourgois, 1995 [1975].
W ou le souvenir d'enfance. Paris: Denoël, 1975.
Pérez Santiago, Omar. "Bolaño. El coraje del Cult-Pop." *Utopista pragmático*, no. 109 (August–September, 2003). www.letras.mysite.com/
"Incoherencias de Larry Rohter en *NYT* sobre Bolaño." *Proyecto Patrimonio* 2009. www.letras.s5.com
Pettinà, Vanni. *Historia mínima de la Guerra Fría en América Latina*. Mexico City: El Colegio de México, 2018.
Piccato, Pablo. *A History of Infamy: Crime, Truth, and Justice in Mexico*. Berkeley: University of California Press, 2017.
Piglia, Ricardo. *El último lector*. Barcelona: Anagrama, 2005.
"Theses on the Short Story." *New Left Review* 70 (2011): 63–66.
Pino, Miriam. "Enigma de (Poe)sía: 'El burro' de Roberto Bolaño y 'Gas de los matrimonios' de Eduardo Espina." *Literatura y Linguistica* 19 (December 2007): 101–113.
Podolski, Sophie. *Le pays où tout est permis*. Paris: Transédition, 1979.
Pollack, Sarah. "After Bolaño: Rethinking the Politics of Latin American Literature in Translation." *PMLA* 128, no. 3 (May 2013): 660–667.
Poniatowska, Elena. *Fuerte es el silencio*. Mexico City: Ediciones Era, 1980.
Porta, Antoni García "A. G." "Disculpen lo personal." *El País*, July 16, 2003. https://web.archive.org/web/20110621070341/http://sololiteratura.com/bol/bolanodisculpen.htm. July 3, 2020 (accessed July 6, 2020).
 Antoni García "A. G." Interview for the Bolaño Archive. March 2013. www.cccb.org/es/multimedia/videos/entrevista-a-antoni-garcia-porta/211166 (accessed July 6, 2020).
Premat, Julio. *¿Qué será la vanguardia?* Beatriz Viterbo, 2021.
Prieto, Martín. "La liberación de Valdés, severo golpe para el régimen de Pinochet." *El Pais*, July 15, 1983. https://elpais.com/diario/1983/07/15/internacional/427068002_850215.html
Quezada, Jaime. *Bolaño antes de Bolaño. Diario de una residencia en México (1971–1972)*. Catalonia, 2007.
Rabih, Alameddine. *An Unnecessary Woman*. New York: Grove Press, 2013, 261–262.

Ramírez Figueroa, Juan Carlos. "Bolaño en víspera de la tormenta de mierda." Abbreviated version of *Diario La Segunda* (June 5, 2018). https://cramirezf.medium.com/bolaño-en-vispera-de-la-tormenta-de-mierda

Ramírez-Pimienta, Juan Carlos, and Juan Pablo Villalobos. "Detección Pública / Detección Privada: El periodista como detective en la narrativa policíaca norfronteriza." *Revista Iberoamericana* (June 2010).

Rebolledo, Javier. *A La Sombra de Los Cuervos: Los Cómplices Civiles de La Dictadura (In the Raven's Shadow: The Dictatorship's Civilian Accomplices)*. Santiago de Chile: Ceibo Ediciones, 2015.

Richard, Nelly. *Eruptions of Memory: The Critique of Memory in Chile, 1990–2015*. Translated by Andrew Ascherl. Cambridge, UK: Polity Press, 2019.

Residuos y metáforas (Ensayos de crítica cultural sobre el Chile de la Transición). Santiago de Chile: Editorial Cuarto Propio, 1998.

Ríos Baeza, Felipe Adrián. "Eclipsamientos: Nuevas 'políticas de la amistad' en 2666, de Roberto Bolaño." no. 49, *Polígramas* (December 2019): 17–39.

Robbe-Grillet, Alain. *For a New Novel: Essays on Fiction*. Evanston: Northwestern University Press, 1989.

Rodríguez, Franklin. *Roberto Bolaño: El investigador desvelado*. Madrid: Editorial Verbum, 2015.

Rodríguez, Ileana. *Gender Violence in Failed and Democratic States: Besieging Perverse Masculinities*. Comparative Feminist Studies Series. New York: Palgrave Macmillan, 2016.

Rodríguez Juliá, Edgardo. *Mapa de una pasión literaria*. San Juan: Editorial de la Universidad de Puerto Rico, 2003.

Rohter, Larry. "A Chilean Writer's Fictions Might Include His Own Colorful Past." *The New York Times*, January 27, 2009. www.nytimes.com/2009/01/28/books/28bola.html

Rojo, Grínor. "Bolaño y Chile." *Anales de Literatura Chilena* 5, no. 5 (December 2004): 201–211.

Rosso, Ezequiel de. *Una lectura conjetural: Roberto Bolaño y el relato policial [2000]*. Edited by Roberto Bolaño, La tauromaquia, and Celia Manzoni. Buenos Aires: Corregidor, 2002.

Rothberg, Michael. *The Implicated Subject: Beyond Victims and Perpetrators*. Stanford: Stanford University Press, 2019.

Roudinesco, Elisabeth. *Jacques Lacan & Co*. Translated by Jeffrey Mehlman. Chicago: The University of Chicago Press, 1990.

Ruisánchez Serra, José Ramón. "Aporías de la amistad." *Fractal* 15, no. 56 (January–March 2010): 47–62.

La Reconciliación. Roberto Bolaño y la literatura de amistad en América Latina. Textos de difusión cultural, UNAM, 2019.

Sánchez Mariño, Joaquín. "Los rastros y los mitos de Bolaño. Las huellas, en Chile, del escritor que dejó temprano una tierra en la que nunca fue profeta." *La Nación*, Buenos Aires, July 12, 2015. http://letras.mysite.com/jque170715.html

Sanchís, Irma. "Si hubiera otra vida y fuera posible elegir, escogería ser mujer." *Bolaño por sí mismo. Entrevistas escogidas*. Edited by Andrés Braithwaite. Ediciones Universidad Diego Portales, 2006, 79–81.

Santana, Mario. *Foreigners in the Homeland: The Spanish American New Novel in Spain, 1962–1974*. Lewisburg: Bucknell University Press, 2000.

Santiago Papasquiaro, Mario. *Advise from 1 Disciple of Marx to 1 Heidegger Fanatic / Dream with No End*. Translated by Cole Heinowitz and John Burns. Ediciones norteadas / Ediciones sin fin, Barcelona, 2020.

Arte & basura / Art & Trash. Edited by Luis Felipe Fabre. Oaxaca: Almadía, 2012.

Aullido de cisne / Swan's Howl. Mexico City: Al este del paraiso, 1996.

Beso eterno / Eternal Kiss. Mexico City: Al este del paraiso, 1995.

Jeta de santo / Holy Mask. Edited by Mario Raúl Guzmán and Rebeca López. Madrid: FCE, 2008.

Sarduy, Severo. *Cobra*. Translated by Philippe Sollers. Paris: Éditions du Seuil, 1972.

Sarmiento, Domingo Faustino. *Facundo: Civilization and Barbarism*. Translated by Kathleen Ross. Berkeley: University of California Press, 2003.

Saunders, Frances Stonor. *The Cultural Cold War: The CIA and the World of Arts and Letters*. New York: New Press, 2000.

Sauri, Emilio. "'A la pinche modernidad': Literary Form and the End of History in Roberto Bolaño's *Los detectives salvajes*." *MLN* 125, no. 2 (2010): 406–432.

Schidlowsky, David. *Las Furias y Las Penas: Pablo Neruda y Su Tiempo*. Berlin: Wissenschaftlicher Verlag, 1999.

Schwob, Marcel. *Vies imaginaires*. Toulouse: Editions Ombres, 1993.

Segato, Rita. "Las nuevas formas de la guerra y el cuerpo de las mujeres." *Sociedade y estado* 29, no. 2 Brasília (May/August 2014): 341–370.

Sepúlveda, Magdalena. "La narrativa policial como un género de la Modernidad: la pista de Bolaño." *Territorios en fuga. Estudios críticos sobre la obra de Roberto Bolaño*. Edited by Patricia Espinoza Hernández. Santiago de Chile: FRASIS editores, 2003.

Shames, David. *History Reborn: Neoliberalism, Utopia, and Mexico's 20th-Century Student Movements*. Ph.D. dissertation, Boston University, pending defense.

Sheringham, Michael. *Everyday Life: Theories and Practices from Surrealism to the Present*. Oxford; New York: Oxford University Press, 2006.

Silva, José Asunción. 1951. *Nocturno*. Bogotá: Prensas del Ministerio de Educación Nacional.

Siskind, Mariano. "Towards a Cosmopolitanism of Loss: An Essay about the End of the World." *World Literature, Cosmopolitanism, Globality: Beyond, Against, Post, Otherwise*. Edited by Gesine Müller and Mariano Siskind. Berlin: De Gruyter, 2019, 205–236.

Smith, Sidonie, and Julia Watson. *Reading Autobiography*. Minneapolis, MN: University of Minnesota Press, 2001.

Solanki, Tanuj. "The Geometry of the Gaze." *Litro Live*, July 28, 2013. www.litrolive.com/

Sollers, Philippe. *Casanova, The Irresistible*. Urbana: The University of Illinois Press, 2016.

Femmes. Paris: Gallimard, 1983.

Solotorevsky, Myrna. "Anulación de la distancia en novelas de Roberto Bolaño." *Hispamérica, Año* 37, no. 109 (April 2008): 3–16.

El espesor escritural en novelas de Roberto Bolaño. Ediciones Hispamérica, 2012.

Sommer, Doris. *Foundational Fictions: The National Romances of Latin America*. Berkeley and Los Angeles: University of California Press, 1991.

Sorensen, Diana. *A Turbulent Decade Remembered: Scenes from the Latin American Sixties*. Stanford: Stanford University Press, 2007.

Soto, Marcelo. "Yo me siento chileno." Entrevista a Roberto Bolaño. *Revista Qué Pasa*, July 27, 1998. https://garciamadero.blogspot.cl/2007/07//

Soust Scaffo, Alcira. *Escribir poesía ¿vivir dónde?* Mexico City: MUAC/UNAM, 2018.

Spivak, Gayatri. "The Rani of Sirmur: An Essay in Reading the Archives.'" *History and Theory* 24, no. 3 (1985): 247–272.

Steinberg, Sam. *Photopoetics at Tlatelolco: Afterimages of Mexico, 1968*. Austin: The University of Texas Press, 2016.

Steiner, George. *After Babel: Aspects of Language and Translation*. New York: Oxford University Press, 1975.

Stern, Steve J. *Remembering Pinochet's Chile. On the Eve of London 1998*. Durham, NC: Duke University Press, 2006.

Stockwell, Cory. "The Life of the Night: Bolaño, Blanchot, and the Impoverishment of Openness." *Critique: Studies in Contemporary Fiction* 60, no. 3 (2019): 342–356.

"Sovereignty, Secrecy, and the Question of Magic in Roberto Bolaño's *Distant Star*." *The New Centennial Review* 16, no. 2 (Winter 2016): 233–262.

Suleiman, Susan. "The Question of Readability in Avant-Garde Fiction." *Studies in 20th Century Literature* 6, no. 1 (1981): 17–35.

Swinburn, Daniel. "La novela y el cuento son dos hermanos siameses." *Bolaño por sí mismo*. Santiago, Chile: *Entrevistas escogidas*. Edited by Andrés Braithwaite. Santiago, Chile: Ediciones Universidad Diego Portales, 2006, 73–78.

Tabarovsky, Damián. *El fantasma de la vanguardia*. Mardulce, 2018.

Tallón, Juan. "Un tal Bolaño." *Jot Down Cultural Magazine* (2018). www.jotdown.es/2018/07/un-tal-bolano/

Tanner, Tony. *Introduction to Moby Dick*. Oxford: Oxford University Press, 1988.

"Text of the Statement." *New York Times*, May 22, 1971.

Thompson, Hunter S. *Hell's Angels*. 1966. New York: Ballantine Books, 1995.

Thompson, Ruth Anne, and Jean Fitzgerald. "From Mean Streets to the Imagined World: The Development of Detective Fiction." *Martin, Crime and Detective Fiction*, 3–13, n.d.

Thrower, James. *Religion: The Classical Theories*. Washington, D.C.: Georgetown University Press, 1999.
Thurner, Mark. *The Names of Spain and Peru: Notes on the Global Scope of the Hispanic*. Edited by Catherine Davies and Rory O'Bryen. Liverpool: Liverpool University Press, 2020.
Todorov, Tzvetan. *Mikhail Bakhtin: The Dialogical Principle*. Translated by Vlad Godzich. University of Minnesota Press, 1988.
Torres, Vicente Francisco. *El Cuento Policial Mexicano*. Mexico City: Editorial Diógenes, 1982.
 Muertos de papel: Un paseo por la narrativa policial mexicana. Mexico City: CNCA/ Sello Bermejo, 2003.
Trelles, Diego. "El lector como detective en 'Los detectives salvajes' de Roberto Bolaño." *Hispamérica* 34, no. 100 (2005): 141–152.
Trelles Paz, Diego. *La novela policial alternativa en Hispanoamérica: Detectives perdidos, asesinos ausentes y enigmas sin respuesta*. Ph.D. dissertation, University of Texas at Austin, 2008.
Ungurenau, Delia. "Pierre Menard the *Sur* -realist." *Comparative Literature Studies* 53, no. 1 (2016): 114–149.
Unruh, Vicky. *Latin American Vanguards*. Berkeley: University of California Press, 1994.
Valdebenito, Luis Nitrihual, and Juan Manuel Fierro Bustos. "Nocturno de Chile de Roberto Bolaño: Metáforas y Horror." *Letras* 53, no. 84 (2011): 60.
Valdes, Marcela. "His Stupid Heart: Roberto Bolaño's Novels Were a Love Letter to His Generation. But What He Had to Say Many Chileans Didn't Want to Hear." *Virginia Quarterly Review* 84, no. 1 (Winter 2008): 169–180.
Valencia, Sayak. "Capitalismo Gore." *Debate Feminista* 50 (2014): 51–76.
Valéry, Paul. *Monsieur Teste*. Paris: Gallimard, 1946.
Valle, Manuel. *El signo de los cuatro: II, Agatha Christie: Historias sin historia de la naturaleza humana*. Albolote, Granada: Editorial Comares, 2006.
Vallejo, César. *The Complete Posthumous Poetry*. Translated by Clayton Eshleman and José R. Barcia. Berkeley, CA: University of California Press, 1980.
 Obra poética. Edited by Américo Ferrari. Archivos, 1988.
Vallejo, Georgette de. *¡Allá ellos, allá ellos, allá ellos! Vallejo*. Lima: Zalvac, 1978.
Vargas Llosa, Mario. *El viaje a la ficción. El mundo de Juan Carlos Onetti*. Madrid: Alfaguara, 2008.
Varón González, Carlos. *La retirada del poema: literatura hispánica e imaginación política moderna*. Madrid: Iberoamericana/Vervuert, 2020.
Velasco, Juan and Tanya Schmidt. "Mapping a Geography of Hell: Evil, Neoliberalism, and the Femicides in Roberto Bolaño's 2666. *Latin American Literary Review* 42 (2014): 97–116
Vila-Matas, Enrique. "Decirlo Todo." *El País*, January 12, 2008.
Vilas, Manuel. "La poesía de Roberto Bolaño." *Poesía reunida*. Alfaguara, 2017, 9–17.
Villalobos-Ruminott, Sergio. "A Kind of Hell: Roberto Bolaño and the Return of World Literature." *Journal of Latin American Cultural Studies* 18, no. 2–3 (2009): 193–205.

Villoro, Juan. "La batalla futura." *Bolaño por sí mismo. Entrevistas escogidas*. Edited by Andrés Braithwaite. Ediciones Universidad Diego Portales, 2006, 9–20.
"Roberto Bolaño: mito literario a su pesar." *El Periódico*, July 19, 2013. www.elperiodico.com/es/dominical/20130712/roberto-bolano-mito-literario-a-su-pesar-2501951
Volpi, Jorge. *El fin de la locura*. Seix Barral, 2003.
Waldman M., Gilda. "La doble vertiente de la crónica actual de la ciudad de Santiago: Historia del presente y postales en sepia." *Anales de Literatura Chilena* 9, no. 10 (2008): 179–190.
Walkowitz, Rebecca. *Born Translated: The Contemporary Novel in an Age of World Literature*. New York: Columbia University Press, 2015.
Wang Ling. "Interview with the Editor of Bolaño." Zhen Daqian, September 29, 2019.
Warnken, Cristián. "Roberto Bolaño en 'La belleza de pensar.'" Interview at Feria Internacional del Libro de Santiago. Estación Mapocho, Santiago de Chile. 1999. Transcription by René Rojas. *World Literature Today* 80, no. 6 (November–December 2006): 46. www.jstor.com/stable/40159246; https://garciamadero.blogspot.com/2010/06/roberto-bolano-en-la-belleza-de-pensar.html
Westad, Odd Arne. *The Cold War: A World History*. New York: Basic Books, 2017.
The Global Cold War: Third World Interventions and the Making of Our Times. Cambridge; New York: Cambridge University Press, 2005.
Whisnant, David E. *Rascally Signs in Sacred Places: The Politics of Culture in Nicaragua*. Chapel Hill: University of North Carolina Press, 1995.
Wilford, Hugh. *The Mighty Wurlitzer: How the CIA Played America*. Cambridge, MA: Harvard University Press, 2008.
Williams, Gareth. "Sovereignty and Melancholic Paralysis in Roberto Bolaño.'" *Journal of Latin American Cultural Studies* 18, no. 2 (2009): 125–140
Wimmer, Natasha. "Introduction." Roberto Bolaño, *The Savage Detectives*. Translated by Natasha Wimmer. New York: Picador, 2008.
Wolfe, Tom. "'The Birth of 'The New Journalism'; Eyewitness Report by Tom Wolfe." *New York* 5.1. Febrary 14, 1972.
Woolf, Virginia. *The Common Reader*. New York: Harvest, 1984.
Woo, Suk-kyun. "Reception of Chilean Literature and South Korean Intellectual Genealogy." Edited by Axel Gasquet and Gorica Majstorovic, *Cultural and Literary Dialogues between Asia and Latin America*. New York: Palgrave Macmillan, 2021: 103–117.
"Works by Bolaño, Otsuka Released in Persian." Iran's Book News Agency, February 17, 2014. www.ibna.ir/en/naghli/194547/works-by-bola%C3%B1o-otsuka-released-in-persian
Yépez, Heriberto. "De la literatura como botín y la crítica como despojo. A propósito de la co-optación de Bolaño." https://borderdestroyer.com/2016/11/30/de-la-literatura-como-botin-y-la-critica-como-despojo/
Young, Dolly J. "Mexican Literary Reactions to Tlatelolco 1968'." *Latin American Research Review* 20, no. 2 (1985): 513–526.

Zambra, Alejandro. *Formas de volver a casa*. Barcelona: Anagrama, 2011.
   Poeta chileno. Barcelona: Anagrama, 2020.
Zavala, Oswaldo. *La modernidad insufrible. Roberto Bolaño en los límites de la literatura latinoamericana contemporánea*. Chapel Hill: University of North Carolina Press, 2016.
Zhen, Daqian, and Ling Wang. Interview with the Editor of Bolaño. Transcription, September 29, 2019.
Zizek, Slavoj. *The Parallax View*. Cambridge/London: The MIT Press, 2006.
   The Plague of Fantasies. London/New York: Verso, 1997.
Zurita, Raúl. *Anteparaíso*. Santiago de Chile: Editores Asociados, 1982.

Index

African and Asian contexts, 15
Allende Gossens, Salvador, 33, 121, 169
Allende, Isabel, 130
American and French literature, 3
Americas, 88–97
Americas and Europe, 5–8, 10, 13–15, 19
amputation, 273
anti-economy, 92
Argentina, 269–271
Asian and African contexts, 334
avant-garde, 128–129, 312–322

bankruptcy of culture, 273
Baudelaire, Charles (2), 143, 241–242, 261
  and Mallarmé, Stéphane, 265
Baudelaire and Rimbaud, 12
belatedness, 309–310
belief, 267, 273, 277, 281, 284, 289
Berlin Wall, 126, 129
Bolaño, Roberto (3), 32
  legend of, 6
  "linguistic nomad," 32
  myths of, 25
  polyglot, 32
  three trips to Chile, 19–32
Bon, François, 143, 151–152, 156
Borges, Jorge Luis (2), 146, 277, 280, 296
Brodsky, Roberto, 327
Breton, André, 94

Callejas, Mariana, 42–43
canonization, 212–223, 278
Catholicism, 281, 283
Cercas, Javier, 325
chance, 184–187, 189
Chile, 9–10, 12, 14, 16–32
civilians, 34
cloaca, 94
coincidence, 169, 182–183, 185–186, 188–189
Cold War (2), 123, 125–126, 157, 188
collective memory and trauma, 303–311

colonialism, 300–301
commodification of genres, 12
communism, 114–115, 118
complicity, 34–35, 42–43
Cortázar, Julio, 129, 137, 278
cosmopolitanism, 334, 341
crime fiction, 224–225, 228, 233–235
cross-genre writing, 10
crónica, 238–243, 246
Cuba, 115, 118–119, 123

Dadaism (2), 317, 320
deceit, 257
destitution, 91
detectives, detective fiction, detective genre, 224–235
dictatorship (5), 33–34, 46–56, 122–123, 204, 219, 221, 267–268
Don Quixote, 137–138

"El Boom" of the 1970s, 48
Eltit, Diamela, 127
essays and short stories
  and chance, 154–155
  and coincidence, 182–183, 186–187, 189
estridentismo (2), 317, 320
ethics, 276, 278
ethics of writing (2), 198–199
ethnicity and race, 294–302
Europe, 5–7, 79–87
Europe and the Americas, 8, 10
evil (2), 106, 128, 132, 161, 171, 177, 218–219, 230–231, 235, 269, 330
exile (4), 24, 31, 39, 82, 89, 125, 172, 175, 307

Fall of the Wall, 126–133
fantasy, 256
fascism (5), 41, 85, 94, 101, 177, 231
feminicide, 235
flâneur, 102, 143–145, 240, 246
Freedom, 115, 118–119, 133, 172

France, 76, 86, 145–146
French literature, 142–157
French and American literature, 3
friendship and love, 323–332

Garcia Marquez, Gabriel, 177
gaucho, 269–272
gender and sexuality, 285–293
gender violence, 286–288, 290, 292–293
German and Russian precursors, 158–168
ghost, 191–200
globalization, 126, 130
gray zones, 35

Herralde, Jorge, 323, 328
historical and literary-historical, 3, 5, 8
historical avant-gardes (2), 312–314, 317
history, 250–262
horror (2), 42, 46, 229, 244, 249, 255–256, 260
human rights abuses, 34, 47, 56

illness, 9, 101, 135, 143, 155–156, 182, 185, 265, 273
illness and literature (2), 135, 155–156, 182, 185, 265, 273
Imaginary Lives, 146
implicated subject, 38–43
influence studies, 128, 196
infraordinary and visceral realism, 150–152
Infrarealism, 193, 198–199, 317
Intemperie, 90, 92, 94–95
intermedial pressures, 3
intertextuality, 107–108, 262
irony, 170, 215

journalism, 237–249
Joyce, James (2), xvi, 67
Jünger, Ernst, 158, 162, 167, 218
justice, 33, 39, 46–47

Kafka, Franz, 159–160
Kristeva, Julia, 65–66, 76, 107
Künstlerroman, 165

Latin American literature, 134–141
   in Africa, 334
   in Asia, 334, 343
   post 1989, 345
Latin American Long-Poem, 205, 207
   mesmerism, 104, 108
Lemebel, Pedro, 239, 246
Lichtenberg, Georg Christoph, 160
listening, 64
literariness, literary value, 212
"literary" and "non-literary," 3

literary criticism and literary history, 250–262
literary history, 8, 10–12
literary-historical and historical, 3, 8, 12
literary institution and marketing, 192–193
literary market, 128
literature (3), 68, 76, 134, 201, 242, 250, 255
López, Carolina, 328
loss, 307, 309
love and friendship, 323–332

mapping, 3–15
masculinity, 285–286
mass culture, 238–239, 244
media, 57–64
Medina, Rubén, 276, 318, 328
melancholia, 133
Melville, Herman, 96
memory (4), 34, 59, 80, 132, 138, 156, 176, 256, 292, 303–311
mesmerism, 104, 108
Mexico (3), 49, 57–64, 199, 224, 226, 303
Mexico City, 57–64, 116, 120–121, 240, 259, 278
Michon, Pierre, 143, 150, 152
   Vies minuscules (Small Lives), 152
Monsiváis, Carlos, 57, 239, 244
mood, 267, 273
mythopoetic, 205–206, 208, 210–211

narrative coherence, 303, 306
narratives of masculinity, 285, 289, 291, 293
national literature, 88–89, 93
national narrative, 307
neo-avant-gardes (2), 312–313, 315–316, 318
neoliberalism (2), 124, 173–174, 176
New Journalism, 238, 244
1968, 49, 57
1989, 297
"nomadic aesthetics," 32
nomadic existence, 198
nostalgia, 212
novel and canon, 212–223

Padilla, Ignacio, 324
Paris, France, 101–112, 117–118
parochialism, 334
parodic representation, 208
parody, 201–211
Paz, Octavio, 121, 135
Perec, Georges, 143, 148, 150, 153
   and the infraordinary/infra-ordinaire, 150–152
Pinochet Ugarte, Augusto (2), 33, 122, 126, 166, 169, 177, 259
plots of globalization, 142–157

Poe, Edgar Allan, 229
poetic apprenticeships, 7, 9, 12
poetical imagination, 204, 207
poetry (4), 120, 129, 144, 153, 161–162, 167, 191–211, 235, 241, 247, 250, 252, 254, 256, 260
Porta, Antoni García "A. G.," 325
postcolonialism, 300
post-national, 276
post-1989, 345
posthumousness, 297, 309–310, 325
power, 301, 306
propaganda, 116
prose and poetry, 196
prose poems, 10–11
prose poem novels, 9, 12

race and ethnicity, 294–302
racism, 296–297, 302
recursiveness, 170
religion and politics, 275–284
repression, 115, 117, 120, 171, 330
revolution, 105, 115, 118–120, 126, 198
Rimbaud, Arthur, 9, 143
Russian and German Precursors, 158

sadness, 153, 155
Santiago Papasquiaro, Mario, 193, 196, 198–200
Sarduy, Severo, 68, 77, 212, 214
Schwob, Marcel, 143, 146
Imaginary Lives, 146–147
sexual violence, 286–288, 292–293
short stories and essays, 181–190
    and chance, 181, 183
    and coincidence, 183, 185
social memory, 47
Sollers, Philippe, 65–67, 75, 77
sorrow, 250, 307
Southern Cone, 46–56, 58

Spain (2), 79–87, 101–112
Spanish Civil War, 101
spectral haunting, 49, 52, 56
subject, 258, 267, 276
surrealism (3), 129, 317

Tel Quel, 65–66, 68–70, 72–77
television, 242, 244, 248
textual interrelation, 173
Tinajero, Cesárea, 209–210
Tlatelolco, 59–63
Tolstoy, 162
Trakl, Georg, 158, 161–162
transatlantic, 12, 50
transnational, 3–5, 13, 85, 88–97, 307
trauma, 59, 61–62
trauma and collective memory, 303–311
Turgenev, Ivan, 159, 163
Twentieth- and twenty-first-century literature, 4, 7, 10, 302
two 9/11s, Chile, New York, 169–178

UNAM, 58–59

Vallejo, César, 101–102, 110
verse and prose, 3
Villoro, Juan, 325–326
violence (3), 47–48, 55, 59, 79, 85, 124, 171, 173, 177, 196, 224, 227, 230–231, 233–234, 242, 248, 273, 283
    against women, 286, 289, 291
visceral realism and the infraordinary, 150–152
Viscerealist, 71, 75, 203, 209, 211

Western literature, 5
Wieder, Carlos, 209, 235, 257, 265
worlds and worlding, 3–15, 95
World literature, 333–346

Zurita, Raúl, 257